Henry Samuel Boase

The Philosophy of Nature

A Systematic Treatise on the Causes and Laws of Natural Phenomena

Henry Samuel Boase

The Philosophy of Nature
A Systematic Treatise on the Causes and Laws of Natural Phenomena

ISBN/EAN: 9783744675161

Printed in Europe, USA, Canada, Australia, Japan

Cover: Foto ©Andreas Hilbeck / pixelio.de

More available books at **www.hansebooks.com**

THE
PHILOSOPHY OF NATURE

LONDON
PRINTED BY SPOTTISWOODE AND CO.
NEW-STREET SQUARE

THE

PHILOSOPHY OF NATURE

A SYSTEMATIC TREATISE

ON THE

CAUSES AND LAWS OF NATURAL PHENOMENA

BY

HENRY S. BOASE, M.D. F.R.S. & G.S. &c.

Honorary Member of the Royal Geological Society of Cornwall

LONDON

LONGMAN, GREEN, LONGMAN, AND ROBERTS

1860

PREFACE.

In the following pages speculation enters more largely than usual into the treatment of the sciences; and on this account may be repugnant to many, as being too metaphysical. This work, however, is not metaphysical, that is, mystical and visionary, in the ordinary bad sense of the term: on the contrary, it rests solely on the knowledge of natural phenomena. In it the physical sciences are referred to the fundamental principles of *realities;* and not only so, but even the abstract sciences, which are commonly ascribed to the *à priori* ideas of intellectual intuition, are based on the direct interpretation of the rational *forms* of nature. Whatever may be the merits of this work, it is not a hasty and thoughtless production, but the result of many years' diligent study, during which it was, step by step, slowly completed after several successive failures.

In his earnest search after truth, the author has

not hesitated to express his opinions freely, whether heterodox or not, whenever they have been arrived at by legitimate inferences from facts: and as his opinions are often at variance with the highest authorities, they can but have the appearance of an arrogated wisdom, unfavourable to a candid and patient consideration. So far the result of his labours is unhappy: but if, as he would fain hope, some truths have been disclosed, though not the whole truth, his work may for awhile be misapprehended, but will ultimately be duly appreciated. There is this justification for the expression of so firm a conviction of the truth of his conclusions; that the differences of opinion have sprung up, in unexpected quarters, as verifications of the fundamental principle of his system:— and such suggestions are the surest and best characteristics of what Comte calls a homogeneous doctrine.

A work, like the present one, embracing the whole field of scientific knowledge, and venturing on speculations, which in this country have engaged but little attention, must necessarily contain many errors; let these be detected and corrected, and a step in advance will be secured: there must needs be many tentative hypotheses before that happy *guess* be made which shall co-ordinate all our knowledge into a perfect system.

The cultivators of science are still engaged in

accumulating physical facts, according to the inductive method, as recommended by Bacon; and for the most part rest content with recording the facts which they have thus discovered by observation and experimental research. This is an important and indispensable preliminary toward the construction of science: but this is not all that is requisite, it is only the means to an end; and this end, for its accomplishment, requires the interposition of another factor, the logical intellect. So that the facts having been acquired, it is competent for others than their discoverers to generalise them and to determine the relations of this generalisation to another of a higher order:— what it is desired to maintain is, that it does not follow that a discoverer of facts and one who is well acquainted with his special science, is alone qualified for theorising; that in this case, as in most affairs of life, the work is best performed when there is a division of labour. The philosopher, for instance, whose occupation is purely intellectual, and who contemplates the analogies of all kinds of knowledge, is much better qualified for the task of colligation and generalisation.

All this, however, is well understood, and stands on record. "It must never be forgotten," says Sir John Herschel, "that it is principles, not phenomena,— the interpretation, not the mere knowledge of facts,—which are the objects of scientific inquiry." And so Comte observes, "that *facts* do not constitute *science*, though they are its foundation and material; science consists in the systematising of facts under established general laws." Other authors might be quoted to the same purpose: but this, as has been said, is well known; and yet, being known, it is virtually ignored.

There is, however, a growing conviction that theories, not facts, are the great *desiderata* of modern science: the tide is now turning in an opposite direction, and the day may not be far distant, when the method of *deduction*, that of the ancients, will be more honoured than her twin sister *induction*, which has so long enjoyed the pre-eminence. Our knowledge will then be "transplanted out of the external into the intellectual world; and we shall be enabled to push *à priori* reasoning to the utmost limit of particularity, resulting in the form of *individual facts*, of which we might have had no knowledge from immediate experience; and thus we are not only furnished with the explanation of all *known* facts, but with the actual discovery of such as were before *unknown*." These are not the sentiments of a dreaming metaphysician, but of a philosopher; and of one too, who is deeply versed in the physical sciences, and whose soundness of judgment is generally acknowledged.

Philosophy is the subject of the following pages, and it may be well to state here the sense in which this term is understood. Philosophy is the science of the sciences, the *summum genus* of systematic knowledge;—a synthesis of the diversity into unity;—the universal from which by analysis all particulars may be developed and demonstrated. It is the pole-star of knowledge on which the eye of science should ever be fixed in all its wanderings; and which alone can ultimately guide man to the attainment of the ardently desired object of his curiosity,—a knowledge of the Reason in Nature.

If this be a correct statement of the case, such a *prima philosophia* cannot surely be regarded as mythical metaphysics. The sages of ancient Greece believed in the possibility of such a philosophy, and delighted in a Pisgah view of this transcendent object: and day by day it is becoming more and more evident, that their intellectual vision was not a delusion, but the logical anticipation of a glorious truth.

Claverhouse near Dundee: July 1860.

CONTENTS.

CHAPTER I.

INTRODUCTORY REMARKS ON THE SYSTEMS OF PHILOSOPHY.

State of Knowledge unsatisfactory. — What is Science? — The Noun-Substantive and logical Universal of Science. — A universal System of Knowledge the great *Desideratum*. — The fundamental Principles of Philosophy. — Ancient and modern Systems of Philosophy. — Idealism and Realism: the Necessity of their Union. — Absolutism of Germany. — Positivism of Comte. — The Identity of Physical Forces: must end in Dynamism. — Proposed Principle of Power, — a Reason-directed Force. — Definition of Power. — Natural Bodies Dualisms of Powers. — Single Powers non-existent in Nature. — Powers vary in Degrees of Order: so can be systematised. — Correlation defined. — The Archetype of all Dualisms. — How single Powers are manifested, — The Relations in Dualisms formulated. — Powers are *veræ causæ*. — Remarks on Causation. — Conclusion . . . . Page 1

CHAP. II.

THE MINIMA AND MAXIMA OF MATTER, THE ATOMS OF MATTER, AND THE CELESTIAL ORBS, ARE ALL DUALISMS OF PHYSICAL POWERS.

The System of Nature. — Every Universal a *Maximum*, but not an infinite quantity. — Physical Substance or Matter the content of all Bodies. — What is Matter? a Dualism of Attraction and Repulsion. — Ether the physical content of Space is pure Matter. — The Universe originally a Sphere of Ether. — Its attractive and repulsive Powers manifested as Centripetal and Centrifugal Forces. — Gravity and Centrifugy, correlative Forces, co-existent, but independent in their Antagonism. — Gravity generally regarded as *the*

Universal Force. — The forces of the Universe twofold: this Dualism reconciles Kepler and Newton's views concerning the causes of Celestial Motions. — On the Laws of Motion. — On the Conservation of Forces. — The primæval condition of the Solar System. — Its relation to the Universe. — The Origin of Planets by periodical Fissions. — Laplace's Theory. — Comte's Remarks thereon. — Solar System virtually but one rotating Sphere. — The relative Distances, Masses, and Volumes of the Planets. — Has the Sun ceased to evolve Planets? — The Nebular Ring or Photosphere of the Sun. — The Zodiacal Light. — Comets, different kinds of — Their Constitution, and mode of Formation. — The Eccentricity of their Courses: and their liability to Changes of Form. — Astronomy not an Artillery problem. — Conclusion . . Page 35

CHAP. III.

THE MOLECULAR FORCES, COHESION AND HEAT, MODES OR PHASES OF PHYSICAL POWERS.

All Modes of Physical Forces function in some form of Motion. — Molecular Motions individually inappreciable: only manifested in the aggregate. — Molecular Attraction called Cohesion; — Molecular Repulsion, expansive Force or Heat. — The term Micronomy proposed for Molecular Physics. — The Solid, Liquid, and Gaseous states of Matter. — The nature of Latent Heat. — The Spheroidal Form of Boutigny, not a fourth state of Matter. Cohesion a quantitative; Heat a qualitative Force: the former fixed and definite; the latter diffuse and variable. — Condensations of Gases in porous Bodies. — Action of a plate of Platinum. — The Quantity of Heat only determined relatively to a given Standard. — The Zero of Heat unknowable. — The Conduction of Heat. — Expansion. — Motion of Molecules and Motion of Mass modes of the same Phenomenon. — Joule's Equivalent of a Unit of Heat. — Convection of Heat in Fluids. — The ratio of Expansion in Gases. Expansion not an invariable indication of an increment of Heat. — Specific Heats. — Condensation evolves Heat: Heat absorbed on Rarefaction. — Diffusion of Liquids and Gases. — Osmotic Phenomena. — The Sum of Latent and Sensible Heats and Vapours, the same for all tensions. — High pressure Vapours — Paradoxical Effect of. — Caigniard De la Tour's Experiments thereon. — Molecular Attraction. — Crystallisation. — Isomorphism, Dimorphism. — Allotropy. — Conclusion . 71

CHAP. IV.

SOUND AND LIGHT, MOLECULAR AND ETHERIAL UNDULATIONS.

Undulations of Material Bodies.—The Medium of transmitting Force.—The Difference between Sound-waves and Light-waves.—Light not related to Heat and Electricity as Modes of the same Force.—What is Light?—Sir John Herschel's Answer to this Question.—Light, like all other Motions, a Composition of Forces.—According to Comte, Light is something *sui generis:* heterogeneous to Motion.—All Undulations are not audible and visible.—Limitation of the Scale of Sound and Light Perceptions.—The Analogies between Sound and Light. The Origin and Constitution of Sound.—Its various *Media:* that of Air immediately concerned in Hearing.—The Sound-wave a Dualism of Forces.—The Composition of Light not yet understood.—The Colours of the Prismatic Spectrum.—Distribution of Heat-rays and of Photographic-rays in the Spectrum. These two kinds of Rays arranged in an inverse Ratio.—Radiant Heat and Actinism the component Forces of Light-waves.—Heat the Cause or *Primum-mobile* of Light.—Actinism not a chemical Force, but a Mode of Physical Attraction.—Conclusion   Page 104

CHAP. V.

ELECTRICITY AND MAGNETISM, PHASES OF PHYSICAL POWERS, FUNCTIONING IN THE POLAR MOVEMENTS OF MATERIAL MOLECULES.

Electricity and Magnetism, cosmical or universal Forces.—Electrology the least advanced Branch of Physics.—Electricity and Magnetism are not the Noun-Substantives of distinct Sciences.—The various Modes of producing Electricity—Explanation of its Origin.—Electricity a Mode of Physical Repulsion.—Bodies not always in an electrical State. Positive and negative Electricities, are co-existent and co-equal.—Electrical Induction, the Action of contiguous Particles.—The Relations of positive and negative Poles to the Current.—Poles only manifested when Current passes through different *Media.*—Oersted on the Relation of electrical and magnetic Currents. Heat evolved during Magnetisation.—A Current of Magnetism lengthens the metallic Medium: that of Electricity shortens it.—Explanation of these Phenomena.—Diamagnetism discovered by Professor Faraday: supposed to be a peculiar Force.—Professor Tyndal's Experiments thereon.—Magnecrystallic Force: a Crystal under its Influence virtually a Magnetic Needle.—Galvanism; Electro-magnetism; and other Forms of Polar Forces.—Conclusion . . . . . Page 130

CHAP. VI.

CHEMICAL SUBSTANCES, DUALISMS OF PHYSICAL AND CHEMICAL POWERS.

The Union of dissimilar Substances, the characteristic of Chemical Action.—This a kind of Attraction.—Does not act indiscriminately between all Bodies: but is elective.—This Attractive Force called Affinity.—Chemical Affinity and Electricity supposed to be identical.—This Opinion advocated by Davy, Berzelius, and Faraday.—Comte regards this as confounding the Auxiliary with the Phenomenon.—Electricity is a diffusive, decomposing Force; Affinity a condensing, combining Force: can such Opposites be identical?—The mutual Convertibility of these Forces more apparent than real.—Various Definitions of Chemistry.—Chemical Elements, their Nature. The Weight and Volume of each Element specific.—The Elements not Multiples of Hydrogen.—Predisposing Affinity.—Chemical Compounds all Binaries or Dualisms.—Chemical Notations.—The Duplication of Atoms an important Innovation.—Allotropy.—This State of Elements not permanent.—Duplication of Atoms remarkably indestructible.—The Hydrocarbons, basic or neutral, electro-negative and electro-positive; their Combinations as *quasi-elements*, like Cyanogen. The typal and basic Combinations of Nitrogen.—Conclusion 153

CHAP. VII.

ORGANISMS, DUALISMS OF CHEMICAL AND VITAL POWERS.

Life or Vital Principle the efficient Cause of Organic Phenomena.—Opinions concerning this Force.—The most recent that of Dr. Carpenter.—This Opinion evades one Difficulty by creating another equally insoluble.—All Forces said to be one and the same, mutually convertible.—Life is transformed Heat.—The *specialty* of the material Substratum alone determines the Character of the Force.—Whence then this Specialty?—The organic Germ is itself a *living* Organism; Heat cherishes Life, but does not impart it.—Difference between chemical and organic Dualisms.—The Relation of specific Vital Forces to universal Physical Forces.— Death, the Dissolution of the Organic Dualism.— Life not the immediate Producer of Motion—It makes Physical Forces subservient to this Purpose.— Life is a directing, superintending Energy.— It functions in acquiring, appropriating, and utilising other Forces, both physical and chemical.—Dr. Carus on the Nature of Life.—Vital Force a final Cause: so in a sense are all other Forces.— The Development of Organisms.— The vegetative Functions of animated Creatures—Reducible to simple Principles.— Vegetables the intermediate Link between Minerals and Animals. —Animals distinguished by the Attribute of Sensibility.— The Nervous and Muscular Systems of Animals.— Instinct and Knowledge.—On the Transmutation of Species.—Conclusion. Page 182

CHAP. VIII.

MIND, OR CONSCIOUS POWER, THE HIGHEST PHASE OF VITALITY.

Mind and Matter not heterogeneous.—Mind differs from the other Parts of the Organism only in Degree. — The mutual Dependence of Mind and Body.—The Phenomena of Mind the Subject of Psychology.—Brutes have Minds.—The Infant Mind, as regards Experience, a *tabula rasa*.—Primary Knowledge intuitive.—Evidence of the Senses reliable: Inferences deceptive.—Sensation and Perception.—Abstraction, or Mental Analysis of Knowledge.—Experience, acquired Knowledge: communicable by Example, as well as by Precept.—Memory.—The Subjective and Objective Factors of Knowledge.—Intuitive Understanding, or Common Sense.— Perfect Knowledge analogous to Instinct.—*A posteriori* and *à priori* Ideas.—Conceptions or Abstract Ideas—Their Denomination; Colligation; and Generalisation.—The Moral Sentiments, like Perceptions, are the intuitive Data of a higher Knowledge.— Brutes have moral and social Intuitions, or Instincts, as well as Man.—Man, in relation to the Morality of Brutes, stands *in loco Dei*.—The Nature of the Will or Conscious Power.—The Science of Morality or Ethics.—Conclusion 216

CHAP. IX.

THE IDEAL SIDE OF NATURAL POWERS MANIFESTED AS FORMAL KNOWLEDGE: THE LOGICAL INTERPRETATION OF THE REASON IN NATURE.

The rational Forms of Nature give the fundamental Principles of the abstract Sciences.—System, or the classified Order of Degrees, the most abstract Idea of Nature.—The Knowledge of such a System is Science or Logic.—All the Sciences are based on the Principles of Logic.—The Definitions of Logic.—Aristotle's Dictum unjustly denounced.—Logic relates only to the Forms of Things, and not to Things themselves.—Logic, like all Sciences, formed by Induction; and functions by Deduction.—The Character of Genus and Species.—Universals and Particulars.—Extension and Intension.—A Proposition; and its Terms, the Subject and Predicate.—The various Kinds of Propositions.—The Syllogism.—Its three Propositions, the Major Premiss, the Minor Premiss, and the Conclusion.—The cardinal Propositions; how symbolised.—The Quantification of the Predicate. The Formulæ of Logic.—Application of Algebraic Notations to Logic.—That of Professor Boole not satisfactory, but his Suggestion important.—Conclusion . . Page 248

CHAP. X.

THE FORMAL SCIENCES, THE KNOWLEDGE OF IDEAL SYSTEMS.

The Mathematics—Sciences of Number, Space, and Time.—Regarded as the Basis of all the Sciences; but this Character belongs to Logic.—The Early Origin of the Abstract Sciences.—Arithmetic, the Science or Logic of Number.—Geometry, the Science or Logic of Space.—These Sciences might have been immediately derived from Logic.—What is Space?—The Real and Ideal can only exist by and in each other.—Space not a *Vacuum*, but a *Plenum*; the *Form* of the *real* Content gives the Idea of Space.—Space an indefinite *Maximum*, not an Infinite.—The Subject of Geometry is universal Extension, and all particular or subordinate Parts of Extension.—Of Space and Partial Spaces.—What is Time?—Various Conjectures thereon.—No beginning and no ending of Time; but a continuous flowing onwards.—All Events occur in Time.—Time goes on whether anything happens or not.—Time one of the extrinsic Relations of Existence—Conceivable only as an indefinite Past, Present, and Future.—The Formal Succession of Events gives the Idea of Time.—The Analogies between Space and Time.—What is the Science of Time?—Not Rational Mechanics, nor Rational Arithmetic; but a special Science, Chronometry.—Conclusion 273

CHAP. XI.

THE KNOWLEDGE OF CAUSATION, THE SCIENCE OF PHENOMENAL VICISSITUDES.

Introduction: On the Character of Abstract Science.—Arithmetic, Geometry, and Chronometry only concerned with the *exterior*

Forms of Things: but variable Phenomena depend on the *inner* Constitution of Things.—Causes must be searched for below the Surface of Things.—Rational Mechanics only treats of Motion.—The Science of Energetics has been proposed as more comprehensive. —A Science required capable of treating of all Changes, physical, chemical, and vital.—Rational Mechanics, a Branch of such a Science. —The proposed Science of Substance or Hypostatics.—Substance, a pure abstract Idea of Matter, its Attributes those of Quantity and Quality; a Composition of Causes, the abstract Idea of Forces. —Its Definitions, Postulates, and Axioms.—The particular Sciences related to the universal Science of Hypostatics.—Cinematics, the Science of Motion.—Statics and Dynamics.—The Idea of *Vis-inertiæ*.—All Motions Compositions of moving Causes.—Remarks on the Laws of Motion.—Combination, a Kind of Change, gives the Special Science of Rational Chemistry or Chemics.—Organisation, another Kind of Change, gives Rational Physiology or Organics.—Conclusion . . . . . Page 295

CHAP. XII.

RECAPITULATION AND CONCLUSION.

Has the Thesis been proved that the state of Modern Science is unsatisfactory?—Freedom of Discussion necessary for the Advancement of Science.—There are Sciences of Realities and Sciences of Ideas; Concrete and Formal Sciences: the Data of the Former, Facts; of the Latter, Truths.—A Trinity in Unity incomprehensible. —Dualism the Condition of Nature, of which the Mental Faculties partake; and are capable, by consciousness, of apprehending.—Phenomenal Knowledge directly perceived as a *Monism.*—The general Character of Science, the Progression of Knowledge in different Ages, analogous to individual Development.—Review of the various Sciences.—A System of the Sciences.—Conclusion 330

THE PHILOSOPHY OF NATURE.

CHAPTER I.

INTRODUCTORY REMARKS ON THE SYSTEMS OF PHILOSOPHY.

State of Knowledge unsatisfactory. — What is Science? — The Noun-Substantive and logical Universal of Science. — A universal System of Knowledge the great *Desideratum*. — The fundamental Principles of Philosophy. — Ancient and modern Systems of Philosophy. — Idealism and Realism : the Necessity of their Union. — Absolutism of Germany. — Positivism of Comte. — The Identity of Physical Forces : must end in Dynamism. — Proposed Principle of Power, — a Reason-directed Force. — Definition of Power. — Natural Bodies Dualisms of Powers. — Single Powers non-existent in Nature. — Powers vary in Degrees of Order: so can be systematised. — Correlation defined. — The Archetype of all Dualisms. — How single Powers are manifested, — The Relations in Dualisms formulated. — Powers are *veræ causæ*. — Remarks on Causation. — Conclusion.

Is our scientific knowledge in a satisfactory condition? As compared with that of the ancients, has it not lost in *intension*, or conciseness of comprehension, what it has gained in *extension*, or diffusiveness of detail?

The Baconian method of interrogating nature has, indeed, put us in possession of many branches of knowledge which were entirely unknown in the Greek school;

but, with few exceptions, these branches, these *inductive sciences*, as they are called, are mere colligations of facts, scarcely deserving the name of science; and, in truth, the very expression *inductive*, which is assumed as a mark of superior excellence, indicates an imperfect condition;— that they are not yet sciences, but only in the stage of construction.

It may be objected to this statement, that these sciences are called *inductive* to imply that they have been inductively formed by a series of verified generalisations, and also in order to distinguish them from the *deductive* or pure sciences. Such a notion, we think, has originated in an inadequate apprehension of the subject—for every science must necessarily have been attained by the method of induction. In some cases, this process may have been greatly abbreviated by an acuteness of intellect, by a happy guess as it is termed, in detecting the characteristic attribute of the *summum genus;* but in every case, be the process long or short, induction is indispensable in the construction of a science; when, however, a science is completed, when it is indeed a science, it is no longer concerned with induction; it deals not with generalisations, but with amplifications demonstrating by deduction a multiplicity of previously unknown particulars.

It is on this account that we have asserted that, whilst modern knowledge has been greatly extended, it has lost that high standard of perfection which so conspicuously marks the sciences of ancient origin. Should a second advent of the " dark ages " suddenly arrest the progress of knowledge, and benumb the intellect for a thousand years, with what bewilderment would the mind, on recovery from its torpid state, gaze on the records which escaped destruction; a vast collection of interesting, but loosely connected facts, would probably be preserved; a *rudis indigestaque moles*, affording no clue for threading the labyrinth of knowledge. It was otherwise at the "revival of literature." The legacy of the ancient school contained several sciences, logic, arithmetic, and geometry, not fully developed indeed, but vital germs fraught with all their essential principles, and capable, by cultivation, of attaining more than even their present expansion, capable also of becoming instrumental in the acquisition of knowledge. The modern school, under like circumstances, would only bequeath rational mechanics, an important gift, indeed, one enabling us to determine correctly the value of physical phenomena, and capable of ultimately leading to an apprehension of the *reason in nature;* but even this branch of the mathematics, as will hereafter be shown, is not a *universal* but only a *particular* science. Besides this, all is imperfection. Astronomy is as yet only an inductive science; and acoustics and optics are not as far advanced as astronomy, and all the other inductive sciences are mere groups of facts held together by various and often incongruous theories.

In the endeavour to substantiate our assumed position, that modern science is not in a satisfactory condition—we have no desire to overstate the case. It is only requisite to turn to the definitions of the several physical sciences, and to observe how various and inadequate they are to denote their respective subject-matter, to be convinced that the present method of philosophising is as defective as that of the ancients, which we have been taught scrupulously to avoid: the one fails to attain a knowledge of the *genus* by being involved among the *differentiæ* of the *species*; the other, by having too rashly attempted to gain its object, *per saltum*, from the *accidents* of the *species*.

The reason of failure in both cases is obvious. The ancients, led astray by the facility with which they had obtained some fundamental principles, and had constructed sciences thereon, seem to have been under the delusion that the whole domain of knowledge could be taken possession of by the same rapid advance. Not that they were ignorant of the inductive method and of its important functions in the generalisation of facts, for all this is fully and admirably set forth in Aristotle's "Posterior Analytics;" but they also knew that there was a royal road to science, if the intellect were equal to the undertaking, and that a science once attained, could by deduction disclose vast regions of knowledge. They had proved all this by experience; and it is not, therefore, surprising that they preferred the dash of intellectual assaults to the sure, but slow, approaches by regular induction. And why were the later attempts of the ancients disappointed? Why was their success so suddenly arrested? The multitude and magnitude of things are *outward* conditions, and readily furnish to the contemplative mind the fundamental ideas of their respective sciences; but the vicissitude of things, the variable phenomena, depends on *inner* and more hidden principles, which can only be arrived at by long and patient investigations; and failing in this perseverance, the ancients were not qualified for the task which they undertook, and therefore their attempts to construct natural sciences were necessarily futile.

Bacon clearly discerned the rock on which ancient philosophy was wrecked; and he pointed out the proper method for the interpretation of nature, which has been followed to the present time with unabated zeal, and has been rewarded with considerable success. But as deeply enamoured of the method of induction, as the ancients were of that of deduction, moderns have been most exclusively absorbed in the object of their devotion; generalisation has been their chief employment, and with generalisation alone they seem disposed to rest contented; so much so, indeed, that some writers, even on logic, so magnify the office of induction, as to make it the chief, if not the sole, factor in ratiocination. Now all this is very well, if generalisation be the ultimate object of science; if the never-ending search after facts, and the co-ordination of such accumulated details, be all that is required of science, then moderns are properly engaged in their vocation; but if generalisation be only the means to an end, the method of forming science which is afterwards to fructify; then are they wasting their labour in enlarging instead of concentrating knowledge. They have done well in laying sure foundations for science; but the ancients were far more intellectual in discerning the true character of science, though their later efforts were wrongly directed.

Such is the opinion of many who have attentively considered this subject; but, though this has been explicitly recorded, it has not hitherto led to any practical results; on the contrary, the rigid and contracted views of Positivism seem to be almost generally accepted. The careful study of phenomena and of the laws of their production is not repudiated, for they are the requisite preliminaries in every science; but we do think that phenomena and their laws do not constitute the sum total of knowledge; that all Nature is not a mere continuous sequence of phenomena, but that they are severally produced by their respective causes. We are aware that Positivism, in the plenitude of its dogmatism, will denounce this opinion as a relapse into myths and metaphysics; but, we believe, and it is the object of this thesis to endeavour to substantiate our belief, that as surely as things exist in space, and as events occur in time, so certainly is every natural change the effect of a definite cause.

By these introductory remarks we are desirous of intimating the point of view from which we regard the present state of knowledge: and, before entering on our subject, a few remarks on some other topics may serve to render the following exposition more intelligible.

In the first place, as the consideration of the sciences will form so large a part of our subject, it may be as well to state what we understand by the word Science. We do not mean the science of this, of that, or of any other particular subject; but what we wish to state is that which Socrates so accurately indicated and so ably discussed more than two thousand years ago. What is science in itself, or *per se* as it is termed? Science is not unfrequently regarded as identical with knowledge: it is indeed knowledge, but it is something more. Knowledge in itself is the pure resultant produced by the concurrence of the conscious mind and of knowable organic impressions; just as the motion of a body is the product of a moving force and of a body capable of being moved: in either case there is a composition of forces; and the resulting compound is in the one case motion, and in the other knowledge. When knowledge is not pure and simple, but in relation to something else, this knowable something marks the nature of the particular knowledge: now, science is the knowledge of some particular idea — that of System; in short, it is the knowledge of system or systematic knowledge.

We cannot at present enter into details, but in its place it will be fully discussed, so must rest content in the meantime with assuming that science is no other than logic; and hence it is that geometry is the science or logic of space, and astronomy the science or logic of celestial bodies or stars. So that logic underlies every particular science;—inasmuch as it is the mental universal, in which each and all of them must be contained. And thus it comes to pass that every science enjoys in common the methods of logic; that of induction in its formation and classification, and that of deduction in its demonstrative developments; and, corresponding thereto, each science, though essentially one in the indissoluble unity of its antithetic methods, may be viewed under a twofold aspect which divides it into its natural history and physical branches; or, as we would prefer calling them, the phenomenal and casual branches of the science. The one view presents the subject-matter in a statical state, as a synthetic whole or system; the other as a whole analysed into its component parts by dynamical operations.

Every science, therefore, has its noun-substantive or

fundamental idea; and this must be regarded as a logical universal. A universal which cannot be either an infinite or an absolute (that is in a metaphysical sense as an unconditioned), for such are unknowable, and can, therefore, form no part of knowledge. But such a universal is a *summum genus*, the equivalent of all its subordinate genera and species; just as a whole is equal to all its parts. This is the limitation of natural knowledge; all particulars must be related to each other; and these in turn must be related to their universal; and the bond of union in each science is its noun-substantive, which is possessed in common by the universal and all its particulars; the latter having in addition thereto some differential characteristics.

If this statement be correct, not only each science but each of its subordinate generalisations is a distinct universal, for each universal is a diversity in unity; and if so does it not follow that all the sciences may, in like manner, be united into one supreme system or hierarchy? On such a plan, we think that a system of the sciences may be ultimately accomplished; but on the principle of an *absolute unity* all attempts have hitherto failed, and must fail, for the principle is impracticable.

Whether a universal system of knowledge be possible or not, it is a fact that from the earliest dawn of the intellect to the present time, it has been the great *desideratum* of philosophy. The importance of such an object, could it be accomplished, has till of late been very generally admitted; and to deny it is, we conceive, to ignore the utility of science altogether. We know that the individual sciences are of great intrinsic value, and just as oriental pearls, when artistically strung together, according to some beautiful design, have a value far exceeding the aggregate of its individual parts, so a unity of knowledge would have a peculiar value of its own over and above that of the special sciences of which it is composed. The sciences would no longer be independent and insulated, but their filiations toward each other would be known; and this circumstance alone would bring out more clearly the character of each science; by which its definition, and the precise limits of its domain, would be better understood; and each science, aided by a wider field of analogies, could be more successfully cultivated.

Impressed with a deep conviction of the importance of such a system of the sciences, this subject has occupied our attention for the last seven years; during which time three hypotheses have been successively worked out, until they were found inadequate to sustain the required superstructure. In each instance, however, the source of error was detected; and, although each trial proved unsuccessful, yet each was an advance on its predecessor toward attaining a higher principle of generalisation. During the past year, the solution of this problem has been attempted by a fourth method; and the result seems to be worthy of attention.

The principle of the proposed system is that of the fundamental idea of POWER; which is not to be conceived of as a mere efficiency, but as *a reason-directed force:* a power which is a law unto itself. The *real content* of such a power is its principle of activity or force; the *ideal form* of the same, is its reason, whether intuitive or conscious, according to which the force functions; whilst the power itself is the synthesis of the *real and ideal*, an indissoluble union, which is manifested as an essential entity, or individual *being*. By abstraction, however, a power may be regarded on either one or the other side of its existence; and, according to the stand-point from which it is viewed, the knowledge is said to be real, or ideal. Such is the character of a power, or reason-directed force. In nature there are a great many powers, each differing from all others in the peculiar attribute of its force, and in the special law by which the operations of its force are regulated. But the grand and distinguishing character of natural powers is that they are always associated together in pairs or dualisms: there is no such thing in nature as a single insulated power; such a power can only be an unconditioned or absolute being. On this twofold constitution of all natural bodies physical phenomena depend; for it renders action and reaction possible, without which they could not function. And not only so, but in each dualism, the powers are not only co-existent but also directly opposite in their attributes; and it is to this antagonism of forces, that the conditioned character of nature must be attributed; for the constituent powers of natural bodies mutually control and limit each other's energies.

In propounding this principle of *power* as the foundation of a new system of knowledge, no foolish expectation is entertained that we have arrived at the final truth, for the whole history of philosophy forbids such a vain hope; but we trust that we may be permitted to express a hope, without being charged with overweening conceit, that this work, the result of long-continued and intense thought, may prove a step of advance in the right direction, one of the many steps which yet remain before we can expect to arrive at the attainment of a perfect philosophy.

Previous to entering on a more detailed statement concerning natural powers, it may be as well to take a rapid glance at some of the principal systems of philosophy, in order to point out the character of the fundamental ideas by which they have been attempted, and to endeavour to show, aided by our principle of power, the reasons why they have failed to accomplish their purpose. "The tendency of the mind to generalise its knowledge," says Sir W. Hamilton*, "leads us to anticipate in nature a corresponding uniformity, and as this anticipation is found in harmony with experience, it not only affords the efficient cause of philosophy, but the guiding principle of its discoveries." Explain this, however, as you may; the fact is indisputable that this love of the unity of knowledge has been the ruling passion of the human intellect.

In Greece, at a very early period, strenuous efforts were made to discover the ultimate principle of nature; and, as might have been expected, researches were first directed to the external, or phenomenal, aspect of bodies. From this objective point of view each of the four elements (earth, water, air and fire), were successively assayed, and were lastly abandoned for more subtile and abstract principles, which finally led to the adoption of the subjective stand-point, to which we owe many interesting speculations; but above all that of the *divine idea*, the transcendent conjecture of Plato. Thus, even at this

---

* Lectures on Metaphysics. Lect. iv. vol. i. p. 69.

early period, we find philosophy vibrating between the two extreme doctrines of realism and idealism, and during the whole of its course it has never ceased to do so, even down to the present time. This is a fact of great significance; it is a standing evidence in favour of the truth, that *being* is essentially twofold in its entity. The mind operates logically, according to its rational laws, in whatever direction its attention is engaged, and it will find a portion of the truth whether it fixes its gaze on the *real* or *ideal* side of being; but if it desire the whole truth it must not rest content with looking first on one side and then on the other, but by a stereoscopic view, it must conjoin both sides into a synthetic whole. Realism and idealism are the opposite sides of knowledge, just as induction and deduction are the antithetic, but inseparable methods of logic; we may by abstraction sever them and investigate their respective characters, but mental functions and mental phenomena, that is method and knowledge, can neither of them be perfect, but by the concurrence of their correlatives.

In modern times philosophy has been most energetically cultivated in Germany, indeed no other country can lay claim to a philosophy of its own, that is, one which has any pretensions to the high standard of a universal system of knowledge. In Germany idealism has been carried out to its ultimate conclusion; the absolute idea having been posited as the fundamental principle, and the identity of idea and being logically deduced therefrom. This startling result has been regarded in this country, by our matter-of-fact minds, as a *reductio ad absurdum;* and very recently even the Germans themselves have arrived at a similar opinion; at all events it has not yielded the fruitful harvest which a sound philosophy would have doubtless afforded. Regarding German idealism from *our* stand-point we should condemn it as a one-sided view of knowledge, and we should still more object to it because its fundamental principle is not a logical universal, having relation to all parts of its system. This objection respectively applies to the doctrines of Fichte, Schelling, and Hegel, for though each of these differ in many respects from one another, they all agree in positing their peculiar principles as absolutes, and consequently when the attempt is made in either case to evolve therefrom relative existences, the whole subject falls into inextricable confusion. But we need not insist on this; for Sir W. Hamilton has unanswerably demonstrated that there is a gulf between the conditioned and the unconditioned which cannot be bridged over, and that all attempts to do so, must end in *nihilism*. In thus freely expressing our opinion concerning idealism, we have no desire to undervalue the intellectual labours of the Germans; their philosophical speculations are second only to those of ancient Greece, and we believe that they have done more than any other people toward the attainment of a system of the sciences.

Two other attempts at generalisation in modern times require a passing notice; the one is positivism, the other the correlation or identity of physical forces. The best exponent of the former is "The Positive Philosophy" of Comte. In it we learn that its object is to frame a hierarchy of the sciences, and to determine the invariable laws to which all natural phenomena are subjected; and that "the ultimate perfection of such a system would be to represent all phenomena as the particular aspects of a single general fact, such as that of gravitation."

Now such a perfection, could it be accomplished, would be a species of absolute realism. Gravitation is a universal force, consequently it actuates not only masses but also the very atoms or ultimate particles of matter. Under certain conditions gravitation can be manifested by the weight of bodies, or as cohesion or crystallic force; but these and other phases of attraction, which might be mentioned, do not comprise all known forces. Gravitation cannot by any ingenuity be converted into, or become identical with, the directly opposite forces of heat and electricity, which in common with their homologue centrifugal force, always tend from and not toward the common centre, as in the case of gravitation.

No wonder that Comte when he reflected on this incongruity of natural phenomena, was impressed with the hopeless prospect of achieving the perfection of positivism. "There is something chimerical," he says[*], "in attempts at universal explanation by a single law, for our intellectual resources are too narrow, and the universe is too complex, to leave any hope that it will ever be within our power to carry scientific perfection to its last degree of simplicity." This confession is sufficient for our purpose, for it shows that the object of our inquiry is not to be sought for in positivism. It would, however, have been more satisfactory if Comte had not attributed his failure to the imperfection of the intellect, but to the inadequacy of the idea on which he had fixed to sustain his philo-

---

[*] Comte's Positive Philosophy, vol. i. p. 16.

sophy. He begins well with the categorical statement, that his system ought to rest on a single general principle, and when he found that this was impracticable he should have acknowledged his error and not blamed the mental capacity; but he even goes farther yet, he decries the perfection of philosophy, and says that "the value of such an attainment, if possible, is greatly overrated," which ludicrously reminds one of the fable of the fox and the grapes.

It only now remains to ascertain whether the opinion, very current at the present day, concerning the oneness or identity of physical forces, is capable of solving this problem of philosophy. In the "Correlation of the Physical Forces," Grove says*: "The position which I seek to establish is, that the various affections of matter which constitute the main objects of experimental physics, (viz. heat, light, electricity, magnetism, chemical affinity, and motion), are all correlative, or have reciprocal dependence. That neither taken abstractedly can be said to be the essential cause of the others, but that either may produce, or be convertible into, any of the others: thus, heat may mediately or immediately produce electricity, electricity may produce heat; and so of the rest, each merging itself as the force it produces becomes developed. The same must hold good of other forces; it being an irresistible inference from observed phenomena, that a force cannot originate otherwise than by devolution from some pre-existing force."

It is indisputably true, that *some* natural forces are only modes or phases of some one distinct and universal

---

* At p. 15.

force; and such forces are mutually convertible according to the conditions under which they are manifested by their corresponding phenomena:—but that *all* natural forces are indiscriminately capable of being reciprocally changed into each other, is, we conceive, not only contrary to facts, but is inconsistent with that action and reaction which pervades nature, and is the basis of all physical phenomena. In the artillery problem, for instance, could it be said that the force by which the projectile is propelled, contrary to gravity, is the same as that force which continually tends to draw it back again to the earth; or that cohesion and heat, on which the states of matter depend, and which act in opposite directions, are modes of one and the same force, and mutually convertible. Is it not more reasonable to suppose that in these and similar cases the forces concerned are co-existent and opposite, that is, that they are correlatives? And if so, it is quite inconsistent with the very idea of correlation to conceive that its correlatives are identical and capable of reciprocal transmutation. There is great confusion of thought in the whole treatment of this subject, as is evidenced by the fact of grouping *motion* among the single forces; for it is well understood that *motion* is a composition of co-existent motions, the existence of a single motion is purely hypothetical. In truth, a motion is not a reality, but only the abstract idea of a body in motion: the resultant of moving and resisting forces, acting and reacting on each other in different directions.

One and the same kind of force can only act with greater or less intensity in one direction: it is not possible that a force can act and re-act on itself. And if the idea of the identity of all forces be legitimately carried out to its ultimate conclusion, it must necessarily land in a pure, simple, and absolute force. And such a result would be analogous to the absolute idea in which German philosophy was involved: the aspects of these absolutes are indeed different, for one is an idealism, and the other a dynamism; but they are both inconsistent with the twofold constitution of nature, and cannot but lead to the same barren results.

Such, in a few words, are our objections to the principles of former philosophies: and we now proceed to set forth *power*, as already defined, as the fundamental principle of a universal system.

Power is Being: this is an identical proposition, the simplest form of enunciating knowledge. Either term, taken alone, does not constitute a thought; the term being is *that* which *is*, or exists; but what is the *that?* It must be a something, a reality; and when we say that it is a power, the mind rests satisfied, though both ideas are the purest abstractions. But immediately the suggestion arises, what is a *power?* and its definition answers, that it is a reason-directed force, a force which acts according to its innate rational law.

Natural beings, we have already stated, are dualisms of powers. We can, however, conceive of an infinite and absolute power, by positing it as the negation of a natural conditioned power: and by contemplating the transcendent wisdom manifested in the operations of finite powers, we may infer that such a power is omniscient, as well as omnipotent. Thus far, by the light of nature, man may

c

arrive at a conception of a Supreme Power: but if he seeks to know the relation which he, in common with all other subordinate natural powers, bears to the supreme, he desires knowledge which nature cannot impart; he can, therefore, only obtain it through some supernatural channel. Revelation has taught us that Absolute Being, the Great I Am, or Deity, is such a power as we are considering; a reason-directed force, to whom all things are possible according to the counsel of his will, which is the perfection of wisdom. The attributes of power, whether infinite or finite, must not be regarded as a compound, as force *plus* reason; but as an indissoluble union of these, co-existent and co-equal, neither one afore or after the other. These remarks have a theological bearing; they have not, however, been made with this intent, but expressly for another purpose. We are about to enter on the consideration of the dualisms of powers, and it is, therefore, necessary before doing so, to have it clearly understood what is meant by a simple, or single power: and unless we are yet more explicit, it may be supposed that the one, or absolute power, is about to be employed as the element of natural dualisms, a proceeding which would terminate in another form of pantheism, so justly abhorred in this country.

A single independent power, as already stated, does not exist in nature, and if it did, it could not function; for, as in the case of an arithmetical unit, it cannot be reduced to a lower, or raised to a higher value. Its existence can be conceived, but being *ex hypothesi*, out of all relations, it must be as a force inert; and, therefore, unknowable, for a cause can only be manifested by its effects. But since natural powers are dualisms, their internal as well as their external relations are very various; so that it becomes possible to make a general system of such dualisms, a system of nature. Now the very idea of system implies a subordination of orders, according to their degrees; and, as in each dualism the rational forms correspond with their co-existent efficient realities, natural forces necessarily dominate over each other according to the intension of their attributes. If, then, we regard nature only on the quantitative side of its twofold constitution, there is no possibility of associating it with absolute power, as the universal; but viewed on the other side as a hierarchy of powers or beings, systematic knowledge, as ontology, might be admissible, subordination of powers being the principle of such a system. And as one star differs from another in glory, so cosmical beings rise one above another in dignity, till they culminate in man, whose attributes are a microcosm, comprehending all others, together with its distinguishing mark of conscious reason. The natural universal is distinguished from the *summum genus* of ontology by its conditioned or finite character; and from the collateral branch of the conditioned, the angelic host, in having material instead of spiritual bodies. Or, in other words, the natural and supernatural are distinct branches of conditioned beings, subordinate to, but not forming part of, the Absolute or Supreme Being.

This association of powers according to degrees of order, which in the voluntary powers is that of authority, and in the involuntary that of necessity or compulsion, may not be readily accepted by those who have been in the habit of regarding universals only in one direction, as wholes made up of similar parts, that is, which only differ from each other in quantity; but when comprehended in its twofold character, in its intension as well as in its extension, it will be perceived that these are only one and the same logical subject, viewed from different stand-points, and are always in the exact inverse ratio towards each other. What we are desirous of showing is that we are not drawing on our imagination, in order to smoothe down a difficulty; but are proceeding logically in our argument by making the predicate of the proposition universal, and the subject particular. Perhaps our meaning may be made plainer by an illustration. Natural powers rise one above another in their domination, each one possessing a peculiar and higher attribute in addition to those of its subaltern; and all, even the highest, man, being subordinate to absolute power, inasmuch as their attributes are finite and inferior: but it does not follow that we must therefore conceive of these powers as parts and parcels of the Absolute; just as parts are of a whole. They may be, however, related thereto by degrees; as different orders are to the head of a hierarchy; or as subjects are to the sovereign in a nation, or as soldiers to their general in an army. And in each case the influence of the supreme power may be said to be over all, through all, and in all; since they are all actuated by the will of the supreme: but they cannot be said to be actually parts thereof. So, likewise, in works of art, we perceive the manual dexterity, and the genius of the artist, and acknowledge them as his works; but no one for a moment supposes that these works are part and parcel of the artist himself. So, in like manner, natural powers bear the impress, some faint similitude of the reason-directed force of supreme power, which forms a bond of relationship on the principle of subordination or hierarchical order; but absolute and conditioned powers have no community of substance, as in the case of a universal subject. This explanation, however, is offered as professedly imperfect; an attempt only to obtain a glimpse of the bond of union which traverses the obscure gulf between the conditioned and unconditioned: and happily for our thesis this subject forms no essential part of our undertaking; natural phenomena are the objects of our inquiry, and these are capable of being arranged as a system of nature.

All natural bodies, whether the vast orbs of the heavens, or the microscopic molecules of matter; whether brute matter itself, or the most perfect organism, man; are all, without exception, regarded, according to our views, as *dualisms of powers*. In the contemplation of nature, the constituents of each dualism may be viewed, either as to their real contents, as antagonistic forces, or as ideal forms; in the former case, the systematic knowledge obtained is called physics or natural philosophy; in the latter, metaphysics or mental philosophy. But these modes of investigating nature are equally one-sided; obtained by a mental analysis of the concrete objects, which are intuitively known to us by perception. These objects or natural beings are very various, and by a knowledge of their differences are capable of being classified: and thus we obtain a system of nature, the subject-matter of natural history.

According to this view natural history is no other than the cosmical branch of ontology; and hence it is that the treatment of each branch of physics is preceded by a description and classification of the special objects of its subject, as has already been pointed out. In metaphysics, however, this relationship between the content and form of the subject is generally denied, its subject-matter being regarded as pure *à priori* truths, independent of all experience; these truths, as the forms or reason in nature, certainly exist previously to their interpretation by the mind; and so does nature herself, and also the mind which is a part of nature; but we cannot conceive the possibility of acquiring any systematic knowledge but through ideas obtained from the system of nature itself. We speak of bodies existing in space, as if this were something real and independent of bodies; and this is one of the highest *à priori* truths; but we shall endeavour hereafter to show that space is the *formal* condition of nature, an abstract idea derived from the dimensions of material bodies, in short, the *form* of nature divested of its real *contents*.

Thus we have seen that even knowledge itself is of a dualistic character, which it necessarily must be as the interpretation of nature; and we cannot express this more simply than by the logical idea of *correlation*, which is a dualism of *correlatives*. A correlation can only exist in the union of its correlatives; which are indissolubly co-existent and antithetically co-efficient; so that the occurrence of one of them necessarily implies the existence of the other; and it is impossible to conceive of either, except in their relationship. For example, in the correlation *family,* and its correlatives, *parents* and *children,* we find all the terms of this statement satisfied. And so, in any material substance, its correlative properties are weight and volume, and vary the proportions of these as you may, the resulting correlation, or substance, varies accordingly. What an absolute or simple power of gravity, functioning as absolute density would be, or what the power of rarefaction, resulting in an infinite *vacuum*, would be, we can form no conception, for we know these powers only in their relations towards each other; and it is not improbable, that their very existence depends on their mutual antagonism.

We propose, then, the following as the universal archetype of all dualisms: —

1st Correlative + 2nd Correlative = Correlation,

which may also be symbolised by the formula

$$A + B = AB.$$

And since the expression of this equation is, in fact, a definition or identical proposition, its conversion may be effected, but such an operation communicates no additional knowledge; but if we change the *plus* sign, and also convert the equation, we can then express either correlative.

$$\text{Thus, } AB - B = A.$$
$$\text{or } AB - A = B.$$

For instance, substitute a concrete for this abstract illustration: —

Body + soul = man.
Man − soul = a corpse.
Man − body = a disembodied spirit.

So likewise, Attraction + repulsion = matter.
Matter − repulsion = attraction.
Matter − attraction = repulsion.

In the first illustration man is destroyed by either analysis: in the one case we get a tangible residuum, which for a while remains in the figure and fashion of a man, though in reality it is only part of a man. The body of a man is a concrete complicated power subordinated to his specific power or humanity; and it is only by the concurrence of these opposite powers that man functions as a living organism; remove the presiding power, and the body falls back into its former state of existence, as chemical substances. In the second illustration we deal with matter, the opposite extreme of natural beings: the former is the highest development of natural complexity, but the latter is the simplest form of a natural dualism; and we are arrived at that point, when one power cannot be separated from another by an actual analysis.

How then is it possible to obtain a knowledge of the constituents of such a dualism? The method is very simple, resting on the principle, that as substances are known by their properties, and causes by their effects, so powers are known by their attributes. In the archetypal formula above given, the dualism is supposed to be in a state of equilibrium, its correlatives being equal; and consequently the correlation is as it were a neutral compound, a *tertium quid;* not characterised by either of its correlatives, but distinguished by its own peculiarity. Now such is only one of the conditions which dualisms are capable of assuming; they may also exist in dynamical states. One of the correlative powers may possess a greater energy than its antagonist; that is, it may be in a *plus* or excited state; up to the point of equilibrium the plus power is *neutralised* or rendered *latent ;* but beyond this point the excess of power is an efficiency, producing phenomena which partake of the character of the predominant power. And thus it comes to pass that this excess is virtually as if the power, to which it belongs, were in a simple insulated state: it is not so in reality, but it manifests its attribute distinctly and individually, and thereby enables us to arrive at a knowledge of its nature.

The constitution of natural bodies is very uniform in one respect,—one power, simple or compound, forms the *basis* or body of the *dualism,* and another its species or *type ;* it is the latter power which alters its relations to the former by various accessions or diminutions of energy; it is the qualitative power, whilst the quantitative or basic power remains stationary. But this difference, however accomplished, frequently occurs, sometimes the one, and sometimes the other power predominating in the dualism; and as the relative proportions of the powers vary, so do the corresponding phenomena: and it is therefore requisite that the *formulæ* should denote these mutations.

The following is not perhaps a correct expression, but it answers the purpose in the meantime, and may be hereafter rectified. Let A stand for the basic, and B for the typal power, and we shall have

$$A + B = AB,$$ the dualism in a statical state.

$B^2 + A = B^2A$, the dualism in a typal dynamic state.
$A^2 + B = A^2B$, the dualism in a basic dynamic state.

By way of further illustration, let us formulate the different states of matter, assuming its composition as given above; which yet remains to be proved.

Attraction + repulsion = matter in a liquid state.
2 Attraction + repulsion = matter in a solid state.
2 Repulsion + attraction = matter as gas or vapour.

Let us suppose that the matter which is undergoing these physical changes is water; as a chemical substance, water has its peculiar constitution, but this must be disregarded or abstracted, and it must, for the present, only be viewed as a material body, actuated by physical powers. These powers are peculiar phases of attraction and repulsion, adapted to the molecular movements of matter, and are commonly known as cohesion and heat.

Cohesion + heat = water.
2 Cohesion + heat = ice.
2 Heat + cohesion = steam.

Or take a chemical substance, and having made abstraction of all its physical or material properties, we have the following:—

Base + acid = salt in a neutral state.
2 Base + acid = salt in a sub, or alkaline state.
2 Acid + base = salt in a super, or acidulated state.

In all these cases it is evident how much more simply and perfectly the variations of composition are expressed by the literal formulæ; the different position of the letters, with their affix, being sufficient to denote the relative condition of each constituent, and also the character of the resulting compound.

In the preceding statement concerning the archetypal correlation, the illustrations have been taken from the real side of being; but the same holds good when the attention is turned in the opposite direction: in the one case, the subject is concerning forces, but in the other, concerning logical forms; the reason in nature, which being interpreted gives abstract ideas. When we say that we have an idea of anything, it is an assertion that we are conscious of or know it; but that which we know is only the ideal *form*, corresponding indeed with its correlative *real*, and, therefore, when we know the one, the conviction is immediate and inevitable that we know the other also; and hence it is that all knowledge is correctly described as being *formal*.

A few instances of correlation on the ideal side of being may suffice:—

$$A + B = AB.$$
$$\text{Object} + \text{subject} = \text{idea}.$$
$$\text{Subject} + \text{predicate} = \text{proposition}.$$
$$\text{Re-action} + \text{action} = \text{effect}.$$
$$\text{Resistance} + \text{force} = \text{motion}.$$

It may have been gathered from what has been already said, that powers are by us regarded as causes; as *veræ causæ*, and not as the mere antecedents of phenomena; and, therefore, before entering on the details of our system, it may be as well to say a few words on the vexed question of causation.

The prevailing opinion seems to be that cause and effect are only an invariable sequence of events; that a cause is nothing more than the antecedent of the consequence; that cause and effect are convertible terms, capable of becoming either one or the other by a species of vibrating succession.

All, however, are not of this opinion; two at least, and they are a host in themselves, have protested against this doctrine. "Whatever attempts may have been made to reason away," says Sir John Herschel*, "the connection of cause and effect, and to fritter it down into the unsatisfactory relation of habitual sequence, it is certain that the conception of some more real and intimate connection is quite as strongly impressed upon the human mind as that of the existence of an external world." And the Rev. W. Whewell† has also observed, "that men cannot contemplate phenomena without clothing them in terms of some hypothesis, and will not be schooled to suppress the questionings which at every moment rise up within them concerning the *causes* of phenomena: to debar science from inquiries like these, on the ground that it is her business to inquire into facts, and not to speculate about *causes*, is a curious example of that barren caution which hopes for truth without daring to venture upon the quest of it."

One of the most talented advocates of Hume's hypothesis

---

* Outlines of Astronomy, p. 264.
† Philosophy of the Inductive Sciences, vol. ii. p. 268 *et seq.*

(viz. that causation is the mere fact of the invariable sequence of one event called the effect after the other called the cause), has at considerable length discussed this subject in his "System of Logic;" great ingenuity has been employed in the adaptation of facts to this doctrine, but too much after the manner of the Procrustean method. And we are inclined to think that no little confusion has arisen from using the word *cause* in different senses, as ably pointed out in Iron's "Dissertation on Final Causes." If invariable sequence can explain the relation of cause and effect, then is day the cause of night, and night the cause of day; for they have this characteristic in perfection, and not only so, but also its other character, that of being mutually convertible, on which the hypothesis places great reliance.

"The Correlation of Physical Forces" is quoted as affording unanswerable arguments in favour of the doctrine of sequence and convertibility. For instance, it is stated that *motion* produces *heat* (or rather the effect of heat, that is, expansion), and *heat* occasions *motion;* again, that *heat* produces *chemical action*, and *vice versâ*. Now, we have no hesitation in asserting that these and similar statements are true, only in part, but not wholly true; and even when in a measure correct, it is only a question of degrees. Heat is not the *cause* of chemical action, but only the cause of a molecular condition which is favourable to chemical action; it is, therefore, only the occasion or means of facilitating combination, whilst the action itself is *sui generis*, as the name *chemical* denotes. And conversely, chemical action is not the *cause* of the extrication of heat, for it can only function in combining different kinds of molecules; but in the act of effecting this union a condensation of molecules takes place, which is a secondary result of a purely physical description, and as such accompanied by the extrication of heat. Chemical bodies are, in common with all other natural bodies, material, and therefore have physical as well as chemical properties; but physical powers cannot produce chemical effects, nor can chemical powers cause physical effects, which we hope hereafter to demonstrate. And as regards the other proposition it is partly true, for the cause is the same in both cases but under different modes or phases. Thus *heat* produces *motion*, it causes the molecules of matter to recede from each other, which is a change of position in space or motion; and if the aggregate expansion be mechanically applied, the multitude of individually invisible motions may be concentrated into the visible motion of a mass. Thus heat does indeed produce motion, and if the moving mass be subjected to friction, heat is in its turn evolved, that is, the aggregate motion will again break up into parts, and by putting the molecules in motion or causing them to repel each other, it reassumes the phenomenon of expansion from which it originated. But we say that such an effect is not equivalent to the energy of the original cause; for, in each repetition of such action and reaction, there is an enormous reduction in degree; and so it will be until the *plus* state, by a continuous progression, is diffused among the surrounding bodies.

"A phenomenon," says Sir W. Hamilton*, "is this. When aware of a new appearance we are unable to con-

---

* Discussions on Philosophy and Literature, p. 585.

ceive that therein has originated any new existence, and are, therefore, constrained to think that what now appears under a new form had previously an existence under others. These others (for they are always plural) are called its cause; and a cause (or more properly causes) we cannot but suppose, for a cause is simply everything without which the effect would not result, and all such concurring the effect cannot but result." Even a motion itself is not one thing; but it is a composition of diverse motions, each of which co-exists in the compound, retaining its independent character. This is an abstract principle of rational mechanics; and if this abstraction be carried up to a higher generalisation, we shall have that of reaction + action = resultant or effect, a principle which includes motion as well as all other kinds of abstract changes, and will be found, if we mistake not, to offer a solution of causation. Let us give it another cast to elucidate the correlation.

Resisting body + moving body = body in motion.
Opposing motion + direct motion = motion.
Re-agent + agent = action.
Passive cause + active cause = effect.

We now stand face to face with our subject, without any extraneous concrete ideas to distract our attention; and it is now evident that, though we speak familiarly of the *cause* of an effect, as if it were only *one*, yet there are in truth *two* causes concerned in *every* effect. The reason of this elliptical mode of speaking, in common use, is now apparent, and it is perfectly justifiable when so understood.

The active cause is the positive or *plus* agent, the passive cause being the negative or latent re-agent; latent, in so far that it is balanced by an equivalent part of its antagonist, but indestructible, effectively co-existing in all its entirety; and this latent cause is, we conceive, the *nexus* in causation, which has been so long sought for in vain, and so defiantly demanded by the advocates of Hume's hypothesis.

The two causes act and react on each other, and the resultant or effect is a composition of causes, the character of the effect depending on the relative proportion of the constituent causes toward each other; and when we regard causes, not as formal abstractions, but as real forces, the resulting phenomena are of a similar character. In short, every phenomenon is the *then* existing condition of natural powers, as it appears to be in its manifestation to consciousness, and when the phenomenon changes, we intuitively refer this change to some alteration in the condition of the natural object, and look around for the cause of this change. We say intuitively or instinctively, for even the brute beast does so, and when it becomes instinctively acquainted therewith, it has acquired knowledge for the direction of its future conduct. Man enjoys also the same empirical knowledge, but he also possesses a higher faculty which enables him to look below the surface of things, and to strive to understand the precise character of the changes, to search out their causes, and also the *modus operandi* of these causes. And as the Mantuan poet has well observed,

"Felix qui potuit rerum cognoscere causas."

Whether we shall in any degree participate in this happy lot depends on the success in establishing our thesis, that all natural bodies are compounds or dualisms of powers, and that powers are reason-directed forces, which are a law unto themselves, the reason in Nature, according to which they function in the production of phenomena; and lastly, that natural powers are *veræ causæ* in their subordinate sphere of operations, that is, derived or delegated efficiencies in relation to absolute power, the Great First Cause.

Some apology may be deemed due for occupying attention with a subject more speculative than is usually brought forward, indeed, in times past, it would have been inexcusable when sufficient data had not been collected for such an undertaking; but now, theories not facts are the more claimant *desiderata* of science; on all sides there is a growing conviction that it is high time to gather together and condense our knowledge into the possible compass of a life-long study. Facts must be digested and assimilated by the logical intellect before science can be organised:—as justly observed by the President of the Royal Society, in his last anniversary address; " In the pursuit of the physical sciences, the imagination supplies the hypothesis which bridges over the gulf that separates the known from the unknown. It may be only a phantom, —it may prove to be a reality." It has also been well remarked by the Rev. James M'Cosh*, that "natural science itself is ever touching on the borders of metaphysics, and compelling physicists to rest on certain

---

* The Intuitions of the Mind, Introduction, p. 7.

fundamental convictions as to extension and force. The truth is, in very proportion as material science advances do thinking minds feel the need of something to go down deeper and mount up higher than the senses can do. Whatever the physicist may think, philosophy is an underlying power, of vast importance because of mighty influence. It is because it is fundamental and radical that it is unseen by those who notice only what is above the surface. Let us see, then, that the foundation be well laid, that the root be properly planted."

CHAP. II.

THE MINIMA AND MAXIMA OF MATTER, THE ATOMS OF MATTER, AND THE CELESTIAL ORBS, ARE ALL DUALISMS OF PHYSICAL POWERS.

The System of Nature.—Every Universal a *Maximum*, but not an infinite quantity.—Physical Substance or Matter the content of all Bodies.—What is Matter? a Dualism of Attraction and Repulsion.—Ether the physical content of Space is pure Matter.—The Universe originally a Sphere of Ether.—Its attractive and repulsive Powers manifested as Centripetal and Centrifugal Forces.—Gravity and Centrifugy, correlative Forces, co-existent, but independent in their antagonism.—Gravity generally regarded as *the* Universal Force.—The forces of the Universe twofold: this Dualism reconciles Kepler and Newton's views concerning the causes of Celestial Motions.—On the Laws of Motion.—On the conservation of Forces.—The primæval condition of the Solar System.—Its relation to the Universe.—The Origin of Planets by periodical Fissions.—Laplace's Theory.—Comte's Remarks thereon.—Solar System virtually but one Rotating Sphere.—The relative Distances, Masses, and Volumes of the Planets.—Has the Sun ceased to evolve Planets?—The Nebular Ring or Photosphere of the Sun.—The Zodiacal Light.—Comets, different kinds of—Their Constitution, and mode of Formation.—The Eccentricity of their Courses: and their liability to Changes of Form.—Astronomy not an Artillery problem.—Conclusion.

WHEN we regard the universe of natural beings in its oneness, we conceive of it as the system of nature, wherein the various species of objects are grouped together in subordinate genera, according to the order of classification.

A *summum genus* must have its own individual characteristic, and, since this is a universal, all its particular subalterns must partake of the same character; conjoined, however, with specific properties, on which their differentiation depends.

Every universal is a *maximum;* that is, it contains every existing thing which possesses its distinguishing mark: this maximum is not an *infinite* quantity, for all that relates to nature is limited, but it is an *unknown* quantity, and therefore indefinite. "The definite and the indefinite," says Sir W. Hamilton, "are the only quantities of which we ought to hear in logic;" and logic is the rational archetype of all the sciences. A universal, therefore, is an indefinite maximum, and so its definition must be assumed; and the same holds good with the minimum part into which this maximum is divided; it can only be regarded as an ultimate unit, incapable of farther division, and which, being indefinite, its value cannot be appreciated. Thus the *maximum divisibile* and the *minimum indivisibile,* the two extreme terms, must be assumed as data in the evolution of every science. Well has it then been said that all our knowledge begins and ends in ignorance; in this life we must rest content with an imperfect knowledge, corresponding with our finite and temporal capacities; but hereafter, when freed from these material limitations, we may hope, as taught by revelation, to know even as we are known.

What then is the universal character of Nature? It is *physical substance* or *matter;* which is the substratum, or basis of all natural bodies: to matter all bodies owe their physical properties, which are manifested as physical phenomena. There are indeed other properties besides the physical, viz. the chemical, and the organic; but these are special, over and above those of matter which are common to all bodies; and which therefore must for the present be set aside, or abstracted, as we have now only to deal with Nature as a *material* universe.

Such a universe of matter is the sum total of everything material, and this *summum genus* is an indefinite *maximum*, divisible into innumerable parts, all of which must be equal to the whole, which, however, is an unknown quantity. And so the *minimum* part of matter is an indefinite, but indivisible unit, but still a part, and as such, endowed with all the attributes of matter, whatever they may be; in short it is a material atom, beyond which, as its name implies, division cannot be carried.

But what is *Matter?* It is usually regarded as an unknown substratum; the basis, or support, of the properties of bodies; a something in which properties inhere, and without which the existence of properties cannot be conceived. According to such a view, matter is the ultimate analysis of all things, but such an analysis is worthless, a mere *caput mortuum;* for having no attribute of its own, it cannot be an object of knowledge. Some think that it is an actual reality, having extension and impenetrability; but such matter is not a substratum divested of all properties, but a concrete natural body.

The whole tendency of modern science points to the probability that natural forces are not only the causes of phenomena, but that they are, in truth, the very phenomena themselves; that is, that all natural bodies are compositions of forces. Boscovich long ago maintained, that the atoms of matter are physical points, or centres of attractive and repulsive forces; and Newton has recorded it as his opinion " that the particles of bodies are either impelled to each other and cohere, according to regular figures, or are repelled or recede from each other; which forces being unknown, philosophers have hitherto made their attempts upon nature in vain."* But Newton's particles were hard indestructible atoms, on which natural forces acted, unknown metaphysical substrata, and not, as the atoms of Boscovich, compositions of forces.

Many object to this dynamical constitution of matter " that it is inconceivable, that attraction and repulsion are unthinkable, unless we first think aggregated matter, as that which is attracted and repelled: to obtain the cognition of matter on this ground, we must, by a *petitio principii*, first think the aggregate; the very thing to be explained."† Now such an objection rests on the old notion of an unknown substratum; and argue as you may with its advocates, they always return again in the endless rounds of this charmed circle. There must be something, they say, to be attracted and repelled; but it is in vain to search for this something, for it is unknowable: now this admission ought to be a sufficient refutation. We only know things by their attributes, and to imagine anything void of attributes, pronounces it to be a nonentity; and to conceive such a condition to be requisite for the action and reaction of forces is tantamount to the abnegation of the reality of Nature.

* As quoted in the Philosophy of the Inductive Sciences, vol. i. p. 251.
† The Ecclesiastic and Theologian. May, 1859.

Abstract from natural bodies all their properties, except their material or physical, and there remains only weight and volume, as the primary properties of matter: now we know that the former depends on gravity or attraction, and the latter on repulsion; the ratio of these properties toward each other may be indefinitely varied, but they can never be dissevered. If a body has weight and volume, what more is requisite to constitute it a material body? And if we conceive of attraction and repulsion, as antagonistic and reason-directed forces or powers, there can be no difficulty in understanding that a material atom is a compound of an unit of each of these forces; and that the aggregations of such atoms form molecules and masses: and the latter thus formed afford a field for the operations of attraction and repulsion in any proportions, and also for the action and reaction of chemical and vital powers.

At all events such a conception of matter may be provisionally conceded; and, in the sequel, we hope to show that the assumption is not improbable. We therefore posit

Attraction + repulsion = matter.

By attraction is understood the power of attraction, an attractive force capable of operating according to an innate rational law of action; and by repulsion, the power of repulsion, a force similarly constituted but of a directly opposite character; and, lastly, by matter is understood a union of these correlative forces, a dualism which has a peculiar character of its own when its constituents are equal, but which partakes of that of either when one or other predominates.

Such being the constitution and character of matter the

question naturally arises, where is such matter to be found? All tangible and visible bodies are material, but they are something more, they are either chemical or organic, and although we can deprive organisms of life and reduce them to chemical substances, we cannot carry the actual analysis any farther by the separation of the chemical from the material properties; it can only be accomplished by mental abstraction. It would, however, be exceedingly interesting if we could detect in nature pure uncombined matter, a dualism of the physical powers in all its simplicity; and unless we greatly err, there is such a substance extensively diffused as interstellar and interstitial *ether*, commonly known as the ether of space, the acknowledged medium by which the radiations of light and heat are accomplished.

The opinion has already been advanced by Grove that this highly elastic fluid is material, that it actually possesses weight, though inappreciable; and he thinks that ether is the vapour of chemical substances, such as might emanate from the sun and its planets, forming an extension of their atmospheres which intermingle in space. This view is very different from that which we have proposed; viz. that ether is pure matter or physical substance; and it may be objected to Grove's view, that such a diffusion of vapours would transfer matter from one celestial body to another, on the principle of the cryophorus; and that in the case of insterstitial ether such a content would seriously affect the chemical constitution of bodies.

According to our conception ether is matter in the state of a highly elastic and permanent gas, an indissoluble compound of attractive and repulsive powers; and consequently it must possess the universal characteristics of matter, weight and volume. In this dualism attraction is the quantitative or basic power, and repulsion the qualitative or typical power; and just as a chemical compound can combine with another element, so ether may become a compound basic power in a more complex dualism. Thus ether or pure matter, in different quantities, may impart the atomic weights to the various chemical elements; the specific powers of which appropriate definite amounts of etherial atoms to frame their bodies, which have definite volumes as crystalline forms. The enormous condensations which must have accompanied such combinations will enable us to explain some interesting phenomena; and we need not be surprised at the amazing energy of such powers, for known chemical action has taught us that gases may be liquefied and even solidified thereby, which have resisted the intensest cold and extraordinary mechanical pressures.

It may seem difficult to apprehend that the highly elastic fluid ether is a material substance: but since solids may be so attenuated as to become inappreciable vapours, it does not require a great stretch of the imagination to conceive that ether may be gaseous matter; and that such a fluid, though its atoms are mutually repulsive, will, when in the vicinity of masses, be coerced thereby, and suffer a corresponding condensation, just as the atmospheres of celestial bodies. Space, therefore, is not a *vacuum* but a *plenum*; and as Grove has observed, the ancient aphorism, *Nature abhors a vacuum*, though metaphorical in expression, contains a comprehensive truth.

The immensity of space is so vast compared with the total volume of celestial bodies, that ether its content, invisible and subtile as it is, must possess an amount of matter by no means inconsiderable in proportion to that of tangible and visible bodies; but whatever may be their relative proportion, these two forms of matter constitute the entire material universe.

Universal matter, then, is one vast dualism of attraction and repulsion, and these powers, as a whole, can suffer no increase or decrease;—the conservation of natural forces being a fundamental principle. But though the physical powers are in this respect invariable and permanent, they have the capacity of altering their relations, by unequal distributions, in different parts of the common system, and these mutations produce the physical phenomena of Nature.

Each material atom is a unit of the central forces attraction and repulsion, which act and react on each other according to their respective laws, the one toward, and the other from, the common centre; and this antagonism causes the atom to revolve on its axis, according to the law of couples. And this statement is equally applicable to the entire system of matter, for it is the generic character which connotes all the parts, as well as the universal itself. Our experience contradicts the notion of a universal equilibrium; for the solar system, the part of the universe with which we are best acquainted, manifests a constant succession of dynamical actions. This is true, but such a condition of things may, in a sense, be regarded as abnormal; it has been brought about by the interposition of specific powers, which have produced the perturbations which we witness; but in all these actions and reactions there is ever a tendency to the restoration of equilibrium, and it is this that occasions the regular sequence of natural phenomena.

The universe of matter may have originally consisted solely of ether—one stupendous sphere of this highly elastic fluid. And supposing this to have been the case, what would have been the condition of such a sphere? The universal power of attraction,—the sum of all the aggregated atoms, would tend toward a common centre, where the whole intensity of the power would be concentrated; and the sum of the universal power of repulsion would be similarly circumstanced, but in a contrary direction, tending from, and not toward the common centre, and therefore radiating to every point of the circumference of the sphere; these forces probably flowed, and continue to flow, in tangential currents, after the manner of electricity and magnetism, by which currents the universal sphere would be maintained in a state of equable rotation. The internal arrangement of such a sphere would not be homogeneous throughout, but would consist of concentric zones, densest toward the centre and rarest toward the circumference; that is, the greatest weight and the greatest volume, being in opposite directions, corresponding with the amount of attractive and repulsive forces, by which these phenomena are produced; just as all correlatives, whether those of real forces or of ideal or logical forms, increase in intension as they decrease in extension, and *vice versâ*, being uniformly in the inverse ratio of each other.

Attraction and repulsion, thus viewed, become the universal physical powers, centripetal and centrifugal forces, which are, therefore, only peculiar phases of attraction and repulsion. The former force is also called *gravity*, and its action *gravitation;* the latter, initiatory or tangential force, but which we shall speak of as *centrifugy*, and its action as centrifugation. Gravity and centrifugy, as correlatives, are necessarily co-existent, co-equal, and co-efficient, at least this is the condition of these forces in their totality, but they are partially subject to unequal distributions; but, however their relations may be changed in this respect, they cannot be entirely severed from each other, for they are indissolubly united together as a dualism of natural powers.

In this case, then, we are at variance with the current opinion on this subject. All treatises on astronomy consider gravity as *the* universal force, the only one with which we are concerned in the consideration of celestial motions; the tangential force being regarded as an initiatory impulse, once and extrinsically imparted to each celestial body, which continues to act for ever, according to the first law of motion *provided* for this special purpose. Without such an assumption, the composition of forces, which orbits of revolution require, could not be accomplished; but why the tangential force should be afterwards set aside in order to maintain the autocracy of gravitation, is not satisfactorily explained. And the reputed origin of tangential force by the *express* interposition of Deity, is an unworthy expedient for such a science as astronomy, which ought not to be involved in such a perplexity as to be driven to the *Deus ex machina* — the last resort of ignorance.

In the " History of the Inductive Sciences," it is observed

that "the conception of Newton, equally bold and grand, disclosed between all the bodies of the universe forces of the *same* kind as those which produce the weight of bodies at the earth;" "and it has been found that the theory of universal gravitation takes up *all* the facts of astronomy, as far as they have been hitherto ascertained." This statement completely subverts our view of the subject; it is requisite, therefore, to make a few remarks thereon, in order to ascertain, if possible, which is correct.

According to Newton, each particle of matter has gravity; and the weight of any mass is the sum of the weight of all its particles, and the force with which two bodies attract each other is directly as their mass, and inversely as the square of the distance. Thanks to Newton, our knowledge of gravity is almost, if not altogether, perfect; but still, as regards astronomical phenomena, it is but one side of the question, it leaves us to contend with centrifugy as a mere assumption. We know that it is the sum of attracting units which makes up the gravity or *weight* of a mass; and why, then, should we ignore that the *volume* of the mass depends in like manner on its units of repulsion? Every mass has not only *weight*, but *volume* also, and it is impossible to conceive a body destitute of either of these properties. Density or specific gravity is a quantity, directly as the weight and inversely as the volume; and specific volume or capacity is a magnitude, directly as the volume and inversely as the weight. Now if it be important in molecular physics to consider not only the force which causes particles to cohere, but also the correlative force which causes them to expand or be driven asunder, to investigate and acknowledge the importance of heat as well as that of cohesion; why in celestial physics should attention be restricted to one force, when we know that two are required in every motion, since it is a composition of forces? We contend that, if gravity be recognised as a universal force, centrifugy is fairly entitled to the same distinction.

Now in maintaining that centrifugy is a distinct physical force demanding particular consideration as much as gravitation, in that the one is concerned as much as the other in every astronomical phenomenon, we are not dealing with a mere fanciful imagination, but with facts. Centrifugal force is a *vera causa*, it enters into the composition of all celestial motions; gravitation tends to draw all the planets to the centre of the solar system; centrifugal force counteracts this endeavour and maintains them in their orbits. It has been well observed by Sir John Herschel, that " that which opposes and neutralises force *is* force; " and it therefore follows that, since gravitation is a force and treated of as a real cause, so centrifugal force, as one of the factors in celestial motions, ought to be dealt with in a similar manner. We are justified in this conclusion by the excellent directions which the above-mentioned able author has given for conducting philosophical inquiries. " In framing a theory which shall render a rational account of any natural phenomenon, we have *first* to consider the agents on which it depends, or the causes to which we regard it as ultimately referable. These agents are not to be arbitrarily assumed, they must be such as we have good inductive grounds to believe do exist in nature, and do perform a part in phenomena analogous to those we would render an account of, or such whose presence in the actual case can be demonstrated by unequivocal signs. They must be *veræ causæ*, in short, which we can not only show to exist and to act, but the laws of whose action we can derive independently, by direct induction, from experiments purposely instituted; or, at least, make such suppositions respecting them as shall not be contrary to our experience, and which will remain to be verified by the coincidence of the conclusions we shall deduce from them with facts."* All these requirements are said to be satisfied in the case of gravitation; and if so, *mutatis mutandis*, the same applies to centrifugal force.

If this point be conceded, it affords an interesting result; it reconciles the apparently discordant theories of the two greatest astronomers, it shows that Kepler and Newton were both right and both wrong—inasmuch as neither of them took into account both sides of the question. Kepler erred in assuming that centrifugal force was *the* energy which *keeps up* the motions of the planets; and Newton, in regarding the force which *deflects* these motions, as the main object of research. " Kepler's forces," says Whewell †, " were certain imaginary qualities which appeared in the motion which bodies had; Newton's forces were causes which appeared by the change of motion. If Kepler's forces were destroyed, the body would instantly stop; if Newton's were annihilated, the body would go on uniformly in a straight line."

This illustration will enable us to put in a clearer light

* Discourses on the Study of Natural Philosophy (209), p. 197.
† History of the Inductive Sciences, vol. ii. p. 19.

our notion concerning the correlative powers, gravity and centrifugy. If the force of Kepler were destroyed the body would lose its volume and collapse into absolute density, a density void of all relations, and therefore a *nonentity* in nature; and if Newton's force were annihilated the body would be reduced to a mere vacuum, void of all ponderous content, and therefore incapable of motion of any sort. This is self-evident, for if a body only gravitates as the sum of its gravitating atoms, and these be taken away, how can it thus function? Unless indeed we return to the "beggarly element" of an unknown metaphysical substratum, and regard this as the body in which forces inhere, which would sadly mar the beauty of Newton's theory.

But there is another argument against the supposed result which would follow on the destruction of Newton's force; viz. that the body would go on uniformly in a straight line. This is based on the first law of motion; but there is another law, that of Galileo, which was arrived at by the investigation of facts, and does not rest, like the former, on the postulated hypothesis of inertia; and according to this law *every* motion is a *composition* of motions or of forces which independently co-exist in every motion. How can these two laws be reconciled? The one contemplates a motion arising from the operation of a single force, the other says that *every* motion is a composition of forces. According to Newton's law of motion also there is action and reaction in every motion. Now from what has been already stated, that all natural bodies are dualisms of forces, and that all, *quoad* their physical or material part, consist of attraction and repulsion; it follows from such a constitution that when these physical forces function as motions, that both forces must independently co-exist in each and every phenomenon; and that such phenomenon must have resulted from the action and reaction of its constituent forces, and according to the character of their relation so will be that of the corresponding effect. This is the view of the case from the realistic stand-point, regarding the motions as *bodies* moved; but dealing with motions as an abstract question, as belonging to rational mechanics, the laws of motion may be thus expressed.

First law. Motion is the composition of independent but co-existent motions.

Second law. Motion is curvilinear, the resultant of its component motions, which act and react on each other from opposite directions.

Third law. Motion approximates to the rectilinear in proportion as one component motion predominates over its antagonist.

No *natural* motion can be *absolutely* rectilinear, for no physical powers, the cause of motion, can be insulated from their dualism; therefore it can only be inferred from the tendency of attraction toward a common centre, and of repulsion directly therefrom, that, if either could possibly act alone, it would operate in a rectilinear direction. In the enumeration of the laws of motion the chronological order of their origin is usually followed, but we have above given the preference to the logical order of their evolution.

On our view of the subject gravity and centrifugy are universal powers, phases or modes of the physical powers attraction and repulsion; powers which are indissolubly associated together, and which exert their peculiar and antagonistic forces according to their respective reason-directing laws; the former acting directly as the mass and inversely as the distance; the latter, directly as the distance and inversely as the mass. This antagonism, ever varying in its actions and reactions, produces the great diversity of motions which are manifested by the celestial bodies.

This conception of a dualism of central forces will render, we think, the apprehension of astronomical phenomena more easy for the student to whom the one-sided view of gravitation, as *the* universal force, has always been a stumbling-block; to the man of science it may be superfluous, because he tacitly admits, and can duly appreciate the *necessity* of the initiatory force. This criticism may be deemed over-fastidious; but when we call to mind that it is only a few years ago when such a man as Faraday did not hesitate to declare his perplexity concerning gravitation, it affords sufficient evidence that our knowledge on this subject is not very definite. Faraday has candidly expressed his opinion that the law of gravitation is at variance with the principle of the conservation of forces; he argues that the increase and decrease of this force, according to the position of a body, seem to indicate a creation and annihilation of force; and if our memory fail not, he came to the conclusion that the phenomenon could not be explained unless by the joint idea of polarity, such as that of magnetism, an antagonism of opposite poles which might throw some light on the subject.

This difficulty is, we think, easily explained on the

view which we are advocating, that gravity and centrifugy constitute a dualism of physical powers. For it follows that since they are both ever present, acting on each other in opposite directions, an additional force in either one or other direction must increase the relative proportion of the corresponding force. For instance, the sun draws a planet, and the planet the sun, and the tendency of this mutual action is to bring the bodies together, but at the same time these bodies mutually repel each other, and the result of this conjoint action and reaction is that the planet occupies a position at a definite distance from the sun, where these forces are in a state of equilibrium. Now, thus circumstanced, the planet is in a condition to respond to any external impulse, whether toward or from the sun, as happens in the case of natural perturbations; but in whatever direction this takes place, the force overpowered, by any intervention, is in nowise diminished in energy; for as soon as the extraneous force is withdrawn the planet regains its original position, precisely as a gas when condensed is restored by its inherent elasticity to its former volume on removal of the condensing pressure. So if a body be forcibly brought nearer to the centre of gravity of another body, the force employed in effecting this is equivalent to an increase of gravity since it acts in the same direction; and so if a body be projected from the earth, the relative proportion of its attraction and repulsion is altered thereby, and when the dominating force is dissipated its inherent gravity comes into play and restores the body to the earth.

The increase and decrease of forces, continual occurrences in every department of nature, are not indications of the creation and annihilation of force, but are only *local* disturbances of co-existing and opposite forces by the variations of their relative proportions; whilst the total amount of these forces in the entire system remains unchanged according to the principle of the conservation of forces.

Let us now endeavour to apply this assumption, that gravity and centrifugy constitute a dualism of correlative forces, to the explanation of some astronomical phenomena, and more particularly of those of the solar system.

The solar system is supposed to have *originally* consisted of one vast sphere of nebular matter, revolving on its axis, and from which all the parts of the *present* system have been derived by continuous condensation around its centre, accompanied by successive and periodical disruptions at the circumference of the sphere. But before noticing these developments of the solar system it may be as well to inquire concerning its relations with the universal system.

Is the solar system, as a subordinate, immediately and directly connected with the common centre of the universe? Or is it associated with another sun after the manner of binary stars, and this combination in its turn, through ascending series of generalisations, connected with the *summum genus* of the universal system? Many circumstances seem to indicate that the latter is the more probable relationship. The retrograde motions of Uranus' satellites and the great inclinations of their orbits to the ecliptic, point to some disturbing influence on the confines of our system, such as might be induced by the action of a twin sun. The parabolic course also of some comets, which implies that their return to our system is not probable, might by a twin sun be so diverted and curved around its focus as to enable them to complete their orbits by an inverse and retrograde motion.

Our sun not only rotates on its axis, but has an onward course in the heavens, carrying along with it all the parts of its system, and moving at the rate of 150 millions of miles during a terrestrial year. According to M. Argelander, this course tends, by some grand path, towards a point in the constellation Hercules; this apparent path may well seem to be undeviating, when the nearest fixed star is about twenty billions of miles off—a distance almost inconceivable. It is probable that the sun's course is curved like that of other celestial bodies, so that the direction in which it points will vary accordingly. It is not, however, probable that this course lies through the immensity of space, immediately influenced by the central attraction of the universe; analogy rather leads us to expect, that as the solar system is comparatively small and definite, that its orbit will partake of a similar character: even if the diameter of its orbit were three billions of miles, its circumference of about ten billions would find ample space for its revolution and that of its twin sun within the bounds of other stellar systems.

But where is this twin sun to be found? Did we but know its position and motion we might hope to be able to settle our sun's path. It is possible that this sun may only exist as a star so small as hitherto to have escaped observation, as happened in the case of the planet Uranus. It has also been conjectured that this body may be opaque, and consequently only visible by reflected light, and if so, it could but appear as the faintest of nebulæ, for its distance is probably thrice that of Neptune from the sun. This conjecture is so far consistent, that whether a body be *autophotic* or not, it is still capable of acting and reacting on other bodies, according to the laws of central forces; and though the bodies of the twin suns are far apart, their systems, with their enveloping spheres of ether, may be approximated or even overlapping each other, so that their respective currents of undulations may freely mingle and intersect each other, by which the communication of the physical forces would be maintained. But in whatever way the solar system may be connected with other systems, this one thing is certain, that it cannot stand alone, but must be in relation with others, as being an integrant part of the universal system.

The solar system, in its individuality, is supposed to have been originally one rotating sphere. A sphere which, throughout all its parts, was subject to the action and reaction of the physical forces attraction and repulsion, the former concentrating its energy at the centre, and the latter at the circumference; the immediate parts of the sphere communicating together by axial currents of gravity, and by equatorial currents of centrifugy. In this manner all the parts of the sphere are held together, bound, as it were, to the axis of gravitating force, whilst at the equator the parts of the sphere experience a constant tendency to be thrown off by centrifugy. Such a system, though nearly spherical, that is, in a state of equilibrium, would not be homogeneous, but made up of concentric zones, the inner ones gradually increasing in density as the outer ones do in rarefaction; there would, however, be an intermediate zone in which these properties are equal, a nodal region of statical rest, a condition favourable to a momentous change in the system.

We are not able to determine whether the universal sphere of ether was disturbed by the interposition of chemical powers, or whether this cause of differentiation was reserved for our solar system; at all events, the latter seems to have been constituted as an aggregate of chemical substances in a vesicular or nebular state, interpenetrated by, and immersed in, the ocean of ether. Now, by the very act of the formation of the chemical elements by the union of physical and chemical powers, an enormous condensation must have taken place, accumulating gravitating matter at the centre, and extricating an enormous heat, which would flow outwardly as centrifugal force, thereby accelerating the rotation of the sphere. Our idea of rotation is so naturally formed on the spinning round of a solid in which all the concentric parts, though increasing in volume, according to their distance from the centre, perform their revolution in the same time, that it is difficult to imagine the internal condition of a rotating nebular sphere, but in all probability its concentric zones have different times, according to their densities, imparting a spiral arrangement, and such a condition is confirmed by the observed forms of many nebulæ now existing.

The experiments of Professor Plateau[*] on the figures of rotating liquid masses are very interesting, and in some degree are applicable to fluids generally; the condition of aërial motions around rotating bodies also offers a good

---

[*] Taylor's Scientific Memoirs, vol. iv. p. 16.

subject for investigation. But whether the internal motion of the nebular sphere be spiral or concentric, there is a constant tendency of the equatorial fluid part to extend itself uniformly in a given plane; and thus it is that the positions and motions of the now independent portions of the system are all nearly related to the ecliptic. In the case of the sphere, there is a limit to its extension; when the continually increasing centrifugal force, increasing *pari passu* with the central condensation, has reduced the sphere to an extreme state of ellipticity, the tension of gravity will be overcome, and a fission of the sphere produced, which will be greatly facilitated and determined by the nodal zone of equilibrium. This fission would have been immediately followed by a collapse of the inner sphere, and consequently by a renewal of the process of condensation, as the first step in the repetition of a similar series of operations. The detached zone would whirl around in eddying waves, gradually enlarging its undulations until it reached that position in space where the mutual attractions and repulsions, between it and the inner sphere, now become a sun to the outer planetary zone, arrive at a state of equilibrium. The ring would continue to rotate, until by its rupture, which the spiral motion greatly aids, it would be rolled up and gathered together into a distinct planet. The explosion of a bubble of phosphuretted hydrogen, when the air is still, gives an apt illustration of this nebular ring and its subsequent rolling up into a cloud, which only wants the restraint of a central attraction to complete the analogy. We need not, however, follow out the formation of each planet by the successive fissions of the central sphere, nor that of the rings and satellites of the planets by the repetition of a similar process, for this has been already fully described by Laplace in the explication of his celebrated theory.

The theory of Laplace accounts for the rotation of the sun and of the planets in the same direction, and in nearly the same plane, by ascribing them to the original rotation of the primæval system; so far, this is preferable to the notion of an initiatory impulse for each planet by divine interposition, but it gives no insight into the cause of this original rotation, nor into the nature of the condensation which produced the intense ignition. "The cosmogony of Laplace," says Comte *, "seems to me to present the most plausible theory of any yet proposed. It has the eminent merit of requiring for the formation of our system only the simple agents weight and heat, which meet us everywhere, and which are the only two principles of action which are absolutely general." And why are these principles two in number? And why are they general? Because matter itself, the sum and substance of the system, is a dualism of attraction and repulsion, and all the various physical forces are only modes or phases of these powers; one while attraction is manifested as solidity and at another as weight, being called cohesion or gravity according to its mode of action, and so in like manner repulsion may appear as either centrifugy or heat. These antagonistic forces, by their actions and reactions, produce all physical phenomena, and since they co-exist throughout nature, they must be absolutely general.

* Positive Philosophy, vol. i. p. 211

The principle of dualism teaches us that the solar system, in its present condition, is actuated by the central forces in a similar manner as when it was originally one uniform sphere. It now, as then, rotates by the action of the same tangential currents; then, indeed, they traversed a mass somewhat homogeneous, but now they traverse different media, and are consequently modified thereby. Thus from the centre to the surface of the sun the medium is very different from that of the ether of space, and therefore the undulating currents, though capable of being propagated through both media, cannot be so in precisely the same manner; just as molecular undulations as sounds are transmitted through both solids and the atmosphere, though their velocity and other conditions greatly vary according to the medium. What we are desirous of maintaining is that the planets are still connected with the sun by tangential currents of forces, just as when they formed continuous parts, or concentric zones, of the same sphere; that they are thereby maintained in definite positions, which in relation to the sun are those of equilibrium, and that their revolutions are concentric rotations of their parts of the system, all of which are regulated by and centre in the sun; the solar system being still *virtually* but one sphere of revolving ether, the sun and its planets being parts, predominant indeed, but still parts of the same sphere.

From this it follows that rotation on an axis is the one and universal motion produced by the action and reaction of central physical forces, and however varied the different kinds of motion may be, they are but diverse aspects or modifications of rotation.

In a system thus constituted we see why comets in their eccentric courses, crossing many planetary zones, may suffer perturbation in their passage through ether; whilst the planets are less liable thereto, not only on account of the greater density of their bodies, but also because they are moving in the same direction as the ether itself, which is also rotating as part of the solar system.

The view which we have been advocating concerning the relations of gravity and centrifugy in astronomical phenomena is suggestive of many remarks on other parts of this subject; such remarks may, on examination, prove for the most part worthless, still the very process of refuting them may elicit truths which would have otherwise escaped attention.

How came it to pass that the planets, as we recede from the sun, are separated from each other by distances of a progressively increasing ratio? According to Bode's law, if the distance between Mercury and Venus be taken at three, the successive doubling of this number with the common *constant* of 4 for each planet gives the ratio of the planetary distances from the sun. This hypothesis has been found to answer except in the case of Neptune, which makes a breach of the law; this law, however, is wholly *empirical*, it offers no physical explanation of the regularity of an arrangement which cannot be devoid of some rational foundation.

Such an arrangement we conceive was produced in accordance with the construction of the original sphere from which the planets were evolved. As already stated, the tangential currents of central forces which actuated the sphere, by their interferences produced nodal lines, on which ruptures would take place as points of least resistance; these lines, from the centre to the circumference of the sphere, would comprise spaces progressively increasing just as the law of radiation; and consequently the planets when evolved would partake of the same symmetrical arrangement. And if so the position of the planets might possibly have been determined *à priori* by geometrical processes.

On the same principle we account for the enormous volume and the comparatively small weight or gravitating matter in the outer planets, whilst the inner planets are small and ponderous, gravity being in the ascendant in the latter, centrifugy in the former. For the condition of the intermediate *asteroids* we also find some explanation in supposing it to be the intermediate region of the solar system, where the central forces are in a state of equilibrium. Not the original node of the total central forces, but the resulting node from the then existing altered state of the system, and during such a balanced state it might be expected that small accessions of centrifugal force would operate promptly and repeatedly in the successive discharge of small zones, containing but little ponderable matter. Be this as it may, the fact is that the mass of the planetoids is very small, even thirty of them not exceeding a quarter part of the earth's weight. Olbers has suggested the idea, that these numerous planetoids have been produced by the explosion of a planet which ought, according to Bode's law, to have existed between Mars and Jupiter. But granting the possibility of such an occurrence, the fragments ought to have returned, and circulated around their original centre of gravity.

In the consideration, however, of the distances, volumes,

and weights of the planets, there are many irregularities which are not fully resolved by the above explanation. For instance, Neptune is not as distant from the sun as the increasing ratio of the adjacent planets would lead us to expect; and, moreover, Neptune has one-third more matter and double the specific gravity as Uranus, whilst their volumes are very nearly equal. As the existence of a twin sun is uncertain, we cannot speculate on the probable influence of such a perturbation on the outer region of our system. But chemical forces may be *veræ causæ*, which must not be overlooked. We know that many substances in a state of vapour are highly rarefied, and yet condense into dense liquids and solids; whilst, on the other hand, some vapours are very ponderous, and yet when solidified form substances of low specific gravity; and between these extremes there are great variations. It does not follow that the chemical elements known to us exist in any other planet, and the awanting numbers in the scale of chemical equivalents are sufficiently numerous to afford a great variety of unknown chemical elements. And if so, the corresponding variety of physical properties, which such elements would possess, might afford data for the explanation of some of the planetary peculiarities.

The great latitude which has been permitted in astronomical speculations, is our only apology for venturing to offer *a* reason, but probably not *the* reason, why our earth alone of all the inner planets has got a *moon*, and why, coincidently with this circumstance, the distance between the earth and Mars is almost double that between the earth and Venus. This would seem to indicate that there is a planet awanting between the earth and Mars; and may not the moon be that planet, drawn out of its orbit by some extraordinary occurrence? We search in vain for a physical, but may there not be a chemical cause? The waters, which now cover so large a portion of the earth's surface, could not have existed as a chemical compound, but only as oxygen and hydrogen during the intense heat of the earth long after its formation, nor could they have combined until the earth had experienced a great reduction of temperature; but when their union did take place, the explosion must have been stupendous. Could not the recoil of such an explosion have been sufficient to have drawn the adjacent small planet, Luna, within the influence of the earth's attraction?

The sun which originally, as the entire solar sphere possessed a radius of probably not less than 10,000 millions of miles, has, by successive fissions and separations of planetary zones, been reduced to a diameter of 882,000 miles; and its period of rotation has by the same events been brought down from about 200 years to less than twenty-six days. Recent observations render it probable that at least one planet exists between Mercury and the sun; but it is an interesting question whether the formative process of the sun has yet terminated, whether the production of new planets may be still looked for. The appearance of the sun indicates that the first stage of such a process has been commenced; it is, however, not improbable that its present annular zone, and even succeeding ones, may be permanent like the rings of Saturn. The present ring is of a nebular or cometic consistency, and acts the part of a *photosphere*, by becoming brilliantly illuminated by the impinging rays proceeding from the mass of the sun. Between this photosphere and the atmosphere of highly elastic vapours immediately resting on the sun, there must be a zone of ether; the sun and its elastic envelope, including the ether, could not be visible, but the rays darting from this intensely heated mass, and impinging on the vesicular substance of the photosphere, would produce a most dazzling effulgence, just as dust or filings projected into a highly heated, but invisible gas, immediately become luminous. The sun's heat and light have been attributed to combustion, to showers of aerolites falling on the sun, and to many other causes; but on the principle of "least action," the phenomenon is better explained by that process of condensation which is going on at the centre of the system. The vaporous state of the sun's atmosphere has been established by the experiments of Arago on the polarisation of the sun's light, and such an atmosphere would be subject to similar currents from the equator to the pole, as take place on our planet, accompanied by whirlwinds — stupendous exaggerations of our tropical tornadoes. Such vortices, viewed by us, would have the appearance of spots like those which occur on the sun, they would suck in and be filled with ether, just as the interior of a whirlpool is filled with common air; and, consequently, the radiations through the ether would be invisible, but striking on the compressed sides of the vortices, the reflected rays would render the sides luminous. These spots are confined to a limited region on each side of the sun's equator, and their increase and decrease, according to Schwabe, are subject to a periodical cycle.

The curious and interesting phenomenon of the zodiacal

light was long regarded as the outer portion of the sun's atmosphere, but, according to Laplace*, this is a dynamical impossibility, for it could not extend, he says, more than one-third of the distance between the sun and Mercury. This limitation somewhat approximates to the node of indifference where attraction and repulsion are in equilibrium—a limitation which S. M. Drach † places at sixteen millions of miles from the centre of the sun. A very prevalent opinion concerning this light is, that it is produced by the circulation of a stream of meteors around the sun, which are individually too small to be discerned otherwise than as diffused nebular light, but which periodically coalesce into larger bodies and become manifested as showers of falling stars. According to our view of the solar system, the zodiacal light may receive another explanation. The vast expanse of ether within the bounds of this system is an important constituent part thereof, and since it is an elastic fluid, it must, in accordance with the laws of such, experience condensation around every centre of gravity; and consequently the most considerable compression in the vicinity of the sun, the general centre of the system, in other words, the amount of condensation would be according to the sum of attraction mutually exerted between the sun and its ethereal atmosphere. The substance of such a spheroid of compressed ether would probably be much inferior to that of the rarest comets, but still sufficiently dense to be illuminated by the sun's rays. The lenticular form of the zodiacal light is such as might be expected to result from the great

---

* Encyclopædia of Physical Science. Art. Zodiacal Light.
† Times Newspaper, Feb. 2, 1859.

velocity of the sun's rotation; and its position, a little removed from that of the ecliptic, is in accordance with this view. It may also be remarked that the existence of such a region of condensed ether around the sun would account for some of the changes which comets undergo when in the vicinity of this luminary. This explanation is not inconsistent with the view recently advanced by Professor Olmsted of Yale College. "He agrees with Laplace in thinking that this light is a nebular body revolving in the plane of the solar equator; and, from long and careful observation, he is of opinion that it has a period of something less than a year; and in the position assigned by him to its orbit, showers of shooting stars may happen in April and November." *

Before concluding these brief and cursory remarks on astronomical phenomena, we must not lightly pass over that extraordinary class of cosmical bodies which, as comets, form so interesting, yet erratic, part of the solar system; they have already furnished the means of becoming better acquainted with its constitution, and will probably, when better understood, be instrumental in solving many momentous problems.

Comets move in ellipses of various degrees of eccentricity, and also describe other figures of the conic sections; and this enables us to divide them into three classes, the elliptical, the parabolic, and the hyperbolic comets. Elliptical comets might also be termed solar, as their orbits are confined to our system; that is, these bodies not only at their perihelion describe a regular curve, but also

---

* Mrs. Somerville's Connexion of the Physical Sciences, p. 449.

F

at their aphelion, which is within the limits of the sun's attraction. Whilst, however, the planets form ellipses but little removed from circles which are arranged concentrically around the sun, the solar comets revolving in ellipses of extreme eccentricity must necessarily intersect the planetary orbits, and consequently be seriously affected by their occasional proximity, though this is in some measure diminished by the plane of the cometary orbits being greatly inclined to the ecliptic. As regards the substance of comets they all possess enormous volumes in comparison to their weights; a constitution which also characterises the outer planets, but which in the comets is greatly exaggerated; indeed their substance is so rare, that stars even of small magnitude have not only been seen through their tails, but even through the densest part — their nucleus or head. They probably consist of a gaseous elastic fluid, rendered somewhat opaque for the better reflection of light, by the diffusion of the vesicles of volatile liquids. Such a material body, though capable of retaining its individuality, would be so sensitive to extraneous influences as to be perfectly Protean in form. And such is the case with comets: — one while they are gathered together into regular spheres, at others greatly elongated; sometimes the lighter part trails behind like the tail of a rocket, and this will continue as the comet approaches the sun; but after its perihelion the tail will take precedence of the body. The reason of the latter curious condition is, that the denser part of the comet must needs be opposite to the sun, according to the law of gravity; and the lighter part must be in the contrary direction, elastic fluids becoming rarer and rarer as they recede from the centre of attraction: so that in reality the position of all the parts of a comet, in relation to its centre of gravity, remains unaltered. It has been ascertained that the nucleus of comets becomes much condensed as it approaches the sun; which from their elastic constitution might have been anticipated: and such an occurrence must be accompanied by an evolution of heat, which accounts for the extraordinary splendour of some comets in such a position; an antophotence similar to that of the sun, and having the self-same origin, that of material condensation.

Strongly contrasted as planets and comets are, both in their constitution and in their movements, there is every reason to believe that, as parts of the same system, they have been produced by the operation of the same causes, under different conditions: central condensation by the influence of gravity evolves centrifugal force, which tending outward, throws off a portion of the revolving sphere; and since all these portions are not similar, they manifest that the action has taken place under different circumstances. The regular coherence of the sphere, and the gradually increasing pressure of centrifugy, would quietly separate the planetary zones; but the presence of rarer and less coherent matter, at the circumference of the sphere, would modify the result; such matter might at any time, more especially during periodical paroxysms, be hurled off by centrifugal force, and be propelled with prodigious violence resembling the flight of a rocket. Such discharges might take place during the evolution of each of the planets, and their orbits would vary accordingly, corresponding with the periods of their *birth*. This, however, is only conjecture, but it is consistent with facts; rotation causes liquid spheres to become more and more oblate, till they become a mere plane, and then throw off a ring, that is if the rotation be equable and the material sufficiently coherent; but if violent the parts fly off at a tangent. We cannot pause to show how well this explains the positions of the inner or elliptical comets: but there is one circumstance relating to Halley's comet, which may be noticed. It is the only one of all the known periodical comets, which moves in a contrary direction to that of the planets, that is, against the order of the signs; and it is worthy of remark, that its orbit extends beyond that of Neptune, where a counter action may be in operation, such as a twin sun might produce, and which would also account for the retrograde motion of Uranus' satellites. The existence of a twin sun would account for the orbits of the parabolic comets: such comets, whether projected originally from the system of our sun, or from that of the other sun, would follow a course almost straight, in the region intermediate between the two systems, where the forces of both are nodal; but on coming within the more direct influence of either sun, their course would form re-entering curves, and thus by inverse operations, may be alternately restored to either system, revolving around its respective sun. And so likewise hyperbolic comets may not be wanderers through boundless space, traversing all the systems of the universe, but the bonds of union between our twin system and some other analogous system, which though far removed from each other, may be periodically encompassed by these visitors; that these comets do not call once for all, and then desert us for ever, though their visits are, like those of angels, few and far between.

From this hasty sketch of the application of the principle of dualism to astronomy, it is hoped that sufficient has been said to show why we consider that this science is not an artillery problem, as is generally supposed. "The identity of weight and the moon's tendency toward the earth," says Comte*, "places the whole of celestial mechanics in a new light. It shows us the motion of the stars as exactly like that of projectiles, which we have under our immediate observation. If we could start our projectiles with a sufficient and continuous force beyond the resisting atmosphere, we should find them the models of the planetary system, or in other words, astronomy has become an artillery problem, simplified by the absence of the resisting medium, but complicated by the variety and plurality of weights."

The inadequacy of an initiatory impulse, as a *primum mobile*, and as a counterpoise to the continuous force of gravitation, has been discussed and shown to be superfluous; since, in nature, there is a co-existent and opposite force, which provides all the antagonism which gravity requires in order to function as astronomical phenomena. If the earth, as well as the moon, did not exert a mutually repulsive, as well as a mutually attractive power, toward each other, they would inevitably come together; to prevent this the tangential force must be continuously applied; one artillery discharge would not be sufficient, an incessant succession of discharges would be required to balance the

* Positive Philosophy, vol. i. p. 181.

continuous currents of gravitation. This is well illustrated by the familiar toy of the pea and tobacco pipe, and also by a ball playing on the top of a water jet; in both cases the rotating projectiles can only be maintained in an elevated and definite position, by continuous impulses. Comte, in his analogy, postulates the absence of a resisting medium which cannot occur; for the *ether* of space meets us in every part of the solar system, an important material constituent without which physical forces could not operate. Now such a medium, if astronomy were a mere artillery problem, would as surely cause a planet to fall, as an ordinary projectile; whereas we know that the orbits of the planets, though continually perturbed, are perpetually conserved as *instantaneous* ellipses.

This subject is very interesting, but we must conclude with pointing out how the natural powers thus far obtained are related in their respective dualisms.

Attraction + repulsion = physical substance or matter.
Gravity   + centrifugy = celestial bodies or stars.

The action and re-action of the correlative forces of matter produce physical phenomena, and the correlation, matter, is the subject or noun-substantive of physics. So the stars, using the term in its largest sense, are particular forms of matter, and as such the subject of the particular physical science, astronomy. Descriptive astronomy is the natural history of the stars depending on definitions and classification; physical astronomy regards the internal constitution of the stars, as compounds of gravity and centrifugy; and a knowledge of the action and re-action of these forces constitutes celestial mechanics.

CHAP. III.

THE MOLECULAR FORCES, COHESION AND HEAT, MODES OR PHASES OF PHYSICAL POWERS.

All modes of Physical Forces function in some form of Motion. — Molecular motions individually inappreciable: only manifested in the aggregate. — Molecular Attraction called Cohesion. — Molecular Repulsion, expansive Force or Heat. — The term Micronomy proposed for Molecular Physics. — The Solid, Liquid, and Gaseous states of Matter. — The nature of Latent Heat. — The Spheroidal Form of Boutigny, not a fourth state of Matter. Cohesion a quantitative; Heat a qualitative Force: the former fixed and definite; the latter diffuse and variable. — Condensations of Gases in porous Bodies. — Action of a plate of Platinum. — The Quantity of Heat only determined relatively to a given Standard. — The Zero of Heat unknowable. — The Conduction of Heat. — Expansion. — Motion of Molecules and Motion of Mass modes of the same Phenomenon. — Joule's Equivalent of a Unit of Heat. — Convection of Heat in Fluids. — The ratio of Expansion in Gases. Expansion not an invariable indication of an increment of Heat. — Specific Heats. — Condensation evolves Heat: Heat absorbed on Rarefaction. — Diffusion of Liquids and Gases. — Osmotic Phenomena. — The Sum of Latent and Sensible Heats and Vapours, the same for all tensions. — High pressure Vapours — Paradoxical effect of. — Caigniard De la Tour's Experiments thereon. — Molecular Attraction. — Crystallisation. — Isomorphism, Dimorphism. — Allotropy. — Conclusion.

HAVING considered the forces of gravity and centrifugy, as modes of the universal dualism of the physical powers, attraction and repulsion; and having shown that these reason-directed forces are the immediate causes of celestial phenomena; we now turn to the consideration of physical powers, under a different aspect, as molecular forces, the causes of the different states of matter.

The changes of material bodies, which take place as molecular motions, are so minute that they cannot be individually seen and measured: — these constitute the subject matter of molecular physics, a science much more complicated than astronomy, and, consequently, not so far advanced in its development; but one which, notwithstanding its intricate character, is making good progress in consequence of the superior advantage which it enjoys in the privilege of experimenting, by which it is enabled to reproduce its phenomena at pleasure, for the verification of observations.

We proceed in the first place to inquire into the nature of the forces which actuate the molecules of material bodies. These forces produce *motions*, and it is thereby determined that they are phases of *physical powers*, for it is the characteristic attribute of such powers to cause motion, that is, change of position in space. The forces which we now have to deal with do not exert their influence over vast extents, from common centres, though they are fundamentally modifications of the same universal attraction and repulsion; but, having a different field of action, they assume a different aspect. The molecules of matter attract each other, and become aggregated together into various forms, and the force by which this is effected, is called *cohesion:* the molecules, however, thus aggregated, never come into actual contact, but are kept apart, at various distances from each other, by a repulsive energy, inherent in the molecules, and co-existent with cohesion; a mode of repulsion which is distinguished from centrifugy as expansive force or *heat*. Cohesion and heat are, therefore, the correlative phases of physical forces, as viewed in relation to molecules, just as gravity and centrifugy are phases of the same universal powers, in relation to cosmical masses or stars. The terms *cohesion* and *heat* are so firmly established that we shall continue to use them, though the former gives a very inadequate idea of the attraction concerned in liquids and gases; we should have preferred such terms as those of *synogy* or *synogetic* force, and thermacy or thermotic force.

Whilst engaged in preliminary remarks, we may also notice what appears to us an ill-advised and unsystematic attempt to construct a science of heat, as *Thermotics*. The analogy which seems to have suggested the attempt is that of dynamics in rational mechanics: but if such a proceeding were sanctioned, we ought, according to this rule, to have also sciences of centrifugy and of gravity, which would be superfluous, since astronomy is comprehensive enough to embrace all these considerations; and so molecular physics includes within its scope all that need be known concerning heat and cohesion, the correlative powers of its dualism. It would, however, be convenient if we had an individual name for molecular physics: this is good as far as it goes, just as we speak of celestial physics to mark another branch of general physics; but which is better distinguished by the special name of astronomy. So molecular physics ought to have a particular name, and we think that of *micronomy* might answer the purpose. Then *micronomy* would be the science or systematic knowledge of small things or *molecules*, as *astronomy* is that of celestial masses or *stars*.

When treating of a rotating body, or system of bodies, we saw that the central forces were unequally distributed; that whilst gravity prevailed at the centre and centrifugy at the circumference, these forces at the intermediate part of the system were in a state of equilibrium. Molecular forces also are capable of a similar unequal distribution; but the circumstances being different, the phenomena by which they are manifested assume different characters. We deal not now with an entire system made up of many parts and concentrated around a common centre; but we regard distinct individual parts of the system, and find that in such limited portions of matter the molecules may be one while under the influence of an excess of cohesion, and at another of heat; or they may be in a statical state, these forces being equal. So that we can consider molecular bodies under three distinct forms, commonly called *the states of matter;* the solid, the liquid, and the gaseous or vaporous; and it is now admitted that it is physically possible for all bodies to be capable of existing in either or all of these states.

In considering the changes of bodies from one state to another; we naturally view them from our every-day, or common sense stand-point: surrounded as we are by the effects of gravity, we are more impressed by the state of solidity than of the others; and so we ordinarily speak of the melting of solids, and the boiling of liquids; and thus Miller in his Chemistry says, that "all gases may be regarded as the vapours of liquids of an extreme degree of volatility.' The course of nature, however, seems to have been the reverse of this: originally all material things existed as highly elastic fluids, and the solids and liquids which we now see around us are condensations from the normal gaseous condition by the interposition of extraneous forces. When we treat of chemistry, this will be more fully explained; but in the meantime it must be borne in mind that each element has a material or physical body of a specific atomic weight and of a definite volume; and hence it is that the different kinds of molecular substances vary so greatly in their physical properties according to the relative masses of the chemical atoms, as is well illustrated in the case of the specific heats of different bodies. For, of course, if the molecules to be moved differ in weight and volume, they will require the application of different amounts of force to change their condition. Recent researches have shown that the weights of equal volumes of most gases (and of vapours when sufficiently removed from the point of liquefaction), are in the ratio of the chemical equivalents; but in the case of liquids and of solids no such relation obtains. In solids the molecules are frequently arranged in symmetrical forms, varying greatly in volume, and a careful attention to their atomic volumes as well as their atomic weights, would give a mean result, which might explain the physical properties of many substances.

Let us briefly illustrate the relations of the correlative molecular forces, in the three states of matter, as ice, water, and steam. Ice is a crystalline solid in which cohesion predominates over heat; the latter force is also present and acts the part of the passive or resisting force in the composition of forces, the material body or dualism of physical powers. By the predominance of cohesion in ice the molecules are brought together and constrained at so many different points that there is little freedom of motion, and that only corresponding to the crystalline axes. At the earth's surface ice melts when the temperature rises above 32° Fahr. and it becomes water; the excess of its cohesive force being balanced by the acquired heat, the molecules are in a statical state and free to obey an impulse in either direction, whether that of heat or cohesion. In the liquid state it is evident that, although neither one nor other of the molecular forces predominates, both are present; for small portions or drops attract each other and run together, and maintain a spheroidal form, but cannot so far cohere as to become solid on account of the repulsive energy of the combined heat. Under ordinary circumstances if water be heated to 212° it flies off in the form of steam or gaseous vapour; in steam heat is in the ascendant, and in consequence thereof its molecules repel each other with great energy, so that cohesion exerts its force inwardly toward condensation, in which respect its action is analogous to that of gravity; and heat, like centrifugy, has an outward tendency, putting the molecules in motion by expansion, which, utilised by mechanical contrivances, becomes a driving power in the industrial arts.

This statement, though correct as far it goes (only pointing out that material bodies melt and boil under ordinary circumstances at definite and unvarying temperatures), yet it leaves out of notice a most important consideration, viz. that such changes do not take place suddenly when the given temperatures are attained, but gradually, during which a considerable amount of heat disappears or becomes passive or *latent*, as it is termed, and is the efficient cause of the change of condition. The operation is very simple. In liquefaction, for instance, the molecules of the solid are held in certain positions by an excess of cohesion, and when they arrive at such a temperature that they cannot be farther moved without changing their relative positions, on which solidity depends, they require sufficient heat to equalise cohesion before they can be maintained in new positions; and so when the liquid returns to a solid the process is reversed.* In vaporisation a similar action takes place, only in comparison to that of liquefaction a much larger proportion of heat is required; but this is accompanied by a corresponding increase in the result, for the molecules are removed much farther from each other, and therefore, as might be expected, require a greater force to preserve them in such a position. These changes of state, like the change of a body from rest to motion, depend on the alteration of the previous relation of its correlative physical forces; if a body at rest is to be moved, the force which keeps it stationary must be balanced or neutralised by an opposite kind of force, and during the accomplishment of this object the latter force will appear to be entirely lost or rendered latent, though in fact it is perfectly efficient, operating in overcoming the force which tends to produce a state of rest. And thus a liquid is like a machine at the point of moving, its forces are statically balanced, and it is ready to obey an excess of either of its forces, attraction or repulsion; becoming either solid or gaseous, according to the character of the predominant force, just as the machine, under like circumstances, either moves or falls back into a state of rest.

We must not omit to notice the *spheroidal* form which liquids assume when poured on very hot metallic surfaces, which has been carefully investigated by M. Boutigny, who regards it as a new or fourth state of matter: but we cannot accept his conclusion; for although the appearance is very curious, it is not singular; it is still that of a liquid in an unusual position. It seems to belong to the same class of facts as liquid globules on repulsive surfaces, as dew on the leaves of plants, drops of oil on wet paper, of mercury on the table, and the like; in all of which gravity being equipoised, the attraction of cohesion between the molecules of the liquid comes into play and arranges them around a common centre, which produces the globular form. The concomitant phenomena of spheroidal heat, such as the reduction of temperature in the interior of the globular liquid by its superficial evaporation, and others, are secondary results arising from the ordinary relations of liquids to heat. The main circumstance, the elevation of the spheroidal liquid above and completely out of contact with the heated metal, seems to depend on the evolution of high pressure vapour, in the first instance, which may be continued by the same, or by a current of highly heated air, as when the experiment is performed on wire gauze over the flame of a lamp. In short, it is precisely of the same character as some paradoxical effects of solid carbonic acid; this substance, though possessing the astonishingly low temperature of $-106°$, may be immersed in water without causing it to freeze, and may even be handled with impunity; whilst iron only at —40° will destroy the flesh as effectually as the actual cautery : but these facts are easily explained, for the solid acid, in fact, never touches either the water or the hand, but is separated therefrom by an atmosphere of its own vapour in a high state of elasticity.

The different states of matter are so distinct and so peculiarly characterised that their consideration, as separate branches of knowledge, is readily suggested; and the more so as by such a method we are enabled to treat of the motions of all the various natural bodies under the three heads of solids, liquids, and gases. These branches of molecular physics are very important, and their cultivation has been promoted by the application of the most profound processes of the calculus; but they still afford a wide field for investigation. The gaseous state of bodies is the one which of late years has been most studied, in consequence of the great importance of *steam*, as a moving power; it is also much more simple in its relations, the predominance of repulsion obliterating those innumerable differences which the atomic weights of molecules occasion in solids by acting in the same direction as cohesion; and hence it is that many generalisations have been arrived at, as those concerning the condensation, expansion, and diffusion of gases. The weights and volumes of bodies are ever varying according to the relative proportions of their constituents, the molecular forces; these, as the results of the actions and reactions of their forces, are important considerations, but let us observe the *modus operandi* of these forces.

In astronomy we have no power to alter the course of nature, the science is purely one of observation; but in micronomy we can subject the objects of study to experiments, we can alter the relations of their correlative forces by the addition or subtraction of either, and note the results. In such experiments it has been found that molecular forces, cohesion and heat, comport themselves very differently. If we take a body having a definite weight and volume, we can augment the latter considerably by placing it near another body which is much hotter, that is, which has an excess of thermotic force; and the increase of its volume will be in proportion to the degree of heat employed. On removing the expanded body from the source of heat, it will gradually return to its original volume; but in all its changes its weight will remain unaltered. Now if we desire to reverse the experiment by placing a body of great density in contact with a lighter body, we find no tendency to an equilibrium of density, for each body retains its original weight. It is true that a similar state of things occurs in astronomy; gravitation is a fixed and invariable quantity in each member of the solar system, whilst centrifugal force is in a continuous current of diffusion from the centre to the extreme limits of the system; and this fixed stability of the one force seems to determine the position of the axis, whilst the outward pressure of the other force causes the equatorial rotation. Thus in the dualism of physical powers, it would appear that attraction, in all its phases, is the quantitative force, whilst repulsion and its congeners are qualitative. But even in the case of gravitation, we see a force concentrated at the centre of a system and acting with its united energy on other bodies; so that turn it as you may, there seems to be a deficiency of explanation in the case of cohesion, the attractive force in molecular physics. There is evidently something awanting akin to the central action of gravity: — we can detect some indications of it, but it looms very hazily.

The weight of bodies can only be altered by adding or abstracting ponderable molecules; but may they not exert attractive and condensing influences on each other, so as to alter the relative weights of their parts whilst the entire weight of the whole is conserved? In searching for a corroboration of this conjecture, the attention must be turned to those bodies which are far removed from each other in density, such as solids and gases. Now we know that when gases are subjected to the action of that very dense substance platinum, they have been found to experience unlooked-for changes. Had this experiment been only tried with one gas at a time, or with gases having no affinity for each other, the resulting phenomenon would have escaped detection. Fortunately, however, the experiment was tried with a mixture of oxygen and hydrogen gases, and still more fortunately, the investigation was conducted by Faraday. In this experiment we find what we are in search of. The great density of the platinum acts as an attracting molecular force, exerting on the adjacent molecules of the gases a pressure, by which a certain amount of condensation is produced, sufficient to bring the approximated molecules within the sphere of chemical action. One condition of success was found necessary—the surface of the metal must be perfectly clean, which may be attributed to the insulating effect of interposed dirt or grease. The delicacy of the manipulation is shown by the fact that if the metal be cleaned by friction and *immediately* plunged into the mixed gases, the action will be retarded by the repulsive influence of the heated metal.

The condensation of gases in porous bodies, such as spongy platinum, charcoal, &c., is, we conceive, of the same character, as is also that of the adhesion of solid bodies to each other and to liquids: capillary attraction, also endosmose and exosmose ascribed to osmotic force, cell-force, and many other kind of influences, which operate in complicated organic structures; all such actions, in as far as they are physical, may be referred to the influence of cohesive force, *diffused* and *extending* beyond the immediate limits of the molecules to which it more immediately belongs. Such an influence, as from a common centre, draws towards itself and envelops adjacent forces of the same kind, and by this aggregate force produces effects which have always seemed marvellous when compared with their apparently inadequate causes.

As yet, however, we only see this subject through a glass darkly; we must await a farther accumulation of knowledge thereon before we can expect to comprehend it: but, in the case of heat, the correlative molecular force, the antagonist of cohesion, we are better acquainted with its modes of operation; it is a qualitative, variable, and diffusive force, and as such capable of being transferred from one body to another.

Our knowledge, however, of even such a force, can, like all other human learning, be only relative. The attribute of heat as a power is to expand bodies, which it effects by adding to the repulsive force of molecules, and thus causing them to recede farther apart from each other. The amount of this expansive power we measure by making a given body partaker of this action, the given body being kept apart, and its degrees of expansion marked on a scale by means of a contrivance called a thermometer. In framing this scale some particular standard must be adopted which is perfectly conventional. So that our knowledge is only relative to this standard, and therefore the idea of an absolute zero of heat, or of an absolute maximum, is a vain pursuit, and contrary to the sound logical principle that the maxima and minima of knowledge are not cognisable.

By the assistance of the thermometer we have been enabled to collect a vast amount of facts concerning the phenomena of thermotic force. In the first place, we learn that not only the different states of matter conduct heat in peculiar manners, but at various rates, and that each kind of substance has a particular conducting power. Thus, when solids are exposed to heat they are affected thereby with different degrees of rapidity, according to which they are called good or bad *conductors* of heat; amorphous solids conduct equally well in any direction, so that it matters not to what part of the body the heat is applied; but this is not the case with solids which have a regular structure. Senarmont ascertained that crystals of the regular system also uniformly conduct heat in every direction, whilst those crystals which do not belong thereto conduct best in directions which are related to their optical axes. So likewise, according to Delarive and Decandolle, woods conduct much better with the grain than across it, that is, better in a direction parallel to the fibres; and, according to Dr. Tyndall, more rapidly in a direction from the external surface toward the centre than parallel with the ligneous rings; all of which facts show that the action of heat in solid bodies is variously modified by molecular arrangements. It is evident that as these arrangements depend in a great measure on the predominance of cohesion, this force must offer greater opposition to its antagonist, heat, in certain directions; that is, there will be lines of lesser and greater resistance. This, however, is not the only modifying circumstance; when a solid has parts varying in degrees of cohesive tension, such in relation to each other are different *media* through which force is always propagated at different rates. It therefore follows that though, in the lines of crystalline axes, the cohesive force would oppose the strongest resistance to any structural change, yet, on account of its uniformity and density, may more readily transmit heat, on the principle of being a better conductor.

But how do solid bodies conduct heat? What is the *modus operandi* of expansive force?—is it by impulsive undulations, by polar rotations, or how is the motion accomplished? Now, in the case of radiant heat we know that the transmission of the force is effected by a succession of vibrating undulations; and when these motions impinge on the molecules of a solid the latter will also be moved; but on account of the difference of the *medium*, the motions will be greatly modified. The repulsive force will be absorbed by the molecules of the solid, that is, enormously reduced in the dimension of its effects or its motions, which instead of being measurable will be inappreciably minute, but by a continuance of the action will be ultimately manifested as an expansion of the solid body. Now, if the entire body expand, it can only be by the enlargement or expansion of its individual molecules; the molecules that are heated by the impinging undulations of radiant heat, by the very act of expansion undergo minute motions which are communicated to adjacent molecules, and thus propagated after the same manner, though not with the same immediate equalising result, as occurs through a series of balls suspended in contact, when either extremity is struck. And hence it is that the densest and most elastic solids are the best conductors of heat; their structures are more uniform and their molecules more closely approximated than solids of an opposite character, so that the minute expansions are more rapidly transmitted.

The degree of expansion depends on the temperature, that is, on the amount of repulsive force or heat present; and so, if on the other hand we can approximate the molecules, that is, reduce the volume of the solid, a certain amount of heat on which the abstracted volume depended will be set at liberty, and appear as an excess or a *plus* state of heat, which will be diffused on adjacent bodies. Thus a rod of iron by rapid hammering may be made red hot, and indeed all malleable and ductile metals by hammering, rolling, or punching, as in coining, become heated, and increase in specific gravity, becoming at the same time harder and more brittle; but by strong heating and subsequent slow cooling their original state will be restored, that is, the effects of the compressing force, applied in the direction and augmentation of cohesion, will be overcome by the application of heat, so that the molecules will return to their normal condition. Count Rumford made some interesting observations on the heat evolved during the boring of cannon, by which two gallons of water were made to boil in two hours and a half; but Sir Humphry Davy performed a much more curious experiment; by causing two pieces of ice to rub against each other *in vacuo* preserved at 32°; sufficient heat was evolved by the friction to melt the ice.

Hence it would appear that the action and reaction of the physical powers are the joint causes of motion as well as expansion, these only differing from each other as effects in the different circumstances under which they occur; the one being the motion of a body or mass, and the other of the molecules which constitute the sum and substance of a body. In these cases moving force and heat, being the *plus* or actuating energies, are commonly regarded as the immediate causes of the body moving or expanding; and as these are convertible effects, so their causes are referred to the same force, repulsion. And thus far we accept the common opinion of the identity and mutual convertibility of forces; for centrifugy, heat, and electricity are, each and all, only modes or phases of the universal physical force *repulsion :* but they must not be confounded with their correlatives, their co-existing antagonists, the various phases of *attraction.*

This analogy between motion and expansion, which now seems to us so apparently self-evident, was long in being clearly understood; it is only of late years, through the researches of Joule and Mayer, that much light has been thrown on this interesting subject. Joule[*] ascertained that the quantity of heat evolved by friction is in the ratio of the moving force expended; and that this is not de-

[*] Philosophical Transactions for 1850.

pendent on the nature of the substances rubbed together, but universally holds good. He found that one pound of water was raised 1° Fahr. by the expenditure of a force equal to 772 lbs. raised one foot in height, communicated to the water by means of a paddle-wheel revolving therein; when mercury was employed a force of 774 lbs. was required to produce a like effect; and when friction between iron and cast iron was used, the equivalent force was found to be 775 lbs. These results so closely approximate, that there is every reason to believe that the number of *foot-pounds* of mechanical work expended is about 775; a number which has been called Joule's Equivalent of a Unit of Heat.

On this view of the subject it is easily apprehended how molecular forces, whether those of the steam-engine or of the animal frame, can function in the visible motions of bodies, and how these again in their turn may return to the condition of molecular movements, individually inappreciable. We know that masses and molecules present very different appearances; they are the *maxima* and *minima* of matter; and so it might be expected that their respective motions would afford a corresponding difference of phenomena: when molecules are united we have a mass, and when molecular expansions are conjoined we have a visible body in motion, and so, conversely, the mass and the motion may be broken up into indefinitely minute molecules and expansions.

We have seen that the transmission of heat through solids by conduction is very various, the force of repulsion in these cases acting under great disadvantage; in solids, cohesion, the antagonist of heat, is in the ascendant, and therefore until this is equalised (which cannot be in solids) the action of heat will produce some modification *quantum valeat;* but it cannot assume its normal mode of action, an outward tendency opposite to that of gravity, because the molecules are under the restraint of a superior power. When, however, bodies are in the liquid state, when the correlative forces, cohesion and heat, are in a state of equilibrium, then the molecules are free to move; and when increased in volume, or expanded by heat, they recede from the centre of gravity and ascend toward the upper layers of the liquid, a movement which is facilitated by the downward movement of the denser molecules according to the law of gravity. This form of the propagation of heat has been distinguished from *conduction* by the name of *convection.* It follows from the nature of this process that if heat be applied to the uppermost surface of a liquid there will be no change of place, and the heat will not be even gradually extended downward by diffusion, if the liquid can freely evaporate. The experiment usually adduced to prove that water does in some small degree conduct downward, is objectionable; in it, conduction by the vessel's sides has been guarded against, but the radiation through the liquid remains; and the impinging rays on the bottom of the vessel must produce some small effect, which to this extent cannot but vitiate the result.

Liquids regularly expand by given increments of heat until they approach a change of state, the boiling point; when various irregularities occur, but not so great as those which attend the melting of solids. Gases, like liquids, transmit heat by convection; and since in their constitution cohesion is completely overborne by repulsion, they are free to respond to the action of heat, each addition of which produces a corresponding equivalent of expansion. The *ratio* of expansion for gases, and for vapours when sufficiently remote from the boiling point of their liquids, has been found to be about $\frac{1}{490}$th part of their volume for each degree of Fahrenheit. According to the experiments of Regnault and Magnus, the coefficient of expansion is not rigidly uniform for all gases, the expansion being greatest for those most readily condensible, whilst for the gases which have resisted all efforts to liquefy them scarcely any appreciable difference can be observed. This is as might have been expected, cohesion being completely neutralised in the perfect gas, but capable of producing some perturbations near the point of liquefaction.

When bodies change their state, as in liquefaction and in vaporisation, it has been stated that definite quantities of heat are combined with the molecules in a latent state, which is the cause of the molecules being retained in their new positions. And so, likewise, when the temperature of any body is changed without producing a different state, it is found that they all require different amounts of heat to bring them to the same temperature, that is, to the same relative degree of expansion; which could not well have been otherwise, for if each chemical substance has a peculiar and definite atomic weight, different amounts of repulsive force must necessarily be required to affect them in an equivalent manner. This has been empirically arrived at in investigating the phenomena of specific heats; it was found that by multiplying the atomic weights of bodies into their respective specific gravities, a near approximation to a *constant* number was obtained, which clearly indicated that the specific heats were subject to some particular law. These investigations, however, are as yet in their infancy, so that a satisfactory explanation cannot be expected; but we think that in the consideration of this and other physical questions concerning molecular phenomena, the atomic *volumes*, as well as atomic *weights*, will prove to be important *data*.

Expansion, as a general rule, denotes an increase of temperature; but there are exceptions thereto, as in the notable instance of ice and some other substances, which on solidifying expand and become lighter, so as to float on their respective liquids, showing that at a less temperature they have a greater volume. Hence we learn, that whilst it is the normal character of heat to expand bodies, this effect may be also obtained by the reaction of its correlative force cohesion, which by aggregating the molecules around particular axes, may produce an enlarged volume by peculiar *structural* arrangements. This anomaly, then, which is one of structure, interferes with the uniformity of relations between specific heats and specific gravities: such complications are very perplexing, but they are invaluable, as leading to a closer scrutiny of nature, and may ultimately teach us the necessary compensations to be made in our explanations.

The weights and volumes of bodies are continually varying, and are the manifestations of the actions and reactions of molecular forces. In gases (which, according to our view, is the normal condition of matter), repulsion or thermotic force is at a maximum, and any circumstances which tend to alter their volume must cause a corresponding alteration in the relative proportion of their molecular forces.

When we exhaust the receiver of an air-pump, the temperature within falls, which is the reverse of what happens when air is compressed into a smaller volume: in the latter case, the denser air being reduced in capacity, heat is set free, which being in a *plus* or energetic state diffuses itself on surrounding bodies, until equilibrium is restored; in the former, the reduced quantity of air expands and fills the entire receiver by its innate elasticity or repulsive force, which was previously restrained by the ordinary pressure of the atmosphere, and its specific heat undergoes a corresponding increase, so that it absorbs heat from around, in order to attain the common temperature.

At first sight this operation seems to be very puzzling; for one is apt to imagine that when air is rarefied, its increased volume being attained, the process would seem to be at an end; but it is not so. The capability of an almost indefinite expansion is the characteristic of the gaseous state, and however much the gas may be compressed, this property is ever present; and when the restraint is removed, by its elasticity it increases in volume, its specific heat being at the same time augmented; so that the degree of heat which before maintained it at the surrounding temperature is quite inadequate for this purpose, so that it becomes colder, and therefore as a recipient of heat abstracts it from adjacent bodies, according to the usual process of the equalisation of heat between bodies at different temperatures. We know that as we ascend in the air it becomes more rare, and the temperature gradually falls, so that in the upper regions of the atmosphere, which are exceedingly rarefied, an intense cold prevails. Some curious speculations have been brought forward, particularly by Fourier, concerning the temperature of space: the degree of cold is supposed to be below any hitherto ascertained at the earth's surface; but even this is probably too high. Above the perpetual snow line the atmosphere itself is so rare a medium that the sun's rays pass freely through it without heating, and the heat communicated from below by convection must be quite inadequate to make any impression, and even if it did would be dissipated faster by radiation into space, which on account of its extreme rarity must have an insatiable capacity for heat.

We know the amount of pressure in pounds-weight on the atmosphere at the earth's surface; and supposing the height of the atmosphere to be fifty miles, its volume is reduced by this pressure to about one-millionth part: and from these data we may calculate what the density would be at the centre of the earth, supposing the whole of our planet to consist of air. This is not a vague and objectless speculation: it may give a more definite notion concerning the constitution of the comets, which seem to be aëriform; and enable us to understand the Protean changes which they undergo, one while expanding and at another condensing, according to their position in relation to denser bodies, by the attraction of which they suffer compression when in their vicinity.

The extremes of rarefaction and of condensation which gaseous bodies are capable of experiencing afford an endless variety of curious and useful applications: these conditions may be produced by purely physical forces, or by chemical forces, or by both conjointly; but our remarks must now be restricted to the first mentioned.

Gaseous bodies, that is, gases and vapours, mutually interpenetrate or become diffused through each other with great facility; but the greater the difference in their specific gravities, the greater the rapidity with which the lighter gas is transfused. It is also a curious fact, first made known by Dalton, that each gas is to another as a vacuum, affected only by its own pressure; and thus it is that the independent existence of each causes the total volume to be increased or diminished according to the quantity of each gas present; so that whilst they are equably diffused throughout each other, there is no *actual* interpenetration.

It is for this reason that the vapour of water exists in the atmosphere at all temperatures, even below that of the freezing point of water; the higher the temperature the greater the weight of vapour in a given volume of air, and consequently the greater the *tension* of the vapour; and this goes on in a rapidly increasing progression, until the temperature reaches 212°, when the tension is equal to the pressure of the atmosphere, and the water flies off freely in the state of steam. It is worthy of remark that the low vapour of water at 32° has a larger amount of latent heat than the same *weight* of ordinary steam at 212°. This curious fact was first made known by Watt, who gave it the following expression: When latent heat is added to sensible heat, the sum is a constant quantity for the same vapour at all temperatures. This statement is sufficiently correct for practical purposes, but not absolutely so; for M. Regnault has shown that the sum increases as the temperature rises, by a constant quantity of 0·305 for each degree of Fahrenheit.

As the pressure of the atmosphere varies, so does the boiling point of liquids rise and fall; and so, in accordance therewith, liquids may be exposed to high temperatures without being converted into vapour, provided they are subjected to the requisite amount of pressure. And the same holds good with the melting of solids; the greater the pressure, the more heat is required for the change of state. This is evidently owing to the resistance of a force antagonistic to heat; a force which, acting in the *direction* of cohesion, must favour its operation, and so far opposes heat by requiring a larger amount of the latter before it can become efficient. When liquids have been thus superheated, on the sudden removal of the pressure highly elastic vapour rushes out of the aperture with great impetus; and on this principle Perkins constructed his steam-gun. The hand may be plunged into a stream of high-pressure steam, as it escapes in a jet from the boiler, without being injured; a curious fact, and one which remained long unexplained; but now it is known to belong to the same category as the cooling effect of air suddenly rarefied during the exhaustion of the receiver of an air-pump: the enlarged volume requires heat to satisfy its increased capacity, which it absorbs rapidly from adjacent bodies; and thus the hand in the above case is for the instant cooled rather than heated.

Thus we learn that a liquid under great pressure may be heated far above its boiling point without sustaining a change of state: such a condition is tantamount to an increase of cohesive force, for pressure acts in the direction opposite to that of repulsion. In connection with this subject, M. Cagniard de la Tour has recorded some extraordinary circumstances. It was long known that vapour subjected to pressure is reduced to the liquid state by a reaction which has just been explained; but it occurred to him that, provided a sufficient space be allowed above the liquid, the whole might be converted into high-pressure vapour; and he not only verified this conjecture, but also ascertained the amount of pressure required for the purpose. Alcohol, with an empty space equal only to one and a-half time its volume, was entirely converted into vapour at a temperature of 404° and a pressure of 119 atmospheres. Water required four times its volume, and such a high degree of heat and pressure that the glass tube was decomposed and disintegrated by the steam.

Startling, however, as these experiments are, they are perfectly consistent with our knowledge: we can conceive of no limit in the degree of compression of highly heated vapours than the volume of the liquid state itself at a corresponding temperature. At this point it would be a superheated liquid, but should it become somewhat more expanded, it would become high-pressure vapour of the greatest possible density.

Our attention has been for some time engaged in the consideration of that branch of molecular physics in which repulsive force, as heat, has been in the ascendant; a force so energetic and continually varying, that the natural history view, or outward descriptions of its objects, are lost sight of in the absorbing interest of searching for the causes of its physical phenomena; and we have seen that, although heat is the predominant, it is not the sole cause, and that we cannot arrive at satisfactory explanations without taking into account the actions and reactions of both the correlative causes, cohesion and heat; the one tending to condensation, the other to rarefaction. We must now, however, take a brief view of the other branch of the science, in which cohesion is in the ascendant, and we shall find that it has a very different character: this force tends to a state of rest in rigid solidity, and presents an aspect which calls more for description and classification, and much less for physical considerations; and therefore its objects, if less interesting, are capable of being better known.

When molecular attraction or cohesion predominates in bodies, it functions in the production of those morphic forms of matter called *crystals*. In crystals the molecules are symmetrically arranged around one or more axes of aggregation; and the nature of this arrangement seems in a great measure to depend on the primary forms which the molecules of each chemical element possess. Each molecule, then, according to its crystallographic system, has definite poles, by which it is united and held together with other molecules, according to the laws of polarity. Now, in consequence of this axial arrangement of the molecules, a body will be variously affected by extraneous physical forces, according to the direction of their application, the degree of fixidity of the molecular poles on different axes offering a corresponding resistance. This subject has of late years been much studied, as has also the determination of all possible forms by increments and decrements on certain planes and angles, which is treated of under "Crystallography," a subdivision of this branch of Physics.

Very different substances may crystallise in the same forms, but they are not called *isomorphous;* this term being restricted to similarity of form, when conjoined with analogous chemical constitution. Different substances having the same form may perfectly resemble each other, when they belong to the regular or tessular system; but when they belong to other systems, their forms are not exactly similar, for a measurement of the angles of prisms and octahedra shows considerable differences in the length of their axes; and in the case of two oblique systems, such crystals may appear to be very like, but their axes are variously inclined toward each other. Mitscherlich, to whom we are indebted for much information on this subject, has been led to conclude, that whilst crystalline forms depend on a physical grouping, and not on the chemical nature of the atoms, yet that the same number of atoms of analogous chemical substances, when combined, always produce the same crystalline form. "If Mitscherlich's law," observes Professor Miller[*], "be confined to compound bodies, the facts which have been supposed to militate against it will prove a remarkable corroboration of its truth, as they show that the number and collocation of the atoms may overcome the tendency of some elementary components to assume different forms. It also shows that it is unsafe to infer isomorphism in the elements, simply from the occurrence of isomorphism in the compounds which they form."

---

[*] Elements of Chemistry, vol. i. p. 109.

We are not as yet in a position to determine, *à priori*, what forms will result from the combinations of given elementary forms; though this would seem not to transcend the sphere of geometry, nor yet to ascertain why the molecules of some chemical elements have the same crystalline forms; whilst the number of material atoms in each chemical atom is so disproportionate, as in the case of carbon and of gold, which crystallise similarly, though the weight of the latter is sixteen times greater than that of the former. But doubtless some law of physical aggregation is followed in these cases; and if the molecular form of each element were determined, applied geometry ought to give all the possible combinations, provided the volumes of such elements remained unaltered during aggregation; for of course a change, in this respect, would produce a corresponding disturbance. There is, indeed, every reason to believe that such changes do occur when the weight of the element is considerable, that is, is composed of many material atoms, for in such cases condensations around common centres, being various, would favour the production of different crystalline forms.

That such a condition is not only possible but probable, is demonstrated by the well-known phenomenon, *dimorphism*, which consists in the same substance crystallising not only in many congenerous forms, but also in forms which are geometrically incompatible, belonging to different systems. This is not a chemical change, but one purely physical; though the new arrangement may be such as to facilitate chemical affinities which were not possible in the original condition. To give an instance of dimorphism. Sulphur is found native in oblique rhombic octahedrons; and these crystals are comparatively hard, do not readily change on exposure to the air, and have a density of 2·05; but when these crystals are melted and slowly cooled, prismatic forms are obtained, which belong to the fifth or oblique system, whilst the original octahedrons belong to the fourth, or prismatic system of crystals. The density of the prismatic crystals is only 1·98, and they are not permanent in the air, but soon lose their transparency; and although they retain for awhile their prismatic form, the coherence of their molecules is so slight, that when pressed they easily crumble into powder, which under the microscope is found to consist of minute rhombic octahedra.

The following may be the explanation of these changes. The octahedral form may be the normal crystal of sulphur, that is, of this chemical element, that in which cohesion is exerted with its fullest force; and hence a corresponding degree of hardness, density, and persistency. In the prismatic crystals, however, the molecules arrange themselves differently during the gradual recovery of their cohesion from the melted state, by which difference of form they acquire a greater volume, and consequently diminished density; and this new arrangement being a state of instability, the molecules are capable of regaining the normal state, in which their centres of gravity are in firmer positions. It is possible that the prismatic crystals may be aggregations of the octahedra, but we are inclined to think that the change is much more fundamental, that these crystals are different arrangements of the material atoms which form the body or basic power of the chemical element sulphur.

Many facts concerning dimorphism and trimorphism might be adduced, all pointing in the same direction and capable of a similar explanation; all depending on cohesion, and varying as this force is modified by the relative proportions of repulsive force in the substances. Indeed, what is commonly called the three states of matter is, in fact, but an example of trimorphism, in which the molecules of the same substance are arranged in three different forms, according to the proportions of their correlative forces — cohesion and heat.

Dimorphism, trimorphism, and similar terms, however, are more correctly restricted to variations of crystalline forms; and the term *allotropy* has been employed to denote those physical changes which bodies are capable of undergoing without affecting their chemical compositions. The subject of allotropy has of late years attracted much attention; and it bids fair to throw much light on several phenomena which have hitherto been involved in much mystery. The allotropic states of carbon, sulphur, and phosphorus have been carefully investigated, and they may, we think, be all explained by the relative condition of molecular forces; the phenomena of altered density and hardness have been already alluded to, but those arising from the influence of light and electricity will be noticed hereafter; since, however, these are only modes of physical forces, it might be expected that they would undergo analogous variations according to the molecular structure of bodies.

In addition to the physical changes which allotropy presents, it has been observed that though the substances have the same composition, they do not comport themselves in the same manner when subjected to chemical reagents. This, however, cannot be adduced in favour of a transmutation of bodies; it is only one of the many instances in which affinities are modified by physical conditions. Chemical elements have a definite and indestructible constitution, and combine together in definite proportions; but there is a sphere of action within which only chemical forces can operate, and physical forces greatly influence this condition. Connected with allotropic changes, there is one circumstance which must not be lightly passed over; it is an important fact, and may, if followed up, lead to important results; — we allude to the capacity of a solid body to render heat latent, as in the changes of *state* by liquefaction and vaporisation, as occurs in the production of Schrotter's phosphorus. The varied appearances of sulphur, when melted at different temperatures, may be found to give similar indications; indeed, whenever the molecules of bodies are retained in new positions force must be employed in producing such a result; and this force is absorbed in the operation, and thus becomes neutral or latent, but is again manifested when the body reverts to its former state.

There can be little doubt that many substances will be found to be susceptible of allotropic modifications, as our researches are extended; and, indeed, a large body of scattered facts seem to belong to this category. Thus, the altered condition of artillery, after frequent discharges, and of metals long exposed to friction, to incessant vibrations or percussions; of metals at different temperatures, as zinc, which is one while so malleable as to be rolled into sheets, and at another so brittle as to be easily pounded; and so likewise many metals, glass, earthenware, and other substances, if rapidly cooled from a state of fusion are hard and brittle, but slowly cooled, or annealed, they lose this property; all these and many other similar facts are kinds of allotropy, that is, metamorphoses of molecular arrangements.

All these cases of allotropy refer to solids; our knowledge on this subject in regard to liquids is very limited. The varied appearances of melted sulphur at different temperatures have been already alluded to, as also the anomaly of water expanding before it reaches the melting point. It is not surprising that liquids as well as solids should experience allotropic changes; but it is very curious that we should find notable instances of such changes in gases, the great elasticity of which seems to be opposed to such alterations. It is, however, now very generally admitted that *ozone* is allotropic oxygen; and it is very probable that those gases which acquire energy by exposure to light, are rendered allotropic by *actinism;* the altered condition of gases, which are condensed by the contact of solid bodies, may possibly undergo a similar change beyond that of a reduction of volume.

In thus endeavouring to reduce all our knowledge concerning the aggregation and expansion of molecular bodies under the general head of Micronomy, or Molecular Physics, we do not refuse the subdivision of this science into many subordinate branches. It may be well to arrange the facts, concerning solids, liquids, and gases, under distinct heads, and, provided each of these is considered, both phenomenally and causally, the constituent forces determined, and the motions resulting from all the changes in the relations of these forces, then each may form a subordinate science; but we protest against taking either force in a *plus* state, and treating of its actions as a proper science.

The various subjects connected with molecular physics are too numerous to be noticed in this general view; but, from what has been already stated, it will be readily understood how we should treat these subjects.

Before turning to a fresh topic, let us gather together, as we proceed, a summary of the natural dualisms which have been considered, and also of their dependant sciences.

Dualism of Physical Powers: —
 Attraction + Repulsion = Matter or Physical Substance.

Phase of Physical Powers as Central Forces: —
 Gravity + Centrifugy = Celestial Masses or Stars.

Phase of Physical Powers as Molecular Forces: —
 Cohesion + Heat = Molecules.

The science of Physical Substance is Physics; that of the Stars, Celestial Physics, or Astronomy; and that of Molecules, Molecular Physics, or Micronomy; and the variable phenomena of which these sciences treat are all some kinds of motion.

CHAP. IV.

SOUND AND LIGHT, MOLECULAR AND ETHERIAL UNDULATIONS.

Undulations of Material Bodies.—The Medium of transmitting Force.—The Difference between Sound-waves and Light-waves.—Light not related to Heat and Electricity as Modes of the same Force.—What is Light?—Sir John Herschel's Answer to this Question.—Light, like all other Motions, a Composition of Forces.—According to Comte, Light is something *sui generis*: heterogeneous to Motion.—All Undulations are not audible and visible.—Limitation of the Scale of Sound and Light Perceptions.—The Analogies between Sound and Light. The Origin and Constitution of Sound.—Its various *Media*: that of Air immediately concerned in Hearing.—The Sound-wave a Dualism of Forces.—The Composition of Light not yet understood.—The Colours of the Prismatic Spectrum.—Distributing of Heat-rays and of Photographic-rays in the Spectrum. These two kinds of Rays arranged in an inverse Ratio.—Radiant Heat and Actinism the component Forces of Light-waves.—Heat the Cause or *Primum-mobile* of Light.—Actinism not a chemical Force, but a Mode of Physical Attraction.—Conclusion.

THE motions of natural bodies are caused by the actions and reactions of the physical powers, attraction and repulsion; and it is by these phenomena alone that the physical powers are manifested; and, as these phenomena assume different aspects according to the kind of natural bodies with which they are associated, so the physical powers, as objects of knowledge, present themselves under corresponding phases or modifications. Thus, when the motions of the celestial orbs are studied, the powers of attraction and repulsion are manifested as gravitation and centrifugal force; but when we turn from the distinct and measurable motions of the stars to the minute and individually inappreciable motions of molecules, the physical powers assume a very different aspect, and we distinguish them accordingly as cohesion and heat; still they are, like the astronomical forces, phases of the same universal powers, attraction and repulsion.

The phenomena resulting from the action and reaction of astronomical and molecular forces would, at first sight, seem to exhaust all possible motions of material bodies; and so they do, as far as regards the continuous change of place in space; and as such motions are, in relation to each other, the maxima and minima of all *continuous* changes of place, they form a *universal*, which ought to be capable of affording one common science of physics. There is, however, a great convenience in treating of astronomy and micronomy as distinct sciences; and as this method is firmly established, it would be a needless innovation to propose their conjunction; but it is not improbable that it may be attempted, should a generalising spirit become in vogue.

Passing, then, from the consideration of *progressive* motions, of rotation and revolution, and of contraction and expansion, we proceed to inquire into those limited motions of successive repetitions, which vibrate forward and backward, which kind of oscillations are known as undulations. All bodies seem to be capable of undergoing such movements; therefore, they are universal; and since all motions are caused by the universal physical powers, undulations must necessarily be attributed to the operation of some peculiar modes or phases of these powers.

When the various kinds of undulations are attentively considered, it will be perceived that they belong to two great heads, which comprise all these phenomena: the one includes the vibrations of all *material molecules*; the other, those of the *atoms* of that subtile fluid, the *ether* of space. Undulations may also be divided into such as are manifested to the consciousness, as *sound* and *light*; these would comprise the greater part, and by far the most important, but not the whole of these phenomena.

Undulations are, therefore, the means by which force is transmitted through various *media*; and as they pass from one kind of medium to another, they give rise to a diversity of actions and reactions; thus, we note the velocity with which they transmit their exciting force, its direction, and the varying intensity of its energy; the dimensions and frequency of the undulations are also interesting objects of observation. If it were not for sound and light, we should be ignorant of most things, and of the events which are passing around us, for it is through their agency chiefly that matter and mind are brought into communication; so that this subject is one of the most important that can engage our contemplations.

Sound, as the perception of *sonorous* undulations, seems to have been clearly apprehended; but the notion concerning light is still very vague. Light is no longer indeed regarded as a corpuscular entity, but still there is a lingering tendency to view it as something real in itself; thus, it is commonly spoken of as a peculiar kind of force, and as such placed in the same category as heat and electricity. And not only so, but a strange notion concerning it has of late been current, and which is said to have originated with George Stephenson: viz. that the light of our gas and coal-fires is a re-manifestation of the sun-light of remote ages, which had been absorbed and fixed by primeval vegetation;—a notion which virtually reasserts the corpuscular theory, which has been repudiated by modern science. Would any one maintain that the musical sounds which now charm our ears, are identically the same as those which delighted the antediluvian world? As sounds, they are indeed similar vibrations, but they are not sounds evoked from a dormant state. Perhaps we lay too much stress on this point, but we have done so, because light is regarded by many as a specific force, and as such, capable of existing in a latent state, according to the above fanciful conjecture.

All, however, are not of this opinion: "The question," says Sir John Herschel[*], "What becomes of light? merges itself into the more general one, What becomes of motion? And the answer on dynamical principles is, that it continues for ever. No motion is, strictly speaking, annihilated, but it may be divided, and the divided parts made to oppose, and in effect destroy each other. A body struck, however perfectly elastic, vibrates for a time, and then appears to sink into its original repose; but this

---

[*] On the Absorption of Light by Coloured Media. As quoted in the Connexion of the Physical Sciences, p. 197.

apparent rest is nothing else than a state of subdivided and mutually destroying motions, in which every molecule continues to be agitated by an indefinite multitude of internally reflected waves, propagated in every possible direction, from every point in its surface, on which they successively impinge." This is well stated, and is sound doctrine; we only differ from it as to the manner in which the fact is expressed. We see in a motion only a composition of forces, of which one is in a *plus* state; when this is diffused by innumerable subdivisions, and a state of equilibrium is restored, the motion is apparently destroyed, whilst the forces constituting the equilibrium still exist and are indestructible, though, on account of their equipollence, they cannot function in visible motion.

The luminous and sonorous vibrations are only particular forms of material movements, which as physical phenomena occur in nature, whether they are perceived by sentient creatures or not: they are the phenomenal appearances of natural dualisms or composition of forces, which are co-existent and opposite.

The sciences of light and sound, optics and acoustics, have been rightly conceived and constructed; and each of them has, in common with all true sciences, two logical branches, the phenomenal and the causal. The former branch of each science has been carefully examined and arranged: so that we need not dwell thereon; but the causal or physical branch, more especially that of optics, is as yet imperfect; and will require our more particular attention.

This view of the subject is contrary to the positive

philosophy, and has been condemned by Comte.* " Physicists," he says, " must abstain from fancifully connecting the phenomena of light and those of motion : the supposition, now become classical, that sound and colours are radically alike, is a wild imagination. It is much better to leave such a pursuit of scientific unity, and to admit that the categories of heterogeneous phenomena are more numerous than a vicious systematising tendency would suppose. The phenomena of light will always constitute a category *sui generis*, necessarily irreducible to any other: a light will ever be heterogeneous to a motion or a sound." Comte admits the connection of sound with the vibrations of material media; and also the direct application of rational mechanics to explain its phenomena: and had he realised the idea, now so generally accepted, that the ether of space is an elastic *material* fluid, he would, perhaps, have acknowledged the analogy between sonorous and luminous undulations. These vibrations do, indeed, differ from each other in their respective lengths, velocities, and other particulars : but all such differences may be fairly referred to the diverse characters of the *media*, the one ponderable and the other imponderable, which constitute the fields of their respective operations.

In treating of acoustics and optics, it must be remembered that these sciences do not deal with all possible molecular and etherial vibrations; but only with those which affect the organs of hearing and of sight, as sound and light. This limitation is a defect, in regard only to the physical motions; but, as regards audible and visible

* Positive Philosophy, vol. i. p. 269.

vibrations, it is provided for by the special definitions of these sciences. It is well known that the vibrations of bodies do not always produce sounds that can be perceived by the human ear; and such inaudible vibrations occur beyond both extremes of the musical scale: some being so slow and grave, and others so rapid and acute, that they cannot be heard; though it is probable that such make conscious impressions on the organs of other creatures. At all events, this holds good with corresponding etherial vibrations; for some nocturnal animals evidently see distinctly, when objects are to us barely visible; and others can endure such a brilliant light, as would produce in us temporary blindness.

In the case of light, as compared with that of sound, the scale of perceptions is very limited, which is not surprising, when the inconceivable rapidity of the luminous vibrations are taken into account; a condition not favourable to very nice discriminations; still though there is but one octave of colours in place of the many octaves of musical sounds; the analogy between the different kinds of vibrations is very close. For if the notes of an octave be simultaneously struck, there is a distinct musical sound, which comprises, and may be separated into its component notes: and so, pure white light may be subdivided into the colours of the spectrum; which may be reunited so as to restore the white light again. And in both cases, the notes and the colours only differ from each other in the number and length of the vibrations of their respective media. The ratios of the vibrations, both of harmonic sounds and of colours, are also analogous: for as there are in any octave harmonics of the fundamental note, vibrating in simple relations to produce a concord; so in the spectrum there are three primary colours, which are distinctly defined, and which by their union give clear white light. Musical notes struck in succession can be distinctly heard; because, though each differs in the number of its vibrations, sound of all kinds travels at a uniform speed in the same medium; and are therefore heard in the order of their production at any distance: if it were otherwise music would be impossible. And so in the case of colours; though the vibrations of each also differ, their respective rays all meet the eye at the same instant. As regards degrees of intensity, sonorous and luminous vibrations are similarly circumstanced; the volume of sound, and the brilliancy of light, depend on the amplitude of the vibrations; a strong force producing corresponding action on the material content of either medium. So likewise the pitch of musical notes, and the body or tone of colours, vary with the rapidity of the vibrations; the quality of both sensations depending on the molecular constitution of the bodies from which the undulations are reflected.

In short, both sound and light are manifested to the consciousness by impressions made on the respective organs of sense by physical impulses communicated through the undulations of the appropriate medium; and therefore we find, as might be expected, that the vibrations of both kinds are similarly constituted, and that they follow similar laws of action, though the precise analogy may not be, in all cases, easy of determination. Let us then, in the first instance, consider the constitution of sonorous undulations, in order to determine the nature of the forces which compose the dualism, sound; which is, as already stated, the phenomenal appearance of a composition of forces; and also to determine the manner in which these forces act and react on each other: and then, if there be truly an analogy between sound and light, the knowledge of the nature of sound ought to enable us to answer the question, What is light?

In the case of sound, the vibrations are occasioned by any sudden impulse, such as a blow, an explosion, or the like, communicated to substances which possess some degree of elasticity. The active or aggressive force, which disturbs the equilibrium of the medium, urges a certain number of molecules forward in the direction of the force, thereby exerting a pressure which produces a certain amount of condensation, according to the intensity of the force; this condensed portion of the medium becomes, in its turn, virtually a force acting on the molecules immediately before it, on account of its *plus* or excited state, and when relieved by diffusion or transmission from this condition, the correlative force of the dualistic medium recovers from the constraint: and its liberated energy exerts itself as elasticity, and reacts in the opposite direction, causing an expansion or rarefaction of those molecules which had been previously condensed. This action and reaction, being confined to a circumscribed portion of the medium, produce an oscillating movement forward and backward, making a complete vibration. Of course, all these movements greatly vary according to the medium in which they take place, and according to the part of the medium, whether its surface or its substance, on which they operate; but under whatever circumstances they occur, these movements are all fundamentally the same, the forms of the phenomena may be those of condensation and rarefaction, of depressions and elevations, and the like; all of which are reducible to the simple expression of action and reaction, which characterise the functions of co-existing and opposite forces, in all phenomena.

In this statement, we have referred to no particular medium for the sonorous vibrations; but, practically, the air is always the medium through which direct communication takes place with the auditory nerves; though it often happens that the air is not the body which primarily vibrated. The initiatory vibrations may be transmitted along various kinds of substances for the greater portion of the distance between the place of excitement; but before they can become audible as sounds, they must be propagated to the air contained in the organ of hearing: so that the air is either originally, or ultimately, the medium of communication. Although air, on account of its great elasticity, and of its susceptibility of responding to the gentlest impulses, is beautifully adapted for the transmission of sounds, yet these travel much slower in air than in many other media; thus the velocity of sound in air is 1090 feet per second, in water four times as much, and in iron it is more than sixteen times that in air; indeed it has likewise been found to vary in air itself according to its density. The degree of loudness also varies as the density of the air, so that no sound follows an impact in an exhausted receiver.

We have already repeatedly stated that a force of any kind, which approximates the molecules of bodies by condensation, acts in the direction of attraction, and thus acting must counteract the energy of the co-existing and opposite force, repulsion; and, in so far as it thus acts, it balances or renders passive an equivalent of the latter force, which however, though rendered latent, is not destroyed, and immediately restores the original volume on the removal of the aggressive force. And this *modus operandi* of correlative forces is, we think, in accordance with the phenomena of vibrations; and if so, we find in these peculiar motions a dualism of forces, analogous to that of all the other physical phenomena which have previously engaged our attention. Indeed this must necessarily follow, or our position cannot be maintained, that all natural bodies, whatever be their varied condition, are dualisms of forces; that, in as far as such bodies are material, their forces are some modes or other of the universal physical forces, attraction and repulsion, all of which function only in some forms of motion. According to this view of the subject, sonorous vibrations are peculiar motions of matter, and consequently their constituent forces must be some dualism of correlative physical forces, that is, of forces which co-exist in this particular phenomenon. The correlative forces of a sonorous vibration are evidently an impulsive compressing force and a reacting elasticity, by the concurrence of which the dualism is produced. Perhaps it may be as well, in order to mark more clearly our meaning, to denote the former force by a special name, and temporarily for this purpose it may be designated as *epipallism*, an impulsive force causing vibrations, and its correlative force may be called *elasticity*, with which we are already familiar. But call them what you will, they are distinct phases of physical forces, co-existent and antagonistic, which is all that is requisite for forces to be able to act and react, and so produce corresponding phenomena; and we therefore symbolise this correlation as

Epipallism + elasticity = sonorous vibration or sound.

Now, let us turn our attention to luminous vibrations, an inquiry of a more delicate character, and one concerning which we have much yet to learn; so that the subject must be approached more cautiously.

Etherial vibrations produce on the organ of sight the sensation called light; and the science or systematic knowledge of light is called Optics. The phenomena of light, as to their outness or external aspect, have been extensively and successfully investigated: a vast fund of very curious and interesting facts has been accumulated, concerning the reflection, refraction, interference, polarisation, and other conditions of the luminous rays; but we need not enter into these details, as they have already been well described by others. But, concerning the constitution of light, what it is essentially in itself, what are its correlative forces, and the nature of the internal actions and reactions which these produce, we have yet much to learn; and it is, therefore, to the causal or dynamical branch of optics that our enquiry will be chiefly directed, in the hope of deriving some aid from the principles of our system.

According to the *emission* theory of Newton, light is a corpuscular body, consisting of particles of impalpable tenuity which are incessantly radiating from luminous bodies with a velocity of about 198,000 miles in a second of time. According to the *undulatory* theory, there is throughout space, an ether, or exceedingly elastic fluid, capable of being thrown into undulations, that propagate themselves with astonishing swiftness: — such undulations are produced by luminous bodies, just as the air is thrown into pulsations by sonorous bodies; and, as these undulations, or light-waves, reach the eye, they cause the sensation of light. The latter theory is satisfactory as far as it goes; but it does not, like that of Newton, tell us what light is, it only informs us that when issuing from a luminous body it is propagated through space by undulations.

In the case of sound-waves, we know that they have their origin in the exercise of some physical force; and those who regard light as a specific force, like that of heat or electricity, may suppose that it is this force emanating from luminous bodies which occasions the light-waves. It is, however, evident that this does not answer the question, What is light? For a luminous body is already in a state of luminous undulation; it only differs from ether, and our atmosphere, in being a different medium, intensely agitated by vibrating motions, which are being diffused on all sides from a common centre by radiation. What we want to know is, when we objectify a light-wave, its internal composition; — what is it in itself? We know it is a peculiar motion, and every motion is a composition of forces; it cannot be a single force, for in nature there is no such thing, and if there were, would be unknowable. Light is, therefore, a natural dualism, and as such must consist of correlative forces; the object of our search then is clearly defined, we must endeavour to ascertain what these forces are, which conjoined make the correlation, light.

Newton, pondering on the reason of the uniform series of colours in the rainbow, and in the prismatic spectrum, saw clearly that they were in some way related to pure white light; and he ultimately arrived at the conclusion, that light is a compound of the prismatic colours; and this conjecture was confirmed by the reproduction of white light, when by means of lenses he gathered all these colours together into one focus. The result, having the Baconian criterion of an *experimentum crucis*, for a time gave the corpuscular theory of light the preponderance in public estimation; but the undulatory theory has since explained the phenomenon in a satisfactory manner; the vibrations of the different coloured lights have been measured, and been found to vary in magnitude from about 37,640 to 59,750 within the length of an inch, and in velocity from 458 to 727 billions of pulsations per second; the lower part of each series beginning at the red colour, and the higher terminating in the violet. If, then, the various prismatic colours be light-waves, only differing from each other in the length and velocity of their motions, they are not individual and independent entities, but only the *maxima* and *minima* conditions of the self-same thing: these modifications of the light-wave, being dissimilar in their properties, produce corresponding variations in their physical impressions on the retina of the eye, and are, consequently, distinguished in sensation as particular colours.

But then comes an important consideration, How are these colours presented in a regular series? And how comes it to pass, that many substances have specific colours, which they permanently retain under the same circumstances? These points cannot, as yet, be perfectly explained: but in the mean time it is not difficult to conceive, that the subordinate parts of each entire light-wave, which is a universal or individual system, may be distinct vibrations of exceeding minuteness, varying from each other in dimensions and energy, according to their relative positions in the *universal:* in that part of the light-wave which is most condensed, the subordinate vibrations would be shortest and slowest; and in the most rarefied part, the longest and most rapid. And between these extremes, as in every regular co-ordination, whether physical or logical, there will be a gradual passage from one to another: this is on the principle of that antithesis, in which extension and intension increase and decrease in the exact inverse ratio of each other; the point at which these diverging series cross being one of equilibrium.

When by means of any peculiar construction, as that of a prism, a light-wave, during its passage, is refracted, the subordinate parts of the undulation are so projected on a plane, as to render each distinctly visible; thus, a species of analysis is performed, separating the component parts of the entire light-wave, which parts, having different degrees of refrangibility, appear at corresponding positions in the spectrum as a series of various colours. But when the light-waves fall on bodies which do not produce this prismatic or iridescent phenomenon, but only exhibit one colour, either simple or compound, this must be referred to the peculiar molecular constitution of the body, which reflects one of the subordinate vibrations of the light-wave, whilst the others are involved or diffused through its interstices. That the specific colour of a body is attributable to its molecular condition, can scarcely be doubted; for we have it in our power, by heat and otherwise, to alter the molecular arrangement; and when this is done, the colour is, more or less, affected thereby: thus, many oxides and sulphurets of brilliant colours, when heated become gradually darker and clouded, till at last they are perfectly black, but return to their original colour on cooling.

"In addition to the ordinary prismatic colours described by Newton, Sir John Herschel * has discovered a set of very dark red rays, beyond the red extremity of the spectrum, which can be only seen when the eye is defended from the glare of the other colours by a dark blue cobalt glass: and he also found that beyond the extreme violet there are visible rays of a lavender grey colour, which may be seen by throwing the spectrum on paper moistened by a solution of carbonate of soda."

The illuminating power of the different rays of the spectrum varies with the colour: the most intense light is in the mean yellow ray. Doubtless in light-waves as in sound-waves, the range of vibrations which affect the organs of sense, does not mark the limit of these motions: some may be so slow and others so fast as not to produce distinct impressions on the optic nerve; and the above-mentioned experiments show that such vibrations extend beyond the limits of the spectrum ordinarily visible;

* Mrs. Somerville's Connexion of Physical Sciences, p. 181.

and the means employed to render them visible produce new reactions, which modify the velocities of the abnormal vibrations; by which contrivances many other perturbations might be obtained within the limits of the spectrum. Sir David Brewster is of opinion that the spectrum actually consists of only three primary colours, red, yellow, and blue; and that the other tints are produced by the variable overlapping of these primary colours.

These and many other curious circumstances concerning colours might be enumerated; but sufficient have been noticed to make it evident that colours alone do not comprise all our knowledge concerning light-waves: we must, therefore, now turn our attention to some other circumstances, in relation to luminous undulations.

Light is essentially the same, whatever may be its origin; but in our inquiries into its nature we deal with that light which proceeds directly from the sun, and which we speak of familiarly as the sun's rays. The brilliant light of the sun is not only capable of exciting the sensations of all the colours of the rainbow, but when it impinges on us, it also produces the feeling of heat. The co-existence of light and heat in the sun's rays is a well-known fact. But it was Sir William Herschel who first pointed out their relative distribution in the solar spectrum: he found heat to predominate in the dark space a little beyond the red extremity, and from thence to decrease gradually towards the violet; beyond which its presence could not be detected. From which it was concluded, that the calorific rays vary in refrangibility, and that those beyond the extreme red end of the spectrum are less refrangible than any rays of coloured light. And since his time, it has been ascertained that the calorific spectrum exceeds the luminous, in the ratio of 42 to 25[*]; and that its maximum point is only slightly thrown out of the straight line which the solar pencil would take had it not been interrupted by the prism.

Wonderful as these phenomena of colour and heat are, yet there are others of another kind also related to the sun's rays, with which we must become acquainted before the constitution of the light-wave can be determined. It was long known that vegetation is retarded and feeble when deprived of the direct influence of the sun's rays, as when overshadowed by dense foliage, or in deep caverns, where only a diffused light can penetrate; and this was attributed to the absence of heat: but now we know that the sun's rays impart something more than heat, and that this may be intercepted whilst the heat-rays are allowed to pass, and yet the plants will not thrive. This principle of activity has been distinguished by the name of *actinism;* and it has been found that it not only exerts an influence over vegetation, but also over chemical combination, which is, indeed, in all probability, the immediate cause of its influence on the functions of plants.

The action of the sun's rays in facilitating many combinations had been often noticed and recorded; but these facts were only regarded as curious and inexplicable occurrences. Sir Humphry Davy and Wedgewood attempted to apply the action of light on the salts of silver, in copying various objects, but their success was not sufficiently promising to induce them to persevere in their

---

[*] Mrs. Somerville's Connexion of Physical Sciences, p. 238.

experiments. This subject has been taken up of late years by Niepce, Daguerre, and Talbot, and carried to great perfection by various artists, as a species of light-drawing, called photography; an art which has been developed with almost unparalleled rapidity.

The precise nature of *actinism* is as yet an unsolved problem; but, whatever this force may be, it clearly does not belong to the same category as heat, for it not only makes its appearance at the opposite ends of the solar spectrum, but also possesses very distinct and antagonistic characters; it is, therefore, reasonable to infer that it is a phase or mode of attraction, which is strongly corroborated by its property of promoting chemical combinations.

Colour and heat enter into the constitution of the solar spectrum, which has been long known, but it is only of late years that it has been discovered that the new ray-force, actinism, also plays a conspicuous part therein. Actinic force occupies in the spectrum a position directly the reverse of that of caloric; it is at a maximum in the colourless space beyond the violet rays, and gradually diminishes as it approaches the red extremity of the spectrum, where its presence is too feeble to be detected. So that the positions of the actinic and calorific forces are as opposite as are their respective attributes; for heat repels, or causes the molecules of bodies to recede from each other; whilst actinism tends to their approximation, as indicated by its facilitating chemical actions.

Thus we have seen that the solar spectrum consists of a series of colours like those of the rainbow, situated between the two extreme colours of red and violet: but this is not all. Superadded to these colours are the antagonistic forces, heat and actinism, which are both present in each of the coloured spaces, but in different proportions. The calorific rays* extend beyond the red extremity, and the actinic rays overlap the violet extremity; and if the linear dimensions of these three parts of the spectrum be taken, the colorific, calorific, and photographic rays will be found to be in the proportion of 25, 42, and 55; so that the entire spectrum is more than twice as long as the visible part. These proportions, however, are somewhat modified by the material of which the prism is made.

Having thus briefly stated the general features of the case, let us now endeavour to apply our notion of the dualism of powers to these facts, and to ascertain whether the etherial vibrations, or light-waves, can be reduced to our logical correlation, which is a composition of coexistent and antithetic terms. Of the three sets of phenomena in the spectrum, we conceive that the coloured rays are only modifications of the universal light-wave, parts which have no other differentiation than variations in the length and velocities of their oscillations, which depend on their constituent forces being combined in different proportions. All these subordinate kinds of etherial undulations, manifesting themselves as different colours, are the conditioned existences of dualistic powers, which form the subject matter of optics: just as molecules of matter, and their different states, depending on their dualistic powers, cohesion and caloric, are the objects concerning which the science of molecules, or micronomy, treats. Strictly speaking, optics only treats of visible

* Mrs. Somerville's Connexion of Physical Sciences, p. 239.

undulations: but with a distinct proviso, it may be extended so as to include in its subject all etherial undulations, whether visible or not.

The next point to be determined, having settled the natural history or descriptive branch of optics, is to ascertain the nature of the correlative forces which produce these phenomena: and having ascertained the constitution of this peculiar composition of forces, or dualism, it then remains to investigate the varying relations of these forces in the different modifications of these etherial undulations. These forces we conceive to be, as may have been anticipated, radiant heat and actinism, the already acknowledged causes of two sets of phenomena displayed in the solar spectrum. The relative positions of these forces, actinism and radiant heat, (or thermicity, as it may be called,) in the spectrum, constitute a parallelogram of forces which may be illustrated by a very oblong diagram, bisected by its diagonal: each triangular portion, thus formed, will represent either force; and also shows their relative proportions in any particular part of the spectrum. It is evident, on considering such an arrangement, that one force increases as the other diminishes, and *vice versâ:* and on cutting off a given portion, say a quarter part, from both extremities, it will be found that one part consists almost, but not entirely, of thermicity; and the other, of actinism. And if the intermediate moiety be divided into bands by lines drawn parallel with the ends of the diagram, it will be apparent that there is a central part in which the forces are equal, corresponding with the *most* luminous, or yellow part, of the spectrum; whilst in the bands on either side of this central part, one or other of the correlative forces predominates. In the red bands it is heat, and in the violet actinism; in the extreme bands the corresponding force prevails almost to the exclusion of its correlative: but it is, according to our notion, a physical impossibility that these forces can be absolutely separated, so as to exist as simple natural forces.

Now from this statement it follows, that in whatever relative proportion these forces be conjoined, the result is a dualism, having characters which will vary according to its composition. The vibrations at the extreme parts of the spectrum derive their properties from the excess of their characteristic force; and the quality of their motions is such as to be incapable of producing any sensible impression on the optic nerve: though at the same time either *plus* force is readily manifested by its peculiar attribute; the one by its effect on the thermometer, the other on chemical tests. On the other hand, the central vibrations of the spectrum are visible, as coloured bands, and are very differently constituted from those at the extremities; their component forces being either equal or nearly approximating thereto, a condition which seems to be requisite for the production of optical phenomena.

In the case of sound, we know that it is propagated from all bodies in a state of sonorous vibration; and that such a state may be originated by any physical impulse. And so, in like manner, light is communicated by all luminous bodies; but it can only be primarily excited by the impulse of an intense heat. At a moderate temperature, bodies are not visible in the dark; but when gradually heated until they become strongly ignited, they are first of all faintly luminous, which goes on increasing till they at last give out a brilliant light. Heat then is the cause, or *primum mobile*, of light: it is this repulsive force, as thermicity or radiant heat, which imparts the initial impulse to the etherial fluid; and it is the reaction of actinism on the ether, when liberated by the transmission of the aggressive force, which completes the etherial undulation, which may or may not be manifested as light, according to the character of the undulation. The greater the intensity of the exciting cause the more vivid the light, and the more energetic is the thermicity associated with such light. Even in the case of feeble phosphorescence, (such as that of decaying wood, fish, and the like,) it is probable that the luminous appearance depends on the heat evolved by continuous chemical action; the heat concerned therein is at a *minimum*, as in the case of violet light, which, modified by particular conditions, gives those opalescent and spectral appearances, which have of late attracted so much attention.

The name actinism has the merit of not expressing any particular hypothesis, but simply the fact that it is a ray-force, or one of the forces of the sunbeam; and on this account we have retained it: but concerning actinism itself, it unfortunately is generally supposed to be a chemical force, which it certainly is not, according to our understanding of such a force; and therefore we must guard against such a conception. Actinism is to us merely a mode of physical attraction, the inseparable antagonist of radiant heat in etherial undulations or light-waves: it is precisely analogous to the force which causes the condensation of gases in porous bodies, and which also is accompanied by chemical actions; but this cohesive force, or attraction of cohesion, is not affinity or chemical force; but like actinism it is only a phase or mode of physical force producing an approximation of molecules, which is favourable to chemical action.

This view of the subject, the antagonism of peculiar phases of physical forces in the sunbeam, enables us to explain some anomalies, and also many phenomena which have been observed in chemical and electrical actions, when modified by the influence of the sun's rays.

At an early period in the history of Photography, it was expected that those countries which enjoy cloudless skies and bright sunshine would afford pictures of superior excellence, and the most skilful artists were sent out for this purpose; but they met with the most signal failures; the lines of the pictures, instead of being sharp and well defined, were very indistinct. Now it is not probable that there is any variation in the relative proportions of the forces in light-waves, however these may vary in intensity; but a bright sunshine, instantaneously and simultaneously with its actinic or photographic action, imparts a considerable warmth, which, by a rapid accumulation on the plate, produces a repulsive state, which is unfavourable to chemical action; and though not sufficient to entirely suspend the latter, yet it renders it very irregular.

We see something similar to this in the effects of the sun's rays on vegetation at different seasons. In spring the predominance of vapours in the air and the coldness of the soil, reduce the intensity of the rays, producing that degree of tension that favours actinic action, and which seems to be especially conducive to the succulent functions in the early growth of plants; but during the arid parching heats of autumn, when the more solid parts of plants are ripening, the repulsive force of heat is favourable in another direction; for, by expanding the organic structures it promotes the movements of molecules which are requisite both for physical and chemical changes. That the defect in photographical operations is attributable to the disturbing influence of an opposite or repulsive force, is rendered probable by the fact that by increasing the delicacy of the chemical preparations, the difficulty is obviated; the greater susceptibility to change enabling the picture to be produced before the heating has become sufficient to be detrimental; and perhaps the same result might be obtained by directly intercepting, or counteracting the antagonistic energy, by using such coloured glasses as would reduce the heating power of the sun's rays, whilst a free passage is afforded to actinism.*

In conclusion, then, to sum up the contents of this chapter, the subject-matter of the sciences of acoustics and of optics is material undulation: that of the former being molecular, of the latter, etherial. Acoustics, then, is the science of molecular undulations; optics, that of etherial undulations. And the correlative forces which constitute these material motions, and which by their actions and reactions produce their respective phenomena, are in the case of acoustics, impulsion or epipallism, and elasticity — peculiar phases of attraction and repulsion; and in the

---

* Mr. Robert Hunt has written fully on the subject of Actinism, and although we have not made special quotations, we have been largely indebted to him for our information thereon.

case of optics, actinism, and radiant heat or thermacy. As in the following correlations,

Epipallism + Elasticity = Molecular Vibrations or Sound.
Actinism + Thermacy = Etherial Vibrations or Light.

This may not be a correct view of the subject, but it has at least a consistency, a homogeneity of doctrine which is greatly in its favour.

CHAP. V.

ELECTRICITY AND MAGNETISM, PHASES OF PHYSICAL POWERS, FUNCTIONING IN THE POLAR MOVEMENTS OF MATERIAL MOLECULES.

Electricity and Magnetism, cosmical or universal Forces. — Electrology the least advanced Branch of Physics. — Electricity and Magnetism are not the Noun-Substantives of distinct Sciences. — The various Modes of producing Electricity — Explanation of its Origin. — Electricity a Mode of Physical Repulsion. — Bodies not always in an electrical State. Positive and negative Electricities, are co-existent and co-equal. — Electrical Induction, the Action of contiguous Particles. — The Relations of positive and negative Poles to the Current. — Poles only manifested when Current passes through different *Media*. — Oersted on the Relation of electrical and magnetic Currents. Heat evolved during Magnetisation. — A Current of Magnetism lengthens the metallic Medium: that of Electricity shortens it — Explanation of these Phenomena.—Diamagnetism discovered by Professor Faraday: supposed to be a peculiar Force. — Professor Tyndal's Experiments thereon. — Magnecrystallic Force: a Crystal under its Influence virtually a Magnetic Needle.—Galvanism; Electro-magnetism; and other Forms of Polar Forces. — Conclusion.

THE last phases or modes of the physical powers, attraction and repulsion, which remain to be examined, are electricity and magnetism. These forces are cosmical, or universal, for all descriptions of material bodies are subject to their influence: as regards electricity, this circumstance has been long known; but it is only recently, through the researches of Faraday, that we have learnt that magnetism is not restricted to iron and a few other metals, but is capable of entering into relation with all bodies. This character of universality is an important fact; one which may ultimately enable us to arrive at a clearer apprehension of these forces than we have at present.

The phenomena manifested by the operation of electricity and of magnetism on various bodies are polar; that is, they assume different aspects in opposite directions, as in the case of the north and south poles of the magnet, and of the positive and negative electricities. The electric spark, and the direction in which the magnetic needle points, and many similar and curious facts, are very impressive; but in regarding them, the attention has been more fixed on the forces as causes, than on the phenomena themselves; a method of proceeding which has not usually been followed in the treatment of the inductive sciences. This we consider to be faulty; but we need not dwell on this topic, as it has already been discussed, when we gave our reasons why thermotics ought not to be acknowledged as a science; and for the same reason we do not think it correct to speak of the sciences of electricity and magnetism. Forces by their actions and reactions produce phenomena, as causes do effects; and it is the latter only which are dualisms or composition of forces, which can become the objects of systematic knowledge: the idea of a system is incompatible with that of an individual force, which cannot function without being in relation to some other force; and it is such relations only which give the subject-matter of a science.

We conceive therefore that whilst, on the one hand, it

is requisite that these physical forces, electricity and magnetism, should be investigated, in all their characteristics, their modes and velocity of transmission, and their relations to other forces; yet when all this has been accomplished, it does not put us in possession of two sciences; for as Comte has justly remarked, "facts do not constitute science, though they are its foundation and material. Science consists in the systematising of facts under established general laws; and regarded in this way, electrology is the least advanced of all the branches of physics. Those who have occupied themselves with imaginary fluids, as the causes of electrical and magnetical phenomena, have transferred the general laws of rational mechanics to the mutual action of their molecules; thus making the body under notice a mere *substratum*, necessary for the manifestation of the phenomenon, but unconcerned in its production, with which office the fluid is charged. It is clear that mathematical labours so baseless can serve no other purpose than that of analytical exercise, without adding a particle to our knowledge: they have borne no share in the great discoveries of the present day; though the discoveries, once made, have been afterwards attached to the hypothesis." *

If we have not misunderstood this passage, Comte points out the importance of studying electricity on a wider platform; that its influence, whether an imponderable fluid or a force, is not alone to be regarded in the consideration of the phenomenon; that there is some reaction between it and the bodies with which it is associated,

* Positive Philosophy, vol. i. p. 278.

which must not be overlooked. At least, this is the conclusion at which we have arrived, whether it coincides with that of Comte or not: the transient movements of the molecules of bodies during the transmission of electricity, are strictly speaking the subject-matter of a physical science, but not the forces which cause the phenomena. If it be so, to what condition of material bodies are we then to direct our attention in this research?

The subject of physics, which treats of the phenomena arising from the action and reaction of physical forces, is in all cases *motion*: and as the modes of these forces vary, so must the resulting motions assume different aspects. And in thus following out the various phases of physical powers, we have already considered the rotations and revolutions of celestial bodies, the changes of states in matter, atomic and molecular undulations; and now, lastly, there remain those polar motions or *polarity*, the actions and reactions produced by electricity and magnetism.

By polar motions, in this sense, we do not mean the distinct and independent movements of magnetised or of electrified bodies, the mere responses of the positive and negative poles of such bodies; but we understand thereby a general and combined arrangement, in which both forces are engaged. Polar forces are the correlatives of a dualism: which must, therefore, be inseparably co-existent and directly opposite, in the character of their attributes. Now all these characteristics are fulfilled in electricity and magnetism; so that if our reasoning be correct, we are irresistibly compelled to accept them as the dualism of forces, which is required to function in polar motions.

It will be no easy task to make this view of the subject

meet all its requirements; such a co-ordination, however, is necessary to complete the system of physical forces; and though, in some instances, it may seem to run counter to present notions, yet it will, we think, be found to renconcile many apparent inconsistencies.

Thus, in a few words, we have endeavoured to set forth what we conceive to be the relation subsisting between electricity and magnetism: and which receives no little support from a modern discovery; viz., that whenever a current of either of these forces is established, a current of the other is simultaneously produced, which flows in a direction at right angles to the original current: a fact which impressively calls to mind the relative positions of gravitation and centrifugal force; but which is nowise surprising, when we know that these central forces are only particular modes of the universal physical forces.

We now proceed to enter more into detail concerning electricity and magnetism; which of course cannot be an exhaustive account, but only sufficiently circumstantial to serve the purpose of our inquiry. And, in the first place, we will direct attention to electricity, which, as already remarked, is an all-pervading force in nature. Its universality seems to be such, that it may be elicited from all kinds of matter; and by any operations which may produce a molecular change in the condition of bodies. Thus, friction of any kind, between dissimilar substances, or even between the same kind of substance in different conditions, or even simple contact of some bodies, will suffice to evolve electricity; and the same happens when bodies change their state, when heated, or when chemically acted on; in short, any disturbance of molecular arrangement.

Now, in all these cases, there must be a disturbing force, be it great or be it small, which occasions these molecular motions. What becomes of this motion; and of the force by which it was produced? The forces employed in these operations do not arrest attention, we are so much occupied with the curious phenomenon which follows; but let not this applied force be lightly passed over: and, in order to simplify our remarks, let *heat* be selected as the agent.

Formerly, heat, a modal variety of repulsion, could not have been clearly understood in such an operation: but, since the researches of Joule have taught us that heat may be measured by the work performed, through the medium of a machine, our notion concerning it has become much more definite. When, therefore, a given force, as heat, acts on the molecules of a body and puts them in motion, the molecules perform the part of a *medium*, transmitting force by continuous repetition of limited motions, and may consequently be regarded as a machine in motion, which transmits power as long as the application of the *primum mobile* continues, but falls back to a state of rest as soon as the oscillating action and reaction ceases. The heat during its transition may become so diffused, as to produce no sensible effects; but if of sufficient intensity, it will, on its escape from this medium into another, manifest itself as a distinct force, as appreciable as when it entered into the molecular body. Must this force, then, appear again as heat? As some kind of *repulsive* force it must certainly appear, for the principle of the conservation of forces requires thus much; but it does not follow that the phase of repulsion will be that of heat;—for the character of the force will depend on the manner of its transmission; that is, it will be modified according to the nature of the molecular motions. Thus heat, as well as the impact of another body in motion, may cause the molecules of a body to vibrate, and this motion will issue from the body as sonorous undulations; and so also when the molecules are affected by polar movements in a continued series of alternate mutations, then electrical phenomena are evoked, either as positive or negative effects, when its passage is through *different* media, or as currents when the polar actions are uninterruptedly continuous.

On this view of the subject, electricity is that phase of repulsion which this universal force assumes when molecules are actuated by polar motions; and it passes on from molecule to molecule by the alternate movement of their poles, just as radiant heat and mechanical impulses are transmitted by undulations; and being a repulsive force, the action of which has an outward tendency, its presence is commonly more conspicuous on the surface of bodies. The different conditions of molecular movements are the phenomena which indicate an alteration in the *modus operandi* of their efficient causes: and for this reason, we properly discriminate between the different phases of the same forces; and for this reason we one while call the repulsive force heat, and at another electricity, though at the same time admitting that they are ultimately one and the same power.

It has already been observed that electricity is a universal force, that is, a force capable of entering into relation with all natural bodies; but it does not follow from this that all bodies are constantly in an electrical state, as is generally supposed, or that all that is requisite to excite electricity is to alter the statical state of bodies in this respect. It is, indeed, probable that currents of electricity, perpetually excited by the action of the sun's rays, may circulate around the earth's equator, as continuously as magnetism flows in an unceasing stream, in the direction of the north and south poles; and if so, of course all bodies must be more or less exposed to this electrical action. But we do not think it expedient to regard bodies as containing combined electricity either positive or negative, and classifying them according to this supposed constitution. All bodies may be electrically excited, for the molecules of all are capable of polar motions; but they are not always in this condition, owing to the interposition of various antagonisms, so that bodies cannot be supposed to be always in an electrical state.

All molecules must be regarded as having two distinct electrical poles, the positive and the negative, and so accordingly we commonly speak of a positive and of a negative electricity. Franklin considered these electricities as only the opposite states of one and the same force; whilst Dufay and others have maintained that they are two distinct fluids. Faraday*, in his Researches in Electricity, says, " that he has sought for evidence capable of sustaining the theory of two electricities rather than that of one, but has not been able to perceive a single fact which could be brought forward for such a purpose; or, admitting the hypothesis of two electricities, he could not detect the slightest grounds for believing that one electricity in a current can be more powerful than the other, or that it

* Philosophical Transactions, Series v., 1833.

can be present without the other; or that one can be varied, or in the slightest degree affected, without a corresponding variation in the other. And judging from facts only, there is not as yet the slightest reason for considering the influence, which is present in what we call the electric current, as a compound or complicated influence. It has never been resolved into simpler or elementary influences, and may perhaps be best conceived of as *an axis of power having contrary forces, exactly equal in amount, in contrary directions.*"

These conclusions of Faraday are invaluable. At first sight, the latter clause seems to be a contradiction of the former, for if there are no facts indicative of two electricities, how comes it to pass that the electrical current is composed of contrary and equal forces? This is very difficult to conceive, and the idea of such an efficiency, exerted in contrary directions, approximates very nearly to that of the positive and negative electricities, which are supposed to be co-existent but opposite forces. Doubtless Faraday himself has a clear apprehension of such an axis of power, which others very competent to judge have indeed accepted as an important hypothesis; we confess, however, that we are unable to reconcile the apparent contradiction, but we must strive to grapple with the difficulty, and consider how far it may be rendered consistent with our notion concerning natural forces.

Much of the perplexity arises, we think, from the misapprehension of the nature of electrical and magnetic polarities. In both cases, one kind of pole attracts the other; and poles of the same kind uniformly repel each other. When bodies are under the influence of either electricity or of magnetism, they give indications that one extremity is the positive, and the other the negative pole; and divide these bodies as often as you may, still each end has an opposite pole; and this there is every reason to believe would hold good, even could we arrive at the ultimate molecules of the body. After having broken up a body in this manner, if we put the parts together again so as to reconstruct the body (which to a certain extent is practicable in the case of the magnet), this might be done so as to give the body the form of a long chain, each link having two poles, and being united to the adjacent links by opposite poles, and in this manner the entire chain would become virtually one body, having a positive pole at one extremity and a negative at the other. In the next place, make a closed circuit by bringing the two ends of the chain together, and there is no longer a distinction of poles, the force moving in a continuous current; the previous character is not destroyed by this arrangement, for break the continuity of the chain at any part, and the opposite poles immediately reappear. From these facts, we conclude that both electricity and magnetism are forces which move in concentric currents around certain axes; that the movement in currents is the normal function of these forces, from which they never depart; and that, when they assume a different aspect, as when they respectively exhibit the phenomenon of poles, the departure is more apparent than real. The current still flows on in a continuous re-entering stream, but its course is no longer through one but different *media*; and in its transition from one medium to another, a great change takes place, a perturbation which is manifested as the opposite poles of an axis. All bodies, whether electrified or magnetised, are thus affected, exhibiting opposite poles, beyond which the current-force is continued by induction; which is no other than the mode in which the current progresses in a different medium; and the direction of such inductions tends to the union of opposite poles, as shown in the magnetic field, when the lines of force are rendered apparent by the arrangement of fine particles of iron. In these currents, the force is exerted in one direction; and when any part of such current is broken, the end of the body which points in this direction is called the positive pole, and the opposite, or re-entering end, the negative pole. If a more powerful pole be forcibly held in any direction near a weaker pole of the same kind, both poles will be in a state of antagonism; and if the weaker pole can move, it must assume the direction of the stronger, which being opposite is equivalent to repulsion, or the reversing of its original direction.

According to this interpretation, the movement at the negative pole must be co-existent, opposite, and, as Faraday states, co-equal with that of the positive pole; whatever takes place at one pole must have a simultaneous coincidence in all things, except a contrariety of position and direction. We cannot, therefore, regard the poles, either of electricity or of magnetism, as indicative of two forces, but only as certain conditions of one and the same force. This is a conception which is not at first glance easily understood, but as we become familiar with it much of the perplexity disappears. The current of such a force is its onward propagation, by the alternate movement of the molecules on their axes, forward and backward; and there is another correlative force present which maintains the molecules in their position, forming the axes, as it were, on which the molecules turn; and when the aggressive or moving force is transmitted onward, the other, or *tangential* force, reacts, and is the means of restoring the original arrangement. Now this polar excitement and transmission may occur with either force, as one or other of the correlative forces predominates. Thus if the action of a repulsive force produce an electrical excitement, a current of electricity will be evolved; but simultaneously therewith another current must be elicited tangentially thereto, and as there is only one other polar force known, viz. magnetism, we cannot escape the conviction that electricity and magnetism are the correlative forces concerned in the polar motions of molecules. Such a notion would have appeared very absurd in the infancy of our knowledge concerning these forces; but since the important discovery of Oersted concerning the intimate relation of electricity and magnetism, and the subsequent extension of this subject by the researches of others, we are prepared to accept such an association as has been suggested.

It is now well known that a closed current of either force is simultaneously accompanied by a current of the opposite force tangentially thereto, and that whichever force is in the ascendant, it revolves around the other force, which forms a fixed axis for the rotation; just as in a celestial body the discharge of centrifugal force causes an equatorial movement around the poles of the body, which are maintained as a stable axis of motion by the force of gravitation. Now what we are desirous of establishing is, that electricity and magnetism are not only thus associated in co-existent currents, but that whilst the energising force is progressive, the reacting force, in a state of tension, is equally concerned in the polar phenomena. At all events, the poles of either force cannot be two things, but only aspects of one and the same; for we cannot conceive of forces existing always in the same relations.

Should this suggestion be deemed worthy of consideration, it will be found to point to the same dualistic constitution which we have found to obtain in all the other conditions of material bodies; and if we admit that the dualism of polar forces consists of electricity and magnetism, we accept them as modes or phases of the universal physical forces, attraction and repulsion. Electricity thus offers itself in polar motions, as a phase of repulsion tending to expansive diffusions; whilst magnetism, a phase of attraction, is a more permanent and coercive force; and when we consider these antagonistic relations, we find a ready explanation of many curious circumstances connected with these forces. Thus during magnetisation, heat is produced, indicating an approximation of molecules by an increased attraction: similiar to that which takes place on the compression of a body; intimating, as we have said, that magnetism is a phase of attraction, and consequently acts in the same direction. On the other hand, when a magnet is heated, it loses its virtue; some say that this only occurs under certain conditions, but Gauss has set this at rest by his excellent researches; the fact is now established, that magnetism is always diminished by heat, and, at elevated temperatures, is entirely subverted. We say *subverted*, and not *destroyed;* for heat being a repulsive, and magnetism an attractive force, the former, when it predominates, renders the latter *latent* or passive, either as magnetism, or as some other mode of the same force, for forces are indestructible. Joule, who discovered the evolution of heat during magnetic induction, observed that the entire volume of the magnet is not altered; for what it gains in length, it loses in breadth; showing that the magnetic coercion is curiously analogous to the rolling of a bar, or the drawing of a wire. The molecules are arranged and contracted by the coercive current in one direction, and extended in the opposite; and in like manner many of the results obtained by Becquerel and Wertheim, by subjecting magnetic bars to torsion and hammering, may be explained. These illustrations might be greatly enlarged, but they suffice to show the relation between magnetism and the molecular constitution of bodies. Electricity also is concerned in corresponding phenomena; but as these are necessarily of an opposite character, they require an explanation the reverse of the former. Thus, when a current of electricity is passed through a wire, the tendency is to shorten it, and to increase its thickness: its repulsive force counteracts and subverts the constrained state of the molecules, occasioned by the elongating *compression* of the wire-drawing process; and the molecules, being set at liberty, rearrange themselves in the normal condition of the metal.

When the molecules of bodies are under the influence of polar motions, how comes it to pass that we have not always both electrical and magnetic phenomena, if these forces co-exist? whereas we commonly find, that only one of these forces is manifested at a time: if repulsive force prevails, the resulting phenomena are electrical, but if the opposite force is in the ascendant, the phenomena are magnetic. Now this is perfectly analogous to all the other kinds of physical motions which have been already considered; and in which the correlative forces of each dualism, according to their respective relations, produce corresponding effects. Thus, in the different states of matter, solids, liquids, and gases, each condition respectively depends on the relative proportions of the dualistic forces, cohesion and caloric: and if we seek to know why these conditions so greatly influence electrical and magnetic phenomena, the answer is ready at hand, when we remember that the forces concerned therein, as well as those relating to the different states of matter, are fundamentally identical; being all modes of the same physical powers, attraction and repulsion, differing only from each other in their *modus operandi* on molecules. From such a stand-point, we see that when magnetism coincides with the attraction of cohesion, they mutually facilitate each other's action, because they operate in the same direction; as is beautifully illustrated by the behaviour of crystals of different systems when suspended in the magnetic field: but if magnetism be resisted by the counteraction of repulsive heat, then it sustains a corresponding reduction of energy. And, *mutatis mutandis*, the same remarks apply to electricity, in its concurrence with different kinds of physical forces: thus, in the electrolysis of chemical substances several illustrations will readily suggest themselves.

By the researches of Faraday we have learnt that ordinary electrical induction is in all cases " an action of contiguous particles," a species of polarity, and not a mutual influence of either particles or masses at sensible distances. It is, indeed, as already stated, an extension of polar motions into different *media*, through which the forces tend to complete a circuit, by which the poles of bodies become parts of, and involved in, a continuous current. And it follows that when by *induction*, (as well as in the case of *conduction*, in which this condition is more grossly apparent,) the circuit is completed, an antagonistic current must necessarily be called into existence, which assumes a tangential arrangement. Should this reasoning be admitted, it offers a solution of those diamagnetic phenomena, for the knowledge of which we are indebted to Faraday.

Some have thought that bodies are magnetic or diamagnetic only in virtue of possessing different degrees of magnetism; and this was Faraday's first view of the subject: but he has seen reason to question it, and he now regards the movements of diamagnetics in the field of force as due to a peculiar influence different from that of ordinary magnetism. *Diamagnetism* manifests itself when non-magnetic bodies are placed between the opposite poles of a magnet; it cannot be called into activity by any other condition, as electricity and magnetism can, by various modes of excitement. On this and other considerations we are inclined to think that it is decidedly different from magnetism, but we do not think that it is a peculiar and *unknown* force: it acts as a polar force, equatorially to the axial current of magnetism, which is the characteristic of *electricity;* and on this account we are disposed to regard the latter and diamagnetism as identically the same force.

In the magnetic field, between the poles of a magnet,

the curved lines of force meet in closed currents in the air by *induction;* and when this is once effected, a counter current of electricity ought also to be evoked tangentially thereto: and thus it comes to pass that diamagnetic bodies suspended between the poles of the magnet, move slowly at first, but quicker subsequently as the current becomes established; and lastly arrange themselves in an equatorial position, which corresponds to that which they would assume under the influence of *electricity.* If the bodies placed in the magnetic field be capable of forming part of the magnetic circle; that is if, like iron, their molecules are susceptible of being magnetically polarised, then they will take up a contrary, or axial, position in the direction of the magnetic current, of which they will form a part. This explanation may prove to be insufficient, but at all events it has the merit of rendering the multiplication of forces unnecessary; and this tendency to simplicitly is no bad criterion of scientific validity.

Professor Tyndal* has also diligently investigated this subject, and has illustrated the relations of bodies to the separate poles of the magnet by some interesting experiments. He has shown that a diamagnetised body is capable of assuming a condition peculiar to each pole, that is, of a dual excitation; and he therefore gives the preference to Faraday's original hypothesis, that diamagnetic bodies, operated upon by magnetism, possess a polarity "the same in kind but the reverse in direction of that acquired by magnetic bodies." In passing we may remark, that this definition is not very inapplicable to electricity.

* Philosophical Transactions, vol. cxlv. pp. 38, 40, 51.

As regards Professor Tyndal's experiments, if it be remembered that the curved lines of force, which proceed from either pole of the magnet, are parts of continuous currents, which broken at any point by the interposition of a different medium must manifest opposite poles with their respective characteristics, we may expect to find the phenomena to vary accordingly: the poles of the interposed body, now forming part of the magnetic current, must agree or not with the poles of the magnet, according to their relative positions; that is, each part of the chain of polar motions, whether the molecules of the interposed air or of any body involved therein, is, as it were, a separate magnet, and consequently each and all are subject to the laws of magnetism.

The same indefatigable experimenter has made known a number of facts concerning the departure of both magnetic and diamagnetic bodies from their normal positions, when placed between magnetic poles of a triangular form. Had these departures only taken place in the case of diamagnetic bodies, the result would have been most perplexing: but as it is, we have only to explain the phenomena of magnetic bodies in this peculiar position; and then we shall be able to understand those of the other kind, since they must be of a directly opposite character. Why then do magnetic bodies, above and below such pointed poles of a magnet, change the axial to the equatorial direction? It can only be attributed to a peculiar arrangement of the lines of force in the magnetic field, produced by the brush-like form which the currents must assume on issuing from, and re-entering at, the pointed poles of the magnet: which arrangement admits of the direct lines of force passing in an uninterrupted stream; whilst the other lines, both above and below, must be greatly perturbed by the crossings of diverging rays. However this may be accomplished, the fact indicates that the current is uniformly flowing in one and the same direction, and therefore on the upper and the under lines must necessarily point in opposite directions; whilst the co-existent and opposite electrical current, whatever the modification of the magnetic current, must undergo a corresponding change. A more distinct and definite description of such a complex arrangement may be given by geometers in a diagram: all we can do is to point out the probability and the possibility of a system of intersecting currents, when viewed in different positions, presenting appearances of a directly contrary aspect.

It has been supposed that the diamagnetic force is the same as that by which *crystals* are actuated when in the magnetic field, and which affords phenomena varying in character as the axes of the crystals are optically positive or negative: whilst on the other hand Plücker ascribes these phenomena to the action of a peculiar force, entirely different from that of magnetism or of diamagnetism. Faraday*, in his almost exhaustive researches in electricity, has carefully investigated the subject of *crystallic force:* and he obtained results different from those of Plücker, concerning the relation of the optical axes to magnetic action. Plücker's force is equatorial, whereas that of Faraday is axial, which he has named the *magne-crystallic force.* "This force," says Faraday, "is not only axial; but

---

* Philosophical Transactions, Series xxii. 2469, 2472, 2479.

it is doubtless resident in the particles of the crystal: it is such that the crystal can set with equal readiness and permanence in two diametral positions; and between these there are two positions of equatorial equilibrium, which are of course unstable in their nature. The magne-crystallic force does not manifest itself by attraction or repulsion, but gives *position* only. The law of action appears to be that the *line* or *axis* of this force (being the resultant of the action of all the molecules) tends to place itself parallel, or as a tangent to the magnetic curve or line of magnetic force, passing through the place where the crystal is situated."
In a later communication Faraday* observes that "the aptitude of a magne-crystal, when in the magnetic field, to assume a maximum conductive state in a given direction, makes it similar in action to a permanently magnetised sphere; and therefore however diamagnetic it may be, and however slight its magne-crystallic condition, still it will *set* in a definite direction."

On this topic we would venture to suggest that a piece of iron is so molecularly constituted that it readily transmits magnetic force in any direction; so that when placed in a magnetic field, if it be free to move, it will arrange itself axially in the direction of its *length*:— but a crystal is different, it conducts best in the direction of its crystalline *axes*; on these lines it assumes a definite position, and is therefore in this respect virtually a magnetic needle, and may be substituted for the ordinary steel needle with advantage, in some circumstances, as pointed out by Faraday. But, like iron, the crystal is not coercive,

---

* Philosophical Transactions, Series xxx. 3384, 3385.

and therefore does not retain the magnetic property when removed from the closed current, as in the case of steel. Surely this fact cannot intimate that magnetised crystals are actuated by any peculiar force, such as the name magnecrystallic force would seem to imply? We can only see in this circumstance that cohesion, the attractive force which unites the molecules, exists in greater intensity on certain lines or axes of crystals, producing a structure favourable to the passage of magnetism; or, in the more usual mode of expressing it, crystals are better conductors of magnetism in the direction of their axes. Now magnetism and cohesion are analogous attractive forces; and as similar forces coinciding in tendency, they do not retard, but facilitate each each other's actions; so that it might be expected that magnetism would follow the axes of crystals in preference to all other directions.

It seems to us to be unnecessary to dwell on those various forces of electricity and magnetism which are evolved under different combinations. The most interesting, that of galvanism, is a continuous current of electricity, evolved by chemical actions: in all of which a change in the position of the molecules of bodies must take place; and such changes give rise to a diffusion of repulsive force, functioning in polar motions, which, by the peculiar arrangement of the apparatus, is conveyed away by conducting wires. There is, therefore, no difference *in principle* in this mode of excitation from that of others by which electricity is evoked into activity, as when the molecules are disturbed by mechanical actions or by heat; in each case very different arrangements are required: but whether electricity be excited by friction, heat, or chemical action, it is in all cases one and the same kind of force.

Whenever there is a closed current of either electricity or magnetism, as already stated, the correlative force is immediately called into existence, and may be manifested in a direction tangentially thereto: in correspondence with this fact various kinds of apparatus have been invented to exhibit the resulting phenomena; and we speak of the forces thus concerned as electro-magnetism, and magneto-electricity, according to the force employed for the excitation of its correlative. The phenomena are very interesting and instructive: but they do not afford any facts different from those which we have been considering, and therefore cannot furnish us with any additional information for the illustration of our subject.

In conclusion, therefore, we will only observe that the forces of electricity and magnetism cannot, on our view of the subject, become the subject-matter of special sciences. To be in accordance with the other physical sciences, and more particularly with that of astronomy which is the farthest advanced toward perfection, these forces should be related to some form of physical substance, some kind of material body, which must exhibit such peculiar motions as do not come under those which have already been enumerated as rotations, expansions, and undulations. In the case of both electrical and magnetical actions, we find that the bodies subjected thereto do exhibit strikingly different motions, which have been called polar; and we therefore conclude that polar motions are the characteristic phenomena produced by the correlative forces of electricity and magnetism. We cannot, in every case, demonstrate that in polar motions both these forces are concerned, but we know the very general fact, that when force manifests itself it can only be because it is in a *plus* or dynamical state; whilst the other force is rendered latent or equalised by a portion of the plus force, up to which point both forces are necessarily unknown, as neither is in a condition to function. So that, although it cannot be always proved, we are justified in concluding that all polar motions are dualisms or compounds of electricity and magnetism. The science, therefore, which comprises the consideration of these forces, as astronomy does those of gravitation and centrifugy, must be the science of polar motions, which may be called *Polarity*. It may be objected to this term that it is already associated in our minds with an idea of antagonism, which is common to all physical phenomena; if so, another may be invented: but it would seem to be preferable to abandon the use of this term in a sense which is at best very confused, and to restrict it to the above-mentioned definite purpose.

CHAP. VI.

CHEMICAL SUBSTANCES, DUALISMS OF PHYSICAL AND CHEMICAL POWERS.

The Union of dissimilar Substances, the characteristic of Chemical Action. — This a kind of Attraction. — Does not act indiscriminately between all Bodies: but is elective. — This Attractive Force called Affinity. — Chemical Affinity and Electricity supposed to be identical. — This Opinion advocated by Davy, Berzelius, and Faraday. — Comte regards this as confounding the Auxiliary with the Phenomenon. — Electricity is a diffusive, decomposing Force; Affinity a condensing, combining Force : can such Opposites be identical ? — The mutual Convertibility of these Forces more apparent than real. — Various Definitions of Chemistry. — Chemical Elements, their Nature. The Weight and Volume of each Element specific. — The Elements not Multiples of Hydrogen. — Predisposing Affinity. — Chemical Compounds all Binaries or Dualisms. — Chemical Notations. — The Duplication of Atoms an important Innovation. — Allotropy. — This State of Elements not permanent. — Duplication of Atoms remarkably indestructible. — The Hydrocarbons, basic or neutral, electro-negative and electro-positive; their Combinations as *quasi-elements*, like Cyanogen. The typal and basic Combinations of Nitrogen. — Conclusion.

HITHERTO our attention has been solely occupied with the consideration of the physical powers, which are universal or cosmical forces, pervading all material bodies; for matter itself, or physical substance, is a dualism of these powers. Various as physical phenomena are, throughout the different departments of nature, they all depend on the modes or phases of physical powers, which function as peculiar kinds of material motions; thus, we have central motions, undulations, and polarisations, but all are modifications of one and the same physical motion, or change of position in space.

Chemical, not physical, changes are, however, now to form the subject of our inquiry; and we shall have to deal with more complex dualisms of powers. Dualisms, not of two simple antagonistic powers which alone were capable of interchanging their relations in such a protean manner, so as to produce an infinity of phenomena; but dualisms, the basic or ponderable part of which consists of the more simple physical dualism actuated by specific influences or *chemical powers*.

But before entering on this subject let us take a hasty glance at the prevailing opinions concerning chemical force, and concerning the character and object of chemistry; an introduction which will render our view more intelligible.

The first and most obvious characteristic of chemical force is its tendency to draw together and unite dissimilar substances, so as to form new and homogeneous compounds. It was by a comparison of the changes which attend chemical actions that Newton was led to conclude that chemical combinations cannot be conceived of in any other way than as an attraction of particles. This notion was much opposed, particularly in France; but it at last gained ground, and the term *affinity* was adopted instead of that of *attraction*. There can be but little doubt that *chemical* force is essentially an *attractive* force; but it possesses something more than this generic character, it has also a peculiar or specific difference; it is not only an attractive, but also an elective force, for it does not unite all substances indiscriminately, but as an elective affinity it manifests a preference in the order of its operations. At the end of the last century the doctrine of elective affinity had assumed a systematic form, when it was assailed by Berthollet, who maintained that affinity is not elective, but depends upon the relative quantities of the substances employed, and other physical conditions. After a long discussion it is, however, now decided that although affinity is greatly modified by various circumstances, and even altogether suspended, yet when it can take place it is exerted with different degrees of energy and preferentially between some substances to the exclusion of others.

"The close connection[*]," observes the author of the "Philosophy of the Inductive Sciences," "between chemical affinity and the crystalline attraction of elements cannot be overlooked. The forces which hold together the elements of a crystal of alum are the same forces which make it a crystal. There is no distinguishing between the two sets of forces." "The regular forms of bodies," says Berzelius, "suppose a polarity which can be no other than an electric or magnetic polarity. This being so seemingly inevitable, we might expect to find the electric forces manifesting some relation to the definite directions of crystalline forms. Mr. Faraday tried, but in vain, to detect some such relation." It is now the general opinion that chemical force and electricity are identical: and if affinity and cohesion are the same force, it follows that

[*] Philosophy of the Inductive Sciences, vol. i. p. 353.

crystalline force and electricity must also be identical; since things that are equal to a third are equal to one another. The recent investigations of Faraday concerning magne-crystallic force may seem to sanction the idea that polarity is concerned in both cases: — there is much in common between crystalline and polar forces, but, as we have already remarked on this subject in the last chapter, we need not now renew the discussion.

In modern times, the identity of chemical affinity and electricity has had many eminent supporters. Davy claimed the credit of having first advanced this doctrine; but this, whether justly or not, has been disputed: he certainly was, however, the first who gave the hypothesis a tangible form, and supported it by a series of brilliant experiments. Since then, Berzelius has most ably advocated this opinion, and reduced it to a more definite system. And Faraday, in his valuable "Researches in Electricity," has completed the inquiry by demonstrating the equivalence of chemical and electrical actions; a fact which seems to have carried with it such conviction, that the doctrine is *now* very generally received as an established truth.

The electro-chemical hypothesis is not, however, universally acknowledged. "Though chemistry," says Comte*, " is united to physics by electricity more than by any other agency, it must yet be remembered that the two sciences are distinct, and that there should be no confounding of chemical with electrical phenomena. When our predecessors regarded *heat* as the chief agent in composition

---

* Positive Philosophy, vol. i. p. 335 *et seq.*

and decomposition, they did not pervert such a consideration to the point of assimilating chemical to thermotic effects. We, however, confound the auxiliary with the phenomenon itself; and pervert chemistry by confounding it with electrology. Berzelius has frankly declared that cohesion, properly so called, admits of no electrical explanation, nor is affinity or the tendency to combination any better explained by the electro-chemical theory. Electrical phenomena in physics are eminently general, offering only differences of intensity in different bodies; whereas chemical phenomena are essentially special or elective, and therefore every attempt to make chemistry, as a whole, enter into any branch of physics, is thoroughly anti-scientific." This is strongly expressed, but it contains an important truth sustained by sound reasoning. Electricity is a phase of the universal force repulsion, one of the correlative forces of the physical dualism; and the physical forces only function in various kinds of motion: whereas chemical force or affinity is not a physical force; it does not operate in any kind of *motion*, but in the *combination* of heterogeneous molecules. So far from *electricity* and *affinity* being identical forces, they seem rather to be diametrically opposite: — the one being eminently an expanding, heating, and dissipating force; the other a condensing and aggregating force.

Before quitting this subject, there remains to be noticed another, and the latest opinion concerning the nature of chemical force. Grove considers this force as not only identical with electricity, but also with all the other physical forces; on the ground, as already stated, that they are all capable of mutual conversion into each other. It is not very surprising that in electrolysis, a definite amount of electricity should liberate a corresponding equivalent of chemical elements; or that the union of these elements should evolve electricity. The forces concerned are the antagonists of one another, the one in direction of attraction, the other of repulsion; and it therefore follows that when chemical union takes place it is accompanied by an evolution of repulsion, which under certain conditions manifests itself as polar or electrical motions: and in turn when electricity operates, its repulsive action on the compound produces a state unfavourable to union, and so its chemical constituents are set at liberty. In short, such cases are only instances of action and reaction, which necessarily imply the co-operation of opposite influences: and if so, it follows from this circumstance alone that electrical and chemical forces are antithetic, having nothing in common.

Since the conception which has been hitherto formed concerning the character of chemical force is so indefinite, it is not to be wondered at that the various attempts which have been made to define chemistry have proved inadequate to express the nature and the objects of the science. One of the best definitions of chemistry is that of Dr. Thomson, in his system, now out of date: "Chemistry," he says, "is a science, the object of which is to determine the constituents of bodies, and the laws which regulate their combinations." Turning to a few modern books within our reach, we read in Peschel's "Physics," that "chemical attraction is the exercise of the molecular forces on the actions of dissimilar bodies." "Chemistry," says Scoffern, "is the science which investigates the quality and constitution of matter in all its relations, except those affecting visible motion." Comte's definition chemistry is that it "relates to the laws of composition and decomposition, which result from the molecular & *specific* mutual action of different substances." Lastly, we look in vain for information thereon in Professor Miller's recent work on this science; perhaps an intentional omission, considering chemistry as yet incapable of being defined. As Comte* has observed, "every science falls short of its definition; but a real definition is the first evidence that science has attained some consistency, for it then measures its own advancement from one epoch to another; and it always keeps inquirers in a right direction, and supports them in a philosophic progress." Now, during the inductive formation of a science, a *real* definition can only be a happy anticipation; but when a science has arrived at maturity, it and its definition ought to be the equivalent of each other, the reciprocally convertible terms of an identical proposition.

Such is a brief statement concerning the nature of chemical force and of chemical science as now generally understood, and which, as may have been gathered from our remarks, we are not prepared to accept as satisfactory. Whether we have anything better to offer remains to be decided, when we have submitted our views thereon; but whether approved of or not, they have resulted from, and are in accordance with, the principles of our universal system.

Guided by the analogy of the physical sciences, that is

---

* Positive Philosophy, vol. i. p. 294.

of those sciences which treat of the varied motions of material bodies, chemistry may be defined as the science or systematic knowledge of chemical substances, and of their *combining* actions and reactions on each other. Just as material *motions* from the subject-matter of physics, so material *combinations* are the objects of chemistry: these two branches of knowledge are perfectly distinct. Physical attractions and repulsions occur in all natural bodies; for all are fundamentally material or physical: and thus it happens that all chemical substances possess characteristic physical properties. But the peculiar, or *specific*, properties of chemical substances must not be confounded with the *generic* or physical: we treat not now of the latter, but of those differential attributes, derived from or belonging to the specific powers, one of which forms a constituent of every chemical element.

All chemical substances have been resolved into a comparatively few simple bodies or *elements,* as they are called. Elementary substances are only conventionally accepted as simple, as long as they remain undecomposable; and so it has come to pass that not only substances supposed to be simple have been proved to be otherwise, but even those which at one time were deemed compounds are now acknowledged as chemical elements. This at first sight would seem to involve the subject in utter confusion; but it has not practically had this effect: it necessarily requires occasional changes, but these are easily made, without deranging the entire system. When, therefore, we hereafter state that elements are individually actuated by their respective specific force, we do so under the *proviso* that they are indeed *bonâ fide* elements; should such, however, prove to be not simple, but combinations of elements, then that which was supposed to be a simple force, becomes a composition of specific forces; our knowledge thus becomes more accurate, without any sacrifice of principle.

What then is a chemical element? It is, like all other natural bodies, a dualism of powers. One of its correlative powers is a complex power, matter, the physical dualism; it is the quantitative basis or body of the element, and thence its physical properties: whilst the other correlative power is the actuating qualitative principle, which imparts to the element its specific chemical character. Here then we see a grand advance in the system of nature: the dualisms are no longer varied modes of the same binary and universal powers, and as such universally related as parts or units of the same whole, but as chemical elements they each possess an *individuality*, which is not communicable. A mass and a molecule of matter only vary in magnitude; and however their figurative forms may be modified, or however diversified the manner and directions of their movements; in short, whatever may be their differences, they are parts of one and the same dualism of physical powers, attraction and repulsion: not so the chemical elements, however they are combined together, and whatever may be the multitude of complications resulting therefrom, each and every element retains its individuality, and phœnix-like may be restored again to its pristine condition.

Each element, then, has its specific power: and thus we have to admit the existence of many chemical powers; whilst physical powers are only two, universal attraction and repulsion. Substance, as already stated, is the logical correlation of its correlatives, quantity and quality:—physical substance, or matter, is a dualism of attractive and repulsive powers; and chemical substance is a dualism of matter and chemical power. Every chemical element, as a peculiar substance, has a material body actuated by a specific energy: but although the bodies of all the elements are material, it does not follow that they are perfectly alike in all cases: and so it is found that they all differ from each other in quantity, each element having a body of a peculiar and definite weight. The reason of this difference is, we conceive, that the specific force of each element is capable, like the specific vital principles of organisms, of appropriating a given number of material units, or atoms, and arranging them in the construction of its *own* body or molecule: and in the exercise of chemical force, according to its innate rational law, it assimilates only a definite number of atoms to form its peculiar atomic weight; and symmetrically disposes these atoms, in a more or less regular manner, to constitute its specific volume. And as these specific *weights* and *volumes* vary for each chemical element, so do their physical properties exhibit corresponding variations. So likewise in the characters of the very elements themselves, that is, of their specific forces, we perceive and may anticipate the nature of chemical functions generally: they are definite, elective, and eminently attractive; joining together and condensing atoms into compounds.

Chemical powers, then, when operative, function in *combination*, which partakes largely of the nature of attraction, but is distinguished therefrom by a specific peculiarity. These powers may be regarded as numerous species of the genus attraction; each of them possessing the generic character, together with some peculiarity, which marks their differences as species; and in this manner, we conceive, the universal and particular attractive powers, physical attraction and chemical forces, may be capable of systematic arrangement. And since chemical powers are thus seen to act in the direction of attraction, that is, having a uniting and condensing tendency, we can understand how sometimes these different forces may promote each other's operations; and at others be unfavourable: all depends on the manner of their concurrence.

This view of the constitution of chemical elements may seem at first sight very similar to one which has been propounded by the Reverend Dr. Macvicar, in his "Elements of the Economy of Nature," an ingenious and very suggestive work published three years ago; the subject of which has just been laid before the British Association at Aberdeen, and reported as follows: — " Suppose an analogy of function in the entire series of chemical agents, implying an analogy of corresponding structure. The only constituent atom, or truly simple element, is something lighter than hydrogen, and a physical rather than a recognised chemical agent. The universal ether, an ancient doctrine, now sanctioned by modern science, constitutes the medium of light and radiant heat, and is composed of particles all similar to each other, and animated by attractive and repulsive forces, like the molecules of common bodies. Affirming the query of Newton as to whether the molecules of dense bodies may not be composed of particles of the medium of light, a molecular theory resulted, which satisfied and explained, to a wonderful extent, the well-known atomic weights of chemical agents. The principle on which Dr. Macvicar conducts his synthesis of molecules is that of statical equilibrium or symmetry. The first in the series is a molecule composed of five particles of light or ether; three to form an equator and two to form the poles. This molecule, when viewed in relation to its own exquisite mechanical structure, and to the medium of light in which it continues to exist, gives as its mechanical and optical properties the same as those which characterise hydrogen. And in this manner, according to the number of atoms of ether, each chemical element is formed."

Our notion concerning chemical elements was arrived at long before we became acquainted with the above views; but as a point of priority this is of no consequence, as there is a great difference between us. We conceive, as Dr. Macvicar does, that the atoms of ether or pure physical substance, according to their definite number, constitute the weight of each element, and that the crystalline form of each element depends upon the symmetrical arrangement of the etherial atoms: and here, if we have not misapprehended the statement, his explanation ends; a definite structure implying a corresponding chemical agent. But according to our view, this definite structure is only the body of each element, the *basis* or reacting principle in the dualism; the actuating principle which determines the weight and volume of the body being a *specific force*, different from all physical forces: we seem therefore, to agree, when the question is only viewed on the side of its ponderable matter; but this is, we think, only one half of the question; the elements are not only physical, but also chemical, a composition of co-existent and opposite forces.

From what has been now stated, we are prepared to understand why the chemical elements are not multiples of hydrogen;—the lightest of the elements, and the one which is generally adopted as the atomic standard of unity. Prout, indeed, maintained, with great ability, that the elements are multiples of hydrogen; but the elaborate experiments of Berzelius, Turner, and others brought forward so many exceptions thereto, that this notion was abandoned; very recently, however, strenuous exertions have been made to revive Prout's theory, but there still remain so many outstanding facts, that the probability of their success is very remote. In the mean time, hydrogen can only be accepted as a relative unit, as a standard with which the atomic weights of all the other elements may be compared. Could it be determined how many atoms of pure matter, or ether, entered into the composition of a chemical atom or molecule of hydrogen, and the actual weight of such atoms, our knowledge on this subject would be perfect: but we must rest content with a conventional standard. Let it then suffice to assume, that each molecule of hydrogen is composed of one hundred or a thousand atoms of ether; and if the cyphers be marked off as decimal-points, there would, on this plan, be no alteration in the notation of the present hydrogen-scale; the decimals, however, would not be read as the fractional parts of a *hydrogen atom*, but as integrant *material atoms*, thereby removing the anomaly of dividing atoms, which seems to have suggested the notion that all the elements must be multiples of hydrogen. Such a notion is well avoided, for it is tantamount to the assertion that all substances are ultimately composed of hydrogen; and it therefore also implies the possibility of the *transmutation* of bodies: — a doctrine inconsistent with the stability of nature, and incompatible with a science of chemistry.

When chemical substances are in a gaseous state, they have been found to have a definite relation towards each other in their volumes; combining volume for volume or some multiple of a volume. In many cases, also, the specific gravity of a gaseous element corresponds with the atomic weight, hydrogen being unity in both instances: and, indeed, when we consider how predominant repulsion is in the gaseous state, and the uniformity of the law of expansion in all gases, it might have been expected that atomic weights and specific gravities would have been universally identical. Some have maintained that it is so, and that this ought to be the regulating principle in determining atomic weights. In his " Radical Theory of Chemistry," Mr. Griffin has extensively illustrated this subject; and has imparted to his argument, at least, the appearance of probability. Having, however, carefully weighed it, we are not disposed to accept it; for, throughout nature, whilst considerable reliance may be placed on the definite character of weight, there is no dependance on that of volume, it is so very variable: and not only so, but the very elements that require great alterations, in the scale of chemical equivalents, in order to maintain the aforesaid identity, are the ones which are subject to allotropic changes, such as oxygen, sulphur, and phosphorus: and therefore we are inclined to accept them as departures from the very prevalent condition, that the specific gravities and atomic weights of gases are identical; and not as affording sufficient grounds for the duplication of oxygen's atomic weight. This conclusion, the doubling the oxygen-equivalent, however, has been arrived at on other considerations; and is, at the present day, very generally adopted: but of this more hereafter.

Before entering on the consideration of chemical actions and reactions, let us endeavour to understand clearly how chemical elements stand in relation to each other. In the case of physical dualisms, the antagonistic forces are indissolubly conjoined in the same body; they cannot exist in an insulated state, as distinct individuals: and the only way in which their individuality can be inferred, is by either of them being dynamically predominant, so as to impart its characteristic to the resulting phenomenon. Now in the case of chemical substances or dualisms, this is very different; even the single elements have a complex constitution, as already stated, and as dualisms can enjoy an independent existence. But still each element, as a single chemical force, as a unit of power, cannot function;— it cannot act and react on itself: therefore there must be a concurrence of two or more elements, before there can be any *combination,* any subject-matter for chemistry. We must know the elements, or we cannot tell what forces are concerned in chemical phenomena; but the knowledge of the latter is the more immediate subject of the science.

When two chemical elements are brought within the sphere of action, they combine to form a compound; one of these performs the part of the *basic* or reacting force in the new dualism; and the other, that of the *specific* or *typal* force; so that the resulting compound is a composition of forces, which, in this case, can be demonstrated by the analytical separation of its constituents, and their exhibition in an insulated state. Call to mind what has already been said concerning the relations of physical forces in the different states of matter; and the same will be found to hold good in the condition of chemical forces, when in compounds their ratios vary. Some elements manifest in an eminent degree a *basic* character; whilst others have a stronger tendency to become *typal:* but all, as regards the entire series, indicate such a relationship, that in respect to any given element, some are basic and others typal, according as they come before or after one another in the series; a characteristic so well marked, as to have suggested the arrangement of Berzelius, the electro-positive and electro-negative elements following a corresponding order.

Binary combinations thus formed become in their turn constituents of new compounds; either the *basic* or *typal* force may be compound, and the other simple; or both correlative forces may be compound. And these compounds also may unite into still more complex combinations; a process which may be carried to many repetitions, involving compounds within compounds, but always following the same archetypal principle as the elements. Thus an acid and an alkali may have very complicated constitutions, and yet combine in the ratio of one equivalent each to form a salt; the basic and typal constituents of which are related to each other in the same manner as in the simplest oxysalt, or as in a binary haloid. In all these cases, the constituent forces being equal, the salts are neutral; that is, neither constituent imparts its characteristics to the compound, which as a *tertium quid* has its own individuality: but when either the typal or the basic force is in excess, say as a double equivalent, then the resulting compound manifests the character of the predominant constituent. This remark reminds us of an observation of J. S. Mill* concerning the character of chemistry; and we will notice it here, as it serves to elucidate the nature of chemical actions. "The chemical combination of two substances," he says, "produces a third substance with properties entirely different from those of either of the two substances separately, or both of them taken together. This explains why mechanics is a deductive or demonstrative science, and chemistry not. In the one, we can compute the effects of all combinations of causes from the laws which govern those causes when acting separately; because they continue to observe the same laws when in combination which they observed when separate. Not so in the phenomena which are the peculiar subject of the science of chemistry." Again, "In mechanics if a body be propelled in two directions by two forces, it moves in a given time exactly as far as the two forces would separately have carried it; and is left precisely where it would have arrived if it had been acted upon first by one, and afterwards by the other force; which law is called the composition of forces."

According to our view of the subject, this disparage

---

* System of Logic, vol. i. p. 400.

ment of chemistry has arisen from a misapprehension of chemical phenomena; the cases are not exactly parallel, which makes the difference more apparent than real. In the case of mechanics, the antagonistic forces are applied to a *given* body; in that of chemistry they are themselves only regarded as making up the body itself: apply the chemical forces through the medium of a *given* body; and the results will be perfectly analogous. Add an equivalent of sulphuric acid to an equivalent of sulphate of soda, and we get bisulphate of soda; a combination as far advanced as a single force can effect in the change of composition: next add thereto an equivalent of soda, and a similar amount of change will be produced in the opposite direction. Lastly, act on the sulphate of soda by adding equivalents both of acid and alkali, not successively but simultaneously, and the same result will be obtained, a neutral salt; precisely what would have been arrived at, if it had been acted on first by one force and afterwards by the other: in short, it is a composition of forces, in which the basic and typal forces, though different, are nevertheless co-existent in all their entirety.

The predisposing affinity of one substance for another, (for a compound which does not as yet exist in the mixture, but which tends to become formed,) has been ably advocated by Berzelius and others, and applied to the explanation of many perplexing facts. Comte ridicules this opinion as metaphysical and incomprehensible; forgetting that he himself sanctions a common expression in rational mechanics, "that forces are only motions produced or *tending* to be produced." Some of these facts are certainly at present inexplicable, but many of them might be solved without having resort to *catalysis*, or any other unknown mode of action. For instance, the evolution of hydrogen gas by the action of dilute sulphuric acid on iron is commonly adduced as a case of *predisposing* affinity. We know that iron decomposes water at a high temperature, combining with its oxygen and liberating the hydrogen; all therefore that is required to enable it to produce the same effect at a low temperature, is an additional force, just sufficient to turn the scale between action and no action; and such a force may exist in the state of condensation of the combined water in the hydrated sulphuric acid; and if so the water may be directly decomposed by the iron, and the resulting oxide uniting with the acid, may induce an increase of compressive or aggregating force which would tend also to facilitate the action of the predisposing affinity.

The physical condition of chemical substances forms a most important consideration in most chemical phenomena; hence, one of the oldest maxims is, "that bodies do not act on each other unless in a state of solution." This is not universally true; but so generally acknowledged in practice, that by far the greater number of re-agents are kept ready at hand in the liquid state. The reason of this is sufficiently evident; the statical condition of liquids permits their respective molecules to be easily intermingled and brought within the sphere of mutual action. Gases also freely diffuse throughout each other, but their molecules being far apart is not a condition favourable to combination; the molecules of solids, on the other hand, are so firmly and closely aggregated, that unless their cohesion be physically overcome, chemical forces cannot become operative; and thus it is that heat is such a valuable agent in promoting combinations. From this statement it must not be concluded, that the energy of chemical forces is feeble; but that the different conditions of bodies more or less modify their action: for chemical affinity between some gases is so intense as to reduce these substances to the liquid and even the solid state, accompanied by a disengagement or expulsion of heat; an effect which the coercion of the greatest cold and mechanical pressure, which ingenuity can devise, has failed to accomplish.

According to the notion above advocated, that all chemical compounds, whether of simple or complex substances, are all *binaries* or dualisms, their constitution may be expressed by the simple formula of our universal correlation,

$$A + B = AB.$$

At present, there are a great many ways of expressing the same compound, in consequence of the difference of opinion concerning its constitution. For instance, water was long regarded as a binary, atom for atom, of oxygen and hydrogen, and as such, formulated as HO; which agrees well with our formula, intimating that it is a neutral compound, in which its constituents, $H + O$, are co-existent and opposite forces. But now, water is more commonly written as H^2O; or, according to the notation of Laurent and Gerhardt, as $\genfrac{}{}{0pt}{}{H}{H}O$; the equivalence with the original notation being maintained, by doubling the atomic weight of oxygen, thus making it, on the hydrogen scale, 16 instead of 8, which number has been so long in use in this country. The principal reason for this change seems to rest on the fact, that water consists by measure of two volumes of hydrogen and one of oxygen, condensed into two volumes: a circumstance which we are inclined to consider as unimportant, for throughout the range of chemical substances, we find weight a permanent, and volume a variable condition; and which ought not for a moment to be put into competition with the comportment of water under electrolysis, which strongly supports the opinion that it is a compound of atom for atom, and not two of hydrogen and one of oxygen, which the new theory maintains.

Besides, this theory introduces a greater complication, both in the composition of substances, and in their formulæ; which ought, if possible, to be always avoided: and unless we are greatly mistaken, to go no farther than the other compound of oxygen and hydrogen, binoxide or peroxide of hydrogen, an incongruity meets us, or at least an appearance which is inconsistent with the character of the compound. If water be H^2O or $\genfrac{}{}{0pt}{}{H}{H}O$, then is this peroxide, H^2O^2 or $\genfrac{}{}{0pt}{}{H}{H}O^2$; this notation indicates that the constituents are in a state of equilibrium, two equivalents of one force united with two of the other force; whereas the substance is in a highly dynamical state, energetically acting on and imparting oxygen to, other bodies; and is, therefore, much better symbolised by HO^2, according to the old notation.

Moreover, on this view of Gerhardt and others, many other equivalents besides oxygen must be doubled; more, we believe, than have hitherto been deemed necessary: and then all the metallic bases of the oxysalts must be supposed to exist in two proportions, and denoted, according to the analogy of water; a complication, which is, we think, much better avoided. Now the two basic atoms, in this trinal system, are supposed to be incapable of existing in an uncombined state, as single atoms; but that whilst in combination they can be disunited, so as to be separately replaced by other substances: assumption on assumption, not resting on facts, but framed to suit the hypothesis. Gerhardt's duplication of metallic atoms in protoxides, is said to give a satisfactory explanation of the hydrated and anhydrous states of these substances. Thus potassium, K, acts on water, $\genfrac{}{}{0pt}{}{H}{H}O$, replaces one equivalent of hydrogen and becomes $\genfrac{}{}{0pt}{}{K}{H}O$, or hydrate of potassa: but this is impossible, according to the hypothesis; for oxygen O, is but one atom, and $K + \frac{1}{2}$ of O, or $H + \frac{1}{2}$ of O, can neither represent potassa nor water, and therefore $\genfrac{}{}{0pt}{}{K}{H}O$ cannot be hydrate of potassa. And not only so, but we are told that hydrogen as H cannot exist in an insulated state, but that it must be evolved as $\genfrac{}{}{0pt}{}{H}{H}$. But this dilemma is escaped by supposing that one atom of potassium cannot decompose water, it must, like that of hydrogen in water, be employed as two atoms $\genfrac{}{}{0pt}{}{K}{K}$, and then the formula of action and reaction will stand as follows, $2\left(\genfrac{}{}{0pt}{}{H}{H}O\right) + \genfrac{}{}{0pt}{}{K}{K} = \genfrac{}{}{0pt}{}{K}{K}O + \genfrac{}{}{0pt}{}{H}{H}O + \genfrac{}{}{0pt}{}{H}{H}$. This begging the question is a roundabout way of evading a difficulty; and after all, the notation is much inferior to the old method, $2HO + K = KO + HO + H$. We cannot now trace out this trinal notation; but we have followed it out in all its bearings: in some cases, its solutions are very plausible; but they are outbalanced by a greater number of objections.

In making these remarks, it must not be supposed that we reject the notion of the duplication of atoms: the duplication, many times repeated, not only of simple, but also of compound molecules, seems to be well established; and is in accordance with the varying magnitudes of molecular masses in physics. That the same element, or the same compound, should be aggregated into molecules, consisting of two or more atoms of the same kind; and that as such they should act not only physically, but also chemically, with varying degrees of energy, is what can be easily imagined; but since analysis has established the fact, it must not be questioned: what we have to do is to study the phenomena under these complicated relations. The modification which oxygen, sulphur, and phosphorus undergo in some conditions of their molecular arrangement, seems to depend on some such duplications of their atoms, or of some internal disposition in their individual atoms, called *allotropy*. Schönbein, a very successful investigator of this subject, has given the name of *ozone* to the allotropic form of oxygen. Its properties are different from those of ordinary oxygen; but still the difference is only in the degree of energy, such as might be expected from the approximation of the oxygen-atoms by some condensing influence.

Whether oxygen gas does undergo any change of volume during the production of ozone, has not been recorded, as far as we can ascertain; though it is probable that its molecules are more closely arranged: an increased density, as occurs in allotropic phosphorus and sulphur, would explain the alteration of its properties. It is possible that ozone may be produced during the action of a platinum plate on oxygen gas. Condensation doubtless takes place in this case; and if this be accompanied by the formation of ozone, the increased facility of combination which the mixture of oxygen and hydrogen gases experiences would be accounted for. The fact could be easily determined, either by observing the change of volume in the oxygen gas; or, what would be still better, by placing the ozone-test in contact with the platinum.

Ozone resembles in many respects deutoxide of hydrogen, but according to the experiments of Schönbein, it does not contain any hydrogen; indeed the properties of the hydrogen-compound are only those of liquid oxygen, such as an excess of this element might impart.

In all such cases of metamorphosis, there is no transmutation of one element into another, but only a physical change of structure, which so far modifies their chemical properties, exalting or depressing them, according to circumstances: in all such cases, however, there is one thing in common, the allotropic condition is subverted at high temperatures; the repulsive force so separating the atoms as to enable them to assume their normal arrangement. At least, such is the behaviour of the elements in respect to heat when in an allotropic state; but if the duplication of the atoms of elements in compounds be an allotropic condition, it is of a much more permanent character, in consequence of the presence of other elements; for such have often a remarkable indestructibility.

The double atoms of the elements enter into the composition of some of the most interesting combinations; and of these none is more important, or of more frequent occurrence, than the duplications of carbon. This element, as C^2, unites with nitrogen forming cyanogen, C^2N; a union so intimate and enduring, that this substance enters into a great variety of combinations, as a quasi-element analogous to chlorine; and not only cyanogen, but also its compounds, are capable of duplication: thus we have Cy, Cy^2, Cy^3; and also CyO, $(CyO)^2$, $(CyO)^3$, the cyanic, fulminic, and cyanuric acids. So likewise carbon, as C^2, may assume also a typal position in compounds, whilst the basic constituent may also be duplicated, as in the hydrocarbons, H^2C^2. The hydrocarbons are of frequent occurrence in organic compounds, and are capable of undergoing duplications to an astonishing number of repetitions: each addition of such duplex atom imparting a gradation of physical properties, corresponding with the progressive ratio of duplication; as is shown in the successive increase in density, and in the elevation of the boiling point.

These basic hydrocarbons, each of which is a distinct compound, severally enter into union with a typal compound of the same elements in different proportions. For instance, with HC^2, an electro-negative substance, analogous to sulphur, phosphorus, and arsenic, and capable, like these, of forming acids by combining with oxygen: thus, $H^2C^2 + HC^2 = H^3C^4$; and again, $H^3C^4 + O^3 = H^3C^4O^3$, and all their respective homologues only differ from each other according to the number of duplications of the basic hydrocarbon; the typal constituent remaining unaltered.

Again, we have the same hydrocarbons uniting with another distinct and characteristic compound of hydrogen and carbon, as H^3C^2, in which the basic hydrogen is in the ascendant; forming a corresponding electro-positive quasi-element, which is analogous to the alkaline and basic metals, combining also with oxygen to form oxides, which, united with acids, become salts: thus, $H^2C^2 + H^3C^2 = H^5C^4$, and $H^5C^4 + O = H^5C^4O$; lastly, $H^5C^4O + HO = H^6C^4O^2$. So that if these three quasi-elements HC^2, H^2C^2, H^3C^2, were severally distinguished by a special name and symbol, (as in the case of cyanogen, Cy,) all the multiplied homologues of the ethers, hydrocarbons, and fatty acids, might be more simply expressed: which would greatly facilitate the labours of the student in the acquisition of this complicated branch of the science.

In order to simplify our statement as much as possible, we did not allude to the fact that the electro-negative and the electro-positive constituents are also capable of duplication in the same manner as the neutral hydrocarbons; we cannot, however, enter into details, but must rest content with pointing out, that the same discriminating notation for the higher powers of each substance will be found generally applicable.

It has already been noticed that substances vary in their electrical relations to those substances above and below them in the scale; so that the same substance may occupy a basic or typal position in compounds, according to the character of the substance with which it is united. Thus nitrogen is capable of combining with the more *typal* or electro-negative substance, oxygen; and also with the more *basic* or electro-positive substance, hydrogen; forming in each case a series of compounds which differ in properties according to the degree of preponderance of the associated element. In the one case the series is NO, NO^2, NO^3, NO^4, NO^5; and in the other the series is HN, H^2N, H^3N, H^4N: three members of the latter series are as yet unknown as insulated substances, ammonia, H^3N, being the only one with which we are actually acquainted; but the analogy of the carbon series, C^2, a substance very analogous to N in its combining relations, renders it not improbable that this hypothetical series may be ultimately substantiated. The analogous series of duplex carbon, C^2, is as follows: HC^2, H^2C^2, H^3C^2, H^4C^2. The characteristics of different parts of these series are deserving of particular attention. The beginning of each series is *negative* in respect to the latter part, which becomes eminently *positive;* and it is curious that not only in these, but also in the oxygen series, the *odd* numbers are distinguished by possessing the strongest marked properties: this is a curious circumstance, but one which accords well with the principle of our system, viz. that equal forces neutralise each other, so that their special attributes do not appear in the compound; whilst unequal forces, when combined, manifest the characteristic of the predominant or *plus* constituent.

The usual notation of compound substances may in the more simple cases be easily interpreted; but in very complicated cases it is a difficult task to reduce this empirical expression into a rational formula. And this circumstance alone shows the necessity of adopting some simple expression for each distinct class of complex substances; such as we already have, with great advantage, for cyanogen, Cy: which, however, compared to the substances alluded to, has a very simple composition, C^2N.

If the binary constitution of compounds, according to the formula $A + B = AB$, were adopted; it would, we think, greatly facilitate the attainment of a more satisfactory notation: in our introduction, it was pointed out how the basic and typal *plus* condition, in different compounds of the same substances, might be indicated; this in many, more particularly physical, cases might be advantageous; but it is not required in chemistry, for in its compounds, whether simple or complex, the position of the symbol in the notation marks whether it be basic or typal, and the numerals affixed to either constituent clearly shows which is in the ascendant. In addition to these guides, the knowledge that the atoms of elements may be frequently duplicated, so as to act in the compound as single atoms (and capable as such of being transferred into various combinations), may ultimately lead to the establishment of a more simple and a better system than now prevails. But this cannot well be the work of an individual: it should be performed by the concurrence of several chemists, in order to give it due authority.

This discussion, however, is drawing us beyond our limits; we will, therefore, conclude with remarking, that chemical forces, in every compound, must necessarily be antagonistic: even when the constituents are very similar, as in alloys, combinations of oxides, and even of different oxides of the same metal; for as there is, in all these cases, action and reaction, there must be antagonism, though of such a feeble character as to give no well-marked indications thereof. And, that in chemical actions, we have the broad and well-defined distinction which separates them from physical actions, that the opposite forces by which they are accomplished may be exhibited in a distinct state of individual existence: so that their characteristics may be carefully examined and determined; not inferentially, as in the case of antagonistic physical forces, but by actual observation and investigation.

In conclusion, then, it may be observed that chemical substances are objects of chemical science. The arrangement of these objects forms the preliminary step or natural history branch of chemistry; and this accomplished, the consideration of the specific forces, whether simple or compound, which make up the constitution of these objects, and the determination of their *modus operandi* when they act and react on each other in the production of chemical phenomena, bring us acquainted with the dynamical or causal branch of the science. And when the science is completed by the application of both the logical methods of induction and deduction; then, by a knowledge of the rational laws by which these forces are directed, we should be able to determine the nature of a compound before it has been experimentally demonstrated:—a result which has already been actually attained in the case of the combinations of many hydrocarbons; for not only the equivalent numbers of their constituents were foreknown, but the prevision was carried to the extent of determining the specific gravities and boiling points of unknown liquids.

CHAP. VII.

ORGANISMS, DUALISMS OF CHEMICAL AND VITAL POWERS.

Life or Vital Principle the efficient Cause of Organic Phenomena.— Opinions concerning this Force.—The most recent that of Dr. Carpenter.—This Opinion evades one Difficulty by creating another equally insoluble.—All Forces said to be one and the same, mutually convertible.—Life is transformed Heat.—The *specialty* of the material Substratum alone determines the Character of the Force.—Whence then this Specialty?—The organic Germ is itself a *living* Organism; Heat cherishes Life, but does not impart it.—Difference between chemical and organic Dualisms.—The Relation of specific Vital Forces to universal Physical Forces.—Death, the Dissolution of the Organic Dualism.—Life not the immediate Producer of Motion—It makes Physical Forces subservient to this Purpose.—Life is a directing, superintending Energy.—It functions in acquiring, appropriating, and utilising other Forces, both physical and chemical.—Dr. Carus on the Nature of Life.—Vital Force a final Cause: so in a sense are all other Forces.—The Development of Organisms.—The vegetative Functions of animated Creatures—Reducible to simple Principles.—Vegetables the intermediate Link between Minerals and Animals.—Animals distinguished by the Attribute of Sensibility.—The Nervous and Muscular Systems of Animals.—Instinct and Knowledge.—On the Transmutation of Species.—Conclusion.

THE physiological researches of the present day all tend to the conclusion, that organic phenomena cannot be fully explained, either on chemical or physical principles; for largely as these principles enter into the consideration of such phenomena, yet after the elimination of all relating thereto, there are many outstanding facts, neither few nor unimportant, that must be referred to some other principle. Call this special influence, which directs the functions of organisms, Life, Vital Principle, Vitality, or what you will; still the fact of its existence, though it has often been ignored, is now acknowledged by the highest authorities.

Concerning the precise nature of this *vital force*, however, there has been, and still is, a great diversity of opinions; but we will restrict ourselves to those which are now most prevalent. Some suppose that each kind of creature, whether vegetable or animal, has a *specific principle of vitality*, which it has derived from its parents, and which in some mysterious manner is transmitted from generation to generation; so that each individual is a portion of the common stock of vitality belonging to its own species. According to this view, the germ-cell, in which each individual originates, is the production of its parents; and however minute it may be, it is potentially adequate to the development of the future creature, whether it be an animalcule, or the largest of animals.

This hypothesis, in the opinion of other physiologists, is irrational. They admit that the *germ-cell* is an animated organism, but they cannot conceive that its minute vital force is capable of producing the mature creature; and to meet this difficulty, they suppose that the materials which are incorporated into the living structure, by nutrition, contain vital force in a dormant state, which is evoked into activity by becoming organised. So that as the creature grows, it acquires, *pari passu*, an increased amount of vitality, equivalent to its enlarged functions.

And lastly, according to Dr. Carpenter*, "the vital force which causes the primordial cell of the germ first to multiply itself, and then to develope itself into a complex and extensive organism, was not originally locked up in that single cell, nor was it latent in the materials which are progressively assimilated by itself and its descendants; but is directly and immediately supplied by *heat*, which is constantly operating upon it; and which is transformed into vital force, by its passage through the organised fabric that manifests it." But afterwards he affirms that he "no more regards *heat* as the *vital principle*, or as itself identical with the vital force, than that it is identical with electricity, or with chemical affinity; nor does he in the least recognise the possibility that any action of heat upon inorganic elements can of itself develope an organised structure of even the simplest kind. The pre-existence of a living organism, through which *alone* can heat be converted into vital force, is as necessary upon this theory, as it is upon any of those currently received amongst physiologists; and it is the *specialty* of the material substratum, thus furnishing the medium or instrument of the metamorphosis, which in his opinion establishes, and must ever maintain, a well-marked boundary between the physical and the vital forces. Starting with the abstract notion of force, as emanating at once from the Divine Will, we might say that this force, operating through inorganic matter, manifests itself as electricity, magnetism, light, heat,

---

* Philosophical Transactions, 1850, p. 752.

chemical affinity, and mechanical motion; but that when directed through organised structures, it effects the operations of growth, development, chemico-vital transformations, and the like; and is farther metamorphosed through the instrumentality of the structures, thus generated, into nervous agency and muscular power. If we *only* knew heat as it acts upon the organised creation, the peculiarities of its operations upon inorganic matter would seem as strange to the physiologist, as the effects here attributed to it may appear to those who are only accustomed to contemplate the physical phenomena to which it gives rise. The variety of organic forms called forth by the agency of heat, which may be regarded as the products of its operation upon living germs, does not present any real obstacle to the reception of this doctrine; since in any hypothesis, which assumes a common force as operative in the living kingdoms of nature, it is necessary to admit that this force is modified in its actions by the properties of the germ; just as that the general force of chemical affinity manifests itself differently in the reactions of each elementary and composite substance."

This doctrine of Dr. Carpenter concerning the nature of vital force, is a legitimate corollary of the principle, now so generally accepted, that natural forces are mutually convertible; and we have quoted it at some length, because it is clearly and intelligibly expressed, and will enable us the better to set forth our views concerning vital force, by contrasting them together.

It has been more than once stated, that one universal force can be no other than an *absolute;* and being thus placed out of all relations, it cannot come within the limits of human knowledge; consequently there must be a dualism of forces, in order to render action and reaction possible, which are the requisites of *all* phenomena. Now Dr. Carpenter in some measure provides for this objection, since he regards such a force as emanating directly from the Divine Will; and as operating through inorganic matter, and through organised structures, assuming thereby the different aspects of physical, chemical, and vital forces. Such a conception may be formed; but even admitting its probability, it leaves our knowledge equally imperfect; it only strives to evade one difficulty by starting another, leaving us as far as ever from an explanation of the nature of living organisms. It calls in the aid of various pre-existing substrata, as the necessary *media* for the differentiation of Divine force; but what we want to know, is the inner nature or essence of matter, of chemical elements, and of organic germs: have they not also proceeded from the Divine Will? and whence comes it to pass that they can impart to one and the same force such varied aspects? An organism is throughout its whole existence a living body, a body actuated by a vital force or life; the *basis* or substratum of such an organism is a *structure* consisting of chemical substances, which serves as a resisting force, or *point d'appui*, in concurrence with which the vital force acts; and thus results that action and reaction which functions as a living creature. In short, an organism, like all other natural bodies, is a dualism of forces, which are co-existent and opposite; and if such a dualism be invaded by an extraneous force, as heat, such a force may modify vital actions, but the changes produced can only be physical. Heat then is not the cause of vital force, for the organism possesses it already: it is, however, a very able coadjutor, for it facilitates another, and a lower order of actions, the chemical; by which inorganic materials are assimilated and rendered fit for the growth of its organic body, by the appropriating and constructing influence of the vital force. When the organism dies, that is, when life departs from the material body, heat does not vivify, nor can it form organic compounds; but it only hastens chemical actions, by which the constituents of the organism are returned to the chemical kingdom of nature, from which they were derived.

Organisms, therefore, possess vitality as a necessary part of their constitution; for when deprived thereof, they are no longer organisms, but only *organic remains*. It is true, that this vitality can only become efficient under certain conditions, and if these be awanting, it remains dormant as in the case of eggs; and still more remarkably in the seeds of plants, which after lying deeply buried in the soil for ages, have vegetated when brought near the surface.

It remains, therefore, still to inquire, What is the nature of this vital force or principle of vitality? Dr. Carpenter is quite correct in the parallel which he draws between organisms and chemical elements; for they are analogous dualisms, consisting of material bodies, actuated by specific forces; and both are the objects of special sciences: but we do not agree concerning the nature of chemical forces; we believe that they are actual specific powers, independent existences, as set forth in the last chapter; whilst he regards them as one and the same force, modified by the peculiar substance of the individual elements. So on his view, instead of many specific forces, we have an equal number of different substances, *substrata*, which variously affect the unknown universal force which emanates from the Divine Will. Now if we accept the common notion concerning matter, that it is some unknown substratum in which properties, and consequently chemical properties, inhere, we still require to know the cause of the difference which characterises the respective chemical elements; which makes them to variously differ from each other, and from the matter with which they are conjoined. This difference of properties cannot be ignored; it must necessarily be referred to the effects of various causes, which as energies, influences, forces, or whatever you may choose to call them, must each of them enjoy its peculiar attribute, which is manifested as a particular property. An element then is matter possessing some peculiar property which is chemical; consequently the element is a chemical substance; and it is therefore superfluous to seek for the extraneous origin of that which already exists in the body itself, and which constitutes its essential individuality.

The prevalent opinion concerning the oneness and universality of force is indeed very fascinating in its apparent simplicity; but it is in truth very complicated and indefinite when subjected to a searching investigation. How beautifully simple is the doctrine, in its enunciation, that all natural forces are fundamentally one and the self-same force, the omnipotence of Deity; and that, therefore, however varied these forces are in appearance, they are all mutually convertible: but when we attempt to apply this doctrine, we are met by the complication, that this universal force can only be manifested under different aspects, through the *medium* of peculiar *substrata*. Now these substrata, and the changes they undergo, are the phenomena which we are contemplating; we are striving to ascertain what these things are in themselves, what those forces are which they evidently possess, for without such they could not act and react on each other, in the production of phenomena: for every effect must have its cause. When these substrata are chemical and organic substances, we distinguish their peculiar forces as chemical and vital: and to say that such forces are only modifications of a general force, when in relation to such substances, is no explanation at all; it is a mere evasion of the question, which is, What is it that originally made these bodies chemical and organic? or in other words, What are the causes of their peculiar attributes?

What forces are ultimately, in themselves, we know not, it is beyond the scope of human knowledge; for all our knowledge is relative, and we can only know forces by their effects: so far we may attain to an explanation of the constitution of natural bodies; and the doctrine which we are advocating seems to explain, but perhaps not satisfactorily, the nature of organisms, when it defines them as "chemical bodies actuated by specific vital powers."

In the organic dualism of powers, there is a marked difference which distinguishes them from the chemical dualisms. In the latter the body or basic power of the dualism is material or *physical;* and hence it is that chemical substances, besides their specific, also possess physical properties: in the organic dualism, the body is *chemical;* that is, a compound of physical and chemical powers, a complication of forces manifesting corresponding phenomena, and exerting a powerful antagonism against the specific force or vital power, by which however they are constrained and subordinated, according to its innate directing reason, which is its rational law of action. There is also another and a grand distinction between chemical and organic dualisms: the union of the constituent powers of the former is indissoluble; but in the latter case, the powers may be disjoined, the specific force departing, we know not whither, as a matter of natural knowledge; whilst the body remains, as an aggregate of chemical bodies, which follow the laws of their order. We are prepared to understand, in some measure, by the circumstance of the complication of nicely balanced forces, the separation which occurs on the dissolution of organisms; still it has the appearance of a departure from that progress toward perfection, which marks the different conditions of creatures in the ascending scale of nature: it is a perplexing thought, that whilst chemical elements are permanent and imperishable during the course of nature, that the higher order of beings, organisms, should only enjoy a limited existence; and that then "the place which knew them, should know them no more." It is a mystery; but whilst we contemplate it, the attention is arrested by a diversity in the capacity of organisms, which operates as a partial compensation in their favour: they have the peculiar faculty of propagating their species, by which provision the permanence of their kindred is established; so that whilst the individuals themselves die, they *ever* live in their descendants; an arrangement which seems to accord with the conservation of forces, so conspicuous in the other departments of nature.

On a former occasion it was stated that chemical powers are related to universal attraction, as *species* are to their *genus;* that these specific forces all partake of an attracting and condensing tendency, but that as species they also possess the differential characters of peculiar elective and combining properties. And in like manner, a relationship may be discerned between vital powers and universal repulsion; as specific forces, they have the generic character of repulsion, a similar instability, and given to incessant changes, tending to a continual outward expansion in growth and multiplication. Thus by these specific relations of chemical and organic powers to the universal physical powers, we conceive that it is possible to establish a System of Nature: the dualism of powers, *attraction* and *repulsion,* forms the universal basis, the *summum genus* of all material bodies; which is diversified on the side of *attraction* by *specific chemical powers,* and on that of *repulsion* by *specific vital powers.*

Life then, on this view, is the continued union of the constituent forces of the organism; death is the dissolution of this union. Life has been likened to the flame of a lamp, which is sustained as long as nourishment is supplied to the wick; and the communication of flame to other lamps, without any diminution of its energy, has been adduced as no unapt illustration of generation:—could the flame renovate its own organism, that is, the lamp with its combustible contents, and also produce other lamps of the same kind, the analogy would hold good: as it is, however, the simile does not assist our knowledge.

In contemplating the growth of the higher orders of organisms, whether vegetable or animal, from the earliest stage of its existence as a primordial cell to its state of maturity, the circumstance that most rivets the attention is the gradual development of its structure, accompanied by a corresponding increase of its vital energies. And so on a general survey of animated nature, we find evidence of a similar order of progression throughout the whole system; broken, indeed, into subordinate groups, as if the process were being tried over and over again on different types, but still sooner or later resuming its onward course towards perfection. Thus each organic function seems to be ever tending toward a higher development, not only in the several stages of each individual organism, but in creatures of different kinds, as they rise one above the other in the scale of nature; and this not only obtains in the functions of *growth* and *reproduction* which are common to all organisms, but also in those of *muscular movements* and *nervous sensibility*, and even in those of the *instinctive* and *intellectual* faculties. In every creature, however, varied as its functions may be, these do not result from the operation of as many distinct and independent influences or faculties, for each creature has only *one* specific principle of activity; and however varied and elevated its actions may be, these only denote the peculiar attributes of its specific power, and mark its degree in the systematic arrangement or hierarchy of natural powers.

In attempting to comprehend the nature of vital force, (which may in the same individual, as in the highest developed organism, man, produce such diversified operations,) it is requisite to divest ourselves of the ordinary notion concerning force. What we understand by *force*, is any influence which is efficient in producing some kind of *change*;

CHEMICAL AND VITAL POWERS. 193

but the more common notion concerning force is that which gives *dynamical* impulse to bodies, imparting some kind of motion, and called accordingly physical force. Many of the changes which organisms undergo are purely physical, variously modified by their peculiar structures; but all subordinated to the vital principle: thus, various capillary attractions and osmotic diffusions, also muscular and nervous motions, are mechanically performed according to physical laws: and yet are so directed, in subjection to the creature's vital principle, as to operate in opposition to the law of gravity. In short, vital force is not a principle, whose effects can be *weighed* and *measured;* though it is associated with a material body as its correlative power, which possesses physical properties: but it is a self-directing and superintending principle, which controls the physical and chemical forces of its body, turning them to account for its own purposes; thereby working out and performing the functions of its body, according to predetermined intelligent designs. It is not, therefore, surprising, that a force which can act with such authority should be capable of developing a body of even considerable magnitude from a microscopic germ-cell: its successively increasing size and strength do not immediately depend on the continual accession of energy by the conversion of physical force into its own essence; but by its domination over accumulated material forces, whose efficiencies are made subservient to its enlarged requirements. An organism is a *dualism* of powers, which function by their mutual action and reaction; and under this joint influence it *acquires, appropriates,* and *utilises* such substances as

O

are fit for its purposes, and fall within the limits of its operations.

Dr. Carus*, in his "Essay on the Kingdoms of Nature, their Life and Affinity," after recounting the several processes in the development of a perfect plant from its seed, remarks, "Thus closes the circle of its being, in that form out of which it first issued. Throughout this chain of phenomena, we find a certain determinate succession, a regularity which compels us to refer these movements to the operations of one internal and universal principle, in which all the others are comprehended. It is evident that this internal, this essential and efficient principle, can be no *single* thing, such as the body of the plant, the chemical change of its substance, or the circulation of its sap, and still less the effect of external influences, but rather all these together; a something in which all these inhere as their common cause, and which we characterise as a unity by the generic appellation, *life*. Hence it is easy to perceive how erroneous it would be to suppose the plant first organised, and life added to it as an attribute, and consequently as something extrinsic. On the contrary, life is necessarily the original principle, and the body one of its particular phenomena; conceived, therefore, not as permanent, but as perpetually changing: and this idea of it is conveyed in the term *formation*, inasmuch as it signifies a thing not only formed, but forming itself." This view of Dr. Carus is in some respects similar, though not precisely the same as ours. According to our view, an animated being is twofold in its constitution, but es-

---

* Taylor's Scientific Memoirs, vol. i. p. 224.

sentially one in its compound individuality: as long as this union is maintained, the creature lives or has life; the action and reaction of its constituent forces being manifested as the phenomena of life. During life, the chemical and physical forces, of which the organic body consists, are variously affected by the condition of the medium in which they are placed; and also by the controlling influence of its vital force, which may be variously distributed throughout the system, energising one part more than another, and yet, however unequally diffused, being ever one and the self-same individual power.

From what has been stated, it is evident that we not only maintain the existence of *specific vital powers*, which, like the specific chemical powers, form and energise their own bodies according to definite designs; but also, that these powers are *final causes*, varying their modes of action according to circumstances, so as to accomplish predetermined purposes. We must, therefore, dwell awhile on this subject, and give our reasons for accepting the notion of final causes, which is at present in great discredit. And by way of introduction, we will quote a passage from Dr. Roget's Physiology*, not a very recent authority, but one which, we think, still expresses the current ideas thereon. "However natural it may be to conceive the existence of a single and presiding principle of *vitality*, we should recollect that this, in the present state of our knowledge, is only a fiction of the mind, not warranted by the phenomena themselves, in which we

* Encyclopædia Britannica, 1842.

perceive no such diversity; and therefore inadmissible, as the result of a philosophical induction. We find that vitality ceases in different textures, at different periods prior to the total extinction of life; a phenomenon which appears scarcely compatible with the unity of any such power. Attempts have been made to reduce the phenomena of the *inorganic* world to a single primordial law; and they possibly may prove successful: but no such approximation can yet be attempted, with any prospect of success, between the muscular, the nervous, the sensational and the organic powers; nor can we establish any kind of association between them, but by the consideration of another, and a totally different class of relations, namely, those they bear to the general object which they combine to produce. This, however, is to substitute *final* for physical causes, which are the only legitimate objects of philosophical analysis, and the true basis of the physical sciences."

It is true that some textures of the body retain signs of vitality longer than others, after the creature's death, which may seem inconsistent with the unity of vital power; but it must be remembered, that though the vitality of each creature is indeed one, yet it pervades all parts of the system, but in different degrees of intensity; and it does not follow, that if the centre and source of this energy be destroyed, that all the parts of the system should simultaneously collapse, as in the discharge of accumulated force in an electrified body. It rather resembles the force by which machinery is propelled, the parts of which do not immediately come to a state of rest when the moving power is detached, but they continue to move by their *vis inertiæ* until restored to their original condition. The universal convertibility of physical forces was not an accepted doctrine when Dr. Roget hesitated to receive it as "a primordial law;" but since then, speculative ingenuity has boldly attributed all description of organic powers "to a single physical power." We have already expressed our dissent to this doctrine, and endeavoured to demonstrate that there can be no such thing as a simple physical power; all natural bodies being dualisms of powers. When we maintain that vital forces are *final causes*, it is evident that the same holds good with all other forces, since we make no distinction, in this respect, between vital and physical causes. We are therefore ready to abandon the term *final* altogether, as being, according to our views, *superfluous;* for all forces are regarded by us as *reason-directed* powers, which only act according to rational laws. In every regular series of phenomena, however extensive, the *plus* state or energy of any body in the series is a cause of the effect which is manifested in the succeeding phenomenon; and this physical energy is some particular force, which in its action is regulated by its innate law, its rational guide, which determines its operation according to a definite design. So that all causes are, in truth, *final causes*, whether physical, chemical, or vital: the physical and chemical are said to act necessarily, because under precisely the same conditions they always produce the same effects; whilst the vital have in some of their operations a *choice;* but as this choice is always exercised with the intention of accomplishing some given purpose, the vital must be *final* causes, be they good or bad, wise or unwise.

It is no new idea, that the principle of life, the *anima*, is a directing, superintending influence, regulating the functions of its body according to a rational design. Even Dr. Carpenter*, whilst advocating the relationship between physical and vital forces by means of a mutual convertibility, admits that the organism's "assumption of its complete and perfect structure is the result of that perfect harmony and balancing of the several forces of growth, multiplication, and transformation, which indicates, in the most distinct and unmistakable manner, the controlling and sustaining action of an intelligent mind, acting in accordance with a determinate plan." We, however, do not suppose that the rational designs that are worked out in the several organisms are *immediately* effected by the superintending of an intelligent mind. All natural bodies, and of course the powers of which they consist, have emanated from Deity; and, as His works, bear the impress of His intellectual potency: each natural power is not only endowed with a peculiar kind of force, but also with a rational faculty, according to the capacity of which it is able to put forth and exercise this force: that is, a force acts according to its *knowledge*, be it *latent* or apparent, instinctive or *acquired*; and according to its designs only can it function; for knowledge and efficiency must have a corresponding relation in every natural power. Doubtless, the origin and continuance of all things must be ultimately ascribed to a First Cause; but with this we are not concerned at present: we are striving to interpret the immediate causes of natural phenomena; and must search for

---

* Philosophical Transactions, 1850, p. 773.

them in the things themselves; otherwise we do not untie, but cut the Gordian knot.

For these reasons we differ from those who ignore *final* causes; or rather we believe that, in a sense, all causes are final: for all natural powers are rational forces, acting as the means to effect certain determinate ends. Desirous that our meaning should not be misunderstood, at the risk of being deemed tedious, we repeat that natural powers are of two distinct kinds. One kind of power acts compulsorily, or in a predetermined manner, according to the laws of its inherent, but unconscious, reason; or of necessity, as it is usually termed; and the resulting phenomena are, under the same conditions, uniform and invariable. The other kind acts not passively and instinctively, but according to acquired knowledge, that is, *consciously*; and has a freedom of choice in its actions, the exercise of this choice being regulated by some intelligent design, whether good or evil. We are justified, therefore, we think, in regarding *powers* not merely as forces, but as reason-directed forces: for whether they act *consciously* or *unconsciously*, they can only do so according either to *instinct* or to *knowledge*; that is, according to reason, which may *voluntarily* or *involuntarily* superintend the creature's actions. Both these kinds may be conjoined in the same vital power: and since this power is capable of existing in different phases in the same organism, the concurrence of these with the complex material forces, which constitute the resisting power of the dualism, must necessarily produce, by the number of forces which come into play, an almost infinite variety of vital phenomena. And, that these should often baffle all our attempts at explanation, is not surprising;

for we know how many intricate variations of the atmosphere, which are purely physical, and therefore comparatively simple, have hitherto remained unsolved.

There is, however, no occasion to be disheartened at the slow progress that has been made in lifting the veil which conceals the mysteries of life. Our knowledge on this subject is, indeed, as yet indistinct and incoherent: we have a multitude of interesting facts, which is, day by day, increasing; and what is more important, there are very many centres in various departments of the subject, around which there has been great and systematic aggregations, which are rapidly tending to a common generalisation. We must, therefore, strive to realise this union by some happy induction: and though attempt after attempt may fail, we must not desist at the dictates of a "barren caution, but still dare to venture upon the quest of truth."

One grand generalisation has been accomplished in physiology, which has given a firm basis to our knowledge, a fixed point of departure, by which we may ascend to higher and more intricate departments of the science: we allude to what has been called the organic or vegetative functions of animated bodies. These processes are peculiarly corporeal, but universal: they form the sum total of existence in the vegetable kingdom; and also make a considerable but subordinate part of the phenomena exhibited in the animal kingdom. Each kind of these functions manifests in different creatures an almost endless variety; and this circumstance affords one of the most interesting considerations in comparative physiology: it enables us to trace in the continuous series of animated beings, as they ascend one above another in the scale of nature, a progressive development of each function, and of its corresponding organ, until it has from the simplest condition attained to its highest perfection; an illustration in the whole system of nature of that unfolding of diversity out of unity, which characterises each individual organism in its gradual growth, from a primordial cell to a state of maturity. If it were not for the continuity of this natural chain of sequences, the great variation of the links when remote from each other would be incomprehensible: but by this systematic development of nature, we are able to grapple successfully with the complicated subject of organic functions.

A knowledge, however, of their individual characters, and of the order of their relations toward each other, only constitutes the introductory or natural history part of this department of physiology: there remains for consideration the causal or dynamical part of the science, by which we learn the nature of the forces concerned in these functions, and the laws which regulate their actions. This topic has been already in a great measure anticipated. The organism consists of a material body, a compound of physical and chemical forces, and of a specific vital force, which controls and directs the actions of its body, according to its own peculiar rational design. The ultimate composition of the bodies of all organisms is very similar, the essential elements being very few in number; but these are associated together in such varied proportions, both mechanically and chemically, that the resulting structures are exceedingly diversified in appearance. All these diversities depend on the peculiarities of the presiding vital power: but multitudinous as these specific powers are, there are certain methods of operating which are common to them all, and which are so few in number as greatly to simplify the comprehension of the subject. Each and all of the vital powers have the faculties of *acquisition, appropriation,* and *utilisation;* and in the exercise of these faculties, however varied the means employed, and the circumstances under which they operate, the organism acquires additional materials, or food, from the *medium* in which it is placed: then it appropriates this food by a process of assimilation, distributing and arranging it either for the growth, or farther development, of its structure; and lastly, it utilises the organs thus formed, by causing them to perform their respective functions.

Now during the actions and reactions which take place during organic functions, though they partake one while of a physical, and at another time of chemical characters, must not be regarded as wholly appertaining to the material body of the respective organism; but to this, in concurrence with vital power. It is true that after a creature is dead, many peculiar physical and chemical changes may take place, that are decidedly organic; but they have been effected in consequence of the material medium having a particular structure, which was derived from the operation of vital power: such media may have for awhile peculiar influences, but unless renovated they cannot endure; and such renovation can only take place in a living body. In truth, all the physical influences exerted on an organism from without, and all those changes within, relating to weights and volumes and motions of any kind, are purely material, that is, physical and chemical: but they are all modified by the peculiar structures of organisms; and these peculiarities depend upon the arrangement of materials which is effected by vital power: and thus it is that the physical and chemical powers become subjected to the vital. Osmotic and capillary actions are very conspicuous in organic functions;—they are indeed effected by physical forces, but you will look in vain for precisely the same actions in the inanimate world: we therefore contend, that if these phenomena require special media for their manifestation, the forces concerned in the production of these media are indirectly the causes of their occurrence. Just as man can externalise his operations, so as to produce outside his body a machine fashioned of material, that is of physical substances, and can actuate it by physical forces, so as to produce various works of art: no one would hesitate to assert that man is the artist, and not the physical forces; for they can only thus operate through the medium of a peculiar arrangement, in which they had no immediate concern.

In the first stage of organic functions, the body of the organism acts physically in the acquisition of food, during which process the vital force is either passive, as in plants, or it is active in directing the performance of higher functions in procuring this food, and conveying it into a position, where, like in the case of plants, it may be physically absorbed or acquired. This accomplished, chemical changes, the process of appropriation, commence; changes, which for the most part, like those of the physical, can only take place in an organic medium; and so far only in concurrence with the operation of vital powers; and assimilation being performed, and distribution having been physically made according to the respective structures of the organism, then the controlling influence of vital power, acting according to a rational design, repairs and fashions the various organs for the continuance of their functions; and the cycle of its operations is completed when the utilisation of its corporeal forces is effected.

Such is organic life on the lowest or simplest platform of existence, a universal phase of vital powers, which may be regarded as their generic attribute; and in proportion as specific differential properties are added thereto, organisms exhibit a corresponding progression in the system, until they culminate in *man*, who is a very microcosm, monopolising in himself all the leading types of vital powers, which are separately manifested in the distinct orders of existence.

In the earliest stage of its existence, every kind of organism is exceedingly simple in its structure. A primordial cell, the production of a pre-existing organism, is the visible body which is actuated by an associated and invisible principle of vitality, and it is the dualism of these that constitutes a distinct and independent being. A cell which does not possess such a principle can only live as part and parcel of another organism; but when vivified it becomes a new individual of the same species. During the development of such a germ-cell, though it should ultimately attain the gigantic stature of an oak, an elephant, or a whale, the animating principle is one and the self-same vital power: by successive divisions, and subsequent growth, the cell may become enormous masses of agglomerated cells; but the same power which superintended their formation, pervades and actuates them all. This notion closely accords with that of Mr. Paget, who under the name of *germ-force* designates the power which each germ possesses to develope itself into the perfection of a specific form; but, if we mistake not, we so far differ, that his germ-force is a general or common force; whereas ours is a multitude of specific forces. What is usually called cell-life, is the cycle of changes which cells undergo: this makes up the entire existence of some organisms, whilst it is only concerned in part in the functions of organisms of a higher order. Cells absorb their nourishment from the medium in which they are placed by the osmotic action of the cell-walls; and the contents of the cells are intermingled to promote the function of assimilation, by a species of circulation or *cyclosis*; a shadowing forth of that more perfect flux and reflux of fluids so distinct and conspicuous in higher organisations. The cellular structure enters more or less largely into the composition of all organisms: indeed it is generally considered that all the varied tissues are derived from successive transformations of cells. Microscopic researches have taught us that, simple and uniform as cells seem to be at the first glance, they are in reality very diversified: that in many organs, there are cells which are purely generative, being only engaged in the production of a different class of cells; and that it is the latter alone which discharge the special function of the organ, whether that of secretion or of motion; and the function being discharged, these cells become effete, and are eliminated from the system as inorganic materials.

Now such changes, though for the most part physical and chemical, are not entirely so; for if the organism dies they cease, and other changes of a different character supervene: so that it is evident that the concurrence of the principle of vitality and of the corporeal forces is necessary for the continuance of organic functions. The vital force not only presides over and directs the formation of peculiar structures, which are instrumental in greatly modifying chemical and physical actions, producing phenomena which cannot occur under any other conditions; but it actually dominates over the corporeal forces, counterbalancing their constant tendency to rest and rigidity by a species of repulsive energy, which imparts to the organism a continuous state of activity, a reiterated cycle of successive processes, so peculiarly characteristic of the vital principle.

The relation of the antagonistic forces in an organism is, however, so nicely balanced, that it is readily reduced to a state of equilibrium by an alteration of the condition of the medium in which the creature is situated. Temperature is the condition which most frequently exercises a modifying influence over the vital functions; and on this account there is a provision of nature, by which many creatures find protection against the interference of the medium by a capacity of evolving internal heat; and of constructing such coverings for their bodies as are adapted for their native climate, and variable according to the seasons. Indeed it is very probable that in all organisms, during the active performance of their functions, heat is simultaneously evolved, and retained long enough by the immediate cellular structure to facilitate the continuance of chemical changes, and to preserve the products in such a state of mobility, as may enable them to perform the requisite transfusions and circulations. When such provisions, on the other hand, are inadequate for the preservation of such a degree of heat as is necessary for these functional changes, a condition is produced which increases the attractive antagonism of the corporeal forces; and in consequence of this preponderance, the vital force becomes passive, and though still feebly acting in its lowest state, as mere cell-life, its more conspicuous functions are suspended. Thus on the approach of winter, trees shed their leaves; the lower animals become dormant, and even some of the higher classes hibernate; in short, all creatures which depend on *extraneous* heat as an accessory force to counteract the tendency to a state of rest in aid of the vital energy, all such must necessarily succumb for a season, whilst this auxiliary is withheld; but their vitality is not destroyed, but only overborne by adverse circumstances; and as a compressed gas regains its elasticity on the removal of pressure, so they start again into active life with renewed vigour on the return of a more propitious temperature. Not only heat, but moisture, food, and many other things are requisite for the continuance of life, but neither of these, nor all collectively, constitute the vital principle, but are only the conditions necessary for the exercise of its activity: and when such conditions are present, the specific vital power, and the complex corporeal power of the organism, so act and react on each other, as to perform all that is needful for its existence. The corporeal power is almost identical in all beings, variations of the same physical forces and of a very limited number of chemical forces, but the specific vital forces are very numerous and very dissimilar; and each, therefore, out of the same materials fashions its peculiar structural form, adapting it to its particular order in the system of nature.

In vegetables, the vital force seems to be very equably diffused throughout the system of each individual; and complicated and extensive as its particular form may be, its structure consists of but few tissues, which are more or less uniformly prolonged throughout all parts of the body: and the vegetable functions, in like manner, though much diversified in detail, are all reducible to those of growth and propagation. It is this simplicity which makes vegetables the connecting link between the mineral and animal kingdoms: a bond of union which is corroborated by the important fact, that vegetables alone can convert mineral into organic substances; so that the bodies of all animals are derived *immediately* or *mediately* from those of vegetables.

In animals the vital force assumes the additional attribute of sensibility, a higher development of self-directive energy than occurs in vegetables: though even in these there are many remarkable instances of irritability, both accidental and periodical, and of the tendency of parts to move, and even elongate themselves towards places more favourable for vegetation; all of which nearly approximate to passive or instinctive sensibility. In animals, however, this characteristic is more clearly defined, though it varies much in degree during its progressive ascent from the protozoa to man; and, according to its degree, in this respect the specific vital powers evolve corresponding bodies, capable of discharging higher and more complicated behests. Thus in the Acrita there are no special organs of sense or of muscular motion; and if they are sentient to external influences, it must be by a uniform and diffused sensibility, such as may possibly be found to exist in vegetables, which must in this case be regarded as the lowest degree, or *zero*, of sensation; a vanishing or *minimum* point of this attribute. In the Nematoneura, the rudiments of a nervous and muscular system have been demonstrated: they evidently possess a general sense of touch, and the faculty of locomotion; and judging from the eccentricity of their motions they are self-directive, regulating their movements according to circumstances. In the Homogangliata, sensibility is greatly advanced, accompanied by a high state of development of the nervous and muscular systems, more especially of the former, as is shown by a series of double ganglia or brains: they not only enjoy a high degree of the locomotive faculty, but also a great degree of freedom, or choice, in the selection of their movements, in consequence of the special senses with which they are endowed; as those of touch and of sight, and in some cases probably those also of hearing, taste, and smell. On this scale of being, the spontaneous actions seem to be all performed intuitively and instinctively; the impressions on the senses being responded to by a reflex and involuntary action of the nervous centres:—their *instinct*, indeed, is of the highest order, but still there is no indication of their actions being guided by *acquired* knowledge, as in those animals that are endowed with conciousness. Lastly, in the Myelencephala or Vertebrata, sensibility attains its highest development; and *pari passu* the organisation exhibits a corresponding degree of perfection: but even in this class, there is great diversity in the capacities of the several senses. All its members are, in some degree, conscious of the impression made on their senses; and this consciousness is knowledge, which differs from instinct, or latent passive knowledge, in that the latter acts necessarily or compulsively in a definite manner; whereas the former is an *acquired* rule of action, which may be applied or not, as the creature chooses:—and hence its liberty. From which it follows that the greater the amount of knowledge which a creature possesses, the greater its degree of freedom; hence the preeminence of man in this respect; and the reason of his predominance over all other creatures,—for knowledge is power: a creature can only act, that is, its specific vital force can only act according to its rational guide, whether this be *instinctive* or *acquired* knowledge. Some of the higher orders of the Vertebrata, though brutes, are so intelligent, possessing so much experience, and making such good use of this acquisition, that we cannot refuse to this high development of consciousness the name of mind; it is not indeed a rational mind, it cannot look below the surface of things, and interpret the reason in nature; but it is nevertheless an *understanding* mind, which knows things intuitively as they appear to be, a *common sense*, the lower platform or substratum of the human mind. This subject, however, must be reserved for a separate chapter.

Hitherto we have spoken of sensibility as the highest attribute of vital power, without any particular mention of the muscular and nervous systems, the instruments by which this mode of vital power becomes efficient. In the same manner, as the vital force superintends and directs the fabrication of its organic body, in order to perform its special functions; one, while framing these on one general or common plan in which there is no differentiation of organs for each particular duty; and at another time, according to the degree of the specific power, fashioning a peculiar organ, or even combination of organs for each special function; so the vital forces of the higher grades follow a similar plan in the construction of their bodies: having a higher attribute they must provide the instruments for its manifestation, and these instruments must correspond with the rank of the specific power in the system of Nature. If a specific power has a capacity of directing or willing any particular motion, it must be provided with a special apparatus for the performance of its designs: it cannot of itself perform physical actions, such as motion; but it can frame an organ, a muscle for instance, which having certain attachments to fixed points will, when it undergoes contraction, produce motion according to its mechanism. But this contraction must have an exciting cause; and hence the necessity of the association of the muscular and nervous systems: the nerves communicate to the muscles the *stimulus* required, and when this is imparted, the muscle is excited to act, which it does by contraction. Every time this action takes place, a certain member of the cells in the structure of the muscle undergo an important change; and are incapable of again performing the same function, and therefore their remains, as dead or useless matter, are removed from the system; this change is doubtless chemical, produced by the influence of the nervous fluid, analogous to that of electricity; combination is a combining condensing force, evolving the opposite physical force which is transmitted by the mechanism, in the form of the motions produced. The nervous fluid seems to be also a phase of physical force evolved during the combining actions in various parts of the organism; a force which one while is manifested as *organic heat*, and at another time as *nervous influence;* as the latter, it may be greatly diffused and generally operative, or it may be restricted to definite centres, which communicate with particular muscles by means of nerves leading to and from these centres. In such centres, there will be a certain intensity of force, which is subject to the direction of the creature's vital power, which acts, either intuitively, producing the regular and predetermined actions of the natural functions; or consciously, that is, subject to the individual's choice, whether according to reason or caprice: in the former case the action takes place through the reflex nerves without the creature's knowledge; in the latter it proceeds from a higher and more energetic centre, in consequence of the impressions conveyed thereto by nerves of sense having entered into consciousness.

So that motions are accomplished by the muscles: some of these motions are more or less incessant and entirely removed from the control of the will, and are therefore excited by the reflex action of the nerves; and some are subject entirely to the will; whilst others are capable of both voluntary and involuntary action. But in all these cases, the actions are local and partial; and it is through the instrumentality of the nerves, that the vital force determines these special actions according to the purpose of its designs, whether the creature is conscious of its intentions or passively influenced by its reason-directed force.

If we have been so fortunate as to have expressed ourselves intelligibly (which on such a complicated subject is no easy matter), it will be perceived that our conception of the *modus operandi* of vital power is twofold. In organic or vegetative functions, it acts according to its rational laws, in the same manner as physical and chemical powers; and this holds good whether these functions occur either in plants or animals: but in the higher functions of animals, which are under the influence of the nervous system, the vital force has two modes of action; one similar to that of the vegetative, and the other not so bound down to a given course of action; for having a knowledge or consciousness of several modes it is capable of selecting between them, or in other words, it has a freedom of choice. These different modes are fundamentally one and the same: and if the expression be allowable, we may say that the vital force in all cases acts according to its *knowledge* of its rational designs; though this knowledge is sometimes passive or *latent*, and at other times, sensible or *conscious*. But of this more hereafter.

From what has now been said concerning specific vital powers, it will have been gathered that we advocate the permanence of species: we do not believe that true *specific powers* can by any process of development be transformed from a lower to a higher species. The same species, as in the case of man (who is the only organism which is definitely indicated in the Scriptures as a distinct species, and there is no other possible source of information on this subject), may present great varieties, by long residence in different climates, and other modifying circumstances: but however greatly the two extreme tribes of human beings may differ from each other, they have all characteristics which broadly distinguish them from all other species of animals; and it is not within the limits of our lengthened experience, that any inferior creature can, by development, become a man; or that man can be *actually* degraded to the condition of a brute beast.

It is indeed very possible that many kinds of animals, as the dog, though presenting varieties exceedingly unlike each other, may all be derived from a common stock; their differences having arisen from the long continuance of peculiar conditions: and this is rendered the more probable by the marvellous transformations which are effected by the breeders of cattle and by the horticulturist. In all such transformations, however, we do not see any confirmation of the notion promulgated by Lamarck, that by gradual development all creatures may have been derived from a lower grade.

The line of demarcation between plants and animals is indeed very obscure; and so it is between most contiguous genera of organisms: they seem to *fine* away into each other almost imperceptibly; a process which nature seems to delight in, and which is so exquisitely beautiful in luminous phenomena. Still, in all this intimate blending together, there are certain broad and well-marked differences, which we have no reason to believe ever have been, or possibly can be, metamorphosed into each other: a fish and a mammal may fly like a bird, and a mammal and a bird may frequent the water like a fish; but the structure of these different organisms are so different that we cannot conceive that any mode of existence, however varied, could convert one into the other. It is true, that we see as wonderful transformations in the metamorphosis of various creatures: but in all such cases provision is made in the structure of each for such developments, in order to adapt them for successive modes of existence; this being the normal character of these particular species.

Each adopted species should be regarded as only provisionally true, until it be proved to be a variety. But even when species are correctly established, they cannot, like chemical elements, be manifested as individual realities: in the one case there is a fixity of character, which renders this possible; in the other there is an endless variation, in accordance with the attributes of growth and reproduction.

In our present state of knowledge, we cannot mark the limits of the varieties which make up definite species, except in the case of man; and therefore those who are now actively engaged in investigating this difficult subject are well occupied: hitherto their labours have been so far successful as to have greatly reduced the number of previously acknowledged species, which doubtless is still greatly exaggerated. But the tendency of their labour seems to be toward the revival of Lamarck's hypothesis, which, if substantiated, would reduce all our specific to one universal vital power. Differentiations when carried to extremes lead to a confused and perplexing state of knowledge, but such unifications as an original oneness of animated beings, and the identity of all natural forces, tends to an absolutism which to the human intellect is equivalent to an abnegation of all knowledge.

CHAP. VIII.

MIND, OR CONSCIOUS POWER, THE HIGHEST PHASE OF VITALITY.

Mind and Matter not heterogeneous.—Mind differs from the other Parts of the Organism only in Degree.—The mutual Dependance of Mind and Body.—The Phenomena of Mind the Subject of Psychology.—Brutes have Minds.—The Infant Mind, as regards Experience, a *tabula rasa*.—Primary Knowledge intuitive.—Evidence of the Senses reliable: Inferences deceptive.—Sensation and Perception.—Abstraction, or Mental Analysis of Knowledge.—Experience, acquired Knowledge: communicable by Example, as well as by Precept.—Memory.—The Subjective and Objective Factors of Knowledge.—Intuitive Understanding, or Common Sense.—Perfect Knowledge analogous to Instinct.—*A posteriori* and *à priori* Ideas.—Conceptions or Abstract Ideas—Their Denomination; Colligation; and Generalisation.—The Moral Sentiments, like Perceptions, are the intuitive Data of a higher Knowledge.—Brutes have moral and social Intuitions, or Instincts, as well as Man.—Man, in relation to the Morality of Brutes, stands *in loco Dei*.—The Nature of the Will or Conscious Power.—The Science of Morality or Ethics.—Conclusion.

It is a proposition, says Dugald Stewart [*], equally certain and indisputable that " the phenomena of mind and those of matter appear to be more completely heterogeneous than any other class of facts within the circle of our knowledge." Body and mind are indeed generally regarded as the antithesis of each other: that they are the opposite

[*] Encyclopædia Britannica. Preliminary Dissertation, p. 10.

poles of animated beings, and capable of being separately contemplated, cannot be denied; but we do not recognise that broad line of demarcation between them which is commonly believed to exist.

In the usual acceptation of the terms body and mind, the former is the living visible organism which discharges all the animal functions; whilst the latter is some *unknown* spiritual existence dwelling therein, and exercising all the faculties of consciousness:—the mind, in short, is conceived to be something *sui generis*, requiring to be treated of separately from physiology; and has, therefore, been erected into the distinct science of psychology. This distinction may be convenient in many respects; but if maintained, these sciences should be regarded as the branches of a more general science, such as that of biology: in this case, however, we should have to contend with the same perplexity as occurs in statics and dynamics, the continual transition of one into the other; for conscious and unconscious are only distinguishing features, or different phases, of the self-same vital power: and, as we shall soon see, even the most exalted phenomena of consciousness are capable of becoming passive or intuitive, that is, of conversion into the unconscious state.

Mind is the intelligent or intellectual faculty, but still it is the self-same power which actuates the body and participates in all the organic functions. It is a phase, the highest phase, of vital power, and as such is immediately related to the highest development of the body, the cerebral organ; the function of which is only concerned with physical force in its most exalted phase, as the nervous fluid: and it is only by the concurrence of this corporeal nervous organ and the conscious vital force that those actions and reactions take place that are manifested as mental phenomena. So that, as our organism is not one thing but a composition of forces, it follows that every part of this whole must be similarly constituted: the mind therefore is not an indwelling influence, but a dualism of forces, the highest phase of organic existence; a diversity in unity, which is the essential condition of all natural beings.

The individuality, or selfhood, of every chemical and vital existence necessarily depends on this dualistic constitution, without which it could not function; and it is the predominant force in such dualisms that imparts thereto their peculiar or specific characters: and as the properties of the latter become more complicated in organisms, so the creature or the subordinate parts of any creature attain a higher degree in the hierarchy of nature. Thus in the higher order of animals, the specific vital power not only possesses a self-directive force, which guides and superintends, according to its rational laws, its vegetative, locomotive, and instinctive functions; but it is also a self-conscious power according to its degree. It may belong to the lowest degree of consciousness, only being aware of its sensations, and responsive to these motives of action, and it may, thus far, be able to choose between various possible modes of accomplishing its desires; and it may not only be conscious of all this, and possess such an amount of understanding as constitutes personal experience; but it may also be rationally conscious, capable of interpreting the reason in nature, the laws by which all cosmical powers are governed; then it becomes a rational will, the highest development of vital power.

The *will* is not only a reason-directed force, but it is capable of becoming conscious of this reason, and of knowing not only that it is a force and can act, but also of knowing for what purpose it acts; and it knows when it has accomplished its designs. Now we say all this of the *will*, as if it were the sole force concerned in causation, because it is the predominant, and therefore the more conspicuous cause of the resulting effects: just as in the motion of bodies, the propelling force rivets the attention to the exclusion of the resisting force, which modifies the result. The *will*, that is, the vital force as a free conscious agent, is intimately associated with the brain, which acts as the corporeal or basic force of the dualism: it is conscious of physical impressions made on the brain, and according to this knowledge it directs and puts forth the efficiency of the cerebral force, which, as nervous energy, is discharged on the muscles to be moved, thereby exciting them into action. This operation is purely physical, and as such must depend on the physical forces of the organism; but these forces are under the control and guidance of the specific vital force, in order to perform such special actions as may conduce to the creature's welfare or enjoyment.

That the concurrence of the will and cerebral force is requisite for the due performance of mental actions, is not only shown in the case of paralysis, when the organic defect renders the mind impotent; but also by the fact that the energy of the mind is as much impaired by excessive mental exertion, as the strength of the body is by any kind of exercise which induces great fatigue. But here we must pause for the present, as we are anticipating our subject too hastily; what we have been desirous of pointing out is, that man, as well as all other creatures, whether guided purely by instinct, or by acquired knowledge, is equally a dualism of natural powers; and however these may function, whether involuntarily and unconsciously, or voluntarily and consciously, there must in all cases be organic action and reaction. This may not always be easily demonstrated; but it is a fundamental truth; and by keeping it at all times well in view, it may ultimately enable us to solve the difficulty. Thus, in a few words, we have endeavoured to indicate the relation which subsists between Matter and Mind: and we now proceed to enter more into details concerning mental phenomena.

Brutes may in a sense be said to possess minds; for they have all the inferior faculties of the understanding, whilst they are devoid of the higher capacities of abstraction and of logical reasoning. Man enjoys the whole range of these faculties, and he alone possesses a perfect mind: we therefore propose to make the human mind the more especial subject of our inquiry, noticing in our progress those faculties that are common to the brute, till we arrive at that point where the two orders of mind part company.

In the earliest dawn of the infant's mind, as far as regards actual knowledge, Locke has well likened it to a *tabula rasa;* ready for the reception of future inscriptions: its condition is analogous to that of the conjugate germ-cells, which are for all creatures so much alike, and apt to assume various aspects according to the influence of their respective specific principles. In what manner does the infant mind begin to function; how is its blank page inscribed with the elements of knowledge? Locke maintained that knowledge is primarily acquired by and through the medium of the senses; and much as this opinion has been combated, its validity has, we think, never been satisfactorily disproved. This idea, however, did not originate with Locke; but it received at his hands such admirable illustration, that he virtually made it his own : "nihil est in intellectu quod non fuerit in sensu," was an old maxim, to which Leibnitz [*] appended the proviso, "nisi ipse intellectus." This addition, at first sight, looks very like nonsense; for how can a mind be within itself? what is meant is, that knowledge may also originate immediately within the mind; that is, that *à priori* knowledge is possible; but of this more hereafter.

If the human or brute mind could not *intuitively* interpret the impressions made on the organs of sense by external objects, knowledge would be impossible; but, as constituted, the creature, when face to face with the outward world, acquires a direct and immediate knowledge of the import of its sensations; that is, as far as regards the outward appearance of objects.

Many have written lightly concerning the value of sensational knowledge, because it relates to phenomena which are ever changing; but inasmuch as it is intuitive, and not liable to the imperfection of logical knowledge, which depends much on the individual reasoning power, it seems rather to be deserving of the greatest reliance. At all

---

[*] Œuvres de Leibnitz, par Jacques, tom. i. f. 59.

events, by common consent, confidence is placed in the testimony of the senses; indeed its veracity will stand the test of the famous criterion of Vincent of Lirens. But surely the senses may be deceived? Certainly not; but wrong conclusions may be drawn from the knowledge thus obtained. Zeuxis painted grapes so naturally that they deceived the birds; whilst he himself, in turn, was deceived by a curtain drawn by Parrhasius: the senses, in both cases, gave a correct testimony that the appearance was the same as would have been afforded by the objects themselves; but the birds and the painter were both deluded because they judged according to experience. Had any doubt arisen concerning the nature of the objects, as when first seen before experience, the sight would not have been trusted alone, but would have been aided by the other senses: but such a proceeding, in the case of experience, would be contrary to an important provision of Nature, by which the intercourse with the outer world is greatly facilitated; viz. that knowledge once acquired is trustworthy, otherwise we should always be doubting, and ever learning. Nature herself is uniform; and on this fact we place great reliance: but she does not provide against human devices, either artificial or moral; these belong to entirely different categories.

If there be no organic defect, sensational knowledge, being intuitive, is invariably uniform; not only for the individual, but for all creatures: and for man it affords the foundation, or primary principles, of all natural knowledge; for all such may immediately or mediately be traced up to this origin.

How, it may be asked, can physical objects and mental

consciousness be brought into communication, so as to produce this presentative knowledge? Each organ of sense is so framed as to be capable of being acted on by peculiar physical agencies; by aërial and etherial undulations, and the like: and the material impacts thus made on the organs are conveyed by the nerves, and produce corresponding physical impressions on the brain. Sometimes these impacts are arrested in their progress towards the brain, and are diverted by a reflex operation, so as only to excite the *efferent* nerves; as in the automatic movements connected with the ganglia of the nervous system: and in this case the impressions on the organs of sense do not enter into consciousness. So that physical impressions may come into concurrence with vital power in two modes: either on the lower, as the unconscious phase; or on the higher, when the creature feels and knows what has happened. Though, in the one case, the vital force is unconscious; still it is a reason-directed force, acting on given impressions according to a predetermined mode of operation: so when this force is conscious, or a will, it regulates its actions according to its acquired knowledge in such manner as it may choose; and when this choice coincides with the ordinary routine of unconscious actions it will be almost passive, that is, only slightly removed from the phenomena of instinct.

This primary mental function is called sensation: and it may be either active or passive, in respect to consciousness, according as it is associated with the automatic or voluntary phase of vital power. It is well known that habit, or intense preoccupation, renders us unconscious of many sensations which must have been produced under the existing circumstances: something more is, therefore, requisite than the ordinary impressions on the nervous centres, before sensations become objects of knowledge.

Sensations are capable of being known, or are cognisable, just as bodies are capable of being moved: and as in the latter case, a moving force must be applied before motion can be produced; so in the former, a conscious or knowing force must act on the knowable objects; a concurrence which results in knowledge. Knowledge, therefore, is no other than a knowable object that is known; as motion, or rather, to speak more accurately, a corporeal movement is a moveable body when moved; in either case the resulting phenomenon is not one thing, but all the forces concerned therein are contained in, or co-exist in, the phenomenon; so that a known object or knowledge is still that which may be farther acted on by conscious force, with various degrees of intensity; it is still as much a knowable object as the original sensation itself. Since, then, sensations partake of the nature of the physical body of the organism, and the consciousness is a phase of the specific vital force, it is evident that the *mind*, on its lowest platform, is as much a dualism as any other organic function; thus conserving the universal correlation of correlative powers.

The *primary* knowledge obtained through the medium of sensation is called *perception;* and the energy of the conscious force concerned therein is *attention:* without some degree of attention there can be no perception. In perception, we get the first glimpse of the mighty import of the ideal or rational side of power; for as the real side, the physical efficiency of power seems to elude our grasp in the higher mental phenomena, consciousness gives us more and more insight into the character of that pure reason, which is the basis of the ideal. As force becomes abstracted from natural powers, reason stands out in stronger and brighter relief; until at length, under the magic influence of consciousness, force vanishes away, and nought remains of power, but the abstract beau-ideals, the designs only of that ineffable genius, which pervades all the works of creation.

But it must ever be remembered that these wondrous manifestations of the human mind are only the interpretations of the reason in nature; a part only, a glorious part indeed, but not nature herself in her entirety. *Abstraction* is but a mental analysis, by which we are enabled to examine the ideal side of nature; and by which we become acquainted with logical forms, the fundamental principles of all rational knowledge. Pure and exact, however, as this knowledge is; it is, we conceive, all derived from our primary and concrete perceptions: fundamental principles are contained therein, just as chemical elements exist in compounds previous to their separation by analysis; but they must be eliminated therefrom by logical methods. When once obtained, we become so deeply impressed by their simplicity, that we are apt to regard them as essentially distinct and independent forms of knowledge, as *à priori* truths, which are only knowable by a species of intellectual intuition: we are, however, inclined to think that perceptions are the only kind of intuitive knowledge, and that as *data*, they enable us to obtain the pure elements by logical processes.

But to return from this digression. Whenever purely

passive sensations take place, instinctive actions follow: they have answered their purpose; the ordinary response has been given, and they are consigned to oblivion. Not so when they have arrested the attention of conscious force, for then perception follows; and when this occurs, knowledge has been acquired, which is more or less perfectly appropriated, according to the degree of attention exercised, and according to the number of the senses engaged in the contemplation. Should the same object be again perceived on another occasion, the same scrutiny is not repeated; the creature already knows it, and a single momentary glance is sufficient to inform him what it is, and his conduct is regulated according to this conviction. When a large experience has thus been acquired, even by the brute, the voluntary actions may be confidently directed thereby: and other brutes of the same kind will depend on their more experienced elder, as an authority which may be implicitly followed; thus obtaining by practical instruction a knowledge, which took their guide a life-long application to acquire.

Experience then is only acquired knowledge, which for the guidance of voluntary actions stands in the place of instinct, (or intuitive knowledge, if it may be so called,) which is the directive principle of involuntary functions. How knowledge, when once acquired, can be retained and made subservient to the will, as its reason-directing influence, we cannot tell; nor do we know how the vital force can develop its organism, and utilise the same for its various purposes; nor indeed, for that matter, can we tell how gravitation can concentrate and retain its energy around a common centre, which increases on every addition to the mass. This, however, we know, that the concurrence of the organic brain is a requisite factor in the operation; for if it be in any way deranged, knowledge is lost; and whether the derangement be a mental defect or a physical inability to function, is of no consequence; for force cannot act without knowledge, and knowledge is powerless without a simultaneous and co-existing force. We do not pretend to offer a perfectly satisfactory explanation of the retention of knowledge in the cerebral region; for we cannot demonstrate corresponding organic phenomena: but if it be, as we suppose, that the concurrence of corporeal, or physical forces, and of conscious force is requisite in all mental functions, it is not improbable that the product of such concurrence may continue to subsist in the cerebral region, if not as a structural, at least as a functional reality. The suggestion which arises on the contemplation of this subject is, that as grosser products are retained around and within corporeal organs, may not the more etherial impressions be retained by the brain, and even be more permanently durable as less gross material. Whether this continuance be unchangeably abiding or periodically renewed, like the products of the vegetative organs, is beyond observation: but the fact is undeniable, that knowledge obtained in childhood remains till old age; and during this long period, the body has been repeatedly renovated, and yet has retained its identity, not only of form and feature, but even of extraneous marks and excrescences both artificial and natural. This is indeed a difficult, but a very interesting problem.

It will have occurred to many that what we are referring

to acquired knowledge, is usually ascribed to *memory*, as a distinct faculty of the mind. Acquired knowledge is the product of the action and reaction of the cerebral and conscious forces; a product which is retained and utilised by the will, as a guide in the exercise of its freedom. Such a function may be called memory, and as the term is so familiar to us, its employment may sometimes save circumlocution; but then it must be distinctly understood that we do not regard it as a peculiar faculty, but only as a *state* of consciousness. When knowledge is imperfect, the memory is confused; but when the attention has been intently rivetted on an object, it becomes well known, and the memory is perfect; and knowledge thus remembered is ever at hand to be utilised by the energy of the same conscious force by which it was originally acquired and appropriated; in like manner as the organs of the body are fabricated, and made to function by the same vital force.

"We remember," says the author[*] of "Psychological Inquiries," "nothing of what occurred in infancy. That part of our life seems afterwards to be a blank in our existence; and it is not unreasonable to suppose that the brain, like some other of the organs of the newly born child, is in an unfinished state, and therefore not fitted to retain the impressions made on it during any considerable period of time." Again, "It seems that impressions made on the organs of sense, and transmitted to the brain, produce some actual change on the minute organism of the latter, and that this is subservient, and in our present

---

[*] At pp. 60, 63, and 67

state of existence, essential to memory." In infancy, man is on a lower platform of existence; his organs and their functions are like those of inferior animals; and even when the senses are developed, they only serve to assist automatic movements by reflex actions; and even in the dawn of consciousness, when *perceptions* are first evoked, they are feeble and transient as the passing shadow; indeed, if they were perfect and abiding, they would be *purposeless*, for the helpless condition of the organism could not avail itself of such knowledge. Nature does nothing in vain; knowledge is not needed by the babe, consequently it acquires none, and the memory is *nil:* but when the child becomes self-conscious, its sensations excite vivid perceptions, accompanied by an earnest curiosity, a craving thirst after knowledge, which is as requisite for the mind as food is for the body: and as it grows in knowledge, its memory acquires strength; and is at no period of life more energetic than during childhood, for then perceptions make the deepest impressions.

Before quitting the subject of perception it may be well to briefly recapitulate what we have said; for as all other kinds of knowledge take their departure therefrom, it is important that we should be rightly understood.

Sensation is one of the factors of perception, the other is conscious force or will, which is one of the phases of vital power, the principle which is concerned in all the animal functions. When the vital force acts instinctively (that is, according to the special laws of its innate but passive rational guide), its energy goes forth in the accomplishment of its purpose by a reflex action of the nervous system; a mode of action similar to that of the physical forces; but when, by the acquisition of the additional attribute of consciousness, the vital force becomes also a conscious force or will, then it perceives and knows the import of the sensations with which it comes into communion; and the result is voluntarily acquired knowledge, a new and independent guide for the regulation of its conduct. The *will,* though a higher phase of vital force, is not dispossessed of the attributes of the lower phases: they are all parts of one and the self-same vital power; and, therefore, within its sphere of activity, it can exercise all its functions.

In respect to the two factors concerned in the mental process of perception, Kant* entertained a notion somewhat similar. "There can be no doubt," he says, "that all our knowledge commences with experience; for what could act upon the knowing faculty, and urge it to movement, but the various objects of sense, which as raw materials are worked up into that knowledge of things which we term experience?" But, as M. Cousin † remarks in his "Lectures on the Critique of Pure Reason," "Kant is very confused on this subject: one while he makes a distinction between sensation and perception, regarding one as the condition of the other; and at another time he refers both to one and the same faculty, the sensory." It was Jacobi ‡ who first detected this inconsistency of Kant; and who distinctly pointed out "that the *moment* of immediateness must remain for the mind the mediating agent, as a basis

---

* Critick of Pure Reason, tr. by Haywood. Introduction.
† At p. 25, 80.
‡ Chalybæus, Spec. Philosophy p. 60.

and condition of development." This Kant evidently lost sight of, relying too much on the one factor of the understanding as the source of knowledge. In this respect he was afterwards surpassed by Fichte, who made Leibnitz's exception, *nisi intellectus ipse*, his rule; and which ultimately terminated in the pure idealism of the German philosophy. On our view, the mind is a dualism, like all other natural powers; and thus viewed, the gulph of absolutism is avoided; we remain within the circle of conditioned relations, making the system of nature the unity out of which all diversity may be evolved. The mind is part and parcel of the living organism: the brain, a corporeal organ, functions physically through impressions communicated to it by the nerves; and the concurrence of its products, or phenomena, with the conscious force results in a diversity of perceptions or primary ideas. In these ideas the organic, or objective, factor is at a *maximum*, and the intellectual faculty, or subjective factor, at a *minimum:* and however the relative proportion of the two factors may vary, yet in every kind of idea (that is, in every kind of interpreted *form* of knowledge) there must be an *object* and a *subject;* for an idea is a correlation of these correlative factors.

The *will* can at pleasure objectify any kind of knowledge, by directing its energy thereon; we say not, as is usual, by fixing its gaze thereon, as if the will operated by a species of intellectual vision: this would not convey our meaning. We rather regard it as a conscious *force*, which adds to the intellectual factor in perception another proportion of its energy, whereby this factor becomes more intensified; and the knowledge becomes thus raised to a higher form; it is no longer a *perception*, but a *conception*.

From this it follows, that although a conception is a higher order of idea or of knowledge, yet it is similarly constituted; having a content and form, an object and subject, and therefore is still related to the same dualistic principle which obtained in a perception, though the factors have different ratios: just as solids, liquids, and gases are modes of the self-same substance; though in each the constituent physical forces vary in their relative proportions.

Conceptions are abstract ideas; and by their filiation to perceptions, it is evident that they are derived from the latter concrete ideas by abstraction; and have therefore no pretension to an independent origin. In forming conceptions there is a degree of intellect required, which transcends the faculties of the brute: we begin now to analyse knowledge, in order to ascertain what it is in itself; whereas the knowledge of brutes is confined to the outward appearance of things. But even in the attainment of this knowledge, the consciousness passively exercises many methods, which are at root the same as those which are voluntarily and designedly employed in higher pursuits. Thus the comparison of perceived objects, as to whether they are like or unlike, evidently takes place, though unconsciously, in all attentive observations: the creature sees at a glance whether it knows the object, or not; and if not, then succeeds a regular investigation by each and all of the senses, which is no other than a mental comparison with such objects as are already known in its experience. Such comparisons are not accompanied by that clear apperception which occurs in the conscious mind in the case of abstraction; it is, however, the same process, though instinctively performed, that is followed in the highest mental pursuits: thus, in logic, positive and negative propositions are only affirmations of similarity or dissimilarity. These tacit and unconscious operations of the instinct show that even on the lowest platform the germ exists in the mind, which may possibly be expanded into perfect intelligence. We have, indeed, many remarkable facts on record concerning the understanding of brutes, that seem to show that they are rational, though not logical creatures; their practical experience intuitively applied, is sufficient for all their exigencies, and though it does not amount to pure reason, it is a clear understanding, which may not be unaptly called *common sense*.

There is another well-marked distinction between man and the brute, in the faculty of speech which the former exclusively possesses; and also in the capacity of intelligibly expressing the language of his speech in written symbols; by which knowledge once acquired may be preserved and accumulated from generation to generation. Objects of all kinds, when represented by appropriate names, the meaning of which has been correctly learnt, may be as distinctly understood as if they had actually become known by personal experience; and thus it is that when the well-informed visit foreign countries, all things seem so familiar to them, that they do not experience those feelings of curiosity and wonder, which so delight the uninformed traveller.

This statement concerning oral and written language may seem to contradict what has just been said concerning mental phenomena, that they are always *immediately* or *mediately* associated with organic actions and re-actions; but when the character of perceptions or primary ideas is attentively considered, it will be found that knowledge obtained in either manner follows a similar process; there are certain impressions made on the senses in both cases: in the one case the impressions are excited by the actual presence of the natural objects, in the other by conventional sounds or visible symbols. Now in the former instance, the interpretation by the conscious faculty is intuitive; we know the objects at once as far as regards their appearance by a direct and immediate knowledge; and so the peculiar impressions made on the senses by the words spoken or symbolised are also directly known, not by an intuitive consciousness, but by an *acquired* knowledge of their meaning, which we have been taught by precept or example. So that ultimately acquired knowledge and instinct are of the same import, as guides of the rational will; the one results from a voluntary, the other from an involuntary operation of the same vital principle, in the phase of the mental faculty; and by these different methods the same purpose is accomplished, the advancement of human knowledge.

The communication of knowledge by oral and written instruction is not confined to the primary ideas; for conceptions and even science itself may be so taught and learnt: thus, man may not only acquire a knowledge of the lengthened experience of his teachers; but also of that which has been accumulated for ages, and handed down by writing or tradition. Such knowledge, however, even in its best estate, has not the certitude of intuitive knowledge, which is not only perfect but invariable: it is liable to a twofold error, either on the part of the tutor or of the pupil; and is for the most part imperfect, being only in a state of development.

When the mind has become familiar with any kind of knowledge, whether that of perception or of conception, that is, when any subject is well known, there is no longer any effort or attention required in becoming conscious of it; or in the performance of actions directed thereby. Such functions have become by *habit*, as it were, a second nature, and are discharged as intuitively and instinctively as those which are purely organic; such a phase of activity is more than that of mere memory, for the acquired knowledge must not only be recalled, but utilised in the performance of particular actions, bodily as well as mental. How long continued and laborious are the practical exercises of the gymnast, and of the musician, before they become expert performers; and, in like manner, how intense the application of the mathematician and of scientific professors, before they attain to a proficiency of their respective knowledge! But when either of them has finished his course of instruction, he can perform the most elaborate tasks, not only without laborious effort, but so easily and intuitively, that though perhaps not absolutely, yet he may be very nearly unconscious of his occupation. In ordinary perceptions this is of constant occurrence, so that what in infancy required much attention and instruction to learn, is in after life a purely *automatic* action of the senses; as, for example, in walking and reading. Thus, hard-earned knowledge, even that beyond the reach of most men, may descend into a species of instinct, similar to that which guides the functions of very inferior animals.

This wondrous result is very consistent with the view concerning vital power which we are advocating. The organic principle is a reason-directed force, which in its lower phase is unconscious of its innate and unerring reason; whilst in its higher phase, it is capable of adding thereto acquired knowledge, as an extra-rational guide, in consequence of its additional attribute of consciousness: this accession of acquired knowledge, which enlarges the creature's field of action, is so appropriated and assimilated by long experience, that it becomes part and parcel of the creature's individual instinct or intuitive knowledge; and as such it is ever prompt to guide and direct the exercise of its efficiency. And thus we learn that physical forces and conscious forces, that is, matter and mind, are but the extreme dualisms of powers; the opposite poles, as it were, of natural bodies.

It has already been stated that by perception we become acquainted with natural objects; and that by distinguishing these objects by peculiar names, man is enabled to communicate knowledge to his fellows: such names, however, only denote the actual objects, as they appear in their individuality to the senses; and are, therefore, purely phenomenal, imparting no knowledge of what things are in themselves. All these objects have peculiar properties, or characteristic attributes, and each kind of property affects some one or other of the senses in a special manner; and thus it is that the properties of bodies become mental objects: and when the conscious faculty diverts its attention to only one particular property, to the exclusion of all others in the various bodies under contemplation, it abstracts this property by a process of mental analysis; and the knowledge thus obtained is an abstract idea, which is secured and appropriated as a mental object by being named. Abstract ideas are the *formal* types by which many primary or concrete ideas may be colligated together into one kind or class; and by a repetition of this act and by denomination, many colligations are obtained, which in turn may be associated together and designated by a general or class name. There is no limit to such a process of generalisation, until the *summum genus* of knowledge, the science of the sciences or philosophy, is attained. The individual sciences are so many subaltern genera; and each of these is a logical universal, which has its own noun-substantive or fundamental idea.

These fundamental ideas, and their rational laws or axioms, according to which they function, are by many regarded not as elements arrived at by the mental analysis of concrete ideas; but as pure *à priori* ideas innate in the mind, and perfectly independent of the sense-perceptions, being manifested only by intellectual intuition. Or in other words, knowledge is supposed to be of two distinct kinds: the one derived immediately from the outer world by the senses, and so termed empirical or *à posteriori*, and partaking of the variableness and incertitude which characterises phenomena; the other, relating only to the principles of things, is regarded as *à priori* and independent, possessing the criteria of necessity and universality. As regards the *universality* of fundamental ideas, inasmuch as each of these ideas is the principle of its own system or logical universal, it must needs be associated with or exist in each and all of such system: and as regards their *necessity*, it can only mean that this form of knowledge, this interpretation of one of the reasons in nature, is a perfect law, which when followed is an invariable guide, necessarily precise and definite; it is not a mere "blind or fated necessity, but a necessity of reason or logical sequence." The criteria of *à priori* ideas, if used in such a sense, are very intelligible; and accord with our notion of the constitution of mental phenomena. *À priori* ideas, we conceive, are the elements of concrete ideas; and consequently must pre-exist in them; though we are ignorant of them, until they have been reached by successive inductions: but when thus obtained they may be re-combined by deduction, so as to demonstrate many particular ideas previously unknown; just as we can unite elements to form chemical combinations, which have not hitherto been detected in nature.

The Rev. Baden Powell has remarked that "pure reason out of his own resources may, indeed, create theories apart from all observations of nature; but to make them applicable to anything in nature, such creations of the mind must necessarily and universally involve *some* small assumption of *material properties*, or mechanical conditions; which can only be in some form or another ultimately derived from observation: what is borrowed may be *very little*; but it must be something." And again, "fundamental ideas are not *à priori*, or antecedent to all experience; they are principles established in the mind by previous abstractions, remotely derived from previous experience."

For these reasons, we accord with those who think that the assumption of the intuitions of the pure reason by a special faculty of the mind is not required to explain the nature of fundamental or *à priori* ideas; it complicates a subject already sufficiently intricate, by introducing an additional, and as we conceive superfluous principle. There has, indeed, ever been a disposition to magnify the rational faculty as a distinct and independent energy, apart from all the other faculties of the mind; a something which can directly see and comprehend logical objects, as external physical objects are immediately apprehended by perception; but such a notion degrades the human intellect to a mere instinct, increasing its certitude doubtless, but removing from it those logical exercises by which the mental, like the corporeal faculties, are urged on to work out their own progress towards perfection. Numerous as the various phases of *knowing* and *willing* are, they are all one and the same conscious vital force or *will*: and though this *will*, according to its degree, whether of the brute or of man, has, in each, various capacities, all of these lie dormant in the first period of existence, and are only gradually developed; just as the various organs of a creature are evolved out of the self-same germ. And it is not, therefore, surprising that the specific power of man should in both cases exercise its faculties in a similar manner; that the mind should increase in knowledge until mere consciousness brightens into the full light of science; just as the germ expands and grows until the body acquires the stature and strength of maturity.

Man is, as Bacon has well said, but the interpreter of nature. He must be indebted to Nature herself, of which indeed he is a part, for the data or primary principles of his knowledge : and having acquired these data, his rational faculty, a reason-directed force which functions by logical methods of which it is conscious, elaborates therefrom the pure elements, or principles, of knowledge.

In the preceding remarks, we have used much repetition, but on so intricate a subject it is not easy to express one's meaning with the precision that is desirable. We will now turn our attention more particularly to that phase of vital power which, as conscious force, acting freely according to self-acquired knowledge, is known as *the will.* Much has been written on this subject, but very unsatisfactorily. The will and instinct are only different phases of the same special force, as this is also a phase of the same vital force which operates in organic functions. *Will* is the phase of vital force which is directed by acquired knowledge; as *instinct* is the same force directed by unconscious reason, or rather by reason of which it is unconscious. And thus it comes to pass, that according to the degree of knowledge, so is the freedom of the will: for knowledge is power; that is, the capacity of acting with corresponding efficiency. It is well known that as our knowledge of nature is enlarged so are we enabled to subject her forces, and make them subservient to our purposes: as is exemplified, in modern times, by numerous inventions; but more especially by those of the steam-engine and the electric telegraph.

This view greatly simplifies our notions concerning *man:* it shows that whilst he is the most exalted of natural beings, he is in no way disconnected therefrom, otherwise than in possessing the additional attribute of a rational consciousness. Even in the extreme case of man's responsibility to a higher power for his conduct, we do not see that dissimilarity between man and the brute, as is usually insisted on: of course, the morality of man is of a higher standard than that of the brute, in accordance with the superiority of his intellect; still, in their character, they are analogous, though not identical. Amongst domestic animals (we might perhaps have said among *all* animals, but we are not so well acquainted with the *feræ naturæ*) we see the laws of nature concerning self-preservation and property followed instinctively, as by man rationally: and likewise we have on record many instances which indicate an instinctive appreciation of social rights and wrongs. And when brutes have been trained up to perform certain actions, they learn submission to the *will* of their masters; so as to do their duty obediently, even when contrary to their inclinations: if they do so with docility, it is well with them; but if they obstinately resist, rebelling against authority, they are conscious that they have done wrong, and knowing the penalty for so doing, they strive to avoid the impending retribution. In short, man stands towards the brute *in loco Dei*, by a delegated power; or at all events by a power, which is the necessary consequence of his superior knowledge. Accordingly man frames laws for the conduct of his dependents; and instructs them therein, by such practical teachings as they are capable of understanding: and when the brute has learnt his duty, and the consequence of disobedience, man expects from him the same submission to his *will* that Deity demands from man under similar circumstances. Are we not then justified in maintaining, that even as regards morality, in relation both to society and to Deity, man is not perfectly insulated from the other works of creation: he differs from them, indeed, as a being of a higher order, enjoying accordingly greater liberty in the exercise of his more exalted condition; but he only differs in dgree: he possesses more attributes than any other natural being; but still he is a part of the same universal system.

Although the *will* is thus connected with other forces, its modes of operation are so various, so free, ond oftentimes so capricious, that the results of its action cannot be calculated upon with any degree of certainty: these actions may be recorded in tables of statistics, and the *data* derived therefrom may serve for abstruse calculations; but the results thereof will not be *truths,* but only *probabilities.* It is, therefore, evident that the phenomena in which such a force is concerned cannot be dealt with like those of the physical, and other unconscious forces; which are not free to choose the special rational guide of their actions, but always under given conditions act in a predetermined manner: if we can have a science of such phenomena, it must rest on very different principles, which cannot relate to what *is* and *must be;* but to what *may be,* and *ought to be:* and this will involve us in an entirely different field of knowledge than has hitherto engaged our attention.

There are three kinds of human knowledge; the absolute, the relative, and the contingent: the source of the first is supernatural, and can only be attained by Divine communication; that of the second is in nature, or rather in that part of nature which is regulated by fixed and immutable laws; whilst the last source arises in the free and variable actions of voluntary beings. Divine knowledge consists of perfect *truths;* natural knowledge, of reliable *facts;* whilst man-knowlege is concerned only with *probabilities,* which partake of the imperfections of all human inventions and institutions. If we frame *anthropological* sciences, they can only serve to show what the actions of man ought to be; and what indeed they would be, if his actions were regulated by the perfect laws which Divine wisdom has promulgated for the guidance of his will: would man but cheerfully submit to these laws, then his conduct would be as perfect, and as logically intelligible, as all the physical operations of nature; because then all natural forces, both voluntary and involuntary, would be governed by the rational laws of the Creator.

The moral sciences are, therefore, only possible when based on the principles divinely revealed; or on those natural principles, which are latently and passively operative in human nature, and of which we have frequent instinctive glimpses: both of which are fundamentally the same, though the latter are very obscure. In constructing such sciences, when we have determined the respective noun-substantive or principle, we cannot do better than fix our attention on the physical sciences and follow their guidance. As the motions of material bodies form the subject-matter of physics, so it will be found that the actions or conduct of voluntary creatures is the theme of moral science. Ethics, a well known and long established science, gives the name, and indicates the character of its contents phenomenally; but it does not point out the inner constitution of moral actions, nor the *modus operandi* by which the varied particulars of its universal are produced: in short, it does not deal with the science of morals in its causal, or, as we should say in physics, its physical aspect. Is then a moral action like a material motion; can it be a composition of forces? And if so, what are these forces and their reason-directing laws?

In the functions of an organism we found a dualism of forces, which could be formulated according to the archetypal correlations; thus:

Organic body + Vital force = Organic function.
Muscular force + Volition = Muscular action.
Material resistance + Muscular action = Locomotion.

Or, to sum up all the subordinates in a general expression,

Corporeal forces + Vital force = Organism,

the science of which is biology, and its branches physiology and psychology.

Now it is evident that Ethics ranges itself as a science parallel with Biology; and is, as we have said, the science of conduct; that is, of voluntary actions: but we have to seek for the forces concerned in producing the resultant, and of which they are the component parts; and therefore must be basic and typal correlatives. We can be at no loss to find the specific or typal force in the *will;* but its correlative is not so apparent: we are inclined to think that it can be no other than *sensation*, which, as appetite, affection, passion, or some other kind of sensation, is the *inducement* or *motive* which enters into concurrence with the *will*, in determining any particular conduct; and all these passive or basic forces may be classed together as *emotions.* So that the forces concerned in moral actions seem to be the *will* and *emotions*: the former the specific force, a phase of vital force; and the latter the basic or corporeal force of the dualism, which, therefore, can be no other than the highest function of organic being. The dualisms may be stated as: —

Emotion + Will = Conduct, or Moral action.

Had we followed the precedent of electricity and magnetism, we might have erected the moral forces into two distinct sciences; and in so doing we should have been also justified by the example of rational mechanics, as follows: —

Magnetism and Electricity.
Statics and Dynamics, branches of Cinematics.
Pathematics and Thelematics, branches of Ethics.

But we do not think it expedient, as already stated, to adopt the constituent forces as principles, on which sciences may be constructed: for the dualism or universal, which is the legitimate subject-matter of systematic knowledge, includes the forces and all that concerns them; which constitutes, indeed, the diversity in unity.

From what has been said concerning the forces engaged in moral actions, we are not to suppose that the personal acts and deeds which are associated with, or immediately follow voluntary determinations, are the subject of moral science; any more than locomotion, or any other muscular operation, can be referred to the forces concerned in the mental process of perception, which precede the bodily functions. The moral phenomenon is produced by the operation of the moral forces, and is as such manifested to the mental consciousness, and as knowledge may become the guide to direct certain corporeal actions or not, according to the desire of the will; just as in the case of ordinary sensational perceptions, it rests with the decision of the will whether this knowledge shall terminate in muscular activity or not: and hence it is that a breach of the moral law is as effectually accomplished by the conception of a sinful desire, as in the actual fruition of the lust. In the case of moral action, the conscious force or will is of a higher order of intelligence than in those sensational perceptions which are associated with the emotions of pleasure and pain; for it not only knows the present emotion, but it is also capable of judging of its tendency to *right* or *wrong*, in consequence of its knowledge, which is either intuitive or acquired according to its position in the scale of morality. In general the will is free and paramount, so that it may act or not, as it may choose according to its moral knowledge; but it is not absolutely so in all cases; for the *pathematic* force may be so intense and overpowering, as to usurp the ordinary dynamic position of the *will*, thus carrying all before it, and imparting its own character to the resulting act and deed. Thus a well-informed and regulated *will* controls and moderates the emotions, even when these springs of action are vehemently excited; whilst a less determined will, under the same circumstances, will be hurried away headlong by the passions. In short, in *ethics* as in *physics*, we must search in the character of the resulting actions for the relation which the constituent forces bear to each other; and according to their relative proportion, so is the aspect of the phenomenon.

It must not, however, be forgotten that the phenomena of *ethics*, like those of all other organic functions, are essentially vital or related to animated beings; and that in the performance of any of these functions there must be a motion from a nervous centre as well as to it; that there must be some kind of corporeal or organic force associated with some phase of vital force in every function of the creature; and that it is only through a knowledge of the functional phenomenon that we can gain an insight into the nature of the forces concerned therein: or, in other words, the forces are causes, and we can only know the latter by their effects, for such is the limited character of human knowledge.

The subject of ethics, taking this term in its largest signification, as including all moral actions, individual, social, and political, is exceedingly interesting; but it would require more space than we have hitherto occupied to impart our views thereon with any prospect of rendering our meaning intelligible. Happily, in the circumstances of the case, this is not necessary: for ethics, as an anthropological science, is so perfectly distinct from the philosophy of nature, that we can avail ourselves of this distinction to postpone its consideration. But before concluding, we cannot refrain from repeating, that though as a science *ethics* is so peculiar, yet it is still an essential part of the universal system; and that, though its principles are largely concerned in human affairs, they are not absolutely restricted to man: for as in man himself the laws of these principles are clearly foreshadowed in his natural estate; so are they fundamentally concerned in the constitution and instincts of conscious brute creatures.

CHAP. IX.

THE IDEAL SIDE OF NATURAL POWERS MANIFESTED AS FORMAL KNOWLEDGE: THE LOGICAL INTERPRETATION OF THE REASON IN NATURE.

The rational Forms of Nature give the fundamental Principles of the abstract Sciences.—System, or the classified Order of Degrees, the most abstract Idea of Nature.—The Knowledge of such a System is Science or Logic.—All the Sciences are based on the Principles of Logic.—The Definitions of Logic.—Aristotle's Dictum unjustly denounced.—Logic relates only to the Forms of Things, and not to Things themselves.—Logic, like all Sciences, formed by Induction; and functions by Deduction.—The Character of Genus and Species—Universals and Particulars—Extension and Intension.—A Proposition; and its Terms, the Subject and Predicate.—The various Kinds of Propositions.—The Syllogism—Its three Propositions, the Major Premiss, the Minor Premiss, and the Conclusion.—The cardinal Propositions; how symbolised.—The Quantification of the Predicate.—The Formulæ of Logic.—Application of Algebraic Notations to Logic.—That of Professor Boole not satisfactory, but his Suggestion important.—Conclusion.

HITHERTO our attention has been engaged in the consideration of natural beings as forces; which are made known to us, as actual realities, by the physical impressions which they make on the senses, whereby they become to us objects of knowledge. This, however, is a one-sided view of nature; these forces are not mere efficiencies, but reason-directed forces, which are a law unto themselves: and as we formerly considered the *forces* apart from their *reason,* we now purpose to direct our attention to the latter, to the ideal side of power; which, as formal principles, are capable of being known as abstract ideas.

In the foregoing survey we saw that, various and multitudinous as natural bodies are, they can be gathered together into characteristic groups, and so classified as to form one common system; and also, that probably this system of nature may be co-ordinated with another system of supernatural beings: but be this as it may, as regards natural bodies, the system of nature is a universal system; it is the highest generalisation of material things, a unity in diversity, and therefore capable of being unfolded into the most minute particulars.

On this systematic principle, each subordinate generic part of the whole may also be regarded as a universal, since it embraces everything of the same kind: so that as Cosmology is the knowledge of the system of nature, that is, of the highest natural universal; so the various natural sciences imply the knowledge of the particular or subordinate universals. Such sciences, however, as their respective names import, relate to forces, the real content of natural powers; or rather, to speak more correctly, they treat of the concrete powers, the realities themselves, though the *form*, by which knowledge only is possible, is concealed by the potential *content*, which is more prominently conspicuous: but when forces and their materialistic attributes are abstracted, we have only the ideal *forms* of nature remaining; the universals of which give the pure exact sciences, systems of fundamental principles.

"With all our admiration," says the late lamented Archer Butler[*], "for the energetic labours of the great

[*] Lectures on the History of Ancient Philosophy, vol. ii. p. 55.

naturalists of our day, and for the advances which the physical sciences are receiving through their combined exertions, we cannot refuse to see,—and in all quarters the conviction is gaining strength,—that the world of ideas is in proportion eclipsed. This huge material universe, with all its labyrinth of laws, seems to fetter and entangle us: we are so overwhelmed by weight and motion, that *matter* and *being* become equivalent terms; and we cannot allow the existence of a world to which these material attributes are not attached." These remarks were called forth on the contemplation of Plato's doctrine of ideas, the eternal laws and reasons of things. There is, however, some indistinctness concerning this doctrine as it has descended to us: but which, indeed, seems to have been original; for Plutarch maintained that the ideas of Plato were not distinct realities, but simply divine conceptions of order; whilst, on the other hand, Aristotle so understood these ideas, as to treat of them as true and real existences. At all events, this twofold aspect of things has always divided philosophy, according as the subject is regarded from the real or ideal point of view: thus, in the present day, some maintain that the world subsists only as ideal forms, manifestations of the thinking intellectual mind; whilst others regard the universe as a world of dynamical forces, functioning, according to laws, as cognisable phenomena.

According to our view of the subject, nature is a system of finite conditioned powers; and in this system alone can we look for *oneness*, which is not an *absolute*, but a diversity in unity or a universal. Each part of this system is a dualism of powers: a single natural power is not known to occur in an insulated or elementary state; and, indeed, probably cannot so exist out of relation with other powers. This combination of powers takes place only between those that are antagonistic: this mutual opposition occasions the limitation to which all natural forces are subject; and it explains why natural bodies can undergo internal changes, as well as those changes resulting from the concurrence of several bodies.

When we regard nature in its totality, as a system or classified arrangement of natural bodies; and by the mental process of abstraction, already considered, eliminate therefrom all the real *content* of co-ordinated *forces*, there only remains the *forms* of these bodies, the reason in nature, which is knowable to the human mind as the idea of order or system. This is the highest generalisation of abstract ideas; and it corresponds with the system of forces: both of which conjoined constitute the system of nature.

But what is system in itself or *per se?* It is the logical order of rational forms, the code of rational laws, which conjoined with specific forces, are powers. These forms of rational powers, when interpreted by the mind, are abstract ideas, pure formal knowledge: and the knowledge of the order, or system, of such forms, is systematic knowledge or pure science; science in itself, the science of the sciences, or Logic.

If we construct a science of a *special* abstract idea, pure science or logic, as the *summum genus*, must underlie and fashion it in all its parts: thus the science of *number* and of *space* are systems of their fundamental ideas; framed on definitions, postulates, and axioms by the logical method of induction; and functioning when thus constructed by deductive demonstrations. The only difference between these sciences and logic is, that some special idea is conjoined with the generic idea of system: thus arithmetic is the science or logic of number; as geometry is the science or logic of space. And so it is in the case of the physical sciences; the principle of order, or system, occurs in all; and, consequently, the science of this principle must be the universal basis on which all are founded: and thus it is that the pure formal sciences are applicable to all concrete knowledge; and therefore are so eminently disciplinary and propædentic.

Logic has of late years attracted considerable attention, having been rescued by several able writers from the contempt into which it had fallen, through the ignorant application of the syllogism. It is to be feared that there is still, with very many, an imperfect apprehension of the character and functions of logic: and this may in some measure be attributed to its being regarded not as a pure, but as an applied science; an art only useful in evolving conclusions by empirical formulæ from all premises whatever, not only from those which are based on statistical averages, but even from those which rest on the vaguest probabilities. Whereas logic can only function accurately and with certitude when its data have been firmly established by its own preparatory processes of induction; and until these premises have been obtained, the conclusions must frequently end in absurdities:—but such must be charged to the incapacity of the workman, and not to his instrument.

The uncertain position of logic cannot be better illustrated than by enumerating its various definitions, which have appeared in recent works on this subject; but we must rest content with three of standard authority. "Logic," says Archbishop Whately*, "is the science of reasoning." According to Mr. John S. Mill†, "Logic is the science of the operations of the understanding, which are subservient to the estimation of evidence; both the process itself of proceeding from the known to unknown truths, and all other intellectual operations, in so far as auxiliary to this." And lastly, Professor Thomson‡ says, "Logic is the science of the laws of thought:"—in some places he speaks of logic as "*pure* logic," and in others he prefixes the words "formal" and "necessary" to the laws of thought; but the simpler expression is the best.

Now it will not, we think, be disputed that *thought* is the product or result of the thinking faculty; and that it is, therefore, analogous to *motion*, which is the effect of a moving force; and if so, this analogy will enable us to express more clearly our comments on these definitions. The science of *motion* is Cinematics. Should we then define cinematics as the science of moving;—or as the science of the operations of moving, which are subservient to the estimation of the change in space, both the process itself of proceeding from a state of rest to motion, and all other moving operations in so far as auxiliary to this;—or lastly, that cinematics is the science of the laws of motion:—it would be evident that there is some deficiency in these definitions. There can be no hesitation in affirming that the ideas of *thought* and of *motion* imply an *opus operatum:* that the science or systematic knowledge of these compre-

* Elements of Logic, p. 1. † A System of Logic, vol. i. p. 11.
‡ Outlines of the Laws of Thought, p. 3.

hends not only their phenomenal appearance, but also the forces concerned therein, and the laws by which they operate. The author of "The Laws of Thought" must have been aware of this distinction, for he observes in another place, that "pure logic enounces the laws we must observe in thinking;" so then the laws belong to the *thinking agent,* and not to the *thoughts,* which result from the activity of the agent: in the above illustrations, therefore, the tentative and probationary definitions do not directly appertain to cinematics, but only mediately as comprising dynamics, the force and the laws of force; and so likewise, the definitions above quoted do not concern formal ideas or thoughts, but the cause, or thinking force, and the laws by which it is regulated when it functions.

When we contemplate nature, and make therefrom certain abstractions, we objectify them or make them objects of knowledge; and as such they become part of the mind, and subject to its conscious faculty: now this faculty is only a phase of vital force, one of the natural forces which act and react according to innate rational laws; but being also a self-conscious force, it is capable of knowing the logical methods which are followed in its rational operations; for whilst all other forces act *instinctively* and unwittingly, the mind, in its intellectual moods, acts voluntarily and *consciously.* Reasoning, therefore, is a free-will exercise of consciousness, according to an acquired knowledge of the rational laws which regulate the entire system of nature; an activity which must pervade all logical operations. But reasoning alone, or the exercise of the thinking faculty, does not give logic, but simply knowledge; nor is logic the formal ideas, but both are conjoined to make logic, which is the knowledge of such a system. The system of forms, therefore, furnishes the objective content of logic, whilst its subjective efficiency is derived from the mind. So that, whilst in the pure formal sciences the whole subject is concerned with abstract ideas, the mind engaged therein is regarded as merely an extraneous spectator, but it is not so; it is the logical mind that enables these abstractions to function according to logical laws, and without it there could be no science; just as in physics its rational laws could not become objects of knowledge unless manifested in phenomena, which are the operations of efficient forces.

If pure abstract system, or the system of abstract ideas, be the fundamental principle of logic, all such ideas can only be related to each other, in regard to the various degrees or order of the system: so that the objects with which logic is concerned are no other than the abstract terms of classification. These objects are successively developed in the process of generalisation; and as they are evolved it is requisite that they should be individualised by appropriate *denominations*, and clearly distinguished by accurate *definitions*. During this development their relations towards each other in respect to extension and intension become manifested as general principles, which, being briefly expressed, are known as *axioms*. And lastly, when the system is completed, and its modes of functioning *postulated*, it is available for the demonstration of many truths which were not discovered during its inductive formation: for this simple reason, that the colligation of a small number of cognate facts is sufficient to enable us to frame subaltern genera; and it is, therefore, possible by the inverse method of deduction to demonstrate those which had not been previously observed. In a sense, the *à posteriori* gathering together and arranging by induction may be called a progression from the known to the unknown; but the *à priori* extension of knowledge by deduction is more especially entitled to this attribute: for when once a science is perfectly established, it opens up boundless regions of truths; as witness the developments of the mathematics.

The transcendental logic of Kant has the pure abstract character which we have ascribed to it; for it is free from all special materials, and from every element of an empirical nature: it seeks to discover the *à priori* principles of the understanding; neglecting all derived and complex conceptions, it fixes its attention solely on the pure logical concepts. But Kant has confused his subject by mixing it up with the consideration of the mental faculties concerned in the production of pure concepts; phenomena which belong to psychology, and which have no concern with logic. It is curious that Cousin*, in commenting on this logic of Kant, whilst admitting the certainty of its *à priori* truths which within these limits make it an infallible science, remarks that "it is entirely void, having no relation to reality; and subject to such inherent weakness, that it can neither assure us of external reality, nor even the reality of our own proper personality." The same objections might be brought against any branch of the mathematics: it is strange that a science should be expected to explain subjects with which it has no concern.

* Lectures on the Philosophy of Kant, p. 76.

This shows, we think, that the character of logic is not rightly apprehended. Some modern writers have described this science as the geometry of thought; because the methods of the mathematics are so conspicuously logical: but, in truth, it is geometry which is the logic of space; for abstract its special *content*, universal extension, and its particular figurate magnitudes, that is its subject-matter or noun-substantive, and all that then remains is its rational *form*, which is logic.

Our definition of logic, that it is the knowledge of pure abstract system, the systematic knowledge of abstract ideas, or in short that it is science, accords very well with the opinion of Aristotle; in whose logic the principle of classification performs a prominent part. Mr. John S. Mill, in his work on logic, dwells long on this topic, and condemns in no measured terms the doctrine of the Stagyrite, as effete and valueless: as " a principle of reasoning suited to a system of metaphysics, once indeed generally received, but which for the last two centuries has been considered as finally abandoned; though there have not been wanting, in our own day, attempts at its revival."

The dividing things into classes, and referring every thing to its proper class is not, Mr. Mill thinks, the office of logic: and the maxim — that whatever can be affirmed or denied of a class may be affirmed or denied of everything included in the class, — the celebrated *dictum de omni et nullo,*— is, he asserts, " a signal example of logical error." On such a purely intellectual subject as this, is it not more probable that it is Mr. Mill, and not Aristotle, who is in error? We have no desire to unfairly criticise Mr. Mill's work on logic; it is a talented production, well calculated to promote scientific *investigation*, and to take a place side by side with the excellent "Discourse on the Study of Natural Philosophy," which indeed it greatly resembles: but it has not, in our opinion, any pretension to the character of a System of Logic.

A quotation will, perhaps, exonerate us from the charge of misrepresentation: for it will show how concrete and materialistic his notions are concerning logic, the whole content of which is *pure* and *formal:* or as some would say, transcendental. "The notion," says Mr. Mill*, "that what is of primary importance in a proposition, is the relation between the two ideas corresponding to the subject and predicate (instead of the relation between the two *phenomena* which they respectively express), seems to me one of the most fatal errors ever introduced into logic. The treatises of logic, produced since the intrusion of this cardinal error, almost always tacitly imply that the investigation of truth consists in contemplating and handling our ideas, or conceptions of things, instead of the things themselves: a doctrine tantamount to the assertion, that the only way of acquiring a knowledge of nature, is to study it at second-hand, as represented in our own minds." Surely in *logic*, we can have nothing to do with the things themselves: they are not the objects with which this science has any concern; if we desire knowledge thereon we must go to *physics*, and not to *logic*. Mental representations are certainly, in a sense, obtained at second-hand; but they do not originate in the mind by the exercise of a fanciful imagination: they are derived from

---

* A System of Logic, vol. i. p. 98.

nature herself; and though not actual *realities*, they are the rational *forms* of things themselves; and if rightly interpreted must correspond therewith. All nature is a dualism of actual *forces* and rational *forms;* and inasmuch as these are co-existent and co-equal attributes of their respective powers, they reciprocally manifest each other, as objects of knowledge: and each kind of objects may become the subject of distinct sciences; the one causal and phenomenal, as physics, the other pure and formal, as logic: the one is concerned with the real and subjective side of nature; the other with the ideal and objective.

In logic the mind is only conversant with those ideas which relate to degrees of order or system: and when it has become cognisant of these objects, it proceeds to their denomination, definition, and classification.

In the development of logic we first accept the ideas of concrete things presented by the senses, as if they were the things themselves, and we denote these *individual* things by names, which though mere mental forms, pass current as the counterpart of the things signified; in adopting such ideas, however, as logical objects, we deal not with the contents of things, but only with their forms. In the next place, we unite together many particular ideas, differing from each other only by some trivial or accidental properties, by some common bond of likeness; and thus we obtain an idea of higher order, and mark its degree by the name of *species*. By similar and analogous repetitions of this process, we acquire a knowledge of many different species; and by the same routine we collect the species into distinct groups, each of which has a common term of agreement, and such groups are called *genera* or classes.

And in like manner we can proceed step by step, colligating classes of the same degree into a new and higher order, until at last, by successive generalisations, we attain to the *summum genus* of the system.

Now each species or genus taken by itself, or abstracted from all higher relations, is a perfect unity or universal, consisting of, and capable of division into, subordinate parts; for by its very constitution it only exists as an aggregate of its subalterns. How many parts make up a universal, is unknown, they may be a select few or a great multitude; but this one thing is certain, they must all possess the same characteristic attribute. And so it comes to pass, that having united particular ideas into a universal, a complex idea, or proposition, is obtained; as $A + B = AB$, which is an identical proposition, in fact, a definition, for it gives the value of either side of the equation, even when converted. Or in other words, as well set forth by Lord Kames*, "The essence of a thing consists of these two parts; first, what is common to it with other things of the same kind; and secondly, what distinguishes it from other things of the same kind. The first is called the *genus* of the thing, the second its *specific difference;* a definition, therefore, must consist of these two parts. To frame, therefore, a definition of any logical idea, we must take the genus of the order in which it stands, and the specific difference by which it is distinguished from other species of the same genus. These two terms give a perfect definition."

A universal is by definition equal to all its parts; but

---

* Sketches of Man, book iii. sect. 4.

both extremes of these parts are indefinite: the smallest part, or individual, can only be posited as an indefinite *minimum indivisibile;* and the totality of the known parts is an indefinite *maximum divisibile,* which approximates to, but is never perfectly commensurate with the universal. Since logic underlies all systematic knowledge, it therefore follows that the same incertitude must belong to the *minima* and *maxima* of every science: and so likewise may be discerned in every science the same principles of *individuation, differentiation,* and *integration* as are concerned in the logical universal.

The universal, whether a *genus* or a *summum genus,* is a diversity in unity, which comprehends all its particular ideas; and the *infima species* in its relations to all the generic characteristics of the system possesses all their attributes, together with something peculiarly its own; or as otherwise expressed by Thomson*, " in the *summum genus* the intension is least, the extension greatest; in the *infima species* the intension is greatest, and the extension least." That is, the attributes of the constituent parts of the system are in an inverse ratio towards each other in the opposite extremes of the universal. From this it is evident that what is called *quantity* in logic is a definite degree of comprehension; the different quantities of ideas have reference to the extent of their signification, which depends on their position in the system. And *quality* in logic is the similarity or dissimilarity of ideas in respect to a certain term of comparison; and the possession or not of such quality makes them a member of, or excludes them

* Laws of Thought, p. 104.

from a given class. Whenever such a similarity is affirmed or denied, the statement of such a comparison of ideas is called a categorical proposition; such a proposition may be a simple expression, as in a definition, or it may be a complex statement comprising an involution of many ideas, which, however, must be reducible into, or accord with the regular formula. The ideas of which a proposition is composed are called its *terms*; the term affirmed or denied is the *predicate*, and that of which the predicate is affirmed or denied is the *subject* of the proposition. If the predicate affects the whole of the subject, the proposition is *universal*, if only a part of the subject, then it is a *particular* proposition; and so the proposition is said to be an *affirmative* or *negative* proposition, according to the character of the predicate. There are, therefore, four distinct kinds of propositions, the universal and the particular affirmative, and the universal and particular negative: as was clearly pointed out by Aristotle; and which we now see to accord well with the essential constitution of ideas, the interpreted *forms* of realities.

Attempts have been made to enlarge this number of propositions, but in vain: for *singular* and *indefinite* propositions are inconsistent with the nature of the logical system. A *singular proposition*, not having a general, but an individual term for its subject, is as the particular of an *infima species*, or the ultimate part of some whole, incapable, like all other *units*, of farther resolution; so that, if we predicate of it, it must be as an indivisible oneness. Again, an *indefinite proposition* is that whose subject has neither a universal nor a particular signification; a particular *quantity*, however, may be understood, but this is the only indefinite. Both these kinds of propositions are therefore superfluous; and indeed the four cardinal ones are capable of including all statements that are logically necessary.

Having thus briefly noticed a few of the leading topics of logic, there remains to say a few words about its *axioms* and *postulates*. As regards its axioms, or principles, they are the expressions of those fundamental relations which subsist between ideas, as parts of a system: they have, like the axioms of all other sciences, the form of self-evident truths; and on this account have been often undervalued. It is an axiom of logic, that a *universal comprises all its particulars:* for it is evident that in a classified arrangement, as long as division and subdivision can be carried on, all the parts resulting therefrom cannot exceed, or fall short of the whole. It is indeed but another mode of expressing the principle of classification; that a *summum genus* contains all its ordinated subalterns: and this principle is no other than that of logic itself: and so it comes to pass that logic being the universal basis of all the sciences, its principle is carried over to these; as we see its equivalent in the axiom of geometry, "the whole is equal to all its parts." Again, the axiom that, *terms which agree with a third term, agree with one another,* is but another expression for one of the principles of classification; viz., that things which are *connoted* by a common mark, are species of the same genus. And simple as this axiom is, it forms the basis of the syllogism, which, in all its legitimate moods, uses a *middle* term for ascertaining the relations of the *major* and *minor* terms. In short, logical axioms are the general expressions of principles, which have been evolved from, and are immediately connected with the very essence of systematic order.

Passing on then from definitions and axioms, it only remains to consider the logical postulates. The former relate to the knowledge of ideas as passive mental objects, or forms of reason; but the latter relate to the results, or conclusions evolved by the mental energy acting thereon, according to the laws of thought; a process by which the unknown become known, an important means for the advancement of knowledge. The *modus operandi* in this process, that is, the logical methods, are capable of being understood; but how the conscious faculty practically performs them we cannot tell; we therefore assume the possibility, and provisionally *postulate* that which cannot be demonstrated. The postulates of logic are, that the mind can so deal with ideas as to construct them into inductive and deductive propositions; that it can manipulate knowledge both synthetically and analytically: these are functions of the logical mind, and we acknowledge them as such; but we can no more explain how the mind performs them, than we can how it perceives ideas; and, mediately through them, the forms of things, the reason in Nature.

Induction deals with various terms, which it combines together into propositions; and these again into others of a higher generalisation; until it arrives at the most comprehensive proposition, which becomes the definition of the science. At any stage of this development, deduction may be employed by a reverse mode of operation; unfolding particulars, even such as were before unknown, from the general propositions. This latter process constitutes that of the syllogism: it consists of three, and only three propositions; viz. the *major premiss*, the *minor premiss*, and the *conclusion*. In the last-mentioned proposition, the subject is called the *minor term*, the predicate the *major term:* in the major and minor premises of the syllogism, the corresponding terms are compared with a common middle term, in order to judge of their agreement or disagreement; and on this account it was called by the older logicians the *argument*.

It has already been stated, that there are four kinds of propositions; and since there are three kinds also in each syllogism, all the possible ways of combining the four cardinal ones, (symbolised by A, E, I, O,) by threes, are sixty-four: but of these numerous moods but a small number are practically employed. The *figure* of a syllogism consists in the situation of the middle term with respect to the two extremes of the conclusion. Four kinds of figures have been described, but it is by many admitted that there are only three which are legitimate: and of these the first figure, in which the middle term is made the subject of the major premiss, and the predicate of the minor premiss, is by far the most definite; and to which Aristotle's dictum is immediately applicable. All valid arguments whatever may be reduced to one or other of these three figures; and probably even to the first alone, by aid of legitimate conversions.

Before quitting the subject of logic, there are some other matters connected therewith, which must not be passed over without remark.

The quantification of the predicate, which has been ably advocated by Sir. W. Hamilton and De Morgan, is virtually excluded from logic according to our view of its constitution: for unless we have greatly erred, logic is a pure formal science; capable, indeed, of application to other subjects, but in its own peculiar sphere it gives results of great certitude, like the mathematics. Hypothetical, conditional, and disjunctive syllogisms, are only tentative processes: the data deal only with probabilities; so that positive conclusions cannot be obtained. And so it follows that if we deal with such indistinct and indefinite data as the toto-partial, and the parti-partial negatives, we cannot expect to arrive at any decisive results. Such an inexclusive quantification of the predicate does not add to our knowledge; for to say that some individual idea is not some other individual idea of the *same* kind, is merely asserting that particulars of a universal are not identical; which indeed the very signification of the systematic term implies. Take, for example, any species, say man; and then to say that some individual, or *this* man, is not some other individual, or *that* man, would be making an unnecessary assertion; and surely such a parti-partial negation could furnish no datum for a syllogism: and if by any ingenuity it could be so employed, it would be a work of supererogation; for simple perception, or a knowledge of the meaning of the words used, would furnish all the necessary information. On this subject, Mr. William Thomson[*] remarks, " that in a list of conceivable modes of predication, the toto-partial and the parti-partial negatives are entitled to a place:"—we cannot concede even thus much, for in a pure science we have nothing to do with the

---

[*] Outlines of the Laws of Thought, p. 179.

possible, or the probable, but only with positive principles. Though not agreeing with him, in his deference of opinion to so high an authority, yet we accept his own deliberate opinion, that "a parti-partial judgment is spurious upon two grounds: it denies nothing, because it does not prevent any of the modes of affirmation; it decides nothing, inasmuch as its truth is pre-supposed, with reference to any pair of conceptions whatever."

All the figures of the syllogism have been symbolised by various schemes of notation: the most recent, and probably the best, is that of Sir W. Hamilton. It is not improbable that logic may hereafter be successfully treated by symbols, as in the case of algebra: for since its principles are so few and abstract, it ought to be practicable. Professor Boole has indeed published, a few years ago, an elaborate work on this subject; more particularly in reference to the theory of Probabilities: this we do not regard as a part of logic; though it is a subject to which this science, in common with the calculus, may be applied. He has not, we think, clearly apprehended and formulated the principles with which he commences; and of course the validity of the whole superstructure depends thereon: it is therefore requisite to state our reasons for arriving at this conclusion.

We have already given the formula $A + B = AB$, as illustrating the constitution of an idea, of a proposition, and indeed of any universal, whether *real* or *ideal*. Perhaps as the compound AB is not a mere *cumulation* of its constituents, but an actual union endowed with distinctive properties, it might have been more correct to have written $A + B = C$: but this does not indicate its composition, which in many cases, especially when the constituents vary in their relative proportions, is very desirable. A still greater objection may be made to it on account of its expression being different from that in mathematical usage; but of this hereafter.

De Morgan* objects to the formula $A + B = AB$, as "confounding the ideas of cumulation and combination: and thinks that the mathematician would stare at an equation $2 + 2 +$ addition $= 4$." It certainly would be monstrous: but for what reason the third particular, $+$ addition, is introduced, we cannot tell; for it is already satisfied by the *plus* symbol between the numerals. The sum, 4, is not a mere cumulation of 2 and 2; nor is water, as he seems to imply, a simple juxtaposition of oxygen and hydrogen: for they are severally a resulting compound, a *tertium quid*, very different in properties from either of their constituents.

In the construction of his logical notation, Professor Boole* commences by proposing " to represent the class of individuals, to which a particular name is applicable, by a single letter as x: and to extend the meaning of the term so as to denote even a single individual of a class." This is objectionable, for although the characteristic mark of any universal or class is possessed by each and all of its members, it cannot be used to represent a single individual of the class: if we find such a mark in an individual, it determines the *class*; but it will not denote the *individual*; this can only be done by appending to the class-

---

* Formal Logic, p. 49.
† An Investigation of the Laws of Thought, p. 28, *et seq.*

mark some discriminating particular. Every whole is indeed made up of lesser parts of the same kind; but these subordinates can only be distinguished from each other, as individuals, by special marks denoting their differences.

In continuation the Professor observes, " If an adjective *good* is employed as a term of description, let it be represented by a letter, as y, which comprehends all things to which the description *good* is applicable; *i.e.* all good things, or the class of *good things*. Let it farther be agreed that by the combination xy shall be understood that class of things to which the names or descriptions represented by x and y are simultaneously applicable." Concerning this mode of notation he adds, "It is not affirmed that the process of multiplication in algebra possesses in itself any analogy with that process of logical combination which xy has been made to represent; but only that if the arithmetical and the logical process are expressed in the same manner, their symbolical expressions will be subject to the same formal law." Again, "The expressions xy and yx equally represent that class of things to which their several members apply: hence we have $xy = yx$." This is advanced as the expression of the first law or logical principle: " which may be characterised by saying that the literal symbols are *commutative, like the symbols of algebra.* This reminds us of Fichte's psychological principle, ego = ego: and it is evidently inconsistent with the character of a class; for whether a class be simple as x or complex as xy, it is an entire whole, or universal, of that kind of things. In the case of individual things which have any one property in common, you may make such an equation; as, a pound of this is equal to a pound of that in *weight;* or, a yard of this is equal to a yard of that in *length:* but to say that the same kind of pound or yard is a pound or a yard, is a superfluous and unnecessary assertion.

In his method of evolving his second logical principle, he follows a process which seems to us very inconclusive. "As the combination of two literal symbols in the form xy expresses the whole of that class of objects to which the names or qualities represented by x and y are together applicable; it follows, that if the two symbols have exactly the same signification, their combination expresses no more than either of the symbols taken alone would do. In such a case, we should therefore have $xy = x$. As y is however supposed to have the same meaning as x, we may replace it in the above equation by x; and we thus get $xx = x$; or $x^2 = x$: which is, in fact, the expression of a second general law of those symbols, by which names, qualities, and descriptions are symbolically represented." This algebraical reasoning is correct as to form, but the assumed data are irrational, and therefore do not give a legitimate conclusion; the two symbols have not the *same* signification: take the things signified as pure abstract ideas of classes, still they are different and distinct classes, and therefore cannot be commutative. If we take the concrete ideas of the class *sheep,* and of the class *white,* which are adduced in illustration, it is perfectly unimaginable to conceive that the combination *white sheep,* expresses no more than *sheep,* or *white* taken alone would do; or that *sheep* and *white* have exactly the *same* signification, in direct contradiction to their respective definitions, and to the previous assumption, that sheep and white are distinct classes of things, and therefore represented by diverse symbols x and y.

"The symbols of logic," he says, are "subject to the special law $x^2 = x$. Now of the symbols of number there are but two, viz. 0 and 1, which are subject to the same formal law. We know that $0^2 = 0$, and that $1^2 = 1$; and the equation $x^2 = x$, considered as algebraic, has no other roots than 0 and 1. Let us conceive, then, of an Algebra in which the symbols x, y, z. &c., admit indifferently of the values 0 and 1, and of these values alone. The laws, the axioms, and the processes of such an algebra will be identical in their whole extent with the laws, the axioms, and the processes of an algebra of logic. Difference of interpretation will alone divide them." Upon this principle the method in the " Investigation of the Laws of Thought " is established.

But what, if our remarks above, on the evolution of the special law $x^2 = x$, have any foundation in truth; what then will become of the principle on which this formal logic is based? The data being invalid, the superstructure cannot stand. We doubt very much the propriety of introducing the symbols of number, 0 and 1, into the formulæ of logic: the signs $+$, $-$, and $=$, are quite legitimate; they are purely abstract and universal, and may be used in connection with a science so perfectly formal as logic; but 0 and 1 are numerals, and belong to arithmetic. If the symbol x represents in logic a particular class, such a symbol can undergo no other variations than are compatible with the notion of a class: whether this class be a universal or a genus, or whatever its degree of rank, it cannot be raised to any higher power by duplication; its attributes are not those of quantity, as in the case of numbers. A class is a whole, and it is indeed so far analogous to an integer number, that it can be divided and subdivided into many fractional parts; but as each particular class has not its like in the universe, as it is one individual thing, like a unit in arithmetic, it cannot function by multiplication.

Though disagreeing with Professor Boole concerning the formation of logical principles and their notation, we think that he has initiated a useful undertaking in his recommendation of the employment of symbols for the illustration of the processes of logic; and in our remarks on his work, it was only intended thereby to use it as a text, whereby our own views might be more clearly unfolded.

To sum up in a few words the result of our inquiry concerning logic, it may be stated, that it is science or systematic knowledge; that is, a knowledge of all abstract ideas relating to *degrees of order*, or system: and since such ideas are only obtained by the interpretation of the relations of bodies in the system of nature, in respect to their ranks in the hierarchy, the idea of *order* might have been adopted as the noun-substantive of logic, the science of order implying a systematic knowledge of order.

CHAP. X.

THE FORMAL SCIENCES, THE KNOWLEDGE OF IDEAL SYSTEMS.

The Mathematics—Sciences of Number, Space, and Time—Regarded as the Basis of all the Sciences; but this Character belongs to Logic. — The early Origin of the Abstract Sciences. — Arithmetic, the Science or Logic of Number. — Geometry, the Science or Logic of Space. — These Sciences might have been immediately derived from Logic.—What is Space ?—The Real and Ideal can only exist by and in each other.—Space not a *Vacuum*, but a *Plenum;* the *Form* of the *real* Content gives the Idea of Space.—Space an indefinite *Maximum*, not an Infinite.—The Subject of Geometry is universal Extension, and all particular or subordinate Parts of Extension.—Of Space and partial Spaces.—What is Time?—Various Conjectures thereon.—No beginning and no ending of Time; but a continuous flowing onwards.—All Events occur in Time.—Time goes on whether Anything happens or not.—Time one of the extrinsic Relations of Existence—Conceivable only as an indefinite Past, Present, and Future.—The formal Succession of Events gives the Idea of Time.—The Analogies between Space and Time.—What is the Science of Time ?—Not Rational Mechanics, nor Rational Arithmetic; but a special Science, Chronometry.—Conclusion.

LOGIC is *par excellence* Science;—the *summum genus* of knowledge, which only needs the adjunct of some differential idea, in order to constitute a specific science:—such differential ideas, if pure abstractions, as those of number, space, and time, give sciences which are universal, inasmuch as their subjects in general apply to all natural phenomena; and which sciences, being well adapted as preliminary disciplines, have been called the mathematics.

The abstractions, on which the mathematical sciences rest, are fundamental principles, or noun-substantives, arrived at by the contemplation of natural objects: but although our knowledge of them has been arrived at *à posteriori*, there can be little doubt that the rational forms previously existed, as the reason in nature, before they were interpreted by us as universal and necessary truths. It was not possible for us to know these truths *à priori* by a species of intellectual intuition; indeed it yet remains to prove that we possess such a faculty: but when once they have been logically evolved from concrete ideas, we can then trace their germs in the universal system of ideas, as clearly as in the system of natural realities; so that from the principles of logic alone it might be possible to obtain them by an *à priori* process; as we will endeavour to show in the sequel.

It must not, however, be kept out of sight that our notion of logic is not that which ordinarily prevails. "The mathematics," says Comte,* "by itself in its abstract purity, signifies *science:* the Greeks had no other, and we may call it *the* science; for its definition is neither more nor less (if we omit the specific notion of magnitudes) than the definition of all science whatsoever; for all science consists in the co-ordination of facts." Again, "The abstract portion of the mathematics is the only one which is purely instrumental, it being simply an immense extension of natural logic to a certain order of deductions."

---

* Positive Philosophy, vol. i. p. 39.

These statements confirm our assumption that logic is *the* science: for abstract the specific notion of magnitudes from the mathematics, and there remains only logic, the knowledge of systematic ideas. In another place, however, Comte has defined the object of the mathematics to be the indirect measurement of magnitudes; or, to determine magnitudes by each other, according to the precise relations which exist between them: it is evident that if the idea of magnitude be omitted from these definitions, there is no objective content, and therefore there can be no relations; but on our view, there remains a content in the idea of systematic order.

It is a curious circumstance, that the most abstract sciences are those which were first constructed: thus logic, arithmetic, and geometry were known to the ancients, but not, chronologically, in their rational order; whilst the natural or concrete sciences are the discoveries of modern times. In the contemplation of nature, it must, at a very early period, have struck the observer, that its objects were of different kinds, very numerous, and greatly diversified both in size and figure: but it was long before these conceptions were distinguished by the general and abstract names of *classes, multitudes,* and *magnitudes;* and still longer before, by abstraction, the ideas of *order, number,* and *space* were determined, and posited as universals, the noun-substantives of the mathematics. We have already dwelt at some length on logic; and we now proceed to make a few remarks on the sciences of number and space: many novel observations thereon cannot be expected.

The *summum genus* of arithmetic is the universal, the sum total or totality of all particular integral numbers, and their respective fractions: and the knowledge of this universal is the science or logic of number. So that the idea of arithmetic, when analysed, gives a numeral *content* and a logical *form;* and when it functions, it is the subjective logical mind which operates on the objective numbers, according to its rational laws: generalising, in one direction, by the inductive method, until all the enumerations of the system have been completed; and effecting calculations in another direction by deduction, a process of *ratioing,* by which the relative value of particular sums is demonstrated. The latter method is the ultimate object of the science; the results of its operations are called calculations; and when used we are said to calculate. We have remarked, that the mathematics might possibly have been derived *à priori* from logic, independent of the system of natural realities; and in the first place we will endeavour to show how this holds good in the case of arithmetic: when naturally derived, it takes place by the abstraction of the idea of numbers from the multitude of surrounding objects; but when logically derived, it is by observing the process of synthesis, by which idea is added to idea, until the entire system of ideas is constructed. A system or classified universal, is a diversity in unity, consisting of many subordinate degrees of order, all rising one above another in value: and the contemplation of such a whole and of its parts varying from each other by regular increments, might have suggested the idea of number, as readily as the multitudes of natural objects: and this idea once secured, the process of enumeration would soon follow; for as the individual is the *minimum* degree of order, so is the unit that of number; and as the species consists of many similar individuals, so each digit is composed of a definite number of units; and so on. Likewise in the case of geometry,—the logical universal gives the idea of the greatest comprehension containing the whole array of subordinate ideas; whilst the limits of each inferior subaltern become successively more and more contracted in respect to the extent of their application: and this idea of limitation, the variation of extension from the highest to the lowest degree of order, is very near akin to the notion of expanse or extension of space. But it must be confessed that knowledge obtained on the realistic side, by noting the dimensions and figures of natural bodies, is a more satisfactory foundation for geometry.

The particular objects of which geometry treats, are the limited forms or figurate magnitudes of space. Now space in its totality, or universal space, is the expanse or extended *form* of the universe, mentally abstracted from all the material contents, or realities, of the system of nature: and if universal space be only an abstract, or *formal* extension, all particular spaces must partake of the same character; and thus we conceive of them as *breadthless* lines, *depthless* surfaces, and *voluminous* figures, *void* of all material content. " By the character of our mind," remarks Comte*, "we are able to think of the dimensions and figures of a body in an abstract way; and we thus obtain an idea of space. This abstraction is now familiar to us; and we cannot conceive of any space, filled by any object, which has not at once volume, surface, and line."

It is usual to speak of space as something *sui generis*,

---

* Positive Philosophy, vol. i. p. 87.

actually existing; a something, or rather a somewhere, in which bodies have been placed; it is admitted that bodies are, chronologically, before space in the order of thought; because we can only conceive of space as the *place* occupied by bodies; yet logically it is supposed to be prior, as a place provided for the reception of created bodies. We are disposed to reject this interpretation *in toto*, as inconsistent with the constitution of the universe. Space is, to us, not an actuality *per se*, nor is it a mere capacity for receiving bodies about to be called into existence: it is only the *form*, the abstract plan or design, of natural bodies, which their forces assume under the influence of their innate rational laws; the real and ideal being co-existent and inseparable, and only capable of existing by and in each other. Space, then, has no actual existence apart from bodies; it is only the modal *forms* of their extension; we may logically insulate these forms by abstraction, and call them *spaces*, and the totality of such *space*, universal space; and thus these abstract ideas may become the objects of knowledge.

This view of the subject will not, of course, be acceptable to those who regard interstellar space, in which celestial bodies are contained, as void of all content: but if it be admitted, as there is every reason to believe, that space is not a *vacuum* but a *plenum* of a material fluid, or ether; then, it is not so difficult to conceive, that it is the idea which arises in our mind of the extended *form* of universal existence which constitutes space.

There is yet another point concerning space, in which we are not in accord with the general opinion. Space is not only spoken of as *infinite*, which in its mathematical sense seems rather to mean indefinite, but also as *absolute:* we proceed to give our reasons for thinking both these terms objectionable.

"Space," observes Whewell*, "is not indeed an object of which we perceive the properties, but a form of our perception; not a thing which affects our senses, but an idea to which we conform the impressions of sense." This we accept as sound doctrine; but we cannot assent to the following. "When we speak of spaces, we understand by the expression, parts of the one and the same identical everywhere extended space. We conceive a universal space, which is not made up of these partial spaces, as its component parts, for it would remain if these were taken away; and these cannot be conceived without presupposing absolute space." This statement seems to involve a contradiction: in one place it affirms that spaces are parts of one and the same space; and in another, that universal space is not made up of partial spaces, for it would remain if these were taken away. This is so inconsistent with the maxims, "that a thing cannot be, and not be, at one and the same time;" and "that the whole is equal to all its parts,"—that we cannot but suspect some inadvertence has occurred in the statement. If particular spaces are parts of one and the same space, the latter is necessarily a logical universal; that is, a *genus* made up of *species:* now take away the species, and the genus must be annihilated; for the parts make up the whole. As we view the subject there can be no annihilation; but it may be objected, that spaces are pure ideal forms, or

---

* Philosophy of the Inductive Sciences, book ii. chap. iii.

abstractions, the mere creations of the mind, and must not therefore be conceived of as actual existences: we answer, that in the case of forces a perfect conservation is admitted; and forces and their correlative forms are indissolubly conjoined in actual realities, or natural beings; if you can take away any partial spaces from universal space, you must at the same time annihilate some portion of natural bodies; for the universe of forces, and the universe of rational forms conjoined, make up the natural universe or system of nature. We can, indeed, conceive of universal space, as a whole, apart from its subordinate parts, and connote it by the generic attribute of extension; and we can conceive of its parts, as all possessing this common attribute, and something more, which make them specific objects of knowledge: but we cannot conceive any of these parts taken away, and yet that universal space would remain intact.

"Absolute space," continues our author, "is essentially one: and the complication which exists in it, and the conception of various spaces, depends merely upon boundaries. Space must, therefore, be not a general conception abstracted from particulars, but a universal mode of representation, altogether independent of experience. Space is infinite. We represent it to ourselves as an infinitely great magnitude. When we say that all bodies and particular spaces exist *in* infinite space, we use an expression which is not applied, in the same sense, to any cases except those of space and time." Now what has been said concerning space as a universal, shows that it cannot be an *absolute* in its usual metaphysical sense: for it is made up of particulars; and an absolute has no such relations. We do not think that such an idea is very applicable to space, which is the formal extension of finite and conditioned existences. Lastly, concerning partial spaces our author remarks, " As space limited by *boundaries* gives rise to various conceptions of *form* or *figure*, every possible form of line, straight line and curve, and of curves an endless number, circles, parabolas, hyperbolas, spiral helices; and plane surfaces of various shapes, parallelograms, polygons, ellipses; and solid figures, cubes, cones, cylinders, spheres, spheroids, and so on:—all these figures have their various properties, depending on the relations of their boundaries; and the investigation of their properties forms the business of the science of geometry."

"Instead of adopting," says Comte[*], "the inadequate account of geometry, that it is the science of *extension*, I am disposed to give, as a general description of it, that it is the science of the *measurement of extension*. Even this does not include all the operations of geometry, for there are many investigations which have not for their object the measurement of extension. But regarding the science in its leading questions as a whole, we may accurately say that the measurement of lines, of surfaces, and of volumes, is the invariable aim, sometimes direct, though oftener indirect, of geometrical labours."

The definition of geometry as the science of space is simpler, and we think preferable: for the idea of space includes everything relating to extension,—all varieties of figures; and all these spaces may be dealt with, both inductively and deductively; and when by the latter process

---

[*] Positive Philosophy, vol. i. p. 86.

their ratios are determined, it is called mensuration. It is not necessary to mention these circumstances in a definition of the science; for the very fact of its being a science implies all this: for every science has a phenomenal and a causal aspect, under each of which the subject-matter of the science must be considered.

The definitions, postulates, and axioms of geometry are so well developed, and so generally known, that we need not dwell thereon; the few remarks which we have to make, not being a proficient in the mathematics, require some apology. But the very fact of this deficiency is perhaps no disqualification for such an undertaking; because an accomplished geometrician would be amongst the last to call in question, and discuss the principles of his science: he has received them, as established data, and found them adequate for all his purposes; and therefore he does not concern himself with their origin or filiations. But our attention being more particularly directed to such subjects, we notice, in comparing geometry with other sciences, that there are some points, more particularly those relating to the totality and unit of extension, the *maximum* and *minimum* of space, which require consideration.

Universal space comprises within itself all particular spaces; it is the system which is equivalent to all its parts, and therefore it must be co-extensive with the whole field of geometry: we, perhaps, lay undue stress upon this point; but if the definition of geometry, as the science of space, be correct, it is requisite that more particular allusion should be made to the fundamental idea of space, than is done in works on this science. Space in its totality is, like all other universals, indefinite in quantity: all we know of it is, that it is a *maximum*, including all ideas relating to space; and all that we can predicate of the *minimum* of space is, that it is an indefinite, but indivisible unit. The extremes of all universals are beyond the limits of our knowledge; this character of the *maximum* seems to be the source of our idea concerning a *limit*, a near approximation to a given integer, but in no instance a perfect integration. It is a curious coincidence that, when we endeavour to form some notion of the figure of universal space, with common consent we imagine it to be that of a sphere; and the sphere of all figures is that which will not admit of absolutely precise measurement; and therefore we are obliged to rest content, in both cases, with the axiom that "what is true up to the limit is true at the limit."

The indefinite *minimum* or unit of space is called a *point*. A point, say geometers, has no dimensions; we maintain that it has, though inappreciably and indefinitely small. According to Euclid, a point is *that which has no parts or which has no magnitude:* but Dr. Simpson has proposed to substitute for this definition,—a point is *that which has position but not magnitude;* objecting to the definition of Euclid, that it asserts only a negative, and is not convertible. But we think that Euclid's is the better of the two: but both are defective, for both ignore the fact that a point is a part of space, and as such, must possess the generic character of the universal, which is extension; and as a matter of course, or of necessity as it is termed, being a part it must have some position in the whole.

A point rightly occupies a very prominent place in the

definitions of geometry; but if we are correct in regarding geometry as the science of space, the definition of space as the subject-matter should have precedence of all: and all that follow ought to be so expressed, as to show their relations thereto. Space is the *formal* extension of the universe. The idea of extension is the generic character or noun-substantive; and therefore all ideas relating to space, all parts or species of this universal, whether large or small, must have some degree of extension: so that a *point*, which all admit has position in space, cannot be devoid of extension; but as a unit of space, it must have a minimum degree of magnitude with all its properties, though inconceivably minute. On this view, we can understand how a point may have *position* in space; but if it has no magnitude, no extended form, there can be no *locus standi* for it; for a position implies the appropriation of some part of space, and such is a partial space for which we are contending. A point, then, is not a *nonentity*, but a formal *magnitude*; and as such it may be represented in practical geometry by a definite figure. These remarks may be deemed hypercritical: but if rigid precision be in any case requisite, it surely must be so in the definitions of a pure exact science.

For these reasons we venture to suggest the substitution of the following definitions for the corresponding ones of Euclid: premising ours concerning space.

Space is the *formal* extension of the universe.

A point is a unit of space, a minimum magnitude known only by its position.

A line is a continuous series of points, having only one appreciable dimension, length or direction in space.

A superficies is a partial space, a magnitude of two dimensions, length and breadth.

A solid is a partial space, capable of being known in all its dimensions of length, breadth, and thickness.

What we are desirous of calling attention to by these remarks, is that all particulars must be related to their universal: and since this universal is the systematic oneness of space (which is the ideal interpretation of the formal expanse or extension of nature), the idea of magnitude, unknown or known, should enter into the consideration of all partial spaces.

Having advanced thus far, step by step, in the investigation of abstract ideas of the highest generalisation, the progress so far has, in some measure, proved to be satisfactory. But the next step, though it still furnishes us with an idea which holds a distinct co-ordinated position in the hierarchy of ideas, involves us in some uncertainty; and consequently occasions much perplexity in its treatment. The idea of *time* is usually regarded, and frequently alluded to, as a fundamental principle, analogous to that of space and of number: but its precise nature and origin, and its science (for there ought to be one based on such a noun-substantive), have not as yet been satisfactorily determined.

What is time? This is a question that has been as often asked as What is science? There have been many answers given, but they are far from satisfactory. It has been said, for instance, that time is a mode of duration, a permanence of existence, a succession of ideas, a numerical sequence or rhythm, and a condition of the sensory: but neither of these statements is very intelligible; and their variety is very perplexing. According to Bishop Gleig *, "Time must be one of three things: either an ideal succession itself; or a certain quality inherent in all objects; or lastly, the relation of co-existence between things that are permanent, and the trains of fleeting ideas which succeed each other in the imagination." And in giving the preference to the last, he states his reasons for objecting to the others, as follows: "It is not the first of these, for in every train of thought one idea occupies no more part of time than a mathematical point occupies in space. Ten thousand such points would make no part of a line; and ten thousand ideas, made to coalesce, would not give any part of time. A point is a boundary of a line, but no part of it: the occurrence of an idea is instantaneous; and an instant is the boundary, but no part of time. Hence a train of ideas, being instantaneous, cannot constitute duration or time. And secondly, that time is not a quality inherent in all objects is likewise obvious; for were ideas as permanent as objects, the notion of time would never have been acquired." These different views, such as they are, being disposed of, there remains the accepted notion, "that time is the relation of co-existence between things that are permanent, and the trains of fleeting ideas which succeed each other in the imagination." It is not easy to know precisely what is meant by this statement. The succession of thoughts in the mind correspond with, and denote a series of periods of time; just the same as the progress of bodies through a series of positions in space: but what the relation is between a train of ideas and things that are permanent, we cannot understand.

* Encyclo. Britan., article Metaphysics.

THE KNOWLEDGE OF IDEAL SYSTEMS. 287

"Time," says Whewell*, "is not a notion obtained by experience. Experience, that is, the impressions of sense and the consciousness of our thoughts, gives us various perceptions; and different successive perceptions considered together exemplify the notion of change. But this very successiveness presupposes that the perceptions exist in *time*. That things happen together, or one after another, is intelligible only by assuming time as the condition under which they are presented to us. Thus time is a necessary condition in the presentation of all occurrences to our minds; we can conceive *time* to go on, while nothing happens in it: but we cannot conceive anything to happen while time does not go on. Time always is, and always is present; and even in thought we cannot form the contrary supposition. Thus *time* is something distinct from the *matter* or substance of our experience; and may be considered as a necessary form which the matter (experience of change) must assume, in order to be an object of contemplation to the mind." Again, "we conceive all particular times to be parts of a single and endless time: and this continually flowing and endless time is what offers itself to us when we contemplate any series of occurrences: all actual and possible times exist as parts in this original and general time. Time is infinite. All limitation merely divides, and does not terminate the extent of absolute time. Time has no beginning and no end; but the beginning and end of every other existence takes place in it."

Sir W. Hamilton † regards time as one of the extrinsic

* Philosophy of the Inductive Sciences, vol. i. p. 121.
† Philosophical Discussions, p. 581.

relations of existence; a quantity which may be considered either as continuous or discrete. "Considered in itself," he says, "time is positively inconceivable, if we attempt to construe it in thought; either, on the one hand, as absolutely commencing, or absolutely terminating; or, on the other, as infinite or eternal, whether *ab ante* or *a post:* and it is no less inconceivable, if we attempt to fix an absolute minimum, or to follow out an infinite division. It is positively conceivable; if conceived as an indefinite past, present, or future: and as an indeterminate mean between the two unthinkable extremes of an absolute least, and an infinite divisibility; for thus it is relative."

The foregoing quotations demonstrate a perfect analogy between the ideas of time and of space. Time as a formal succession is a universal idea, comprising all particulars of the same character: on the principle that a whole is equal to all its parts. We need not therefore dwell thereon; nor on the incompatibility of the ideas of the infinite or absolute in connexion with this subject, as changing time into *eternity*, which has no relation to the past, present, and future of sublunary affairs: for what has already been said of space is equally applicable to time. Since then the formal *extension* of things furnishes the idea of space; and the formal *succession* of events, that of time; we may arrive at many particulars concerning time, by following out its analogy to space, and of course making the requisite allowances for the different character of the ideas.

Thus, in space, extension is regarded as a magnitude having the dimensions of length, breadth, and depth; and so in time, succession is a duration comprising the periods of beginning, continuance, and ending. Likewise, as the parts of extension are figurate magnitudes, or figures, having position in space; so the parts of succession are events having occurrence in time. So particular figures in regard to magnitude are points, lines, surfaces, and volumes; as particular events in their duration are instants, sequences, and periods. And lastly, as particular figures in respect to their position in space may be viewed as inferior, collateral, and superior: so particular events in the occurrence of time, are antecedent, contemporaneous, and subsequent.

Time, therefore, like space, being a universal and fundamental idea, we ought to be able to construct thereon a science analogous to geometry: and such a science should treat of the duration of events, as geometry does of the magnitude of figures; for diversified periods of successive events make up the continuous duration which we call time. Time is a universal of indefinite duration; it is the ideal expression of the total period which marks the vicissitudes of the system of nature: it is an abiding continuance, as long as this universe lasts, just as space is a limiting expanse under the same condition. Time and space, therefore, as the relative forms of natural realities, are possible objects of human knowledge; but when they merge into eternity and infinity, they transcend our ken, for to the *finite* the *absolute* is incomprehensible.

What, then, is the science of time? On the continent, and more especially in Germany, this science is regarded as identical with rational Mechanics, but the most prevalent in this country is that it is rational arithmetic. "There are certain principles," says M. Cousin [*], "that

[*] Lectures on the Philosophy of Kant, p. 52.

are derived from our notion of time: for example, time has but one dimension; different times are successive and not simultaneous. If therefore these spring from the idea of time, this idea must be a pure *à priori* intuition; it is the foundation of our notions of change and motion, which is the change of place. Now we have an entire science which treats of motion; and its propositions, like those of geometry, are *à priori* synthetical: so that mechanical science is founded upon the idea of time, as geometry is founded upon that of space." This reason is not we think conclusive. It is indeed true that motion is one kind of change, viz. that of position in space; but it does not include all kinds of changes, as for example the chemical and vital: and so far from mechanical science being founded on the idea of time, this idea is only concerned as one of the elements in the calculation of velocities, which is but one of the mechanical phenomena.

On this subject Whewell* observes, "It is clear that the perception of motion, that is, change of place, presupposes the conception of time, and is not capable of being presented to the mind in any other way. If we contemplate the same body as being in different places at different times, and connect these observations, we have the conception of motion, which thus presupposes the necessary conditions that existence in time implies." Time is indeed an indispensable element in the consideration of the velocity of motion; it is a conception which must necessarily have been formed previous to the development of the science of motion, for it is one of the instruments,

---

* Philosophy of the Inductive Sciences, vol. i. p. 123.

of which geometry and arithmetic are others, which are requisite for determining the value of its phenomena; time therefore, as Whewell says, is a necessary condition: but it is not the noun-substantive of cinematics, for it is not the generic characteristic, which unites all parts of the science, and forms their most prominent feature.

" The relations of position and figure," says Whewell, "are the substance of the science of geometry: there is in like manner a science of great complexity and extent, which has its foundation in the idea of time. But this science, as it is usually pursued, applies only to the conception of number, which is, as we have said, the simplest result of repetition. This science is theoretical arithmetic, or the speculative doctrine of the properties and relations of numbers." Now this notion is, we conceive, far less reasonable than that which makes the science of motion and of time identical: we state our opinion freely, and subject to correction; but truth is our common object, and in the pursuit of it there should be no undue deference to authority. We therefore venture to suggest that any number, or sums of numbers, can be apprehended without entertaining the idea of time, or concerning ourselves with the successive addition of units, by which the digits and other numerals are formed. The most complex properties of numbers are arrived at by a prolongation of the rational process, similar to that which is used in the formation of elementary propositions: in short, theoretical arithmetic is only a higher branch of the logic of number, or Arithmetic. We can note the succession of our pulse and breathing, or any external succession, without concerning ourselves about their number: but if we desire to compare any of these successions with each other, or with any other known succession, in respect to their frequency, then we call in the assistance of another idea, that of number, and by means thereof render our knowledge more definite. We might in truth mark the frequency of these successions in various ways, so that by sight alone we might apprehend their difference without any numeration, as by several *pendula* vibrating at different rates: and so, likewise, we know the progress of time by mere inspection of the dial, without any conception of number engaging the mind. It is true that in calculating, the operations of the mind, like those of any other agent, are successive events in time: but time continues to flow on without any reference to the number of these events; or whether the mind evolves therefrom the idea of number, and by means thereof proceeds to their definite enumeration. Number then has no concern in the succession of events, which we denote by the word time: it is itself only an idea evolved from the objective form of such successions, by the operation of the subjective mind; and of which noun-substantive perfectly distinct from the idea of time it forms the special science of number.

Time, like number, is a universal or fundamental idea: it is, however, inferior to it in logical order; for arithmetic is required, as an instrument for the definite expression of its phenomena; as it does also that of space in case of its geometric or figurative representations. In short, time is a distinct idea *sui generis*, which cannot therefore be identified either with the ideas of motion or of number: and its science is neither that of rational mechanics, nor of rational arithmetic, but is peculiar, a systematic knowledge of its own idea. Such a science might be called chronology, the logic of time: but this term has already been appropriated to denote the knowledge of past events, the history of all known times. A science of time should comprise all parts of universal time; past, present, and future: whatever periods of time have occurred, or may occur hereafter, ought to find their positions in such a system. As particular magnitudes, in geometry, have definite figures which become the means of measuring others, and of thus enabling us to determine unknown magnitudes by those already known: so the various events, which have durations of known periodicity, are made the standards for determining the periods not only of past events, but also of predicting, by a scientific prevision, the character and duration of events yet concealed in the womb of futurity.

The science of time may be called *chronometry* in order to maintain in it the idea of measurement, which is involved in the term geometry: such a term may perhaps be confounded with the art of making chronometers; but this would be more than compensated for, by avoiding the introduction of an entirely new term. *Chronometry* may be defined the science of time, a systematic knowledge of the succession of events: its highest function would not be either calculation or mensuration, for these belong to other sciences; it would be *prediction*, the determination of future times, by a logical deduction of those partial times already known.

The whole range of such a science must be strictly confined to a knowledge of the duration of events; of what has come to pass, of what is present, and of what may happen hereafter: and in the consideration of such occurrences, their duration, and all relating thereto, is all that we are concerned with; we have nothing to do with the events themselves, as to what they appear to be, or as to what they are in reality; just as in geometry, the abstract forms, and not the bodies themselves, are the legitimate objects of the science. So in the contemplation of the universe, in respect only to the abstract forms of its fleeting events, we perceive that they are in a continuous flux or progression: whilst we are yet considering a passing event, the instant of time in which it occurred is present no longer, but has become part of the past; which will disappear in the abyss of oblivion, unless preserved in the records of history. Some events are momentary, others have various degrees of duration; whilst others, whatever be the lengths of their duration, return again and again in regular series of periodicity. All these take place, side by side, in an antecedent, contemporaneous, or subsequent order, but all are part and parcel of universal time; which flows on, as the duration of the universe, in one continuous current, whether partial events cease, or whether man, who is one of these events, is conscious or not of the progression. The idea of time is only a rational idea or conception of this duration of the universe; which duration is the formal condition of continuous existence, and which will abide as the rational form of succession as long as the universe endures.

CHAP. XI.

THE KNOWLEDGE OF CAUSATION, THE SCIENCE OF PHENOMENAL VICISSITUDES.

Introduction: On the Character of Abstract Science.—Arithmetic, Geometry, and Chronometry only concerned with the *exterior Forms* of Things : but variable Phenomena depend on the *inner* Constitution of Things.—Causes must be searched for below the Surface of Things.—Rational Mechanics only treats of Motion—The Science of Energetics has been proposed as more comprehensive.—A Science required, capable of treating of all Changes, physical, chemical, and vital.—Rational Mechanics, a Branch of such a Science.—The proposed Science of Substance or Hypostatics.—Substance, a pure abstract Idea of Matter, its Attributes those of Quantity and Quality; a Composition of Causes, the abstract Idea of Forces.—Its Definitions, Postulates, and Anxioms. The particular Sciences related to the universal Science of Hypostatics.—Cinematics, the Science of Motion.—Statics and Dynamics.—The Idea of *Vis-inertiæ.*—All Motions Compositions of moving Causes. — Remarks on the Laws of Motion. — Combination, a Kind of Change, gives the special Science of Rational Chemistry or Chemics.—Organisation, another Kind of Change, gives Rational Physiology or Organics. — Conclusion.

ACCORDING to the statements of the last chapter, a pure science is the knowledge of some formal system; the body or content of such a system is an abstract idea of the highest generalisation; and the actuating, or efficient principle of this system is the conscious faculty. The mind obtains the materials by the interpretation of the reason in nature; with which it constructs the system, and then by its logical methods, which it possesses in virtue of its being a conscious part of this self-same reason, it causes the system to function in the elaboration of divers intellectual phenomena.

The laws of thought, the axioms of logical operations, are the types of all natural laws; which indeed necessarily follows if our former conclusion be accepted, that mind is only the highest development of organic existence: for thus being a part of nature, which is made up of dualistic powers, it is subject to the same laws; and being self-conscious, it is capable of becoming acquainted with the reason in nature, as systematic knowledge. Nature itself, with all its varieties of conditioned material beings, is essentially a hierarchy of natural powers; in which all these powers are related to each other according to their degrees of rank. Since, however, every power is twofold, (or one pair of co-existent and co-efficient attributes, potency and reason,) nature assumes a different aspect according to the point of view from which it is regarded. We have already treated of nature as a system of forces, that is, on the potential side; and also as a system of rational or logical forms; but the latter consideration, on the ideal side, has not yet been completed.

We have already seen that in the contemplation of nature, when all its real content, that is, its forces, are abstracted, the ideal form of system alone remains, the knowledge of which is called science, or systematic knowledge: and since pure knowledge is the consciousness of rational and logical ideas, it follows that a system of these can be no other than logic. This system then is the pure formal archetype of reason, which is an integrant part, or moiety of the system of nature; and co-existent with the other and corresponding half, the system of forces, to which it is a law for the regulation of their efficiency. We have advanced yet a step farther in natural knowledge: we have not only ascertained that every science must be necessarily based on the purest and most abstract principle of logic, which is *par excellence* the universal science ; but also that all sciences in relation thereto are particular or special, being only the logic of their respective fundamental ideas. And we have also seen that when these ideas do not relate to specific *realities*, but to specific *formal* abstractions, we have the pure sciences of number, space, and time, which are universally applicable to the concrete natural sciences ; and thus become instrumental in the more accurate determination of natural phenomena.

So far then we are in a position to understand the system, the multitude, the magnitude, and the duration of natural objects; but if we stop short here, our knowledge of nature will be very incomplete. Hitherto the pure sciences which have engaged our attention have treated only of the general external appearances or phenomena, and their relations toward each other, as to order, number, space, and time,—most important considerations certainly, but they do not comprise the whole field of exact knowledge. They are concerned only with the *exterior forms* of things ; but we also desire to know the *interior forms* of things, what they are internally: we crave after a knowledge of the causes of those protean changes, which all things around us are continually undergoing. Now no one can deliberately reflect on these things, and seriously deny that we stand in need of more knowledge concerning the *forms* of things than we at present possess. It is the fashion of many not only to ignore, but to deride with the bitterest sarcasm, all attempts to search out these obscure subjects: but for the sake of truth, we do not hesitate to state our firm conviction, that the abstract ideas of *substance, cause,* and *effect,* are as pure and as universal in their character, as those of number, space, and time.

The abstract ideas of substance, cause, and effect, are all intimately related together; indeed they seem to be integrant parts of one and the same science: just as in physics we have the subject-matter of the science, which may be either the maximum or minimum of material bodies, as the stars or molecules, and the forces of which these are composed, and the phenomena or effects which result from their action and reaction.

But have we not got such a science? We think not: but it has been acknowledged as a *desideratum,* as witness the very recent attempt of Macquorn Rankine to establish a science of *Energetics,* " which if constituted would be the highest abstraction or generalisation attainable in physical research." So says the " Cyclopædia of Physical Science ;" and as far as we can gather from the brief notice therein, *energetics* is only intended to include all kinds of motion, the various modified operations of physical forces; but has no concern with the changes of combination or of organisation. A science of changes, however, cannot be universal, unless it comprises not only the changes of place or of motion, but also those changes which result from the operation of chemical and vital powers.

If we have rightly apprehended the subject, the science required must be universally applicable to all kinds of changes; and since motion is only one kind of change, the noun-substantive of rational mechanics or mechanical science, it is evident that this science is not what we are in search of. Some have thought that mechanical science is based on the idea of time, which being a universal idea is so far plausible: but we have already attempted to show that the idea of time cannot be employed for such a purpose. There is indeed a very close agreement between the ideas of time and of change. Time is related to a succession of events: and change implies some notion of sequence, for there is an antecedence and consequence in the phenomena of every change. But granting this, it is not conclusive that succession is the principle of change as well as of time; it only shows that time is the higher generalisation of the two, and may be instrumental in the illustration of changes, just as number is logically prior to time, but is not identical thereto, merely because successive periods may be numbered.

Periodicity, which is related to time, as magnitude is to space, is a regular series of successive events; and in one sense this may be called a change: but in the strict meaning of the word *change*, or that in which we propose to use it, it does not signify an *alternation*, but an *alteration* of things. When anything experiences a *change* it is not in the same *state*; and it is the *altered* condition which gives rise to the inquiries, What is the nature of the difference which has taken place? and, Whence comes the change? whereas, in the case of time, we only observe the duration and periodicity of events, not the nature of the events themselves, but only their succession; nor are we concerned with the causes of their origin.

We may consider natural things abstractedly as formal bodies or substances: there are several kinds of substances, which are denoted by their specific differences, as physical, chemical, and organic substances; but all may be classed together under the universal or generic idea of substance: and when we seek to know what this pure abstract substance is in itself, we learn that it is the formal counterpart of forces, which together make natural dualisms; and we ascribe to this abstract *substance* the formal attributes of *quantity* and *quality*.

When actual bodies undergo real changes, either within their own bodies, or by the concurrence of two or more bodies mutually acting on each other, knowing the component forces of such bodies, we are able to explain the new phenomena or changes of state, on considering the character of the forces concerned. So in the case of abstract substance, knowing that its attributes are quantity and quality, we refer all the changes which it may undergo to an alteration in the relations of these attributes toward each other: so that to preserve the parallel which we are drawing between abstract and concrete bodies, we consider the attributes as causes or formal forces, which acting and reacting on each other produce effects: and whatever variety of aspects these may assume, they are still the same substance, consisting of the same attributes, in different proportions.

Now in the consideration of a concrete or natural science it was found necessary to treat it both descriptively and rationally; that is, its objects or subject-matter, both in a state of rest and in a state of change, are subjects of inquiry; the former giving us a knowledge of its objects as they appear to be; the latter affording an insight into their constitution, thereby enabling us to discern the causes of the changes. Guided by this analogy, and substituting formal ideas for potential realities, we will regard substance in all its varieties as the subject-matter of a universal science; and consider it under both its phenomenal and causal aspects. Such an inquiry gains some assistance from the character of rational mechanics, which is a particular, or subordinate part, of the universal science in question: for the special science teaches us, that although motions, or changes in place, constitute its immediate objects, the conceptions of substance and forces cannot be altogether ignored; there must always be something, that is supposed to be moving or tending to motion, if it be only a point in space, or an atom of substance which is the minimum quantity or unit of this conception. Even in the enunciation of the laws of motion, the words body and bodies are introduced; and we speak as often of the composition of forces as of the co-existence of motions; this, however, is not correct, for being the laws of an abstract science, there ought to be no reference to realities; it, however, shows what we are insisting on; that something, though even pure formal substance, must be conceived, in order to make our ideas, on such a subject, intelligible.

When therefore we speak of substance, the pure *form* of material bodies is intended, and not the actual bodies themselves, which are not only *forms* but also the real *contents* of bodies, that is, natural forces; the two conjointly constituting natural bodies. In treating then of the abstract science of substance, these forces ought not to be even provisionally employed; their pure forms only are admissible, and these are *causes:* so that we go farther than Comte, when he says " that in mechanics we have nothing to do with the origin or different nature of forces; they are all one, while their mechanical operation is uniform." But we do not agree with him in his condemnation of natural forces, or *veræ causæ*, as old metaphysical notions, rendered obsolete by positivism: for we acknowledge *causes* as the ideal side of powers, of which forces are the real side; powers, the indissoluble union of these, are beings which are manifested to our senses, as natural objects.

A universal science is therefore, we think, awanting, which shall hold a similar relation to its particular or subordinate sciences, that logic does to arithmetic, geometry and chronometry; as a science of a lower degree of abstraction, having a closer relation to natural powers, and bearing a greater resemblance to realities, the form and content more clearly corresponding, all the preceding sciences become subservient to it, or are instrumental in its calculations and mensurations. At first sight this statement may seem to be contradictory to our former assertion, that logic is the basis or at the root of all other sciences; but it is not so: logic is the science of system, the whole of which is obtained by the interpretation of the rational forms of things, the reason in nature. But this interpretation depends on the self-consciousness of the rational mind, which knows not only the import of the rational forms or ideas that it perceives, but also knows intuitively the logical methods by which these ideas function, and by means of this knowledge it is enabled to deal logically with its conceptions. The mind then as a rational power, self-conscious of its own rational forms, which are concerned in the production of knowledge according to its innate laws of thought, can discern its own mode of operating; and since its power is the highest order of all powers, it must possess the attributes of all, and be capable of appreciating the forms of all; but its logical forms only relate to knowledge, which is purely that of the degrees of order or system, but has nothing to do with the cause or reason of that order, or of the nature of that efficiency, by which these orders function inductively and deductively. In short, in contemplating the various forms of natural forces, we can logically arrange them into a system, and we can logically again analyse this system into all its parts; and so far logic is at the foundation of all our knowledge of natural powers, whether on the side of their physical forces as realities, or on that of their rational forms or causes as abstract ideas. But in relation to the constitution and internal changes of things, there is a conception of another kind involved, which is not to be found in the abstract sciences already considered; it is something over and above all the ideas relating thereto, viz. that of *causation*, which is necessary for the comprehension of all those sciences which relate to some kind of change.

If we have been so fortunate as to have made our meaning understood (which may not be the case, for it is not easy to express oneself clearly and definitely on a subject which the mind is as yet only striving to grapple with and master), it will have been seen that although we have not at present such a universal science as is under consideration, yet that it is possible that such a science may be formed, which shall comprise the particular formal or rational sciences relating to motion, combination, and organisation, which are all the modes of natural changes.

Such a science, we conceive, to be in strict keeping with our most perfect sciences, must be that of *substance:* and we would suggest for it the name of *Hypostatics.* As the figurative magnitudes or *figures* of *space* are the immediate objects of *geometry,* so the *changes* of *substance* are the objects that will chiefly engage the scope of *hypostatics.* The dimensions of figures are determined by mensuration, which is the principal function of geometry; as the differences of changes or effects are explained by causation, the function of hypostatics. Every substance, that is, every portion, or partial substances, of universal substance, may be regarded as an effect, for all things are in a continual flux of change; and that which we one instant regard as a phenomenon in a statical state, is the next instant altered in appearance, and becomes a new effect, the cause of which is a subject for investigation. So, in like manner, as the *multitude* and *magnitude* of things have been carefully studied, and the sciences of arithmetic and geometry evolved therefrom; there can be no good reason why a science, such as that of hypostatics, may not be derived from the rational interpretation of the *vicissitude* of things.

In attempting to arrive at such a science, it is requisite, in the first place, to ascertain the nature of substance itself, which is the subject of change: and why, when the change does take place, the substance is still the same, only in a new or different condition; which altered condition, and the cause thereof, require to be determined. The substance which we have now to treat of is universal; it is no special substance which is capable of motion, or of combination, or of organisation; but is pure substance only, having the attributes, equally pure and abstract as itself, of quantity and quality: just as physical attraction and repulsion are the forces, or *veræ causæ*, of matter in the world of realities; which matter also varies in its state or condition according to the relative proportions of its constituent forces: or just as a body in motion is actuated by two forces tending in different directions; the character of which motion depends on the relation of its forces towards each other.

Substance itself, then, is a composition of quantitative and qualitative causes, which are co-existent, but the antithesis of each other: as a universal, it comprises the whole of these causes, which cannot become more or less, consistently with the law of conservation; but particular substances may be differentiated by the proportion in which these attributes are distributed throughout the whole system; just as in the case of logical *extension* and *intension* these attributes being in an inverse ratio to each other, as these vary, so must the properties of the particular propositions to which they belong. It will be seen by this, that we are making a parody of the physical or real side of nature, such as we have already described as a system of forces: and so it must be, for the forces and the rational forms of powers perfectly correspond; the one is that which effects the actual changes, and the other which imparts the *form* of the change according to its rational design.

The axiom of hypostatics, that *every effect must have its cause,* or differently expressed, that *every cause is known by its effect,* conveys the notion that one cause only is concerned in causation; but, as already observed in the introductory chapter, this is an abbreviated form of speech in common use; and which may be justified, since it is the *plus* or efficient cause which is immediately concerned in the change, and which imparts its own character to the resulting effect. So that, virtually, an effect is the manifestation of a single cause: but in truth there must needs be also the simultaneous presence of another, a resisting cause; for without action and reaction there can be no efficiency, in this conditioned world of nature.

Now inasmuch as the substance is only an ideal *form,* the change itself, which substance may undergo, must be also an abstract idea; a *change,* however, which is a single conception cannot be thought of alone, it must be as a change of some substance, just as we cannot form an idea of motion itself, but it must be presented to the mind as something moving, even though that something be only an abstract idea. In all changes, the effects produced are themselves only the substances concerned therein, in some new condition; they are, therefore, invariably compositions of causes, co-existent and antagonistic causes, inseparably necessary for the constitution of the special effect. If the causes concerned in a change be equal, the result is an equilibrium, or neutralisation of the opposite attributes; but if either one or other of the constituent causes be in excess, it imparts its character to the change. In the latter or *plus* state of the change, the effect may become an exciting cause to another change, and so on until the intensity of the excess is diffused through the substances engaged in these operations, and all return to a state of equilibrium.

On this view of the subject, we arrive at the following general principles concerning hypostatics. First *axiom*, Every effect must have a cause. Second *axiom*, Every effect is a composition of causes; consequently, causes are co-existent in and commensurate with the effect. Third *axiom*, Every effect is the result of the action and reaction of its causes; consequently such causes are always opposite or antagonistic. Fourth *axiom*, Effects, in their character, depend on the relation of their causes; hence the nature of a cause is manifested by its effect, or resulting phenomenon.

By this statement it is evident that the axioms of hypostatics comprise the whole content of the laws of motion: we have only to substitute the ideas of moving and resisting causes for the pure causes, the particular for the universal, and the idea of motion or change of place for the more general idea of pure change; and we then obtain rational mechanics, just as logic becomes geometry when to the more general ideas of order, that of space is superadded. This has already been pointed out by Whewell,* who, when treating of the idea of cause, has observed that " the three axioms of causation, now stated, are the fundamental maxims of all reasoning concerning causes, as to their quantities; and it will be shown in the sequel, that

* Philosophy of the Inductive Sciences, vol. i. p. 177.

these axioms form the basis of the science of mechanics, determining its form, extent, and certainty."

From what has now been said concerning the proposed science of hypostatics, some general notion may have been formed concerning its objects and its functions; but before concluding this subject a few more remarks may be made thereon.

In the construction of hypostatics, the course to be pursued must be the same as ought to be followed in every science. In the first place, it may be defined as the science, or systematic knowledge, of substance, which is its noun-substantive, or fundamental idea. This universal substance must be then analysed into its various parts, and each of these parts, in order to their clear recognition, must be determined by their respective definitions, and marked by distinct names, so that nomination and definition are preliminary operations.

We have already marked the fundamental principle of hypostatics by the name of substance, and we define it to be the formal constitution of natural beings or powers, or in other words, the pure *form* of nature: and since all natural bodies are dualisms, it follows that, on their ideal side as well as on the real, they must be similarly constituted; and if so, the more precise definition of substance is, that it is a formal dualism of quantity and quality; and then quantity is the *basic* attribute, and quality the *specific* attribute of substance. The maximum of substance will be its entire system, and its subordinate parts will be masses of various extent; whilst the unit or minimum of substance is an *atom*, that which cannot be subdivided. In all this, it is evident that we are only regarding those abstract terms which we are in the habit of using in connection with material bodies; thus, we commonly speak of an atom or of a molecule of matter, or a material atom, &c.; and of an atom of material or chemical substances. How far we may be able to gather together, and appropriate such abstractions for the purposes of hypostatics, remains to be determined: but we are inclined to think that they include all those general expressions, such as those of agent, reagent, and action; active and passive, action and reaction, equilibrium, and the like: all, in short, which as pure formal ideas, relating to natural bodies and natural powers, are capable of universal application.

The *postulate* requisite for the science of substance, seems to be that it is possible for any given part of substance, which is demonstrable, to be made up of atoms or units of substance, though in themselves inappreciable; and that the change of any substance, which is an effect, may be brought about by an alteration in the relative proportions of its attributes.

Concerning the *axioms* of this science, according to which substances function, we have already made several remarks, and enumerated four of them, which are probably sufficient for all the purposes of the science. To attempt to develope this subject more fully, would involve us in such minute details as would be inconsistent with the character of this work; the object of which is to trace out the filiations of known sciences, so as to collect them into a common system: and in so doing to notice the vacancies therein, and to indicate in what manner these blanks may possibly be filled up. Such an undertaking cannot be expected to be completed by a first attempt, even should the suggestions in any measure prove to be correct: but it may ultimately tend, by the labours of others, to accelerate the advancement of knowledge.

Having now considered the universal science of substance, which is concerned with all descriptions of changes, to which its laws are equally applicable, we now turn to those special kinds of change, which, in addition to the generic character, have specific ideas which make their difference: and on each kind of change we now proceed to make a few brief remarks.

Rational mechanics, or mechanical science, has been long acknowledged as a branch of pure mathematics: we have endeavoured to show that it is not a universal science, like that of space, because its fundamental idea of motion, or change of place, is not an idea of the highest generalisation, appertaining only to one kind of change: and if this be accepted as conclusive, it follows that the science in question is only a branch of the pure science of substance, hypostatics, which is one of the universal mathematical sciences. Rational mechanics is the science of motion, or cinematics, as it ought to be called; this term is much in use, but by most only in connection with statics and dynamics, the two latter so-called sciences having relation to the forces which produce, or tend to produce motion. As already stated, we consider that cinematics, as a science, is adequate for the treatment of all these subjects; just as astronomy comprehends, not only the description of its objects, whether at rest or in motion, but also an explanation of their different conditions, by the dynamical actions of the antagonistic forces which are concerned in the production of all astronomical phenonomena. Statics and dynamics, therefore, are only regarded by us as the relative states or conditions of the *moving* causes, which function as motion; the various kinds of motion are, then, the effects of special causes, and are the objects or subject-matter of cinematics. If we persist in treating of statics and dynamics as special sciences, or distinct branches of science, to be consistent we ought, in the natural sciences, to have sciences of the centripetal and centrifugal forces, as we have indeed now those of other forces, heat, electricity and magnetism, all of which are, we think, contrary to the very principle of a science, which is systematic knowledge: indeed we can only know forces by their effects, and they are always complex composition of forces, which as phenomena are capable of being immediately known as mental ideas.

We are confirmed in our view of the subject in objecting to the present constitution of rational mechanics, by the great uncertainty which prevails in the treatment of statics and dynamics; a perplexing circumstance which has often attracted attention. "Statics," says Comte[*], "was the only possible method in the early days of science: but since Galileo's time, dynamics, the method of seeking the conditions of equilibrium through the laws of the composition of forces, has been more generally followed. At first glance, it does not appear the more rational; dynamics being more complicated than statics, and precedence being naturally to the simpler. It would, in fact, be more philosophical to refer dynamics to statics, as has since been done, but only in the case of uniform motions." "It is usual, however, to consider statics as a particular

[*] Positive Philosophy, book i. chap. iv. sect. 1.

case of elementary dynamics; but simple as may be the operation, and great as may be the practical advantage gained by this method of proceeding, it would be satisfactory to return, if we could, to the method of the ancients; to leave dynamics on one side, and proceed directly to the investigation of the laws of equilibrium, regarded by itself; by means of a direct general principle of equilibrium. A *science* must be *imperfectly* laid down, as long as it is necessary thus to pass backwards and forwards between its two departments."

At all events, it is evident that the principles of science, thus constituted, cannot be rightly apprehended, and it is reasonable to suppose, in such a case, that the defect is not trivial, not a mere imperfection which may be hereafter removed, but that it is radically insuperable; for in any science, much more in a pure science, intelligible clearness and definite precision are indispensable requisites.

Cinematics, the science of motion, treats of the whole system of motions, which comprises all kinds of motion, and their relations toward each other; and this necessarily implies a knowledge of moving causes, and their variable relations; for motion is a composition of *formal* forces or causes. Now every substance capable of being moved, that is, every moveable substance, is actuated by its constituent causes; each of which tends to move the substance in an opposite direction to each other: so that if no motion takes place in either direction, either toward or from the common centre of action, the substance is in a state of rest; and its moving causes are consequently equal, or in a state of equilibrium. Make the smallest addition to the energy of either cause, when in this condition, and the substance will instantly move in the normal direction of the efficiency. Whichever direction the moving substance may take, it is self-evident that if it be required to reverse its motion in the opposite direction, we cannot now accomplish it by the same amount of energy as that which first put it in motion; we must first employ a sufficient power to balance its antagonist, that is, the equilibrium must be restored, and then superadd an excess which will subvert the statical state of the substance, and by its dynamic influence cause it to move in the new direction with a velocity equivalent to the excess employed.

All substances are moveable; indeed universal substance, or the entire system, is not only moveable, but perpetually in motion; but since the moving causes of the system, taken in their totality, are invariably conserved in a state of equality, the resulting motion is so equable, that, like a top when it sleeps, it would, could we see it, have the appearance of being in a perfect state of rest. And even the parts of this universal substance, when constrained by a great excess of the cause tending to the centre, so that in respect to its local position it is rigidly at rest, yet even then, though the antagonist moving causes of the substance are not co-equal, yet they are still co-existent, and their efficiency is not destroyed; they are ever efficient, they neither slumber nor sleep, but are ever ready to start into perceptible activity should extraneous energy interpose to turn the balance in favour of such a phenomenon. A cause then which is equalised by another, whether a moving or any other cause, is not annihilated, but only rendered latent by a kind of neutralisation; and such a condition gives us an important point of departure in all our investigations concerning motions and their causes: we know not indeed the absolute amount of energy which is exerted on either side in any given equilibrium; but, be it large or be it small, it matters not, for all our knowledge can be but relative: but we can determine in any case the amount of energy requisite for bringing any substance into such a statical state; and then starting from this point, we can estimate the value of the actual moving force by the motions produced.

This principle is only one of the many forms resulting from the dualistic constitution which pervades all nature, and which we have symbolised in our archetypal correlation: it is the same as that for which we are indebted to D'Alembert, by which the equations of the motion of any system may be established; and which, combined with that of virtual velocities, enables us to solve very intricate problems of motion. In fact, these mechanical principles may be all referred to the second, or Newton's, law of motion, that of the equality of action and reaction; which in turn may be traced up to the higher generalisation of the antagonism of causes, as enunciated in the third axiom of hypostatics.

There is one notion which has been adopted in rational mechanics, the idea of a *vis inertiæ*, and which is tenaciously retained: it is true that it is no longer considered to have any real foundation, but is valued merely as a convenient expression. The fact is, that it is a monument of our ignorance; but one enveloped in such an appearance of mystic knowledge, that it imposes on the student, and so perverts his understanding as to favour its retention. Some effort should be made to eradicate this notion: there is enough to learn worth knowing; and we need not perplex our youths with learning the conventional meaning of an hypothesis acknowledged to be untenable.

According to the idea of *vis inertiæ*, " all nature is supposed to be inert, motionless, and lifeless, and that action or activity can be impressed on it solely by external energies or forces: but this is not true, for every part of nature is the centre and source of manifold and multiform activities." "But the hypothesis of *inertia* is not only convenient, but necessary for the development of science; for an *inert point* is theoretically required whereon forces may act to produce motions." We are, however, inclined to think that in the case of forces and bodies, moved that is on the real side of nature, no such consideration is necessary: every body that is to be moved must first have its resisting, or statical, force equalised; and this resisting force is not an unknown *vis inertiæ;* and so when it begins to move it starts not from an inert state, but from that of *equilibrium*, in which state it is ready to respond to the external energy or force. And so, *mutatis mutandis*, the same explanation serves for the abstract forms of bodies and forces, viz. for substances and causes: for the real and ideal perfectly correspond, depending on the self-same reason.

This idea of *inertia* is employed even in a higher sense, agreeable with which the first law of motion is frequently called the law of inertia. Bodies being in themselves regarded as *inert*, they only move as they are acted on: so that a body, or an abstract body or substance, when moved by any force, would, if not disturbed, move on for ever in a straight line and with an uniform velocity.

Any substance in a state of *equilibrium* would afford a much more rational point of departure, and would give the same result under the like condition of meeting with no resistance or interference of any kind. We may imagine, but by mental abstraction alone is it possible to consider, what would be the *modus operandi* of any one kind of force; and as we know that each force has its own peculiar direction, of course, if it could be insulated, this line of action would be the only one in which it could act. So far it is perfectly legitimate to form such a conception; for it is necessary, in order to understand the kind of motions which actually take place, to know the character of the individual forces concerned therein. No motion can result from the operation of a single force, there must in every case be action and reaction; for motion is a *composition of forces*: and such motion, therefore, can never be more than an approximation to a straight line; for however one force may predominate, and impart its peculiar direction, it can never be absolutely separated from its co-existent, that is, its correlative force. Such a possibility would stultify the second and third laws of motion. Moreover, whether we deal with real or abstract motions, the condition of the first law of motion, which states, "if not disturbed," requires that which may be imagined, but which never did nor can occur in relation to anything in nature, whether real or ideal. No force of any kind can act but in relation to all around; and hence it is that the result of any action whatever is not pure and simple, but complex; and it is this very complicity which makes analysis possible, on which all science depends.

By this statement we are not denying that we may, by

mental analysis, abstract the single elementary forces; and this way objectify them, and note their peculiar attributes: but what we are desirous of maintaining is, that as such forces are never so insulated, but always occur in pairs or dualisms, it is not legitimate to frame a law concerning that which is non-existent, both as regards the force itself and the condition of its action. A law, whether physical or logical, is supposed to be an expression of that rational rule by which natural phenomena are regulated; it does not relate to things that may be, but to those which actually occur in nature: and for this reason we assert that a law, purporting to be a natural law, must be consistent with the constitution of nature.

We need not here repeat what has been said concerning the axioms of hypostatics ; but must rest content with stating, that it is only necessary to add to their general terms the differential ones which specially belong to motion, and then they become the laws of motion. The latter are usually stated in the chronological order of their development: thus, the 1st is Kepler's, the 2nd Newton's, and the 3rd Galileo's. We have, however, reversed this order, following that of their logical relation : and we are inclined to think that if the established laws of motion had been so arranged, it would have appeared more startling, after Galileo's law of the co-existence of motions, to enunciate the law of Kepler.

Cinematics may be divided into subordinate branches, according to the kind of motions concerned, which are very various, as continuous motions, projections, undulations, and polar motions.

Hypostatics may, in a sense, be called a temporospatial science; but its relations thereto are of a very general and evanescent character: whereas cinematics is very closely related to space and time, and derives great assistance therefrom in the description of its phenomena. And thus it is in each succeeding science; its special idea seems to become more and more complex, connoting a wider sphere of qualities, including as it were all preceding ideas; just as natural beings arise one above another in the complicity of their attributes, until they terminate in man, who is a microcosm of all creatures.

Advancing another step in our progression, we pass from the idea of *motion* to that of *combination*, which relates to those changes which chemical substances undergo; as motion relates to those of physical or material substances.

As motion is not one thing, but a compound of moving forces of a different character, so combination is a compound of distinct combining forces, or rather *causes*. Whenever a chemical change takes place, it is effected by the operation of chemical causes; and the result thereof is a combination, which is another form of chemical substance. The science of combination, therefore, must be a pure science, all the objects of which are perfect abstractions of chemical powers and their relations: such a science must not be confounded with chemistry; and for distinction sake it may be called rational chemistry, or chemics, bearing the same relation to chemistry as cinematics does to physics.

The possibility of establishing such a science as rational chemistry engaged Comte's attention; and he clearly indicated that the success of such an attempt must depend on correctly apprehending the nature of chemical combination. Some of his remarks on this subject, at first sight, seem very startling; but when closely examined are found to be very sagacious. "If," says he[*], "we could not hold at once the grand principle of the dualism which pervades chemistry, and constitutes its homogeneous character, and also the doctrine of definite proportions, I should not hesitate to sacrifice the latter; for it is more important for chemical progress to grasp the great principle of systematic dualism, than to advance our investigations by the use of the numerical rule. Even after this clearing of the field, we could not accomplish the desired generalisation, if we had not taken a new stand in regard to the ternary and quaternary substances. The rigorous dualism which I have before, and in a higher view, shown to be necessary, seems to supply, naturally and finally, the needs of the doctrine of definite proportions." Again: "In an indirect way electricity may operate favourably for chemical science, by its binary antagonism suggesting the extension of dualism among compounds, which as yet are supposed to be more than binary. Berzelius appears to have felt this connection, and he would probably have erected dualism into a fundamental principle, but for his subjection to the old division into organic and inorganic. For a chemical philosophy, we do not want new materials so much as the rational disposition of the details which already abound, by reducing all combinations, according to the principle of dualism, into one body of homogeneous doctrine."

[*] Positive Philosophy, vol. i. p. 331.

The idea of combination is very different from that of cumulation, or even aggregation; it is the union of two distinct chemical causes, the rational forms of chemical powers; and the resulting change, the new chemical substance, is characterised by its own peculiar attributes, which are more or less unlike those of its constituents. In the case of an effect, or of a motion, the causes concerned in the respective change cannot be demonstrated by the dissolution of their union; but it is not so in the case of combination; for each combining or chemical cause, on account of its complex constitution, is capable of an individual existence, so that the nature of each combination can be ascertained by analysis, and the accuracy of the result tested, synthetically, by reunion of the individual constituents. We have said that every chemical combination is a dualism of combining causes; but it does not follow that either, or both of these, are simple; they may, on the contrary, be exceedingly complex; thus either constituent may be reduced successively into many different compounds of a simpler character. But however complex compounds may be, they are, or ought to be, theoretically reducible into two constituents, which, as chemical causes, are co-existent and opposite; one cause being the *basic* or quantitative, and the other the *typal* or qualifying cause. And it is the knowledge of this fact which often leads, in analytical experiments, to the selection of the kind of reagent we employ, according as it is desired to separate one or the other of the ingredients; thus the basic or the typal cause, when in combination, may be removed by substituting another of the same kind which has greater combining energy than the one to be displaced:

and by a repetition of this process, first on the basic, and then on the typal side, or *vice versâ*, we obtain a knowledge of the composition of the original compound. Not an inferential knowledge, as in the case of physical analyses, but an actual demonstration, by obtaining the individual constituents in a state of distinct separation.

Should it be deemed expedient to gather together all the abstract principles of chemistry, and to constitute with them a science of combination, or chemics, the task would not be very difficult when the general science relating to pure changes has been well established; for then all that would be requisite would be to conjoin the special idea of combination to that of substance in the universal hypostatics, and we should have a perfect exemplar for its construction. But, in the meantime, all that we can now do is to point out the position of such a science in the system, and to indicate its filiations with the other sciences, which we have endeavoured to do in the few preceding remarks, but perhaps too imperfectly for any practical application: — we must however hasten on to complete the outline of our sketch.

The only particular kind of change remaining to be noticed for the completion of our knowledge concerning the formal side of nature, is that of organic changes which result in organisation. This kind of change is the most complicated of all, comprising not only motions and combinations, but something more peculiar which characterises its specialty.

Each single chemical or combining cause is capable of an individual existence, that is, apart from all other chemical causes; because it can form a dualism or composition of causes, by union with physical causes, and in such a compound, which is the formal representative of chemical elements, the physical cause or causes become the basic, and the combining cause, the typal or specific constituent; and it is this capacity to form such definite and indissoluble dualisms that enables them to maintain their individuality;—for no single cause or power can exist alone as a natural being. Though each chemical cause can be thus insulated, it is only as a chemical substance, using this term in an abstract sense, yet it is not a combination or chemical compound; it is necessary before such can be obtained that two chemical causes at least should be conjoined, in which union one acts the part of a basic and the other of a typal cause; corresponding with the abstract notion of reagent and agent, without which there can be no combining action and reaction resulting in combination.

Such in a few words is the character of those specific changes called combinations, and from which it may be readily inferred that whilst we can by abstraction restrict our attention to the chemical changes only, yet in actual reality, that is, in chemical bodies, various kinds of motions must at the same time occur, because the basic constituent of each combining substance is a dualism of physical causes which are manifested as the attributes of physical or material substance. Now the character of organisation, though not the same as that of combination, has a considerable analogy thereto; it is twofold, that is, a dualism like all natural things, whether real or ideal: each individual organism consists of a basic and a typal cause; the latter is a specific organic or vital cause, but the former is a very complex chemical substance or combination, and as such not only chemical but also physical. So we see that it is to its complex nature that each chemical cause owes its capability of an individual existence, which is perfectly stable and durable, for it cannot be reduced to a lower denomination; and it is owing to the greater complicity of constitution in organisation, that the latter enjoys a higher order of individuality, becoming a system within itself; so that without the concurrence of any other individual it can undergo and accomplish most intricate and numerous series of changes, which are manifested as the phenomena of organisation.

The idea of organisation, in the abstract, is the universal system of all organic changes; all of which have in common certain generic characters: they are all compositions of chemical or basic causes, and of typal organic causes; and it is by the ever varying action and reaction of these causes on each other that the ever changing phenomena of organisation are produced. But multifarious as these are, they may all be reduced to three grand processes which are mutually related; the phenomena of *acquisition*, *appropriation*, and *utilisation*. The particular parts of this universal organisation are very multitudinous, each of which is differenced from the others by specific attributes, which mark the various species of organisms: these attributes are not respectively mere differences, but such as those of different degrees of order, all related together, but progressively rising one above another, so as to include that which has gone before, with an additional something which is peculiar; so that, by ascending gradations of generalisation, the whole can be collected together into the universal that constitutes the system. Each part of the organisation, that is, each organism as regarded in its individuality, is itself a universal or system of a subordinate degree: and according to its position in the hierarchy of organic beings so is its dignity; that is, the number of its properties by which it is connoted. The specific or distinguishing cause of each organism is unceasingly exercised, as is indicated by the incessant changes which it undergoes, which imply a constant activity of functions: in many individuals, however, there is apparently very considerable suspensions of animation, both periodical and accidental; in many cases we know that the living functions are only partially, but not totally interrupted; and it is not improbable that whilst there is life there are always some changes going on, though inappreciably small.

A grand characteristic of all organisation is, that whilst as a whole its existence is conserved, yet its individual parts are always suffering dissolution: their specific principle becomes detached from the basic or chemical, in consequence of some injury or deterioration; and thus the concurrence of the dualistic causes, that composition of forces so requisite in every organism, is necessarily subverted. The general dissolution, which would follow the unimpeded operation of such a process, has been provided against by the function of *reproduction:* each specific organism has its own peculiar method of effecting this, as well as in all other kinds of functions; and all such differences serve to enable us to discriminate between various organisms. But various and complicated as this function is in all its details, yet, viewed abstractedly, its *rationale* is very simple; and in accordance with the general routine which characterises all functions. Each kind of organism acquires materials from the medium in which it lives, by means of its physical or basic causes, which are subservient to the directing energy of its specific cause: and having obtained its materials by means of the same causes, conjoined with the chemical causes, it selects, therefrom, retaining some, and rejecting others. And after divers manipulations, by which the materials are adapted to its purpose, it directs the employment thereof in constructing organs, according to its peculiar rational designs: such organs, whether the mere enlargement, or reproduction, of former organs, or the development of inferior into higher organs, or even of new and additional organs, are still, in every case, but the self-same organism; and as such continue to be actuated by the same typal or specific cause. And, in like manner the dualism functions, producing certain actions or organic changes, which are means to certain predetermined ends; the whole process terminating in adaptations useful for the welfare of the creature. Now the germ-cell, produced in the function of reproduction, is no other than such an additional organ, which, whilst a portion of the parent, is on the same footing as all other parts of the individual organic system; and, consequently, as such, it is a living organ, though dependent: there remains but the discharge of another function by the same individual vital cause (or by the conjoint operation of another individual organism of the same kind, but the latter need not be insisted on, being only one of the many instances in which the operations of nature are so richly diversified, for the case of hermaphrodites shows that it is not an absolutely necessary condition), by which it acquires a higher condition, that of being able to enjoy an independent state of existence, and to exercise all the functions which its parent previously discharged.

Every organism has commenced its existence as a substance actuated by an animating principle: it cannot originate its own being; its basic part must have been prepared, that is, acquired from chemical substances, and appropriated by some pre-existing cause, as a habitation or indispensable medium for containing and enabling its animating principle to function. The conjunction of these two distinct causes is requisite for every part, as well as the whole system of organisation. So that, even in the discharge of one of the highest and most complex of organic functions, the energising principle follows the universal formula of acquisition, appropriation, and utilisation: a formula which may well be called universal, for it is, in truth, but the expression in other words of the logical methods of definition, generalisation, and demonstration, which pervades all things as the reason in nature. There is then, on this view, no repetition of acts of creation; no continual renewal of the vital principle on the birth of each kind of creature: but each specific life is continued by a propagating faculty which cannot be perfectly comprehended; but which may be as well understood, as any other faculties of natural powers; that is, as causes they can only be known by their effects; which are to the conscious mind facts with which we must rest content in the present finite condition of our intellects.

All organic changes, though following one and the same routine, are capable of being arranged under several distinct heads. The first and most general class of such changes comprises those of growth and reproduction, which, as we have just said, are fundamentally one, having relation to the general idea of increase : just as in arithmetic, the sum obtained by addition and the product arising from multiplication are, at the root, of the same character, being variations only of one and the same principle. The incremental changes of organisation are, like motions and combinations, compulsory according to the innate laws of the causes concerned therein : that is, the causes and all the conditions of a given change being known, we can, under precisely the same circumstances, predict the result which will follow. The organic cause is indeed a reason-directed cause, but on the platform of mere vegetative existence it is a passive unconscious cause, similar to that which is concerned in physical and chemical phenomena, which are usually regarded as definitely conditioned or necessitated. In the case of many organic causes this condition is the sole mode of action : but there are some causes which, in addition thereto, enjoy the faculty of consciousness, which raises them into a higher class of existence. Some conscious organic causes, have, according to their degree, the capacity of perceiving and knowing their sensations, and using this knowledge for the guidance of their actions: and when this faculty has attained its highest development, as not only conscious of the changes relating to the operations of the basic cause with which it is associated, but also rationally conscious of the laws which regulate these changes, it then acquires a corresponding influence over the subordinate causes, making them subservient to its designs; and thus acquiring also the greatest freedom of action, as a voluntary cause or will. Such an organic cause of the most exalted degree is still only one cause: it possesses in common with reason all the lower faculties, which are enjoyed by subordinate organisms; but all these are only various modes of the self-same cause. For since the highest cause comprises within itself all the attributes of the lower causes, it is capable of exercising either of them according to its exigencies. The mind is one kind of organic function, as much as locomotion is another: there can be no line of demarcation drawn between body and mind; throughout all nature there is a gradual ascending scale of being; but all are intimately related together, and united into one common system.

The few abstract principles of biology which have been referred to, may suffice to show in what manner we ought to proceed in attempting to work out a pure abstract science of organics, or the systematic knowledge of organic substances. This includes not only the description and classification of all the abstract ideas relating thereto; but also the explanation of all organic changes, which are only abstract organic substance under new or different aspects. Such a science within its sphere may be as pure and exact as cinematics: its object will be to determine the nature of the various organisms, and their functions by organic causation; as that of cinematics is to determine the various motions by a knowledge of the action of moving causes. And as organics is a very complex science, so it occupies a corresponding rank in the hierarchy; and is therefore capable of availing itself of the other abstract sciences, by means of which its complex character may be rendered much more intelligible, as calculated and measured phenomena.

The result of our investigation concerning the pure sciences is that we have arrived at a series of fundamental ideas; viz. order, number, space, time, substance, motion, combination, and organisation; several of which have been already worked out and established: but if our view of this subject be correct, there are several yet remaining concerning which much must be done before they can be accepted as rational sciences, as will be readily seen in the following enumeration; viz. logic, arithmetic, geometry, chronometry, hypostatics, cinematics, chemics, and organics.

CHAP. XII.

RECAPITULATION AND CONCLUSION.

Has the Thesis been proved, that the State of Modern Science is unsatisfactory?—Freedom of Discussion necessary for the Advancement of Science.—There are Sciences of Realities and Sciences of Ideas; Concrete and Formal Sciences: the Data of the former, Facts; of the latter, Truths.—A Trinity in Unity incomprehensible.—Dualism the Condition of Nature, of which the Mental Faculties partake; and are capable, by Consciousness, of apprehending.—Phenomenal Knowledge directly perceived as a *Monism*.—The general Character of Science, the Progression of Knowledge in different Ages, analogous to individual Development.—Review of the various Sciences.—A System of the Sciences.—Conclusion.

SUCH is the evidence by which we have attempted to prove our introductory proposition — that, the present state of scientific knowledge is not satisfactory; that theories, not facts, are the more clamant *desiderata* of science. How far we have substantiated this charge; and how far we have been successful in our proposed remedy for this unsatisfactory condition of knowledge, must await the decision of others: the system of the sciences, or philosophy, which has cost us so much thought and toil, "may be only a *phantom*; it may prove to be a *reality*."

We are buoyed up with the hope of the latter happy consummation of all our labours by the circumstance that the numerous outstanding facts which we have grappled with (all indeed which we could remember during the investigation,) have all, without a single exception, found a place in our system; and by a knowledge of their relations thus obtained, have received, if not *the* true, at least *a* reasonable explanation. This assertion may excite a smile in those who know, by experience, how easy it is to reduce all things to any standard, by the Procrustean method: we have been from the beginning aware of this tendency of the mind, and have endeavoured to watch carefully against falling into such a fallacy. And yet, notwithstanding all our care, the precaution may have been in vain; for *humanum est errare:* we appeal therefore to the judgment of others on this subject.

Science has two standards of validity; corresponding in this respect with the dualistic constitution of nature, and with the two-sided character of all natural knowledge. Thus we have sciences of facts and sciences of truths; that is, of realities and of ideas: we can only know material bodies, that is, natural beings or existences, mediately through their attributes which belong to the individual powers that constitute natural beings; for all such are not distinct and independent existences, but essentially dualisms of powers. And since each power is a reason-directed force, an efficiency capable of acting according to the law of its innate reason; force and reason are the indissoluble attributes of power, not only co-existent but co-equal: hence it is that facts and truths, though essentially one, may be regarded from different standpoints; the one as relating to actual forces, manifested as natural realities; the other relating to the formal reason, or rational principles which are known as abstract ideas.

So that when we speak of facts being the objects of the

physical or material sciences, and of truths as the objects of the mental or formal sciences, it must not therefore be supposed that facts and truths are completely heterogeneous; for they are only the two-sided views of one and the same rational idea, which objectively is a real fact, subjectively a formal truth.

A *fact* may therefore be defined as the conformity of the real to the ideal; and a *truth*, as the conformity of the ideal to the real: from which it is evident that these terms express one and the same thing from different points of view. But we must not conceive of them as coming under the head of natural dualisms, which may be formulated, according to our archetypal correlation, as

$$\text{Fact} + \text{truth} = \text{fact} - \text{truth, or verity.}$$

The association of fact and truth is not a dualism, but relates to a higher constitution than anything in nature which can be definitely known; it is on the same footing as that of *power*, which is a unity in diversity, as respects its conjoint and indissoluble attributes of force and reason: neither of which can be conceived of as before or after other; but as an actual oneness, which may assume to the finite mind a diversity, according to the side on which it is regarded.

Absolute, or perfect oneness of power, and its attributes, imply a trinity, which may be accepted as a revealed truth, but cannot be comprehended by the human mind; for this simple reason, that it has no relation to any of the data of natural knowledge. Man is a part of nature, and, by his peculiar mental endowment, is capable of interpreting the reason in nature: and, therefore, as every natural thing is twofold, a dualism or composition of two kinds of antagonistic (not consentient) powers, can be readily apprehended, and perfectly comprehended. All this is, we conceive, consistent with reason. In the lower development of the understanding, as mere perception, whether that of the brute or of man, all acquired knowledge is immediate and phenomenal, that is, such knowledge may be characterised as being that solely of *monism;* all things are, to a mind so constituted, just as they appear to be, distinct individualities. The brute cannot rise above this conditioned state of knowledge; thus far, and no farther, is the decree of Deity: and it would be in vain for the brute to thirst after a higher knowledge, if it were possible for it to do so. Man is not restricted to this narrow limitation of knowledge; he possesses the highest form of that natural understanding which he has in common with the brute, and which may be called *common sense;* but he also enjoys an extraordinary sense, or mental faculty, of a higher order, by which he is enabled to look below the surface of things, and to acquire a knowledge of the reason in nature. And what does this learning consist in? It consists in knowing what things are in themselves; that they are not what they seem to be in their phenomenal oneness, but are composed of various and dissimilar constituents: that this oneness is in fact a diversity in unity, and that this diversity, however great, may be reduced into two distinct and antagonistic parts, which by their union make a binary compound or *dualism*.

The sum total then of all rational knowledge is that all natural bodies are *dualisms* (not *monisms,* as the inferior animal intellect apprehends them to be), but the unification of two co-existing and opposite powers, an idea of composition which the rational mind is so framed as to understand, which indeed corresponds with its own constitution: in short, it is the peculiar property of its attribute, and that is all that can be said for any power. But the knowledge of dualism, the two in one, is the limitation of man's mental acquirements; he frets himself in vain in striving to overflow the shores which bound conditioned knowledge; in vain he grasps at the phantom of the Absolute which tantalises his aspirations after higher knowledge: it is unattainable, for this simple reason that the mind, in the present state of existence, has no faculty capable of compassing a knowledge of a trinity in unity; such knowledge is too high for mortal ken, it cannot attain to it; though it may in a more exalted state of existence, when it will know even as it is known.

We must therefore rest content with the knowledge of the dualistic condition of existence; a condition which, as already said, is that of all natural bodies: and so far this accords well with our purpose, for a system of the sciences is only concerned with natural knowledge, which must be worked out by the logical faculty of the mind; whilst supernatural knowledge cannot be self-acquired, but must be imparted by divine instruction.

The dualistic constitution of nature, and the twofold aspect of each of its constituent powers, afford a clue to the character of each individual science, and to the collateral series into which the sciences arrange themselves in the general system. A natural body is a dualism, a unity in diversity, or oneness: and according to the character of its outward appearance, it may be classified in the system of nature; and this descriptive knowledge, or natural history, must needs be the introductory branch of every science, and is attained by aid of the logical method of induction. And, in the second place, a knowledge of the composition of the dualism, shows what it is in itself, and what are the characteristics of its constituents; a knowledge which is the foundation of the physical or causal branch of each science, by which its various phenomena are capable of being explained. In the acquisition of the first branch of a science, all the objects relating thereto are inductively arranged into a synthetic whole or universal, which must necessarily possess some generic character, by which all its parts may be predicated; such a character is the fundamental principle of the science, it is sometimes used as the name or noun-substantive of the science itself, but more correctly this should have reference to the universal and not to its attribute. In the acquisition of the second or physical branch of a science, the immediate subject for consideration is the synthetic whole itself, which by a deductive process is analysed into subordinate classes; and these again into their subalterns, and so on until all its particular parts are developed: — each of these parts is a dualism of powers, as much so as the universal itself; but in each, the constituent powers are united in different proportions, and it is the knowledge of these different relations that enables us to explain their respective phenomena.

These are the principles on which the sciences, or systematic knowledge of dualisms, depend: but inasmuch as all the powers which constitute these dualisms may be regarded either on their real or on their ideal side, that is, either as to their potential contents or their rational forms, the knowledge derived therefrom must exhibit a corresponding difference. The one view will give us forces as the subject-matter of one series of sciences; and the other, the abstract forms of the reason in nature, for another series of sciences: and it is to this double vision, or consciousness of the mind, which can direct its attention either to the content of its ideas which depend on physical impressions, or to the form of its ideas which are its rational principles, that we are indebted for the two series of sciences, the physical and the formal. Although these series of sciences are so distinct that they cannot be confounded, they are, however, intimately connected; oftentimes exhibiting most circumstantial correspondencies. This is not surprising, since they are so closely related:— for, as in natural bodies, the real and ideal are indissolubly conjoined, so that one cannot even exist without the other; so, in the case of the physical and formal sciences, the knowledge of the one is impossible without that of the other.

We have already endeavoured to show that an objective knowledge of nature must have been first acquired, before the pure sciences could have been constructed: the ideas on which these sciences are founded relate only to knowledge which lies on the surface of things, which intuitively apprehended, readily becomes subservient to the logical methods of the rational mind. The contemplation of natural bodies, as a diversity in unity, (however crude and imperfect their early classified arrangements must necessarily have been,) must sooner or later have suggested to the mind the abstract notions of multitude and magnitude, together with all their correlative ideas;

and the possibility of their being gathered together into distinct systems. All the abstract sciences of ancient times, logic, arithmetic, and geometry, are essentially phenomenal sciences, corresponding respectively with that oneness which characterises our knowledge of the appearance of things. The ancients had, indeed, a clear apperception that there is also an *inner* as well as an *outward* nature of things; they hastily formed hypotheses thereon, and put forth divers philosophies, which were intended to acquaint us with the causes of all those physical changes which are manifested as the phenomena of nature. That their failure was signal, is not surprising; for with the exception of some notions, more or less correct, concerning bodies in a statical condition, and in a state of motion, they were not prepared to understand the inner nature of things:— this requires a previous lengthened investigation, not only concerning the constitution of things, but also of the rational laws by which the constituents are governed in their mutual actions and reactions, resulting in natural phenomena.

Thus far then we have traced that *natural history* knowledge, which is external and objective, and almost intuitively acquired (being accomplished, indeed, inductively, but by the almost instinctive operation of the logical mind, which compares things as to their similarity or dissimilarity and arranges them accordingly), but when once acquired it furnishes a variety of abstract ideas, as data for the construction of some pure formal sciences, which for distinction' sake may be called the elementary or *monoformal* sciences: their subject-matter is purely simple, as in the case of logic, arithmetic, geometry, and chronometry;—

which are respectively the sciences of order, number, space, and time. Now such are manifestly pure and simple, or monistic; and not dualistic, as in the case of motion, which is a composition of forces.

Onward the human intellect advances; it has now acquired a knowledge of nature both on its real and ideal side; but this knowledge is, in a sense, purely superficial, and only concerns nature in a statical state of rest: it has nothing to do with nature in a dynamical state, it regards not those incessant actions and reactions which produce continual changes in the appearance of things. Nature is indeed a dualism, but ancient science has only, effectively, dealt with it as a congeries of apparent monisms: by means of ancient science, however, a firm footing has been obtained, and now the intellectual lever can be applied with good prospect of forcing an entrance into the temple of nature, and unveiling all her mysteries.

By a reflex action, the mathematical mind turns its attention on that nature from which it derived its knowledge; and now with logical precision it defines each distinct kind of property by which the various natural bodies are characterised. It investigates, by a searching scrutiny, the changes which bodies undergo in their properties, marks down the varying circumstances under which each kind of property disappears and reappears: the investigation is no longer a vague process of mere observation and record; but each change is calculated, and noted by a definite enumeration; and also measured and delineated with geometrical precision.

Such a knowledge of natural phenomena is an aggregate of physical facts, which should furnish sufficient data for the construction of a physical science. The word physics is in continual use ; we scarcely ever discuss any scientific subject without frequently employing this expression: for whenever astronomy, acoustics, optics, and the like are mentioned, we generally conclude by saying, these and all the other physical sciences. The term physics, in ordinary parlance, seems merely to imply that astronomy, optics, and other special and analogous sciences, have something in common, which may be designated as *physical*: it is only regarded as a convenient bond of union by which they may be held together in one group. This notion, however, is we think anti-scientific, to borrow a phrase from Comte; for, if these several sciences are *specific*, and have a common term, this can be no other than a *generic* term: and, consequently, it must logically follow that physics is the generic science, or universal, which includes all the particular physical sciences as species. Whatever may be the difficulty of establishing such a universal science as physics, it cannot be evaded; — for it is an inevitable necessity.

In reply it may urged that this is a mere metaphysical objection; and that if accepted it will involve us in a world of abstractions; that such nice precision of language is superfluous; that it is sufficient that the conventional use of the word physical is well understood, and very convenient in practice. This and much more might be objected: but it would be more rational, we think, to accept this, and any other philosophical hint, so far as to test its truth; and finding it invalid to state clearly the proof thereof. For the sake of discussing this point, let it be provisionally admitted that physics is a distinct science:

then comes the question, what is it the science of? Before attempting to give an answer, it will be well, in the first place, to call to mind the character of the special sciences; and then we may possibly gain an insight into that which they all have in common, and which ought to be the subject-matter of physics.

Astronomy is the science of celestial bodies or stars: it treats of that form of natural or material bodies, which are of vast magnitude; acting and reacting on each other by their constituent and antagonistic energies, gravitation and centrifugy, which operate as central forces, functioning in motions of rotation and revolution.

Molecular physics or micronomy, is the science of molecules: it treats of atomic forms, the *minima* of material bodies, which act and react on each other by their innate condensing and expanding forces of cohesion and heat; which operate as molecular forces, and function in the various states of matter in all their relations.

Acoustics and optics are the sciences of vibrating molecules and atoms, material undulations which are not progressive motions, but motions which oscillate within limited spaces; and which result from their component forces acting and reacting on each other, producing the phenomena of sound and light.

Lastly, polarity, the science of molecules in a state of polar motions, treats of tangential currents formed by a continuous series of polar actions and reactions produced by their constituent and opposite forces, functioning in the phenomena of electricity and magnetism.

Now, on a survey of all these special sciences, we observe that the objects of each are some *form* or other of material bodies; and that the differentiation in each case depends on this *form*, and the corresponding *phase* of the acting and reacting forces which are concerned therein. Since material bodies are all dualisms of forces, it is almost superfluous to note that all the different forces which are considered in each physical science, are only various phases of the self-same forces, *attraction* and *repulsion:* so that the various motions which these forces produce by acting in a different manner are the physical phenomena which these sciences discourse about; and all these are at root one and the same, as motions or changes of place; their various aspects depending on the peculiar methods by which these motions are accomplished. It is, therefore, the object of each special science to treat only of its individual peculiarity: whilst they all have this in common, that their objects are some *form* or condition of material bodies.

Guided by these considerations, we have been induced to conclude that there may be such a universal science as that of physics; that its subject will be that of material bodies generally or *matter:* and, accordingly, we would define physics to be the *science of matter* or physical substance. The object of such a science would be to gather together everything relating to material bodies, that is, as far as regards their physical properties.

In entering on such an undertaking it may seem to be of a more abstract character than it really is. It is true that pure matter, or ether, stands apart from all other bodies, in that it is immediately inappreciable by the senses (which, indeed, to a great extent, is also the case with a permanent gas, such as hydrogen when greatly rarefied), but this does not make it an abstraction; it is capable of being known by its phenomena; and this is as much as we can assert even of visible and tangible bodies. In dealing, therefore, with every kind of material body, there are certain physical properties which are common to them all; even in the various kinds both of chemical and organic bodies, inasmuch as they are partly material, all such properties are present, but variously modified according to their molecular condition: and in all such cases we can set aside the peculiarities, and only regard those characters which belong to general physics. In this manner we may arrive at a knowledge of various material objects which must be defined; of principles which, as laws, regulate the actions of their constituent forces, and which are expressed as axioms; and, lastly, of postulates which are requisite to explain their *modus operandi*. [We will endeavour to illustrate our meaning by a few details.

Definitions.

1. *Physics* is the science or systematic knowledge of matter.

2. *Matter* is an indissoluble dualism of attractive and repulsive powers, more generally known as physical forces.

3. *Atom*, a unit of matter, a minimum quantity of physical forces.

4. *Mass*, an aggregation of atoms into a distinct body, a part of universal matter.

5. *Material bodies*, masses of various forms.

6. *Properties of matter*, weight and volume.

7. *Weight*, a definite quantity of attraction directly as the number of atoms.

8. *Volume,* a variable quantity directly as the amount of repulsion.

9. *Atomic weight,* an indefinite minimum of weight, an assumed quantity according to some conventional standard of unity.

10. *Atomic volume,* the amount of *extension* of a single atom.

11. *Density,* or specific gravity, a relative quantity, directly as the weight and inversely as the volume.

12. *Capacity,* or specific volume, a relative bulk, directly as the volume and inversely as the weight.

13. *Equilibrium,* or statical state, that condition of matter, when its physical powers are not only co-existent and opposite, but also co-equal.

14. *Force,* or dynamic state, that condition of matter, when one or other of its dualistic powers predominates as a *plus* or energetic force.

15. *Diffusion,* or induction, the progression of a *plus* force towards the restoration of equilibrium.

16. *Motion,* the normal function of matter resulting from the action and reaction of its co-existent and opposite physical forces.

17. *Rest,* the constrained state of bodies by a *plus* resisting force in the directions of all possible motions.

Postulates.

Let it be granted that material atoms are compounds of the physical powers, attraction and repulsion.

And that these forces act on each other tangentially, the one polarly and the other equatorially; by which concentric currents are produced at right angles to each other.

Axioms.

1. Universal matter is a system rotating in perfect equilibrio, depending on the co-equality of its co-existing and opposite forces: hence the law of the conservation of forces.

2. If parts of this statical whole be added to similar parts, the total is of the same denomination.

3. If statical parts be taken from statical parts, the remainders are statical.

4. If dynamical parts (that is, portions of matter, the constituent forces of which are unequal), be added to dynamical parts, the sum or aggregate is similar.

5. If dynamical parts be subtracted from similar parts, the remainders are dynamical.

6. If statical be added to dynamical parts, the aggregate is dynamical.

7. If statical be taken from dynamical parts, the remainder is dynamical.

8. If the dynamical *state* arises from excess of attraction on any given part of universal matter, contraction of volume and increase of density result.

9. If the dynamical state proceeds from excess of repulsion, volume is enlarged and specific gravity diminished.

These axioms have more immediate reference to the condition of the constituent forces; we might have added others applicable to the motions which result from the actions and reactions of these forces; but we cannot now attempt to exhaust the subject, it is only desired so far to touch thereon as to make our views intelligible. In the above-mentioned definitions, axioms, and postulates, the terms *matter* and *forces* have been substituted for *substance* and *causes*, the abstract principles of Hypostatics: — thus this pure science may be made instrumental in working out the concrete science of physics; just as rational mechanics is applied to astronomy.

At the same time, we learn the relation which subsists between the concrete and the formal sciences: the one deals with the *real side* of nature, in which actual forces are concerned, and which function in those tangible and visible changes called physical phenomena; the other with the *ideal forms* of nature, which interpreted by the mind make known the rational principles and laws of powers according to which they exert their reason-directed forces. A complete knowledge of nature cannot be obtained but by a narrow scrutiny of both sides of the question; we must examine both the *real* and *ideal*, and then, synthetically uniting them, we complete the knowledge as far as the human mind can reach. This is not a fanciful idea, but in conformity with astronomy, which requires not only to study the concrete science, as to its actual phenomena, and the real forces of gravitation and centrifugy concerned therein, but also to know rational mechanics in order to conjoin the real and ideal; so in each of the other special physical sciences a similar conjunction must take place. And it will be, we think, also requisite that the sciences of chemistry and biology (which treat of changes which do not come under the head of physics in the restricted sense in which we have used it, as they are not concerned with changes that are motions), should be associated with corresponding formal sciences, such as rational chemistry or chemics, and rational physiology or organics.

First attempts in any new field of research must necessarily be imperfect; but, if any one has only caught a glimpse of the unknown region, ought he not fearlessly to state what he has seen, or thought he saw, regardless of the derision which may follow the detection of his delusion? There has been too much of this sarcasm used of late; it is not a scientific spirit; it may exert an unhappy influence on those who are engaged in the earnest search after truth; for it is inimical to the candid and unreserved expression of individual experience. History has taught us, that even the most eminent men will stumble into reiterated errors; and that it has been in the correction of these errors that some of the greatest advances of science have been effected: sometimes these errors have not only been detected, but corrected by the author himself; as witness those remarkable instances of Kepler, which have held him up as a pattern for future inquirers. And if this be the case, the fear of failure need not restrain any one from the candid statement of any well-considered opinion: *Magna est veritas, et prevalebit.*

Let us then gather together what has been stated generally concerning the sciences, and strive to reduce them to some arrangement, according to the preceding views. In the first place, the highest generalisation of our knowledge concerning the universe is, that it is a subordinate system of beings, a class of Ontology, characterised by its objects as dualisms of natural power. That this system of nature, which may be treated of as Cosmology, is co-ordinated with another subordinate system, or *class* of ontology, dualisms of supernatural powers, the knowledge of which may be distinguished as Pneumatology. Both these classes of dualisms may be discriminated; in the one case as spiritual, and in the other as material bodies: but in both cases they are conditioned beings, not independent and absolute, but compositions of forces. Together these classes constitute a higher class, or *summum genus*, of dualistic or conditioned beings, which gives the science of ontology; this is the whole domain of conditioned knowledge: divine knowledge we can only acquire, as taught by revelation; we cannot understand the *trinism* or *trinity* of absolute unconditioned being, and so we cannot connect the highest grade of being, the supreme power, with the system of ontology.

We are compelled, therefore, to restrict our system of the sciences to that of nature, a subordinate class of the higher system, ontology; and accordingly we define cosmology as the science of natural beings or powers, or more simply, as that of nature.

Now nature affords such a vast field for knowledge, no wonder that ages on ages have passed away without its having hitherto been reduced to one homogeneous system of doctrines: turn which way we will, we are met in every direction by portions only of this system, whose objects are so numerous and interesting, that a life-long study is insufficient for their right comprehension. During these ages, however, thousands on thousands of inquirers have spent their energies in these researches; and have recorded their results: at the same time a succession of their coadjutors have toiled to arrange these results; and to draw therefrom divers rational principles. Time has sped on, and man is still engaged in the same pursuits; the results of which have always tended to a higher and higher generalisation of knowledge in the several departments of nature: and all this inductive pioneering has been a necessary preparation for a final result.

When nature is contemplated, under the present light of accumulated knowledge, we perceive that the most general aspect which it presents to view is that of its phenomenal appearance, that is, as it seems to be, *outwardly:* and in order to make the way ready for a more minute and particular inspection, it is requisite, in the first place, to lay this down as appertaining to all the parts of nature in common. This is not only the most rational plan, but it would seem to be the more natural; for it is that course which the mind has intuitively followed, guided by the innate order of its logical methods. First, then, nature is to be posited as an entirety, as the whole world, or the universe: which first divides itself into the celestial and terrestrial; and the latter into the subordinate classes of the animate and inanimate. Again these classes unfold themselves respectively into the physical and chemical; and into the animal and vegetable kingdoms; each and all of which may be developed into an almost endless variety of genera and species; and so by an inverse order of proceeding, if we successively withdraw the most particular and the most extensive of these groups, it may be likened to the removal of each outward zone of a concentric sphere, until we at last arrive at the more simple central portion on which all were formed, and which possesses only that substantial character which is common to them all. There are various other ways in which the constitution of nature may be illustrated, as by a branching tree or river: but in whatever way it is viewed, it is one system; in its genus or universal, a material body; which is variously differentiated by additional specific properties which render it capable of being arranged according to the principles of classification.

Thus far we arrive at the knowledge of a system of nature viewed outwardly as a system of realities, of divers natural bodies having distinctive properties; the causes of which we are not now concerned with; we know them only as manifested to us by the senses, which testify that they are actual existences. The mind after having long dwelt on this knowledge, becomes aware that this is only a one-sided view which it has taken: and this depends on the very constitution of the rational mind; for every idea it conceives is knowledge, and each idea has not only a *content*, but also a *form*. But long before this knowledge of itself was acquired, the mind by its intuitive functions was conscious that in the system of nature there was not only a hierarchy of realities, but also a system of ideas, which might be viewed apart from realities, and constituted into distinct systems of knowledge. In the adolescence of the human intellect, the Greeks with youthful vigour of mind soon turned from material realities to the contemplation of their ideal forms, and in a wonderfully short space of time, for such an undertaking, got possession of those pure abstract ideas which form the ideal side of nature, as far as relate to her external appearances. And on these ideas they constructed the sciences of logic, arithmetic, and geometry, which have come down to us as a most invaluable legacy; for to these sciences we are indebted in a great measure for the success of modern researches.

So, then, in the study of outward nature we see that

two kinds of knowledge may be arrived at: if we regard it only as a system of nature, we have natural history; if we abstract therefrom only the forms of this system, disregarding the realities which constitute its actual contents, then we have a pure system, all the parts of which are merely degrees of order, which is *the* Science or logic.

Natural history and logic are universal sciences, which are concerned with the objective side of nature: it has already been suggested in this chapter, that the objective view of nature might be well distinguished from the subjective by the respective names of monistic and dualistic; indicating that the former looks at things as they appear to be in their respective individualities, the latter as they are *per se* beneath the surface, as compositions of forces.

Natural history subdivides itself into the sciences of the three kingdoms of nature, mineralogy, botany, and zoology, in as far as they are only descriptive and classificatory: logic underlies the sciences of arithmetic, geometry, and chronometry; each of these being respectively the logic of number, of space, and of time. Like the subordinate genera and species of natural history, these may be successively formed by differentiation: for in the calculations of arithmetic logical processes are necessary, as they are also in the mensurations of geometry, which moreover require the aid of numbers; and lastly in the functions of chronometry, not only logic, but also the processes of number and space, are also requisite. That is, as the sciences develope themselves in the series of complexity, all the earlier or preceding ones may be rendered subservient to their demonstrations.

We must not, however, attempt to conceal, that there

is not that corresponding conformity between the subdivisions of these *concrete* and *formal* sciences, that is necessary to make our scheme as complete as is desirable: between mineralogy, as far as relates to its subordinate crystallography, or rather to its crystalline forms, and geometry, the correspondence is somewhat satisfactory; but in the case of the other sciences the relationship is very indistinct. The above-mentioned abstract sciences seem to be clearly evolved out of the notions which the multitude, the magnitude, and the successions of natural bodies readily suggest to the contemplative mind, and may also even be evolved out of logic itself, as already shown: but we should have liked to find that each subordinate on the real side had its corresponding ideal on the opposite side of each kind of cosmical being. This confused view of the subject shows that there is something awanting to complete the analogy, which holds good in the remaining series of the sciences.

Thus when we investigate the composition of natural dualisms, that is, when we look beneath the surface of things, we find the real and the ideal in a very distinct antithesis:—thus in the universal sciences, we have the concrete phenomenology (not however as yet developed as a distinct science) and the formal hypostatics; the one treating of the actions and reactions of forces which function in actual phenomena, the other, of the relations of pure causes which by causation eventuate in formal effects. Physics subdivides itself into astronomy, micronomy, acoustics, optics, and polarity, all treating of different kinds of motions, and the peculiar phases of physical forces by which they are produced: and opposite to each of these we have the subordinate sciences of hypostatics; — viz. rational mechanics or cinematics, with its various methods adapted to the special forms of motion with which they are concerned. And lastly we have chemistry, which treats of those specific forces which seem to be intimately related to attraction, the basis or quantitative constituent of physical substance or matter, a fundamental principle of physics: whilst biology deals with a very different class of specific forces which are related to the other universal principle of physics, repulsion; as already set forth.

Here, then, on the real side, the specific powers are correctly evolved out of the universal powers, and their position in the general system clearly defined: and the corresponding sciences related to this subject on the ideal side, though not yet acknowledged and worked out, yet seem to be satisfactorily indicated as rational chemistry, or chemics, and rational physiology, or organics.

This is a rapid survey of those sciences, which are commonly called physical or natural, and we will now gather them together in their order.

The trunk of our tree of knowledge, Ontology, has its roots concealed in absolute being, which the unassisted mind cannot know, as is also the case with one of its two branches: — so that human knowledge really begins with Cosmology, the science of corporeal beings. The subdivisions of the latter rest on our correlation, $A + B = AB$. One side of this equation is intuitively known as the monistic phenomenon; the other, as the elements of the dualism, the *veræ causæ* of all actions and reactions: — and these opposite sides of Nature give corresponding sciences.

ARBOR SCIENTIARUM.

ONTOLOGY.
The Science of Conditioned Beings.

PNEUMATOLOGY.   **COSMOLOGY.**
The Science of Spiritual Beings.   The Science of Corporeal Beings.

1st Division, as Monisms.   2nd Division, as Dualisms.

As Real.   As Ideal.

NATURAL HISTORY.   LOGIC.
The Science of Nature.   The Science.

MINERALOGY.   ARITHMETIC.
BOTANY.   GEOMETRY.
ZOOLOGY.   CHRONOMETRY.

On the Real Side, as Forces.   On the Ideal side, as Rational Causes.

PHENOMENOLOGY, the Science of Natural Dualisms.   HYPOSTATICS, the Science of Substance.

Subdivisions of.   Subdivisions of.

1. PHYSICS, the Science of Material Bodies, or of Matter.
   a. ASTRONOMY, the Science of Stars, or Celestial Bodies.
   b. MICRONOMY, the Science of Molecules.
   c. ACOUSTICS, the Science of Sound.
   d. OPTICS, the Science of Light.
   e. POLARITY, the Science of Polarised Molecules.
2. CHEMISTRY, the Science of Chemical Bodies.
3. BIOLOGY, the Science of Living Bodies.
   a. Physiology.   b. Psychology.

1. RATIONAL MECHANICS, the Science of Motion, treats of
   a. Orbital Motions.
   b. Contractions and Expansions.
   c. Sound-waves } Undulations.
   d. Light-waves }
   e. Polar Motions.

2. RATIONAL CHEMICS, the Science of Combination.
3. RATIONAL ORGANICS, the Science of Organisation.

This sketch is confessedly imperfect, still we are inclined to think that it throws some light on an important subject; — viz. the relationship of the principal sciences, both concrete and pure: it shows that whatever department of nature we make the object of our investigation, whether as to its outward appearance, or to its inner constitution, it will be found to have both a real and ideal side; and accordingly as we direct our attention to the one or the other, the knowledge obtained must relate either to forces or ideas; that it must be resolved into either a physical or a formal science. And in order to complete our knowledge of any concrete subject, it is necessary to apply the abstract science in the illustration of its phenomena.

Many of the sciences which we have enumerated have several ramifications, which would require lengthened details even for their bare mention; but this omission is of little consequence, for the position of most of them cannot be mistaken. There is, however, one science which has engaged much attention on the continent, which should not be passed over without notice; viz. Morphology: if this science be viewed as concrete, related to actual material bodies, it would furnish a good substitute for the very uncouth term, natural history, and would greatly improve the appearance of the preceding tabular arrangement. But it sometimes assumes rather the aspect of a pure science: and if this view were strictly adhered to, the science would approximate very nearly to geometry: this is evident when the morphic forms or figures are those of crystals; but when extended to organic forms, the case becomes dubious. Still, when we remember that it is only in certain parts of every science that its objects are *definite* (for at both extremes they are *indefinite*), it is very possible that no parts of space, as manifested by natural bodies, are truly amorphous, that they are always approximations, though these are indefinite. All things considered, however, we are rather disposed to the former opinion, because the term morphology might be used as the science of the outward forms or figures of natural bodies; — the classification of phenomena.

But in our enumeration there may appear to have been a still greater omission; we have not given a place in the system to the important science of Geology: the reason for so doing is as follows. Our planet is one of the stars, one of the many objects which make up the subject-matter of astronomy: its history is that of an individual star from the period of its origin, by solar fission, to the present period of its existence. During this lapse of ages, it has undergone a succession of important changes, which in the days of its youth were vast and momentous; but as it approached maturer years, these changes have settled down to a regular routine, which mark the several stages of its existence. *Now*, it seems to have attained a good old age: the action of the elements, aided by chemical changes, and the continuous accumulation of organic exuviæ, are the same in kind as they have been for many preceding epochs; but the material degradations and reconstructions are more feeble, and the results correspondingly inconsiderable. The study of these changes, the individual history of the earth, forms the subject-matter of geology; and for the successful prosecution of this interesting research, the physical, chemical, and physiological sciences must all render their assistance: it is a vast study, requiring a great range of knowledge; a science, if it can be so called, of a very *complex* character. It rather seems to us to be a historical subject, in the illustration of which many sciences are aptly applied: for we cannot discern in it any fundamental principle, which can become the noun-substantive of a distinct science. The earth, as a natural body, has experienced, and continues to experience, a vast variety of changes; but when we abstract therefrom all the physical, chemical, and organic changes, the result seems to be exhaustive: could we detect one which does not fall within these categories, then we might be able to erect geology into a *primary* science; but failing this, it can only be a history, like that of any other individual creature, or at best a *compound* science.

It is time, however, to draw our subject to a close. We would have gladly entered on the discussion of moral, social, and political topics: but these, as already remarked, are anthropological; — so distinct from physical sciences, that it was deemed expedient to keep them apart.

In conclusion, we would fain express our hope that we have not laboured altogether in vain; that the various views put forward on important subjects, if not accepted, may at least be the means of directing attention into new channels: and if so, they cannot fail to render some good service; for any new direction given to thought is an excellent stimulus for invigorating mental exertion. The frequent antagonism of our opinions to those which now generally prevail, is not favourable for a patient consideration: but though our opinions are so directly opposed to others, they have not been adopted hastily; they have been grounded on natural phenomena, which may, however, have been erroneously interpreted. Such errors have been continually committed; but natural facts are the only source of science; and, right or wrong, we must persevere in attempting the solution of these problems: the very difficulty of the interpretation arouses the intellect to the greatest exertions; and no one has the right dogmatically to determine what can, and what cannot be accomplished; for nature herself is the only limitation of human knowledge. On this subject Lord Bacon has well observed, " Homo enim Naturæ minister et interpres tantum facit et intelligit, quantum de Naturæ ordine, opere, vel mente, observaverit; nec amplius scit, aut potest. Neque enim ullæ vires causarum catenam solvere aut perfringere possunt: neque Natura aliter quam parendo vincitur. Itaque intentiones geminæ illæ, humanæ scilicet *scientiæ* et *potentiæ*, vere in idem coincidunt: et frustratio operum maxime fit ex ignoratione causarum."

We have endeavoured to show that knowledge and power are not only co-existent, but co-equal: as the one increases or diminishes, so must the other; for they are the inseparable attributes of the self-same being. All beings are powers, whether simple or compound; and every power has the attributes of force and reason: without force, reason could not manifest its designs; and without reason, force would have no law for the regulation of its actions. So that, of a truth, *powers* are *veræ causæ*, not mere brute forces, rioting in indiscriminate licentiousness; but powers which are a law unto themselves: and that law is the *reason in nature*, which directs all her forces; and according to which they function in co-ordinated phenomena. In this conclusion, we are in direct antagonism to Humboldt, Comte, and some of the most talented men of this country, whom it would be invidious to mention. There was a time of ignorance, they say, when myths and personifications of forces were excusable; but science has now dispelled all this darkness. "The business of the positive philosophy is, — seeing how vain is any research into what are called *causes*, whether first or final, — to pursue an accurate discovery of natural laws, with a view of reducing them to the smallest possible number: to analyse accurately the circumstances of phenomena, and to connect them by the natural relations of succession and resemblance."

The idea of a law, other than an appointed rule for the regulation of an actual being or power in its operations, is to us inconceivable; and if there be such powers, which as causes are known by their effects, then must such be, in a sense, *personifications;* that is, individual existences. But we must refrain; — our case is now before the scientific world: we repudiate positivism, and the identity of forces; maintaining that all natural bodies are dualisms of powers; and that each power is a reason-directed force.

THE END.

LONDON
PRINTED BY SPOTTISWOODE AND CO.
NEW-STREET SQUARE

LIST OF WORKS IN GENERAL LITERATURE

PUBLISHED BY

MESSRS. LONGMAN, GREEN, LONGMAN, AND ROBERTS

39 PATERNOSTER ROW, LONDON.

CLASSIFIED INDEX.

Agriculture and Rural Affairs.

Bayldon on Valuing Rents, &c.	4
" Road Legislation	4
Caird's Prairie Farming	5
Cecil's Stud Farm	10
Hoskyns's Talpa	13
Loudon's Agriculture	13
Low's Elements of Agriculture	13
Morton on Landed Property	16

Arts, Manufactures, and Architecture.

Bourne's Catechism of the Steam Engine	4
Brande's Dictionary of Science, &c.	4
" Organic Chemistry	4
Creay's Civil Engineering	6
Fairbairn's Informa. for Engineers	7
Gwilt's Encyclo. of Architecture	8
Harford's Plates from M. Angelo	8
Humphreys's Parables Illuminated	11
Jameson's Saints and Martyrs	11
" Monastic Orders	11
" Legends of Madonna	11
" Commonplace-Book	11
König's Pictorial Life of Luther	8
Loudon's Rural Architecture	13
MacDougall's Campaigns of Hannibal	14
MacDougall's Theory of War	14
Moseley's Engineering	16
Piesse's Art of Perfumery	18
Richardson's Art of Horsemanship	18
Scoffern on Projectiles, &c.	19
Steam-Engine, by the Artisan Club	4
Ure's Dictionary of Arts, &c.	23

Biography.

Arago's Lives of Scientific Men	3
Baillie's Memoir of Bate	3
Brialmont's Wellington	4
Bunsen's Hippolytus	5
Bunting's (Dr.) Life	5
Crosse's (Andrew) Memorials	6
Green's Princesses of England	8
Harford's Life of Michael Angelo	8
Lardner's Cabinet Cyclopædia	12
Marshman's Life of Carey, Marshman, and Ward	14
Maunder's Biographical Treasury	15
Morris's Life of Becket	16
Mountain's (Col.) Memoirs	16
Parry's (Admiral) Memoirs	17
Russell's Memoirs of Moore	18
" (Dr.) Mezzofanti	19
SchimmelPenninck's (Mrs.) Life	19
Southey's Life of Wesley	21
Stephen's Ecclesiastical Biography	21
Strickland's Queens of England	20
Sydney Smith's Memoirs	21
Symond's (Admiral) Memoirs	21
Taylor's Loyola	21
" Wesley	21
Uwins's Memoirs	23
Waterton's Autobiography & Essays	24

Books of General Utility.

Acton's Bread-Book	3
" Cookery	3
Black's Treatise on Brewing	4
Cabinet Gazetteer	5
" Lawyer	5
Cust's Invalid's Own Book	7
Hints on Etiquette	9
Hudson's Executor's Guide	10
" on Making Wills	10
Kesteven's Domestic Medicine	12
Lardner's Cabinet Cyclopædia	12
London's Lady's Country Companion	13

Maunder's Treasury of Knowledge	15
" Biographical Treasury	15
" Geographical Treasury	15
" Scientific Treasury	14
" Treasury of History	15
" Natural History	15
Piesse's Art of Perfumery	8
Pitt's How to Brew Good Beer	18
Pocket and the Stud	9
Pycroft's English Reading	18
Rich's Comp. to Latin Dictionary	18
Richardson's Art of Horsemanship	18
Riddle's Latin Dictionaries	18
Roget's English Thesaurus	19
Rowton's Debater	19
Short Whist	20
Simpson's Handbook of Dining	20
Thomson's Interest Tables	23
Webster's Domestic Economy	24
Willich's Popular Tables	24
Wilmot's Blackstone	24

Botany and Gardening.

Hassall's British Freshwater Algæ	9
Hooker's British Flora	9
" Guide to Kew Gardens	9
Lindley's Introduction to Botany	13
" Synopsis of the British Flora	13
" Theory of Horticulture	13
Loudon's Hortus Britannicus	13
" Amateur Gardener	13
" Trees and Shrubs	13
" Gardening	13
" Plants	13
Pereira's Materia Medica	17
Rivera's Rose-Amateur's Guide	19
Watson's Cybele Britannica	24
Wilson's British Mosses	24

Chronology.

Brewer's Historical Atlas	4
Bunsen's Ancient Egypt	5
Haydn's Beatson's Index	11
Jaquemet's Chronology	11
" Abridged Chronology	11
Nicolas's Chronology of History	12

Commerce and Mercantile Affairs.

Gilbart's Logic of Banking	8
" Treatise on Banking	8
Lorimer's Young Master Mariner	13
M'Culloch's Commerce & Navigation	14
Thomson's Interest Tables	23
Tooke's History of Prices	23

Criticism, History, and Memoirs.

Brewer's Historical Atlas	4
Bunsen's Ancient Egypt	5
" Hippolytus	5
Chapman's Gustavus Adolphus	6
Conybeare and Howson's St. Paul	6
Connolly's Sappers and Miners	6
Crowe's History of France	6
Fraser's Letters during the Peninsular and Waterloo Campaigns	8
Gleig's Essays	8
Gurney's Historical Sketches	8
Hayward's Essays	9
Herschel's Essays and Addresses	9
Jeffrey's (Lord) Essays	11
Kemble's Anglo-Saxons	11
Lardner's Cabinet Cyclopædia	12
Macaulay's Crit. and Hist. Essays	13
" History of England	13
" Speeches	13

Mackintosh's Miscellaneous Works	14
" History of England	14
M'Culloch's Geographical Dictionary	14
Maunder's Treasury of History	15
Merivale's History of Rome	15
" Roman Republic	15
Milner's Church History	15
Moore's (Thomas) Memoirs, &c.	16
Mure's Greek Literature	16
Normanby's Year of Revolution	17
Perry's Franks	17
Porter's Knights of Malta	18
Raikes's Journal	18
Riddle's Latin Lexicon	18
Rogers's Essays from Edinb. Review	19
" (Sam.) Recollections	19
Roget's English Thesaurus	19
SchimmelPenninck's Memoirs of Port Royal	19
SchimmelPenninck's Principles of Beauty, &c.	19
Schmitz's History of Greece	19
Southey's Doctor	21
Stephen's Ecclesiastical Biography	21
" Lectures on French History	21
Sydney Smith's Works	21
" Lectures	21
" Memoirs	21
Taylor's Loyola	21
" Wesley	21
Thirlwall's History of Greece	23
Turner's Anglo-Saxons	23
Uwins's Memoirs	23
Vehse's Austrian Court	23
Wade's England's Greatness	23
Young's Christ of History	24

Geography and Atlases.

Brewer's Historical Atlas	4
Butler's Geography and Atlases	5
Cabinet Gazetteer	5
Johnston's General Gazetteer	11
M'Culloch's Geographical Dictionary	14
Maunder's Treasury of Geography	15
Murray's Encyclo. of Geography	16
Sharp's British Gazetteer	20

Juvenile Books.

Amy Herbert	20
Cleve Hall	20
Earl's Daughter (The)	20
Experience of Life	20
Gertrude	20
Howitt's Boy's Country Book	10
" (Mary) Children's Year	10
Ivors	20
Katharine Ashton	20
Laneton Parsonage	20
Margaret Percival	20
Piesse's Chymical, Natural, and Physical Magic	18
Pycroft's Collegian's Guide	18

Medicine, Surgery, &c.

Brodie's Psychological Inquiries	5
Bull's Hints to Mothers	5
" Management of Children	5
" on Blindness	5
Copland's Dictionary of Medicine	6
Cust's Invalid's Own Book	7
Holland's Mental Physiology	9
" Medical Notes and Reflect.	9
Kesteven's Domestic Medicine	12
Pereira's Materia Medica	17
Richardson's Cold-Water Cure	18
Spencer's Psychology	21
Todd's Cyclopædia of Anatomy and Physiology	21

CLASSIFIED INDEX TO GENERAL CATALOGUE.

Miscellaneous and General Literature.

Bacon's (Lord) Works - - - 3
Defence of *Eclipse of Faith* - - 7
De Fonblanque on Army Administration - - - - 7
Eclipse of Faith - - - 7
Fischer's Bacon and Realistic Philosophy - - - - 7
Greathed's Letters from Delhi - 8
Greyson's Select Correspondence - 8
Gurney's Evening Recreations - 8
Hassall's Adulterations Detected, &c. 9
Haydn's Book of Dignities - - 9
Holland's Mental Physiology - - 9
Hooker's Kew Guide - - - 9
Howitt's Rural Life of England - 10
" Visits to Remarkable Places - 10
Jameson's Commonplace-Book - 11
Last of the Old Squires - - 17
Letters of a Betrothed - - 13
Macaulay's Speeches - - - 14
Mackintosh's Miscellaneous Works 14
Martineau's Miscellanies - - 14
Pycroft's English Reading - - 18
Rich's Comp. to Latin Dictionary - 18
Riddle's Latin Dictionaries - - 19
Rowton's Debater - - - 19
Sir Roger De Coverley - - 20
Southey's Doctor, &c. - - 21
Spencer's Essays - - - 21
Stow's Training System - - 21
Thomson's Laws of Thought - - 23
Trevelyan on the Native Languages of India - - - 23
Willich's Popular Tables - - 24
Yonge's English-Greek Lexicon - 24
" Latin Gradus - - 24
Zumpt's Latin Grammar - - 24

Natural History in general.

Agassiz on Classification - - 3
Catlow's Popular Conchology - 6
Ephemera's Book of the Salmon - 7
Garratt's Marvels of Instinct - 8
Gosse's Natural History of Jamaica 8
Kirby and Spence's Entomology - 12
Lee's Elements of Natural History 12
Maunder's Natural History - - 15
Morris's Anecdotes in Natural History - - - 16
Quatrefages' Naturalist's Rambles 18
Stonehenge on the Dog - - 21
Turton's Shells of the British Islands 23
Van der Hoeven's Zoology - - 23
Waterton's Essays on Natural Hist. 24
Youatt's Work on the Dog - - 24
Youatt's Work on the Horse - - 24

1-Volume Encyclopædias and Dictionaries.

Blaine's Rural Sports - - - 4
Brande's Science, Literature, and Art 4
Copland's Dictionary of Medicine - 6
Cresy's Civil Engineering - - 6
Gwilt's Architecture - - - 8
Johnston's Geographical Dictionary 11
London's Agriculture - - 13
" Rural Architecture - 13
" Gardening - - 13
" Plants - - - 13
" Trees and Shrubs - 13
M'Culloch's Geographical Dictionary 14
" Dictionary of Commerce 14
Murray's Encyclo. of Geography - 16
Sharp's British Gazetteer - - 20
Ure's Dictionary of Arts, &c. - - 24
Webster's Domestic Economy - 24

Religious & Moral Works.

Afternoon of Life - - - 3
Amy Herbert - - - - 20
Bloomfield's Greek Testament - 4
Bunyan's Pilgrim's Progress - - 5
Calvert's Wife's Manual - - 6
Catz and Farlie's Moral Emblems - 6
Cleve Hall - - - - 20
Conybeare and Howson's St. Paul 6
Cotton's Instructions in Christianity 6
Dale's Domestic Liturgy - - 7
Defence of *Eclipse of Faith* - - 7
Earl's Daughter (The) - - 20
Eclipse of Faith - - - 7
Englishman's Greek Concordance 7
" Heb. & Chald. Concord. 7
Experience (The) of Life - - 20
Gertrude - - - - 20
Harrison's Light of the Forge - 8
Horne's Introduction to Scriptures 10
" Abridgment of ditto - 10
Huc's Christianity in China - - 10
Humphreys's *Parables* Illuminated 11

Ivors; or, the Two Cousins - - 20
Jameson's Sacred Legends - - 11
" Monastic Legends - - 11
" Legends of the Madonna 11
" Lectures on Female Employment - - - 11
Jeremy Taylor's Works - - 11
Katharine Ashton - - - 20
König's Pictorial Life of Luther - 8
Laneton Parsonage - - - 20
Letters to my Unknown Friends - 13
Lyra Germanica - - - 5
Maguire's Rome - - - 14
Margaret Percival - - - 20
Marshman's Serampore Mission - 14
Martineau's Christian Life - - 14
" Hymns - - 14
" Studies of Christianity 14
Merivale's Christian Records - 15
Milner's Church of Christ - - 15
Moore on the Use of the Body - 16
" Soul and Body - 16
" 's Man and his Motives - 16
Morning Clouds - - - 16
Neale's Closing Scene - - 16
Pattison's Earth and Word - - 17
Powell's Christianity without Judaism - - - 18
" Order of Nature - 18
Readings for Lent - - - 20
" Confirmation - 20
Robinson's Lexicon to the Greek Testament - - - 19
Self-Examination for Confirmation 20
Sewell's History of the Early Church - - - 20
Sinclair's Journey of Life - - 20
Smith's (Sydney) Moral Philosophy 21
" (G.) Wesleyan Methodism 20
" (J.) St. Paul's Shipwreck - 21
Southey's Life of Wesley - - 21
Stephen's Ecclesiastical Biography 21
Taylor's Loyola - - - 21
" Wesley - - - 21
Theologia Germanica - - 5
Thumb Bible (The) - - - 23
Ursula - - - - 20
Young's Christ of History - - 24
" Mystery - - - 24

Poetry and the Drama.

Aikin's (Dr.) British Poets - - 3
Arnold's Merope - - - 3
" Poems - - - 3
Baillie's (Joanna) Poetical Works - 3
Goldsmith's Poems, Illustrated - 8
L. E. L.'s Poetical Works - - 13
Linwood's Anthologia Oxoniensis - 13
Lyra Germanica - - - 5
Macaulay's Lays of Ancient Rome 14
Mac Donald's Within and Without 14
" Poems - - 14
Montgomery's Poetical Works - 15
Moore's Poetical Works - - 16
" Selections (Illustrated) - 16
" Lalla Rookh - - 16
" Irish Melodies - - 16
" National Melodies - 16
" Sacred Songs (*with Music*) 16
" Songs and Ballads - 16
Shakspeare, by Bowdler - - 19
Southey's Poetical Works - - 21
Thomson's Seasons, Illustrated - 23

The Sciences in general and Mathematics.

Arago's Meteorological Essays - 3
" Popular Astronomy - 3
Bourne's Catechism of Steam-Engine - - - - 4
Boyd's Naval Cadet's Manual - 4
Brande's Dictionary of Science, &c. 4
" Lectures on Organic Chemistry 4
Conington's Chemical Analysis - 6
Cresy's Civil Engineering - - 6
De la Rive's Electricity - - 7
Grove's Correla. of Physical Forces 8
Herschel's Outlines of Astronomy 9
Holland's Mental Physiology - 9
Humboldt's Aspects of Nature - 10
" Cosmos - - - 10
Hunt on Light - - - 11
Lardner's Cabinet Cyclopædia - 12
Marcet's (Mrs.) Conversations - 14
Morell's Elements of Psychology - 16
Moseley's Engineering & Architecture 16
Ogilvie's Master-Builder's Plan - 17
Owen's Lectures on Comp. Anatomy 17
Pereira on Polarised Light - - 17

Peschel's Elements of Physics - 1
Phillips's Mineralogy - - - 17
" Guide to Geology - 17
Powell's Unity of Worlds - - 18
Smee's Electro-Metallurgy - - 20
Steam-Engine (The) - - - 4
Webb's Celestial Objects for Common Telescopes - - 2

Rural Sports.

Baker's Rifle and Hound in Ceylon 3
Blaine's Dictionary of Sports - 4
Cecil's Stable Practice - - 6
" Stud Farm - - 6
Davy's Fishing Excursions, 2 Series 7
Ephemera on Angling - - 7
" 's Book of the Salmon - 7
Freeman and Salvin's Falconry - 7
Hawker's Young Sportsman - 9
The Hunting-Field - - - 6
Idle's Hints on Shooting - - 11
Pocket and the Stud - - 6
Pycroft's Cricket-Field - - 18
Richardson's Horsemanship - 18
Ronalds' Fly-Fisher's Entomology 19
Stable Talk and Table Talk - 6
Stonehenge on the Dog - - 21
" on the Greyhound - 21
The Stud, for Practical Purposes - 6

Veterinary Medicine, &c.

Cecil's Stable Practice - - 6
" Stud Farm - - 6
Hunt's Horse and his Master - 11
Hunting-Field (The) - - - 6
Miles's Horse-Shoeing - - 16
" on the Horse's Foot - 16
Pocket and the Stud - - 6
Practical Horsemanship - - 6
Richardson's Horsemanship - 18
Stable Talk and Table Talk - 6
Stonehenge on the Dog - - 21
Stud (The) - - - - 6
Youatt's Work on the Dog - - 24
Youatt's Work on the Horse - 24

Voyages and Travels.

Baker's Wanderings in Ceylon - 3
Barth's African Travels - - 3
Burton's East Africa - - - 5
" Medina and Mecca - 5
Domenech's Texas - - - 7
" Deserts of North America 7
First Impressions of the New World 7
Forester's Sardinia and Corsica - 7
Hinchliff's Travels in the Alps - 9
Howitt's Art-Student in Munich - 10
" (W.) Victoria - - 10
Huc's Chinese Empire - - 10
Hudson and Kennedy's Mont Blanc - - - - 10
Humboldt's Aspects of Nature - 10
Hutchinson's Western Africa - 11
Kane's Wanderings of an Artist - 11
Lady's Tour round Monte Rosa - 12
M'Clure's North-West Passage - 14
MacDougall's Voyage of the *Resolute* 14
Minturn's New York to Delhi - 15
Möllhausen's Journey to the Shores of the Pacific - - - 15
Osborn's Quedah - - - 17
Peaks, Passes, and Glaciers - 17
Scherzer's Central America - - 19
Senior's Journal in Turkey and Greece - - - - 19
Snow's Tierra del Fuego - - 21
Tennent's Ceylon - - - 21
Von Tempsky's Mexico - - 23
Wanderings in Land of Ham - 23
Weld's Vacations in Ireland - 24
" Pyrenees - - - 24
" United States and Canada 24

Works of Fiction.

Connolly's Romance of the Ranks 6
Cruikshank's Falstaff - - 10
Howitt's Tallangetta - - 10
Mildred Norman - - - 15
Moore's Epicurean - - - 16
Sewell's Ursula - - - 20
Sir Roger De Coverley - - 20
Sketches (The), Three Tales - 20
Southey's The Doctor &c. - - 21
Trollope's Barchester Towers - 23
" Warden - - - 23

ALPHABETICAL CATALOGUE

of

NEW WORKS and NEW EDITIONS

PUBLISHED BY

MESSRS. LONGMAN, GREEN, LONGMAN, AND ROBERTS,

PATERNOSTER ROW, LONDON.

Miss Acton's Modern Cookery for Private Families, reduced to a System of Easy Practice in a Series of carefully-tested Receipts, in which the Principles of Baron Liebig and other eminent Writers have been as much as possible applied and explained. Newly-revised and enlarged Edition; with 8 Plates, comprising 27 Figures, and 150 Woodcuts. Fcp. 8vo. 7s. 6d.

Acton's English Bread-Book for Domestic Use, adapted to Families of every grade. Fcp. 8vo. price 4s. 6d. cloth.

The Afternoon of Life. By the Author of *Morning Clouds*. Second and cheaper Edition, revised throughout. Fcp. 8vo. 5s.

Agassiz.—An Essay on Classification. By LOUIS AGASSIZ. 8vo. 12s.

Aikin.—Select Works of the British Poets, from Ben Jonson to Beattie. With Biographical and Critical Prefaces by Dr. AIKIN. New Edition, with Supplement by LUCY AIKIN; consisting of additional Selections from more recent Poets. 8vo. 18s.

Arago (F.)—Biographies of Distinguished Scientific Men. Translated by Admiral W. H. SMYTH, D.C.L., F.R.S., &c.; the Rev. BADEN POWELL, M.A.; and ROBERT GRANT, M.A., F.R.A.S. 8vo. 18s.

Arago's Meteorological Essays. With an Introduction by Baron HUMBOLDT. Translated under the superintendence of Major-General E. SABINE, R.A., Treasurer and V.P.R.S. 8vo. 18s.

Arago's Popular Astronomy. Translated and edited by Admiral W. H. SMYTH, D.C.L., F.R.S.; and ROBERT GRANT, M.A., F.R.A.S. With 25 Plates and 358 Woodcuts. 2 vols. 8vo. price £2. 5s.

Arnold.—Poems. By Matthew Arnold. FIRST SERIES, Third Edition. Fcp. 8vo. price 5s. 6d. SECOND SERIES, price 5s.

Arnold.—Merope, a Tragedy. By Matthew ARNOLD. With a Preface and an Historical Introduction. Fcp. 8vo. 5s.

Lord Bacon's Works. A New Edition, revised and elucidated; and enlarged by the addition of many pieces not printed before. Collected and edited by ROBERT LESLIE ELLIS, M.A., Fellow of Trinity College, Cambridge; JAMES SPEDDING, M.A. of Trinity College, Cambridge; and DOUGLAS DENON HEATH, Esq., Barrister-at-Law, and late Fellow of Trinity College, Cambridge.—VOLS. I. to V., comprising the Division of *Philosophical Works*; with a copious INDEX. 5 vols. 8vo. price £4. 6s. VOL. VI. price 18s.

*** VOL. VII., completing the Division of *Literary and Professional Works*, is just ready.

Joanna Baillie's Dramatic and Poetical Works: Comprising the Plays of the Passions, Miscellaneous Dramas, Metrical Legends, Fugitive Pieces, and Ahalya Baee; with the Life of Joanna Baillie, Portrait, and Vignette. Square crown 8vo. 21s. cloth; or 42s. bound in morocco by Hayday.

Baker. — The Rifle and the Hound in Ceylon. By S. W. BAKER, Esq. New Edition, with 13 Illustrations engraved on Wood. Fcp. 8vo. 4s. 6d.

Baker.—Eight Years' Wanderings in Ceylon. By S. W. BAKER, Esq. With 6 coloured Plates. 8vo. price 15s.

Bate.—Memoir of Capt. W. Thornton Bate, R.N. By the Rev. JOHN BAILLIE, Author of "Memoirs of Hewitson," "Memoir of Adelaide Newton," &c. New Edition; with Portrait and 4 Illustrations. Fcp. 8vo. 5s.

Barth. — Travels and Discoveries in North and Central Africa : Being the Journal of an Expedition undertaken under the auspices of Her Britannic Majesty's Government in the Years 1849—1855. By HENRY BARTH, Ph.D., D.C.L., Fellow of the Royal Geographical and Asiatic Societies, &c. With numerous Maps, Wood Engravings, and Illustrations in tinted Lithography. 5 vols. 8vo. £5. 5s. cloth.

Bayldon's Art of Valuing Rents and Tillages, and Claims of Tenants upon Quitting Farms, at both Michaelmas and Lady-Day ; as revised by Mr. DONALDSON. *Seventh Edition*, enlarged and adapted to the Present Time : With the Principles and Mode of Valuing Land and other Property for Parochial Assessment and Enfranchisement of Copyholds, under the recent Acts of Parliament. By ROBERT BAKER, Land-Agent and Valuer. 8vo. 10s. 6d.

Bayldon's (R.) Treatise on Road Legislation and Management ; with Remarks on Tolls, and on Repairing Turnpike-Roads and Highways. 8vo. 3s. 6d.

Black's Practical Treatise on Brewing, based on Chemical and Economical Principles : With Formulæ for Public Brewers, and Instructions for Private Families. New Edition, with Additions. 8vo. 10s. 6d.

Blaine's Encyclopædia of Rural Sports ; or, a complete Account, Historical, Practical, and Descriptive, of Hunting, Shooting, Fishing, Racing, &c. *New Edition*, revised and corrected ; with above 600 Woodcut Illustrations, including 20 now added from Designs by JOHN LEECH. In One Volume, 8vo. price 42s. half-bound.

Bloomfield. — The Greek Testament, with copious English Notes, Critical, Philological, and Explanatory. Especially adapted to the use of Theological Students and Ministers. By the Rev. S. T. BLOOMFIELD, D.D., F.S.A. Ninth Edition, revised. 2 vols. 8vo. with Map, price £2. 8s.

Dr. **Bloomfield's College and School Edition of** the *Greek Testament :* With brief English Notes, chiefly Philological and Explanatory. Seventh Edition ; with Map and Index. Fcp. 8vo. 7s. 6d.

Dr. **Bloomfield's College and School Lexicon** to the Greek Testament. New Edition, carefully revised. Fcp. 8vo. price 10s. 6d.

Bourne. — A Treatise on the Steam-Engine, in its Application to Mines, Mills, Steam-Navigation, and Railways. By the Artisan Club. Edited by JOHN BOURNE, C.E. New Edition ; with 33 Steel Plates and 349 Wood Engravings. 4to. price 27s.

Bourne's Catechism of the Steam - Engine in its various Applications to Mines, Mills, Steam-Navigation, Railways, and Agriculture : With Practical Instructions for the Manufacture and Management of Engines of every class. Fourth Edition, enlarged ; with 89 Woodcuts. Fcp. 8vo. 6s.

Boyd. — A Manual for Naval Cadets. Published with the sanction and approval of the Lords Commissioners of the Admiralty. By JOHN M'NEILL BOYD, Captain, R.N. With Compass-Signals in Colours, and 236 Woodcuts. Fcp. 8vo. 10s. 6d.

Brande. — A Dictionary of Science, Literature, and Art : Comprising the History, Description, and Scientific Principles of every Branch of Human Knowledge ; with the Derivation and Definition of all the Terms in general use. Edited by W. T. BRANDE, F.R.S.L. and E. ; assisted by DR. J. CAUVIN. Third Edition, revised and corrected ; with numerous Woodcuts. 8vo. 60s.

Professor Brande's Lectures on Organic Chemistry, as applied to Manufactures ; including Dyeing, Bleaching, Calico-Printing, Sugar-Manufacture, the Preservation of Wood, Tanning, &c. ; delivered before the Members of the Royal Institution. Edited by J. SCOFFERN, M.B. Fcp. 8vo. with Woodcuts, price 7s. 6d.

Brewer. — An Atlas of History and Geography, from the Commencement of the Christian Era to the Present Time : Comprising a Series of Sixteen coloured Maps, arranged in Chronological Order, with Illustrative Memoirs. By the Rev. J. S. BREWER, M.A., Professor of English History and Literature in King's College, London. *Second Edition*, revised and corrected. Royal 8vo. 12s. 6d. half-bound.

Brialmont.—The Life of the Duke of Wellington. From the French of ALEXIS BRIALMONT, Captain on the Staff of the Belgian Army : With Emendations and Additions. By the Rev. G. R. GLEIG, M.A., Chaplain-General to the Forces and Prebendary of St. Paul's. With Maps, Plans of Battles, and Portraits. VOLS. I. and II. 8vo. 30s.

The THIRD and FOURTH VOLUMES (completion) are now in the press, and will take up the history of the Duke from the Battle of Waterloo, representing him as an Ambassador, as a Minister, and as a Citizen.

Brodie.—Psychological Inquiries, in a Series of Essays intended to illustrate the Influence of the Physical Organisation on the Mental Faculties. By Sir BENJAMIN C. BRODIE, Bart. Third Edition. Fcp. 8vo. 5s.

Dr. Thomas Bull on the Maternal Management of Children in Health and Disease. New Edition. Fcp. 8vo. 5s.

Dr. Bull's Hints to Mothers on the Management of their Health during the Period of Pregnancy and in the Lying-in Room: With an Exposure of Popular Errors in connexion with those subjects, &c.; and Hints upon Nursing. New Edition. Fcp. 8vo. 5s.

Dr. Bull's Work on Blindness, entitled the Sense of Vision Denied and Lost. Edited by the Rev. B. G. JOHNS, Chaplain of the Blind School, St. George's Fields. With a brief Introductory Memoir of the Author by Mrs. BULL. Fcp. 8vo. 4s. 6d.

Bunsen.— Christianity and Mankind, their Beginnings and Prospects. By Baron C. C. J. BUNSEN, D.D., D.C.L., D.Ph. Being a New Edition, corrected, remodelled, and extended, of *Hippolytus and his Age.* 7 vols. 8vo. £5. 5s.

* This Edition is composed of three distinct works, which may be had separately, as follows:—

1. Hippolytus and his Age; or, the Beginnings and Prospects of Christianity. 2 vols. 8vo. price £1. 10s.
2. Outline of the Philosophy of Universal History applied to Language and Religion: Containing an Account of the Alphabetical Conferences. 2 vols. 8vo. price £1. 13s.
3. Analecta Ante-Nicæna. 3 vols. 8vo. price £2. 2s.

Bunsen.—Lyra Germanica. Translated from the German by CATHERINE WINKWORTH. *Fifth Edition* of the FIRST SERIES, Hymns for the Sundays and chief Festivals of the Christian Year. *New Edition* of the SECOND SERIES, the Christian Life. Fcp. 8vo. price 5s. each Series.

HYMNS from *Lyra Germanica* ......18mo. 1s.

* These selections of German Hymns have been made from collections published in Germany by Baron BUNSEN; and form companion volumes to

Theologia Germanica: Which setteth forth many fair lineaments of Divine Truth, and saith very lofty and lovely things touching a Perfect Life. Translated by SUSANNA WINKWORTH. With a Preface by the Rev. CHARLES KINGSLEY; and a Letter by Baron BUNSEN. Third Edition. Fcp. 8vo. 5s.

Bunsen. — Egypt's Place in Universal History: An Historical Investigation, in Five Books. By Baron C. C. J. BUNSEN, D.D., D.C.L., D.Ph. Translated from the German by C. H. COTTRELL, Esq., M.A. With many Illustrations. VOL. I. 8vo. 28s.; VOL. II. price 30s.; and VOL. III. price 25s.

Bunting.—The Life of Jabez Bunting, D.D.: With Notices of contemporary Persons and Events. By his Son, THOMAS PERCIVAL BUNTING. In Two Volumes. VOL. I. with Two Portraits and a Vignette, in post 8vo. price 7s. 6d. cloth; or (*large paper and Proof Engravings*) in square crown 8vo. 10s. 6d.

Bunyan's Pilgrim's Progress: With a Preface by the Rev. CHARLES KINGSLEY, Rector of Eversley; and about 120 Illustrations engraved on Steel and on Wood from Original Designs by Charles Bennett. Fcp. 4to. price 21s. cloth, gilt edges.

Bishop Butler's General Atlas of Modern and Ancient Geography; comprising Fifty-two full-coloured Maps; with complete Indices. New Edition, nearly all re-engraved, enlarged, and greatly improved. Edited by the Author's Son. Royal 4to. 24s. half-bound.

Separately { The Modern Atlas of 28 full-coloured Maps. Royal 8vo. price 12s. The Ancient Atlas of 24 full-coloured Maps. Royal 8vo. price 12s.

Bishop Butler's Sketch of Modern and Ancient Geography. New Edition, thoroughly revised, with such Alterations introduced as continually progressive Discoveries and the latest Information have rendered necessary. Post 8vo. price 7s. 6d.

Burton.—First Footsteps in East Africa; or, an Exploration of Harar. By RICHARD F. BURTON, Captain, Bombay Army. With Maps and coloured Plates. 8vo. 18s.

Burton. — Personal Narrative of a Pilgrimage to El Medinah and Meccah. By RICHARD F. BURTON, Captain, Bombay Army. *Second Edition*, revised; with coloured Plates and Woodcuts. 2 vols. crown 8vo. price 24s.

The Cabinet Lawyer: A Popular Digest of the Laws of England, Civil and Criminal; with a Dictionary of Law Terms, Maxims, Statutes, and Judicial Antiquities; Correct Tables of Assessed Taxes, Stamp Duties, Excise Licenses, and Post-Horse Duties; Post-Office Regulations; and Prison Discipline. 18th Edition, comprising the Public Acts of the Session 1858. Fcp. 8vo. 10s. 6d.

The Cabinet Gazetteer: A Popular Geographical Dictionary of All the Countries of the World. By the Author of *The Cabinet Lawyer.* Fcp. 8vo. 10s. 6d. cloth.

Caird.—Prairie Farming in America: With Notes by the way on Canada and the United States. By JAMES CAIRD, M.P., Author of "English Agriculture," "High Farming," &c. 16mo. 3s. 6d.

Calvert.—The Wife's Manual; or, Prayers, Thoughts, and Songs on Several Occasions of a Matron's Life. By the Rev. W. CALVERT, M.A. Ornamented from Designs by the Author in the style of *Queen Elizabeth's Prayer-Book.* Second Edition. Crown 8vo. 10s. 6d.

Catlow.—Popular Conchology; or, the Shell Cabinet arranged according to the Modern System: With a detailed Account of the Animals, and a complete Descriptive List of the Families and Genera of Recent and Fossil Shells. By AGNES CATLOW. Second Edition, much improved; with 405 Woodcut Illustrations. Post 8vo. price 14s.

Catz and Farlie's Book of Emblems.—Moral Emblems, from JACOB CATZ and ROBERT FARLIE; with Aphorisms, Adages, and Proverbs of all Nations. The Illustrations freely rendered from designs found in the works of Catz and Farlie, by JOHN LEIGHTON, F.S.A., and engraved under his superintendence. Imperial 8vo. with 60 large Illustrations on Wood, and numerous Vignettes and Tail Pieces.

Cecil.—The Stud Farm; or, Hints on Breeding Horses for the Turf, the Chase, and the Road. Addressed to Breeders of Race-Horses and Hunters, Landed Proprietors, and especially to Tenant Farmers. By CECIL. Fcp. 8vo. with Frontispiece, 5s.

Cecil's Stable Practice; or, Hints on Training for the Turf, the Chase, and the Road; with Observations on Racing and Hunting, Wasting, Race-Riding, and Handicapping: Addressed to Owners of Racers, Hunters, and other Horses, and to all who are concerned in Racing, Steeple-Chasing, and Fox-Hunting. *Second Edition.* Fcp. 8vo. with Plate, price 5s. half-bound.

Chapman.—History of Gustavus Adolphus and of the Thirty Years' War up to the King's Death: With some Account of its Conclusion by the Peace of Westphalia, in 1648. By B. CHAPMAN, M.A., Vicar of Letherhead. 8vo. with Plans, 12s. 6d.

onington.—Handbook of Chemical Analysis, adapted to the Unitary System of Notation. By F. T. CONINGTON, M.A., F.C.S. Post 8vo. 7s. 6d. Also *Tables of Qualitative Analysis,* designed as a Companion to the Handbook, price 2s. 6d.

Connolly.—The Romance of the Ranks; or, Anecdotes, Episodes, and Social Incidents of Military Life. By T. W. J. CONNOLLY, Quartermaster of the Royal Engineers. 2 vols. 8vo. 21s.

Connolly's History of the Royal Sappers and Miners: Including the Services of the Corps in the Crimea and at the Siege of Sebastopol. *Second Edition,* revised and enlarged; with 17 coloured plates. 2 vols. 8vo. price 30s.

Conybeare and Howson.—The Life and Epistles of Saint Paul: Comprising a complete Biography of the Apostle, and a Translation of his Epistles inserted in Chronological Order. By the Rev. W. J. CONYBEARE, M.A.; and the Rev. J. S. HOWSON, M.A. *Third Edition,* revised and corrected; with several Maps and Woodcuts, and 4 Plates. 2 vols. square crown 8vo. 31s. 6d. cloth.

*** The Original Edition, with more numerous Illustrations, in 2 vols. 4to. price 48s.—may also be had.

Dr. Copland's Dictionary of Practical Medicine: Comprising General Pathology, the Nature and Treatment of Diseases, Morbid Structures, and the Disorders especially incidental to Climates, to Sex, and to the different Epochs of Life; with numerous approved Formulæ of the Medicines recommended. Now complete in 3 vols. 8vo. price £5. 11s. cloth.

Bishop Cotton's Instructions in the Doctrine and Practice of Christianity. Intended chiefly as an Introduction to Confirmation. *Fourth Edition.* 18mo. 2s. 6d.

Cresy's Encyclopædia of Civil Engineering, Historical, Theoretical, and Practical. Illustrated by upwards of 3,000 Woodcuts. *Second Edition,* revised and brought down to the Present Time in a Supplement, comprising Metropolitan Water-Supply, Drainage of Towns, Railways, Cubical Proportion, Brick and Iron Construction, Iron Screw Piles, Tubular Bridges, &c. 8vo. 63s. cloth.

Crosse.—Memorials, Scientific and Literary, of Andrew Crosse, the Electrician. Edited by Mrs. CROSSE. Post 8vo. 9s. 6d.

Crowe.—The History of France. By EYRE EVANS CROWE. In Five Volumes. VOL. I. 8vo. price 14s.

Cruikshank.—The Life of Sir John Falstaff, illustrated in a Series of Twenty-four original Etchings by George Cruikshank. Accompanied by an imaginary Biography of the Knight by ROBERT B. BROUGH. Royal 8vo. price 12s. 6d. cloth.

Lady Cust's Invalid's Book.—The Invalid's Own Book: A Collection of Recipes from various Books and various Countries. By the Honourable LADY CUST. Second Edition. Fcp. 8vo. price 2s. 6d.

Dale.—The Domestic Liturgy and Family Chaplain, in Two Parts: PART I. Church Services adapted for Domestic Use, with Prayers for Every Day of the Week, selected from the Book of Common Prayer; PART II. an appropriate Sermon for Every Sunday in the Year. By the Rev. THOMAS DALE, M.A., Canon Residentiary of St. Paul's. Second Edition. Post 4to. 21s. cloth; 31s. 6d. calf; or £2. 10s. morocco.

Separately { THE FAMILY CHAPLAIN, 12s.
{ THE DOMESTIC LITURGY, 10s. 6d.

Davy (Dr. J.)—The Angler and his Friend; or, Piscatory Colloquies and Fishing Excursions. By JOHN DAVY, M.D., F.R.S., &c. Fcp. 8vo. price 6s.

The Angler in the Lake District: or, Piscatory Colloquies and Fishing Excursions in Westmoreland and Cumberland. By JOHN DAVY, M.D., F.R.S. Fcp. 8vo. 6s. 6d.

De Fonblanque.—The Administration and Organisation of the British Army, with especial reference to Finance and Supply. By EDWARD BARRINGTON DE FONBLANQUE, Assistant Commissary-General. 8vo. 12s.

De la Rive.—A Treatise on Electricity in Theory and Practice. By A. DE LA RIVE, Professor in the Academy of Geneva. Translated for the Author by C. V. WALKER, F.R.S. With numerous Woodcut Illustrations. 3 vols. 8vo. price £3. 13s. cloth.

Domenech.—Seven Years' Residence in the Great Deserts of North America. By the ABBÉ DOMENECH. With a Map, and about Sixty Woodcut Illustrations. 2 vols. 8vo. *[Just ready.*

The Abbe Domenech's Missionary Adventures in Texas and Mexico: A Personal Narrative of Six Years' Sojourn in those Regions. Translated under the Author's superintendence. 8vo. with Map, 10s. 6d.

The Eclipse of Faith; or, a Visit to a Religious Sceptic. *9th Edition.* Fcp. 8vo. 5s.

Defence of The Eclipse of Faith, by its Author: Being a Rejoinder to Professor Newman's *Reply:* Including a full Examination of that Writer's Criticism on the Character of Christ; and a Chapter on the Aspects and Pretensions of Modern Deism. Second Edition, revised. Post 8vo. 5s. 6d.

The Englishman's Greek Concordance of the New Testament: Being an Attempt at a Verbal Connexion between the Greek and the English Texts; including a Concordance to the Proper Names, with Indexes, Greek-English and English-Greek. New Edition, with a new Index. Royal 8vo. price 42s.

The Englishman's Hebrew and Chaldee Concordance of the Old Testament: Being an Attempt at a Verbal Connexion between the Original and the English Translations; with Indexes, a List of the Proper Names and their Occurrences, &c. 2 vols. royal 8vo. £3. 13s. 6d.; large paper, £4. 14s. 6d.

Ephemera's Handbook of Angling; teaching Fly-Fishing, Trolling, Bottom-Fishing, Salmon-Fishing: With the Natural History of River-Fish, and the best Modes of Catching them. Third Edition, corrected and improved; with Woodcuts. Fcp. 8vo. 5s.

Ephemera's Book of the Salmon: Comprising the Theory, Principles, and Practice of Fly-Fishing for Salmon: Lists of good Salmon Flies for every good River in the Empire; the Natural History of the Salmon, its Habits described, and the best way of artificially Breeding it. Fcp. 8vo. with coloured Plates, price 14s.

Fairbairn.—Useful Information for Engineers: Being a Series of Lectures delivered to the Working Engineers of Yorkshire and Lancashire. With Appendices, containing the Results of Experimental Inquiries into the Strength of Materials, the Causes of Boiler Explosions, &c. By WILLIAM FAIRBAIRN, F.R.S., F.G.S. *Second Edition;* with numerous Plates and Woodcuts. Crown 8vo. price 10s. 6d.

First Impressions of the New World on Two Travellers from the Old in the Autumn of 1858: with Map by Arrowsmith. Post 8vo. 8s. 6d.

Fischer.—Francis Bacon of Verulam: Realistic Philosophy and its Age. By Dr. K. FISCHER. Translated by JOHN OXENFORD. Post 8vo. 9s. 6d.

B 4

Forester.—Rambles in the Islands of Corsica and Sardinia: With Notices of their History, Antiquities, and present Condition. By THOMAS FORESTER, Author of *Norway in 1848-1849*. With coloured Map; and numerous Illustrations in Colours and Tints and on Wood, from Drawings made during the Tour by Lieut.-Col. M. A. BIDDULPH, R.A. Imperial 8vo. price 28s.

Frazer.—Letters of Sir A. S. Frazer, K.C.B., Commanding the Royal Horse Artillery under the Duke of Wellington: Written during the Peninsular and Waterloo Campaigns. Edited by Major-General SABINE, R.A. With Portrait, 2 Maps, and Plan. 8vo. 18s.

Freeman and Salvin.—Falconry: Its Claims, History, and Practice. By GAGE EARLE FREEMAN, M.A. ("Peregrine" of the *Field* newspaper); and Capt. F. H. SALVIN. Post 8vo. with Woodcut Illustrations from Drawings by Wolf.

Garratt.—Marvels and Mysteries of Instinct; or, Curiosities of Animal Life. By GEORGE GARRATT. *Second Edition*, revised and improved; with a Frontispiece. Fcp. 8vo. price 4s. 6d.

Gilbart.—A Practical Treatise on Banking. By JAMES WILLIAM GILBART, F.R.S. *Sixth Edition*, revised and enlarged. 2 vols. 12mo. Portrait, 16s.

Gilbart's Logic of Banking: a Familiar Exposition of the Principles of Reasoning, and their application to the Art and the Science of Banking. 12mo. with Portrait, 12s. 6d.

Gleig.—Essays, Biographical, Historical, and Miscellaneous, contributed chiefly to the *Edinburgh* and *Quarterly Reviews*. By the Rev. G. R. GLEIG, M.A., Chaplain-General to the Forces and Prebendary of St. Paul's. 2 vols. 8vo. 21s.

CONTENTS.
1. Dr. Chalmers.
2. Our Defensive Armament.
3. Natural Theology.
4. Military Bridges.
5. The War of the Punjaub.
6. The Puritans.
7. General Miller.
8. India and its Army.
9. The Madchenstien.
10. Military Education.

The Poetical Works of Oliver Goldsmith. Edited by BOLTON CORNEY, Esq. Illustrated by Wood Engravings, from Designs by Members of the Etching Club. Square crown 8vo. cloth, 21s.; morocco, £1. 16s.

Gosse. — A Naturalist's Sojourn in Jamaica. By P. H. GOSSE, Esq. With Plates. Post 8vo. price 14s.

Greathed.—Letters written during the Siege of Delhi. By H. H. GREATHED, late of the Bengal Civil Service. Edited by his Widow. Post 8vo. 8s. 6d.

Green.—Lives of the Princesses of England. By Mrs. MARY ANNE EVERETT GREEN, Editor of the *Letters of Royal and Illustrious Ladies*. With numerous Portraits. Complete in 6 vols. post 8vo. price 10s. 6d. each.—Any Volume may be had *separately* to complete sets.

Greyson. — Selections from the Correspondence of R. E. H. GREYSON, Esq. Edited by the Author of *The Eclipse of Faith*. Second Edition. Crown 8vo. 7s. 6d.

Grove. — The Correlation of Physical Forces. By W. R. GROVE, Q.C., M.A., F.R.S., &c. *Third Edition*. 8vo. price 7s.

Gurney.—St. Louis and Henri IV.: Being a Second Series of Historical Sketches. By the Rev. JOHN H. GURNEY, M.A., Rector of St. Mary's, Marylebone. Fcp. 8vo. 6s.

Evening Recreations; or, Samples from the Lecture-Room. Edited by the Rev. J. H. GURNEY, M.A. Crown 8vo. 5s.

Gwilt's Encyclopædia of Architecture, Historical, Theoretical, and Practical. By JOSEPH GWILT. With more than 1,000 Wood Engravings, from Designs by J. S. GWILT. Fourth Edition. 8vo. 42s.

Hare (Archdeacon).—The Life of Luther, in Forty-eight Historical Engravings. By GUSTAV KÖNIG. With Explanations by Archdeacon HARE and SUSANNA WINKWORTH. Fcp. 4to. price 28s.

Harford.—Life of Michael Angelo Buonarroti: With Translations of many of his Poems and Letters; also Memoirs of Savonarola, Raphael, and Vittoria Colonna. By JOHN S. HARFORD, Esq., D.C.L., F.R.S. *Second Edition*, thoroughly revised; with 20 copperplate Engravings. 2 vols. 8vo. 25s.

Illustrations, Architectural and Pictorial, of the Genius of Michael Angelo Buonarroti. With Descriptions of the Plates, by the Commendatore CANINA; C. R. COCKERELL, Esq., R.A.; and J. S. HARFORD, Esq., D.C.L., F.R.S. Folio, 73s. 6d. half-bound.

Harrison.—The Light of the Forge; or, Counsels drawn from the Sick-Bed of E. M. By the Rev. W. HARRISON, M.A., Domestic Chaplain to H.R.H. the Duchess of Cambridge. Fcp. 8vo. price 5s.

Harry Hieover.—Stable Talk and Table Talk; or, Spectacles for Young Sportsmen. By HARRY HIEOVER. New Edition, 2 vols. 8vo. with Portrait, price 24s.

Harry Hieover.—The Hunting-Field. By HARRY HIEOVER. With Two Plates. Fcp. 8vo. 5s. half-bound.

Harry Hieover. — Practical Horsemanship. By HARRY HIEOVER. *Second Edition*; with 2 Plates. Fcp. 8vo. 5s. half-bound.

Harry Hieover.—The Pocket and the Stud; or, Practical Hints on the Management of the Stable. By HARRY HIEOVER. Third Edition; with Portrait of the Author. Fcp. 8vo. price 5s. half-bound.

Harry Hieover.—The Stud, for Practical Purposes and Practical Men: Being a Guide to the Choice of a Horse for use more than for show. By HARRY HIEOVER. With 2 Plates. Fcp. 8vo. price 5s. half-bound.

Hassall.—Adulterations Detected; or, Plain Instructions for the Discovery of Frauds in Food and Medicine. By ARTHUR HILL HASSALL, M.D. Lond., Analyst of *The Lancet* Sanitary Commission; and Author of the Reports of that Commission published under the title of *Food and its Adulterations* (which may also be had, in 8vo. price 28s.) With 225 Illustrations, engraved on Wood. Crown 8vo. 17s. 6d.

Hassall.—A History of the British Fresh Water Algæ: Including Descriptions of the Desmideæ and Diatomaceæ. With upwards of One Hundred Plates of Figures, illustrating the various Species. By ARTHUR HILL HASSALL, M.D., Author of *Microscopic Anatomy of the Human Body,* &c. 2 vols. 8vo. with 103 Plates, price £1. 15s.

Col. Hawker's Instructions to Young Sportsmen in all that relates to Guns and Shooting. 11th Edition, revised by the Author's Son, Major P. W. L. HAWKER; with a Bust of the Author, and numerous Illustrations. Square crown 8vo. 18s.

Haydn's Book of Dignities: Containing Rolls of the Official Personages of the British Empire, Civil, Ecclesiastical, Judicial, Military, Naval, and Municipal, from the Earliest Periods to the Present Time. Together with the Sovereigns of Europe, from the Foundation of their respective States; the Peerage and Nobility of Great Britain; &c. Being a New Edition, improved and continued, of Beatson's Political Index. 8vo. price 25s. half-bound.

Hayward. — Biographical and Critical Essays, reprinted from Reviews, with Additions and Corrections. By A. HAYWARD, Esq., Q.C. 2 vols. 8vo. price 24s.

CONTENTS.

1. Sydney Smith.
2. Samuel Rogers.
3. James Smith.
4. George Selwyn.
5. Lord Chesterfield.
6. Lord Melbourne.
7. General Von Radowitz.
8. Countess Hahn-Hahn.
9. De Stendahl (Henri Beyle).
10. Pierre Dupont.
11. Lord Eldon and the Chances of the Bar.
12. The Crimean Campaign.
13. American Orators and Statesmen.
14. Journalism in France.
15. Parisian Morals and Manners.
16. The Imitative Powers of Music.
17. British Field Sports.
18. Science and Literature of Etiquette.
19. The Art of Dining.

Sir John Herschel.—Outlines of Astronomy. By SIR JOHN F. W. HERSCHEL, Bart., K.H., M.A. *Fifth Edition*, revised and corrected to the existing state of Astronomical Knowledge; with Plates and Woodcuts. 8vo. price 18s.

Sir John Herschel's Essays from the Edinburgh and *Quarterly Reviews*, with Addresses and other Pieces. 8vo. price 18s.

Hinchliff.—Summer Months among the Alps: With the Ascent of Monte Rosa. By THOMAS W. HINCHLIFF, of Lincoln's Inn, Barrister-at-Law. With 4 tinted Views and 3 Maps. Post 8vo. price 10s. 6d.

Hints on Etiquette and the Usages of Society: With a Glance at Bad Habits. New Edition, revised (with Additions) by a Lady of Rank. Fcp. 8vo. price Half-a-Crown.

Holland. — Medical Notes and Reflections. By SIR HENRY HOLLAND, Bart., M.D., F.R.S., &c., Physician in Ordinary to the Queen and Prince-Consort. *Third Edition*, revised throughout and corrected; with some Additions. 8vo. 18s.

Sir H. Holland's Chapters on Mental Physiology, founded chiefly on Chapters contained in *Medical Notes and Reflections*. Second Edition. Post 8vo. price 8s. 6d.

Hooker.—Kew Gardens; or, a Popular Guide to the Royal Botanic Gardens of Kew. By SIR WILLIAM JACKSON HOOKER, K.H., &c., Director. 16mo. price Sixpence.

Hooker and Arnott.—The British Flora; comprising the Phænogamous or Flowering Plants, and the Ferns. Seventh Edition, with Additions and Corrections; and numerous Figures illustrative of the Umbelliferous Plants, the Composite Plants, the Grasses, and the Ferns. By SIR W. J. HOOKER, F.R.A. and L.S., &c.; and G. A. WALKER-ARNOTT, LL.D., F.L.S. 12mo. with 12 Plates, price 14s.; with the Plates coloured, price 21s.

B 5

Horne's Introduction to the Critical Study and Knowledge of the Holy Scriptures. *Tenth Edition*, revised, corrected, and brought down to the present time. Edited by the Rev. T. HARTWELL HORNE, B.D. (the Author); the Rev. SAMUEL DAVIDSON, D.D. of the University of Halle, and LL.D.; and S. PRIDEAUX TREGELLES, LL.D. With 4 Maps and 22 Vignettes and Facsimiles. 4 vols. 8vo. £3. 13s. 6d.

⁎ The Four Volumes may also be had *separately* as follows:—

VOL. I.—A Summary of the Evidence for the Genuineness, Authenticity, Uncorrupted Preservation, and Inspiration of the Holy Scriptures. By the Rev. T. H. Horne, B.D., 8vo. 15s.

VOL. II.—The Text of the *Old Testament* considered: With a Treatise on Sacred Interpretation; and a brief Introduction to the *Old Testament* Books and the *Apocrypha*. By S. Davidson, D.D. (Halle) and LL.D. .... 8vo. 25s.

VOL. III.—A Summary of Biblical Geography and Antiquities. By the Rev. T. H. Horne, B.D. .... 8vo. 18s.

VOL. IV.—An Introduction to the Textual Criticism of the *New Testament*. By the Rev. T. H. Horne, B.D. The Critical Part re-written, and the remainder revised and edited by S. P. Tregelles, LL.D. .... 8vo. 18s.

Horne. — A Compendious Introduction to the Study of the Bible. By the Rev. T. HARTWELL HORNE, B.D. New Edition, with Maps and Illustrations. 12mo. 9s.

Hoskyns.—Talpa; or, the Chronicles of a Clay Farm: An Agricultural Fragment. By CHANDOS WREN HOSKYNS, Esq. Fourth Edition. With 24 Woodcuts from the original Designs by GEORGE CRUIKSHANK. 16mo. price 5s. 6d.

Howitt (A. M.) — An Art-Student in Munich. By ANNA MARY HOWITT. 2 vols. post 8vo. price 14s.

Howitt.—The Children's Year. By Mary HOWITT. With Four Illustrations, from Designs by A. M. HOWITT. Square 16mo. 5s.

Howitt.—Tallangetta, the Squatter's Home: A Story of Australian Life. By WILLIAM HOWITT, Author of *Two Years in Victoria*, &c. 2 vols. post 8vo. price 18s.

Howitt. — Land, Labour, and Gold; or, Two Years in Victoria: With Visit to Sydney and Van Diemen's Land. By WILLIAM HOWITT. *Second Edition*, containing the most recent Information regarding the Colony. 2 vols. crown 8vo. price 10s.

Howitt.—Visits to Remarkable Places: Old Halls, Battle-Fields, and Scenes illustrative of Striking Passages in English History and Poetry. By WILLIAM HOWITT. With about 80 Wood Engravings. *New Edition*. 2 vols. square crown 8vo. price 25s.

William Howitt's Boy's Country Book: Being the Real Life of a Country Boy, written by himself; exhibiting all the Amusements, Pleasures, and Pursuits of Children in the Country. New Edition; with 40 Woodcuts. Fcp. 8vo. price 6s.

Howitt.—The Rural Life of England. By WILLIAM HOWITT. New Edition, corrected and revised; with Woodcuts by Bewick and Williams. Medium 8vo. 21s.

The Abbé Huc's work on the Chinese Empire, founded on Fourteen Years' Travels and Residence in China. *People's Edition*, with 2 Woodcut Illustrations. Crown 8vo. price 5s.

Huc.—Christianity in China, Tartary, and Thibet. By M. l'Abbé HUC, formerly Missionary Apostolic in China; Author of *The Chinese Empire*, &c. VOLS. I. and II. 8vo. 21s.; and VOL. III. price 10s. 6d.

Hudson's Plain Directions for Making Wills in conformity with the Law. New Edition, corrected and revised by the Author; and practically illustrated by Specimens of Wills containing many varieties of Bequests, also Notes of Cases judicially decided since the Wills Act came into operation. Fcp. 8vo. 2s. 6d.

Hudson's Executor's Guide. New and enlarged Edition, revised by the Author with reference to the latest reported Cases and Acts of Parliament. Fcp. 8vo. 6s.

Hudson and Kennedy.—Where there 's a Will there 's a Way: An Ascent of Mont Blanc by a New Route and Without Guides. By the Rev. C. HUDSON, M.A., and E. S. KENNEDY, B.A. *Second Edition*, with Plate and Map. Post 8vo. 5s. 6d.

Humboldt's Cosmos. Translated, with the Author's authority, by MRS. SABINE. VOLS. I. and II. 16mo. Half-a-Crown each, sewed; 3s. 6d. each, cloth: or in post 8vo. 12s. each, cloth. VOL. III. post 8vo. 12s. 6d. cloth: or in 16mo. PART I. 2s. 6d. sewed, 3s. 6d. cloth; and PART II. 3s. sewed, 4s. cloth. VOL. IV. PART I. post 8vo. 15s. cloth; and 16mo. price 7s. 6d. cloth, or 7s. sewed.

Humboldt's Aspects of Nature. Translated, with the Author's authority, by MRS. SABINE. 16mo. price 6s.: or in 2 vols. 3s. 6d. each, cloth; 2s. 6d. each, sewed.

Humphreys.—Parables of Our Lord, illuminated and ornamented in the style of the Missals of the Renaissance by HENRY NOEL HUMPHREYS. Square fcp. 8vo. 21s. in massive carved covers; or 30s. bound in morocco by Hayday.

Hunt.—Researches on Light in its Chemical Relations; embracing a Consideration of all the Photographic Processes. By ROBERT HUNT, F.R.S. Second Edition, with Plate and Woodcuts. 8vo. 10s. 6d.

Hunt (Captain).—The Horse and his Master: With Hints on Breeding, Breaking, Stable-Management, Training, Elementary Horsemanship, Riding to Hounds, &c. By VERE D. HUNT, Esq., late 109th Regt. Co. Dublin Militia. Fcp. 8vo. with Frontispiece, price 5s.

Hutchinson.—Impressions of Western Africa: With a Report on the Peculiarities of Trade up the Rivers in the Bight of Biafra. By T. J. HUTCHINSON, Esq., British Consul for the Bight of Biafra and the Island of Fernando Po. Post 8vo. price 8s. 6d.

Idle.—Hints on Shooting, Fishing, &c., both on Sea and Land, and in the Fresh-Water Lochs of Scotland: Being the Experiences of C. IDLE, Esq. Fcp. 8vo. 5s.

Mrs. Jameson's Legends of the Saints and Martyrs, as represented in Christian Art: Forming the FIRST SERIES of *Sacred and Legendary Art*. Third Edition, revised and improved; with 17 Etchings and upwards of 180 Woodcuts, many of which are new in this Edition. 2 vols. square crown 8vo. price 31s. 6d.

Mrs. Jameson's Legends of the Monastic Orders, as represented in Christian Art. Forming the SECOND SERIES of *Sacred and Legendary Art*. Second Edition, enlarged; with 11 Etchings by the Author, and 88 Woodcuts. Square crown 8vo. price 28s.

Mrs. Jameson's Legends of the Madonna, as represented in Christian Art: Forming the THIRD SERIES of *Sacred and Legendary Art*. Second Edition, corrected and enlarged; with 27 Etchings and 165 Wood Engravings. Square crown 8vo. price 28s.

Mrs. Jameson's Commonplace-Book of Thoughts, Memories, and Fancies, Original and Selected. PART I. Ethics and Character; PART II. Literature and Art. *Second Edit.* revised and corrected; with Etchings and Woodcuts. Crown 8vo. 18s.

Mrs. Jameson's Two Lectures on the Social Employments of Women,—*Sisters of Charity* and the *Communion of Labour*. New Edition, with a Prefatory Letter on the present Condition and Requirements of the Women of England. Fcp. 8vo. 2s.

Jaquemet's Compendium of Chronology: Containing the most important Dates of General History, Political, Ecclesiastical, and Literary, from the Creation of the World to the end of the Year 1854. *Second Edition.* Post 8vo. price 7s. 6d.

Jaquemet's Chronology for Schools: Containing the most important Dates of General History, Political, Ecclesiastical, and Literary, from the Creation of the World to the end of the year 1857. Edited by the Rev. J. ALCORN, M.A. Fcp. 8vo. 3s. 6d.

Lord Jeffrey's Contributions to The Edinburgh Review. A New Edition, complete in One Volume, with a Portrait engraved by Henry Robinson, and a Vignette. Square crown 8vo. 21s. cloth; or 30s. calf.— Or in 3 vols. 8vo. price 42s. Comprising—

1. General Literature and Literary Biography.
2. History and Historical Memoirs.
3. Poetry.
4. Philosophy of the Mind, Metaphysics, and Jurisprudence.
5. Novels, Tales, and Prose Works of Fiction.
6. General Politics.
7. Miscellaneous Literature, &c.

Bishop Jeremy Taylor's Entire Works: With Life by BISHOP HEBER. Revised and corrected by the Rev. CHARLES PAGE EDEN, Fellow of Oriel College, Oxford. Now complete in 10 vols. 8vo. 10s. 6d. each.

Keith Johnston's New Dictionary of Geography, Descriptive, Physical, Statistical, and Historical: Forming a complete General Gazetteer of the World. *New Edition*, rectified to May 1859. In One Volume of 1,360 pages, comprising about 50,000 Names of Places. 8vo. 30s. cloth; or 35s. half-bound in russia.

Kane.—Wanderings of an Artist among the Indians of North America; from Canada to Vancouver's Island and Oregon, through the Hudson's Bay Company's Territory, and back again. By PAUL KANE. With Map, Illustrations in Colours, and Wood Engravings. 8vo. 21s.

Kemble.—The Saxons in England: A History of the English Commonwealth till the Norman Conquest. By JOHN M. KEMBLE, M.A., &c. 2 vols. 8vo. 28s.

B 6

Kesteven.—A Manual of the Domestic Practice of Medicine. By W. B. KESTEVEN, Fellow of the Royal College of Surgeons of England, &c. Square post 8vo. 7s. 6d.

Kirby and Spence's Introduction to Entomology; or, Elements of the Natural History of Insects: Comprising an Account of Noxious and Useful Insects, of their Metamorphoses, Food, Stratagems, Habitations, Societies, Motions, Noises, Hybernation, Instinct, &c. *Seventh Edition*, with an Appendix relative to the Origin and Progress of the work. Crown 8vo. 5s.

A Lady's Tour round Monte Rosa; With Visits to the Italian Valleys of Anzasca, Mastalone, Camasco, Sesia, Lys, Challant, Aoste, and Cogne: In a Series of Excursions in the Years 1850, 1856, 1858. With Map, 4 Illustrations in Colours from Sketches by Mr. G. Barnard, and 8 Wood Engravings. Post 8vo. 14s.

Mrs. R. Lee's Elements of Natural History; or, First Principles of Zoology: Comprising the Principles of Classification, interspersed with amusing and instructive Accounts of the most remarkable Animals. New Edition; Woodcuts. Fcp. 8vo. 7s. 6d.

LARDNER'S CABINET CYCLOPÆDIA
Of History, Biography, Literature, the Arts and Sciences, Natural History, and Manufactures.
A Series of Original Works by

SIR JOHN HERSCHEL,
SIR JAMES MACKINTOSH,
ROBERT SOUTHEY,
SIR DAVID BREWSTER,

THOMAS KEIGHTLEY,
JOHN FORSTER,
SIR WALTER SCOTT,
THOMAS MOORE,

BISHOP THIRLWALL,
THE REV. G. R. GLEIG,
J. C. L. DE SISMONDI,
JOHN PHILLIPS, F.R.S., G.S.

AND OTHER EMINENT WRITERS.

Complete in 132 vols. fcp. 8vo. with Vignette Titles, price, in cloth, Nineteen Guineas.
The Works *separately*, in Sets or Series, price Three Shillings and Sixpence each Volume.

A List of the WORKS *composing the* CABINET CYCLOPÆDIA:—

1. Bell's History of Russia .... 3 vols. 10s. 6d.
2. Bell's Lives of British Poets .... 2 vols. 7s.
3. Brewster's Optics .... 1 vol. 3s. 6d.
4. Cooley's Maritime and Inland Discovery 3 vols. 10s. 6d.
5. Crowe's History of France .... 3 vols. 10s. 6d.
6. De Morgan on Probabilities .... 1 vol. 3s. 6d.
7. De Sismondi's History of the Italian Republics .... 1 vol. 3s. 6d.
8. De Sismondi's Fall of the Roman Empire 2 vols. 7s.
9. Donovan's Chemistry .... 1 vol. 3s. 6d.
10. Donovan's Domestic Economy .... 2 vols. 7s.
11. Dunham's Spain and Portugal .... 5 vols. 17s. 6d.
12. Dunham's History of Denmark, Sweden, and Norway .... 3 vols. 10s. 6d.
13. Dunham's History of Poland........... 1 vol. 3s. 6d.
14. Dunham's Germanic Empire........... 3 vols. 10s. 6d.
15. Dunham's Europe during the Middle Ages................................. 4 vols. 14s.
16. Dunham's British Dramatists .... 2 vols. 7s.
17. Dunham's Lives of Early Writers of Great Britain .... 1 vol. 3s. 6d.
18. Fergus's History of the United States .. 2 vols. 7s.
19. Fosbroke's Grecian & Roman Antiquities 2 vols. 7s.
20. Forster's Lives of the Statesmen of the Commonwealth .... 5 vols. 17s. 6d.
21. Gleig's Lives of British Military Commanders............................. 3 vols. 10s. 6d.
22. Grattan's History of the Netherlands ... 1 vol. 3s. 6d.
23. Henslow's Botany .... 1 vol. 3s. 6d.
24. Herschel's Astronomy .... 1 vol. 3s. 6d.
25. Herschel's Discourse on Natural Philosophy .... 1 vol. 3s. 6d.
26. History of Rome....................... 2 vols. 7s.
27. History of Switzerland .... 1 vol. 3s. 6d.
28. Holland's Manufactures in Metal ...... 3 vols. 10s. 6d.
29. James's Lives of Foreign Statesmen .... 5 vols. 17s. 6d.
30. Kater and Lardner's Mechanics .... 1 vol. 3s. 6d.
31. Keightley's Outlines of History .... 1 vol. 3s. 6d.
32. Lardner's Arithmetic .... 1 vol. 3s. 6d.
33. Lardner's Geometry .... 1 vol. 3s. 6d.
34. Lardner on Heat .... 1 vol. 3s. 6d.
35. Lardner's Hydrostatics and Pneumatics 1 vol. 3s. 6d.
36. Lardner and Walker's Electricity and Magnetism........................... 2 vols. 7s.
37. Mackintosh, Forster, and Courtenay's Lives of British Statesmen .... 7 vols. 21s. 6d.
38. Mackintosh, Wallace, and Bell's History of England........................... 10 vols. 35s.
39. Montgomery and Shelley's eminent Italian, Spanish, and Portuguese Authors 3 vols. 10s. 6d.
40. Moore's History of Ireland............. 4 vols. 14s.
41. Nicolas's Chronology of History .... 1 vol. 3s. 6d.
42. Phillips's Treatise on Geology .... 2 vols. 7s.
43. Powell's History of Natural Philosophy 1 vol. 3s. 6d.
44. Porter's Treatise on the Manufacture of Silk................................. 1 vol. 3s. 6d.
45. Porter's Manufactures of Porcelain and Glass .... 1 vol. 3s. 6d.
46. Roscoe's British Lawyers............... 1 vol. 3s. 6d.
47. Scott's History of Scotland .... 2 vols. 7s.
48. Shelley's Lives of eminent French Authors .... 2 vols. 7s.
49. Shuckard and Swainson's Insects ...... 1 vol. 3s. 6d.
50. Southey's Lives of British Admirals .... 5 vols. 17s. 6d.
51. Stebbing's Church History............. 2 vols. 7s.
52. Stebbing's History of the Reformation.. 2 vols. 7s.
53. Swainson's Discourse on Natural History 1 vol. 3s. 6d.
54. Swainson's Natural History and Classification of Animals .... 1 vol. 3s. 6d.
55. Swainson's Habits and Instincts of Animals .... 1 vol. 3s. 6d.
56. Swainson's Birds...................... 2 vols. 7s.
57. Swainson's Fish, Reptiles, &c. .... 2 vols. 7s.
58. Swainson's Quadrupeds .... 1 vol. 3s. 6d.
59. Swainson's Shells and Shell-Fish....... 1 vol. 3s. 6d.
60. Swainson's Animals in Menageries..... 1 vol. 3s. 6d.
61. Swainson's Taxidermy and Biography of Zoologists........................... 1 vol. 3s. 6d.
62. Thirlwall's History of Greece.......... 8 vols. 28s.

The Letters of a Betrothed. Fcp. 8vo. price 5s. cloth.

Letters to my Unknown Friends. By a LADY, Author of *Letters on Happiness*. Fourth Edition. Fcp. 8vo. 5s.

L.E.L.—The Poetical Works of Letitia Elizabeth Landon; comprising the *Improvisatrice*, the *Venetian Bracelet*, the *Golden Violet*, the *Troubadour*, and Poetical Remains. New Edition; with 2 Vignettes by R. Doyle. 2 vols. 16mo. 10s. cloth; morocco, 21s.

Dr. John Lindley's Theory and Practice of Horticulture; or, an Attempt to explain the principal Operations of Gardening upon Physiological Grounds: Being the Second Edition of the *Theory of Horticulture*, much enlarged; with 98 Woodcuts. 8vo. 21s.

Dr. John Lindley's Introduction to Botany. New Edition, with Corrections and copious Additions. 2 vols. 8vo. with Six Plates and numerous Woodcuts, price 24s.

Dr. John Lindley's Synopsis of the British Flora arranged according to the Natural Orders; containing Vasculares or Flowering Plants. *Third Edition* (reprinted). Fcp. 8vo. 6s.

Linwood.—Anthologia Oxoniensis, sive Florilegium e Lusibus poeticis diversorum Oxoniensium Græcis et Latinis decerptum. Curante GULIELMO LINWOOD, M.A. Ædis Christi Alumno. 8vo. price 14s.

Lorimer's (C.) Letters to a Young Master Mariner on some Subjects connected with his Calling. New Edition. Fcp. 8vo. 5s. 6d.

Loudon's Encyclopædia of Agriculture: Comprising the Theory and Practice of the Valuation, Transfer, Laying-out, Improvement, and Management of Landed Property, and of the Cultivation and Economy of the Animal and Vegetable Productions of Agriculture. New and cheaper Edition; with 1,100 Woodcuts. 8vo. 31s. 6d.

Loudon's Encyclopædia of Gardening: Comprising the Theory and Practice of Horticulture, Floriculture, Arboriculture, and Landscape-Gardening. With many hundred Woodcuts. Corrected and improved by MRS. LOUDON. New and cheaper Edition. 8vo. 31s. 6d.

Loudon's Encyclopædia of Trees and Shrubs, or *Arboretum et Fruticetum Britannicum* abridged: Containing the Hardy Trees and Shrubs of Great Britain, Native and Foreign, Scientifically and Popularly Described. With about 2,000 Woodcuts. 8vo. price 50s.

Loudon's Encyclopædia of Plants: Comprising the Specific Character, Description, Culture, History, Application in the Arts, and every other desirable Particular respecting all the Plants found in Great Britain. New Edition, corrected by MRS. LOUDON. With upwards of 12,000 Woodcuts. 8vo. £3. 13s. 6d.—Second Supplement, 21s.

Loudon's Encyclopædia of Cottage, Farm, and Villa Architecture and Furniture. New Edition, edited by MRS. LOUDON; with more than 2,000 Woodcuts. 8vo. 63s.

Loudon's Hortus Britannicus; or, Catalogue of all the Plants found in Great Britain. New Edition, corrected by MRS. LOUDON. 8vo. 31s. 6d.

Mrs. Loudon's Lady's Country Companion; or, How to Enjoy a Country Life Rationally. Fourth Edition, with Plates and Woodcuts. Fcp. 8vo. 5s.

Mrs. Loudon's Amateur Gardener's Calendar, or Monthly Guide to what should be avoided and done in a Garden. *New Edition*. Crown 8vo. with Woodcuts, 7s. 6d.

Low's Elements of Practical Agriculture; comprehending the Cultivation of Plants, the Husbandry of the Domestic Animals, and the Economy of the Farm. New Edition; with 200 Woodcuts. 8vo. 21s.

Macaulay.—Speeches of the Right Hon. Lord Macaulay. Corrected by HIMSELF. 8vo. price 12s.—Lord Macaulay's Speeches on Parliamentary Reform, 16mo. price 1s.

Macaulay. — The History of England from the Accession of James II. By the Right Hon. LORD MACAULAY. New Edition. VOLS. I. and II. 8vo. price 32s.; VOLS. III. and IV. price 36s.

Lord Macaulay's History of England from the Accession of James II. New Edition of the first Four Volumes of the 8vo. Edition, revised and corrected. 7 vols. post 8vo. price 6s. each.

Lord Macaulay's Critical and Historical Essays contributed to The Edinburgh Review. Four Editions, as follows:—

1. A LIBRARY EDITION (the *Ninth*), in 3 vols. 8vo. price 36s.
2. Complete in ONE VOLUME, with Portrait and Vignette. Square crown 8vo. price 21s. cloth; or 30s. calf.
3. Another NEW EDITION, in 3 vols. fcp. 8vo. price 21s. cloth.
4. The PEOPLE'S EDITION, in 2 vols. crown 8vo. price 8s. cloth.

Macaulay.—Lays of Ancient Rome, with *Ivry* and the *Armada*. By the Right Hon. LORD MACAULAY. New Edition. 16mo. price 4s. 6d. cloth; or 10s. 6d. bound in morocco.

Lord Macaulay's Lays of Ancient Rome. With numerous Illustrations, Original and from the Antique, drawn on Wood by George Scharf, jun., and engraved by Samuel Williams. New Edition. Fcp. 4to. price 21s. boards; or 42s. bound in morocco.

Mac Donald. — Poems. By George MAC DONALD, Author of *Within and Without*. Fcp. 8vo. 7s.

Mac Donald.—Within and Without: A Dramatic Poem. By GEORGE MAC DONALD. *Second Edition*, revised. Fcp. 8vo. 4s. 6d.

MacDougall.—The Theory of War illustrated by numerous Examples from History. By Lieutenant-Colonel MACDOUGALL, Commandant of the Staff College. *Second Edition*, revised. Post 8vo. with 10 Plans of Battles, price 10s. 6d.

MacDougall.—The Campaigns of Hannibal, arranged and critically considered, expressly for the use of Students of Military History. By Lieut.-Col. P. L. MACDOUGALL, Commandant of the Staff College. Post 8vo. with Map, 7s. 6d.

M'Dougall.—The Eventful Voyage of H.M. *Discovery Ship* Resolute *to the Arctic Regions in Search of Sir John Franklin and the Missing Crews of H.M. Discovery Ships* Erebus *and* Terror, 1852, 1853, 1854. By GEORGE F. M'DOUGALL, Master. With a coloured Chart; 8 Illustrations in tinted Lithography; and 22 Woodcuts. 8vo. price 21s. cloth.

Sir James Mackintosh's Miscellaneous Works: Including his Contributions to The Edinburgh Review. Complete in One Volume; with Portrait and Vignette. Square crown 8vo. 21s. cloth; or 30s. bound in calf: or in 3 vols. fcp. 8vo. 21s.

Sir James Mackintosh's History of England from the Earliest Times to the final Establishment of the Reformation. Library Edition, revised. 2 vols. 8vo. 21s.

M'Culloch's Dictionary, Practical, Theoretical, and Historical, of Commerce and Commercial Navigation. Illustrated with Maps and Plans. New Edition, revised and adapted to the Present Time; containing much additional Information. [*Just ready.*

M'Culloch's Dictionary, Geographical, Statistical, and Historical, of the various Countries, Places, and principal Natural Objects in the World. Illustrated with Six large Maps. New Edition, revised; with a Supplement. 2 vols. 8vo. price 63s.

Maguire.—Rome; its Ruler and its Institutions. By JOHN FRANCIS MAGUIRE, M.P. *Second Edition*, revised and enlarged; with a new Portrait of Pope Pius IX æt. 66. Post 8vo. 10s. 6d.

Mrs. Marcet's Conversations on Natural Philosophy, in which the Elements of that Science are familiarly explained. Thirteenth Edition, enlarged and corrected; with 34 Plates. Fcp. 8vo. price 10s. 6d.

Mrs. Marcet's Conversations on Chemistry, in which the Elements of that Science are familiarly explained and illustrated by Experiments. New Edition, enlarged and improved. 2 vols. fcp. 8vo. price 14s.

Marshman. — The Life and Times of Carey, Marshman, and Ward: Embracing the History of the Serampore Mission. By JOHN CLARK MARSHMAN. 2 vols. 8vo. price 25s.

Martineau. — Studies of Christianity: A Series of Original Papers, now first collected or new. By JAMES MARTINEAU. Crown 8vo. 7s. 6d.

Martineau.—Endeavours after the Christian Life: Discourses. By JAMES MARTINEAU. 2 vols. post 8vo. 7s. 6d. each.

Martineau.—Hymns for the Christian Church and Home. Collected and edited by JAMES MARTINEAU. *Eleventh Edition*, 12mo. 3s. 6d. cloth, or 5s. calf; *Fifth Edition*, 32mo. 1s. 4d. cloth, or 1s. 8d. roan.

Martineau.—Miscellanies: Comprising Essays on Dr. Priestley, Arnold's *Life and Correspondence*, Church and State, Theodore Parker's *Discourse of Religion*, "Phases of Faith," the Church of England, and the Battle of the Churches. By JAMES MARTINEAU. Post 8vo. 9s.

Maunder's Scientific and Literary Treasury: A new and popular Encyclopædia of Science and the Belles-Lettres; including all branches of Science, and every subject connected with Literature and Art. New Edition. Fcp. 8vo. price 10s. cloth; bound in roan, 12s.; calf, 12s. 6d.

Maunder's Biographical Treasury; consisting of Memoirs, Sketches, and brief Notices of above 12,000 Eminent Persons of All Ages and Nations, from the Earliest Period of History: Forming a complete Popular Dictionary of Universal Biography. Eleventh Edition, revised, corrected, and extended in a Supplement to the Present Time. Fcp. 8vo. 10s. cloth; bound in roan, 12s.; calf, 12s. 6d.

Maunder's Treasury of Knowledge, and Library of Reference. Comprising an English Dictionary and Grammar, a Universal Gazetteer, a Classical Dictionary, a Chronology, a Law Dictionary, a Synopsis of the Peerage, numerous useful Tables, &c. New Edition, entirely reconstructed and reprinted; revised and improved by B. B. WOODWARD, B.A. F.S.A.; Assisted by J. MORRIS, Solicitor, London; and W. HUGHES, F.R.G.S. Fcp. 8vo. 10s. cloth; bound in roan, 12s.; calf, 12s. 6d.

Maunder's Treasury of Natural History; or, a Popular Dictionary of Animated Nature: In which the Zoological Characteristics that distinguish the different Classes, Genera, and Species, are combined with a variety of interesting Information illustrative of the Habits, Instincts, and General Economy of the Animal Kingdom. With 900 Woodcuts. New Edition. Fcp. 8vo. price 10s. cloth; roan, 12s.; calf, 12s. 6d.

Maunder's Historical Treasury; comprising a General Introductory Outline of Universal History, Ancient and Modern, and a Series of separate Histories of every principal Nation that exists; their Rise, Progress, and Present Condition, the Moral and Social Character of their respective Inhabitants, their Religion, Manners and Customs, &c. New Edition; revised throughout, with a new GENERAL INDEX. Fcp. 8vo. 10s. cloth; roan, 12s.; calf, 12s. 6d.

Maunder's Geographical Treasury. — The Treasury of Geography, Physical, Historical, Descriptive, and Political; containing a succinct Account of Every Country in the World: Preceded by an Introductory Outline of the History of Geography; a Familiar Inquiry into the Varieties of Race and Language exhibited by different Nations; and a View of the Relations of Geography to Astronomy and Physical Science. Completed by WILLIAM HUGHES, F.R.G.S. *New Edition;* with 7 Maps and 16 Steel Plates. Fcp. 8vo. 10s. cloth; roan, 12s.; calf, 12s. 6d.

Mildred Norman the Nazarene. By a WORKING MAN. Crown 8vo. 5s.

Merivale. — A History of the Romans under the Empire. By the Rev. CHARLES MERIVALE, B.D., late Fellow of St. John's College, Cambridge. 8vo. with Maps.

VOLS. I. and II. comprising the History to the Fall of *Julius Cæsar.* Second Edition..........................28s.
VOL. III. to the establishment of the Monarchy by *Augustus.* Second Edition...............................14s.
VOLS. IV. and V. from *Augustus* to *Claudius,* B.C. 27 to A.D. 54...32s.
VOL. VI. from the Reign of *Nero,* A.D. 54, to the *Fall of Jerusalem,* A.D. 70..............................16s.

Merivale. — The Fall of the Roman Republic: A Short History of the Last Century of the Commonwealth. By the Rev. C. MERIVALE, B.D. New Edition. 12mo. 7s. 6d.

Merivale (Miss). — Christian Records: Short History of Apostolic Age. By L. A. MERIVALE. Fcp. 8vo. 7s. 6d.

Miles. — The Horse's Foot, and How to Keep it Sound. *Eighth Edition;* with an Appendix on Shoeing in general, and Hunters in particular, 12 Plates and 12 Woodcuts. By W. MILES, Esq. Imperial 8vo. 12s. 6d.

⁎⁎ Two Casts or Models of Off Fore Feet, No. 1, *Shod for All Purposes,* No. 2, *Shod with Leather,* on Mr. Miles's plan, may be had, price 3s. each.

Miles. — A Plain Treatise on Horse-Shoeing. By WILLIAM MILES, Esq. With Plates and Woodcuts. *New Edition.* Post 8vo. 2s.

Milner's History of the Church of Christ. With Additions by the late Rev. ISAAC MILNER, D.D., F.R.S. A New Edition, revised, with additional Notes by the Rev. T. GRANTHAM, B.D. 4 vols. 8vo. price 52s.

Minturn. — From New York to Delhi by way of Rio de Janeiro, Australia, and China. By ROBERT B. MINTURN, Jun. With coloured Route-Map of India. Post 8vo. price 7s. 6d.

Mollhausen. — Diary of a Journey from the Mississippi to the Coasts of the Pacific, with a United States Government Expedition. By B. MÖLLHAUSEN, Topographical Draughtsman and Naturalist to the Expedition. With an Introduction by Baron HUMBOLDT; a Map, coloured Illustrations, and Woodcuts. 2 vols. 8vo. 30s.

James Montgomery's Poetical Works: Collective Edition; with the Author's Autobiographical Prefaces, complete in One Volume; with Portrait and Vignette. Square crown 8vo. price 10s. 6d. cloth; morocco, 21s. — Or, in 4 vols. fcp. 8vo. with Portrait, and 7 other Plates, price 14s.

Moore.—The Power of the Soul over the Body, considered in relation to Health and Morals. By GEORGE MOORE, M.D. *Fifth Edition.* Fcp. 8vo. 6s.

Moore.—Man and his Motives. By George MOORE, M.D. *Third Edition.* Fcp. 8vo. 6s.

Moore.—The Use of the Body in relation to the Mind. By GEORGE MOORE, M.D. *Third Edition.* Fcp. 8vo. 6s.

Moore.—Memoirs, Journal, and Correspondence of Thomas Moore. Edited by the Right Hon. LORD JOHN RUSSELL, M.P. With Portraits and Vignette Illustrations. 8 vols. post 8vo. price 10s. 6d. each.

Thomas Moore's Poetical Works: Comprising the Author's Autobiographical Prefaces, latest Corrections, and Notes. Various Editions of the separate Poems and complete Poetical Works, as follows:—

	s. d.
LALLA ROOKH, 32mo. ruby type	1 0
LALLA ROOKH, 16mo. Vignette	2 6
LALLA ROOKH, square crown 8vo. Plates	15 0
LALLA ROOKH, fcp. 4to. with Woodcut Illustrations by TENNIEL, in the press.	
IRISH MELODIES, 32mo. ruby type	1 0
IRISH MELODIES, 16mo. Vignette	2 6
IRISH MELODIES, square crown 8vo. Plates	21 0
IRISH MELODIES, illustrated by MACLISE, super-royal 8vo.	31 6
SONGS, BALLADS, and SACRED SONGS, 32mo. ruby type	2 6
SONGS, BALLADS, and SACRED SONGS, 16mo. Vignette	5 0
POETICAL WORKS, People's Edit. 10 PARTS, each	1 0
POETICAL WORKS, Cabinet Edition, 10 VOLS. ea.	3 6
POETICAL WORKS, Traveller's Edit., crown 8vo.	12 6
POETICAL WORKS, Library Edition, medium 8vo.	21 0
SELECTIONS, entitled "POETRY and PICTURES from THOMAS MOORE," fcp. 4to. with Wood Engs.	21 0
MOORE'S EPICUREAN, 16mo. Vignette	5 0

Editions printed with the Music.

IRISH MELODIES, People's Edition, small 4to.	12 0
IRISH MELODIES, imperial 8vo. small music size	31 6
HARMONISED AIRS from IRISH MELODIES, imperial 8vo.	15 0
NATIONAL AIRS, People's Edition, 10 Nos. each.	1 0
NATIONAL AIRS, imperial 8vo. small music size.	31 6
SACRED SONGS and SONGS from SCRIPTURE, imperial 8vo.	16 0

No Edition of Thomas Moore's Poetical Works, or of any separate Poem of Moore's, can be published complete except by Messrs. LONGMAN and Co.

Morell.—Elements of Psychology: Part I., containing the Analysis of the Intellectual Powers. By J. D. MORELL, M.A., One of Her Majesty's Inspectors of Schools. Post 8vo. 7s. 6d.

Morning Clouds. By the Author of *The Afternoon of Life.* Second and cheaper Edition, revised throughout. Fcp. 8vo. 5s.

Morris (F. O.)—Anecdotes in Natural History. By the Rev. F. O. MORRIS, B.A., Rector of Nunburnholme, Yorkshire, Author of "History of the Nests and Eggs of British Birds," &c. Fcp. 8vo. [*Just ready.*

Morris (J.)—The Life and Martyrdom of St. Thomas Becket, Archbishop of Canterbury and Legate of the Holy See. By JOHN MORRIS, Canon of Northampton. Post 8vo. 9s.

Morton.—The Resources of Estates: A Treatise on the Agricultural Improvement and General Management of Landed Property. By JOHN LOCKHART MORTON, Civil and Agricultural Engineer; Author of Thirteen Highland and Agricultural Society Prize Essays. With 25 Illustrations in Lithography. Royal 8vo. 31s. 6d.

Moseley.—The Mechanical Principles of Engineering and Architecture. By H. MOSELEY, M.A., F.R.S., Canon of Bristol, &c. Second Edition, enlarged; with numerous Corrections and Woodcuts. 8vo. 24s.

Memoirs and Letters of the late Colonel ARMINE MOUNTAIN, Aide-de-Camp to the Queen, and Adjutant-General of Her Majesty's Forces in India. Edited by Mrs. MOUNTAIN. Second Edition, revised; with Portrait. Fcp. 8vo. price 6s.

Mure.—A Critical History of the Language and Literature of Ancient Greece. By WILLIAM MURE, M.P. of Caldwell. Second Edition. VOLS. I. to III. 8vo. price 36s.; VOL. IV. price 15s.; VOL. V. price 18s.

Murray's Encyclopædia of Geography; comprising a complete Description of the Earth: Exhibiting its Relation to the Heavenly Bodies, its Physical Structure, the Natural History of each Country, and the Industry, Commerce, Political Institutions, and Civil and Social State of All Nations. Second Edition; with 82 Maps, and upwards of 1,000 other Woodcuts. 8vo. price 60s.

Neale.—The Closing Scene; or, Christianity and Infidelity contrasted in the Last Hours of Remarkable Persons. By the Rev. ERSKINE NEALE, M.A. New Editions. 2 vols. fcp. 8vo. price 6s. each.

Normanby (Lord).—A Year of Revolution. From a Journal kept in Paris in the Year 1848. By the Marquis of NORMANBY, K.G. 2 vols. 8vo. 24s.

Ogilvie.— The Master-Builder's Plan; or, the Principles of Organic Architecture as indicated in the Typical Forms of Animals. By GEORGE OGILVIE, M.D. Post 8vo. with 72 Woodcuts, price 6s. 6d.

Oldacre.—The Last of the Old Squires. A Sketch. By CEDRIC OLDACRE, Esq., of Sax-Normanbury, sometime of Christ Church, Oxon. Crown 8vo. price 9s. 6d.

Osborn. — Quedah; or, Stray Leaves from a Journal in Malayan Waters. By Captain SHERARD OSBORN, R.N., C.B., Author of *Stray Leaves from an Arctic Journal*, &c. With a coloured Chart and tinted Illustrations. Post 8vo. price 10s. 6d.

Osborn.—The Discovery of the North-West Passage by H.M.S. *Investigator*, Captain R. M'CLURE, 1850–1854. Edited by Captain SHERARD OSBORN, C.B., from the Logs and Journals of Captain R. M'Clure. Third Edition, revised; with Additions to the Chapter on the Hybernation of Animals in the Arctic Regions, a Geological Paper by Sir RODERICK I. MURCHISON, a Portrait of Captain M'Clure, a coloured Chart and tinted Illustrations. 8vo. price 15s.

Owen.— Lectures on the Comparative Anatomy and Physiology of the Invertebrate Animals, delivered at the Royal College of Surgeons. By RICHARD OWEN, F.R.S., Hunterian Professor to the College. Second Edition, with 235 Woodcuts. 8vo. 21s.

Professor Owen's Lectures on the Comparative Anatomy and Physiology of the Vertebrate Animals, delivered at the Royal College of Surgeons in 1844 and 1846. With numerous Woodcuts. VOL. I. 8vo. price 14s.

Memoirs of Admiral Parry, the Arctic Navigator. By his Son, the Rev. E. PARRY, M.A. of Balliol College, Oxford; Domestic Chaplain to the Lord Bishop of London. Sixth Edition; with a Portrait and coloured Chart of the North-West Passage. Fcp. 8vo. price 5s.

Pattison.— The Earth and the Word; or, Geology for Bible Students. By S. R. PATTISON, F.G.S. Fcp. 8vo. with coloured Map, 3s. 6d.

Peaks, Passes, and Glaciers: a Series of Excursions by

E. L. AMES, M.A.
E. ANDERSON.
J. BALL, M.R.I.A.
C. H. BUNBURY, M.A.
Rev. J. LL. DAVIES, M.A.
R. W. E. FORSTER.
Rev. J. F. HARDY, B.D.
F. V. HAWKINS, M.A.
T. W. HINCHLIFF, M.A.
E. S. KENNEDY, B.A.
W. MATHEWS, Jun., M.A.
A. C. RAMSAY, F.R S. & G.S.
A. WILLS, of the Middle Temple, Barrister-at-Law, and
J. TYNDALL, F.R.S.

Edited by JOHN BALL, M.R.I.A., F.L.S., President of the Alpine Club. Second Edition; with 8 Illustrations in Chromolithography, 8 Maps illustrative of the Mountain-Explorations described in the volume, a Map illustrative of the Ancient Glaciers of part of Caernarvonshire, various Engravings on Wood, and several Diagrams. Square crown 8vo. 21s.

⁎ The EIGHT SWISS MAPS, accompanied by a Table of the HEIGHTS of MOUNTAINS, may be had separately, price 3s. 6d.

Dr. Pereira's Elements of Materia Medica and Therapeutics. *Third Edition*, enlarged and improved from the Author's Materials, by A. S. TAYLOR, M.D., and G. O. REES, M.D.: With numerous Woodcuts. VOL. I. 8vo. 28s.; VOL. II. PART I. 21s.; VOL. II. PART II. 26s.

Dr. Pereira's Lectures on Polarised Light, together with a Lecture on the Microscope. 2d Edition, enlarged from Materials left by the Author, by the Rev. B. POWELL, M.A., &c. Fcp. 8vo. with Woodcuts, 7s.

Perry.—The Franks, from their First Appearance in History to the Death of King Pepin. By WALTER C. PERRY, Barrister-at-Law, Doctor in Philosophy and Master of Arts in the University of Göttingen. 8vo. price 12s. 6d.

Peschel's Elements of Physics. Translated from the German, with Notes, by E. WEST. With Diagrams and Woodcuts. 3 vols. fcp. 8vo. 21s.

Phillips's Elementary Introduction to Mineralogy. A New Edition, with extensive Alterations and Additions, by H. J. BROOKE, F.R.S., F.G.S.; and W. H. MILLER, M.A., F.G.S. With numerous Wood Engravings. Post 8vo. 18s.

Phillips.—A Guide to Geology. By John PHILLIPS, M.A., F.R.S., F.G.S., &c. Fourth Edition, corrected to the Present Time; with 4 Plates. Fcp. 8vo. 5s.

Piesse's Chymical, Natural, and Physical Magic, for the Instruction and Entertainment of Juveniles during the Holiday Vacation. With 30 Woodcuts and an Invisible Portrait of the Author. Fcp. 8vo. 3s. 6d. harlequin cloth.

Piesse's Art of Perfumery, and Methods of Obtaining the Odours of Plants: With Instructions for the Manufacture of Perfumes for the Handkerchief, Scented Powders, Odorous Vinegars, Dentifrices, Pomatums, Cosmétiques, Perfumed Soap, &c.; and an Appendix on the Colours of Flowers, Artificial Fruit Essences, &c. *Second Edition*, revised and improved; with 46 Woodcuts. Crown 8vo. 8s. 6d.

Pitt.—How to Brew good Beer: a complete Guide to the Art of Brewing Ale, Bitter Ale, Table Ale, Brown Stout, Porter, and Table Beer. To which are added Practical Instructions for making Malt. By JOHN PITT, Butler to Sir William R. P. Geary, Bart. Fcp. 8vo. 4s. 6d.

Porter.—History of the Knights of Malta, or the Order of the Hospital of St. John of Jerusalem. By Major WHITWORTH PORTER, Royal Engineers. With 5 Illustrations. 2 vols. 8vo. 24s.

Powell.—Essays on the Spirit of the Inductive Philosophy, the Unity of Worlds, and the Philosophy of Creation. By the Rev. BADEN POWELL, M.A., F.R.S., F.R.A.S., F.G.S., Savilian Professor of Geometry in the University of Oxford. Second Edition, revised. Crown 8vo. with Woodcuts, 12s. 6d.

Christianity without Judaism: A Second Series of Essays on the Unity of Worlds and of Nature. By the Rev. BADEN POWELL, M.A., &c. Crown 8vo. 7s. 6d.

The Order of Nature considered in reference to the Claims of Revelation: A Third Series of Essays on the Unity of Worlds and of Nature. By the Rev. BADEN POWELL, M.A., &c. Crown 8vo. 12s.

Pycroft.—The Collegian's Guide; or, Recollections of College Days: Setting forth the Advantages and Temptations of a University Education. By the Rev. J. PYCROFT, B.A. *Second Edition*. Fcp. 8vo.

Pycroft's Course of English Reading, adapted to every taste and capacity; or, How and What to Read: With Literary Anecdotes. New Edition. Fcp. 8vo. price 5s.

Pycroft's Cricket-Field; or, the Science and History of the Game of Cricket. Third Edition, greatly improved; with Plates and Woodcuts. Fcp. 8vo. price 5s.

Quatrefages (A. De).—Rambles of a Naturalist on the Coasts of France, Spain, and Sicily. By A. DE QUATREFAGES, Member of the Institute. Translated by E. C. OTTÉ. 2 vols. post 8vo. 15s.

Raikes (T.)—Portion of the Journal kept by THOMAS RAIKES, Esq., from 1831 to 1847: Comprising Reminiscences of Social and Political Life in London and Paris during that period. *New Edition*, complete in 2 vols. crown 8vo. with 3 Portraits, price 12s. cloth.

Rich's Illustrated Companion to the Latin Dictionary and Greek Lexicon: Forming a Glossary of all the Words representing Visible Objects connected with the Arts, Manufactures, and Every-Day Life of the Ancients. With about 2,000 Woodcuts from the Antique. Post 8vo. 21s.

Richardson.—Fourteen Years' Experience of Cold Water: Its Uses and Abuses. By Captain M. RICHARDSON, late of the 4th Light Dragoons. Post 8vo. with Woodcuts, price 6s.

Horsemanship; or, the Art of Riding and Managing a Horse, adapted to the Guidance of Ladies and Gentlemen on the Road and in the Field: With Instructions for Breaking-in Colts and Young Horses. By Captain M. RICHARDSON, late of the 4th Light Dragoons. With 5 Plates. Square crown 8vo. 14s.

Riddle's Copious and Critical Latin-English Lexicon, founded on the German-Latin Dictionaries of Dr. William Freund. New Edition. Post 4to. 31s. 6d.

Riddle's Complete Latin-English and English-Latin Dictionary, for the use of Colleges and Schools. By the Rev. J. E. RIDDLE, M.A. of St. Edmund Hall, Oxford. *New* and cheaper *Edition*, revised and corrected. 8vo. 21s.

Separately { The English-Latin Dictionary, 7s. { The Latin-English Dictionary, 15s.

Riddle's Young Scholar's Latin-English and English-Latin Dictionary. *New* and cheaper *Edition*, revised and corrected. Square 12mo. 10s. 6d.

Separately { The Latin-English Dictionary, 6s. { The English-Latin Dictionary, 5s.

Riddle's Diamond Latin-English Dictionary. A Guide to the Meaning, Quality, and right Accentuation of Latin Classical Words. Royal 32mo. price 4s.

ivers's Rose-Amateur's Guide; containing ample Descriptions of all the fine leading varieties of Roses, regularly classed in their respective Families; their History and Mode of Culture. Fcp. 8vo. 3s. 6d.

r. E. Robinson's Greek and English Lexicon to the Greek Testament. A New Edition, in great part re-written. 8vo. 18s.

r. Henry Rogers's Essays selected from Contributions to the *Edinburgh Review*. Second Edition. 3 vols. fcp. 8vo. price 21s.

1. Thomas Fuller.
2. Andrew Marvell.
3. Martin Luther.
4. Leibnitz.
5. Pascal.
6. Plato and Socrates.
7. Descartes.
8. John Locke.
9. Sydney Smith's Lectures.
10. English Language (Structure).
11. English Language (History).
12. The British Pulpit.
13. Vanity and Glory of Literature.
14. Ultramontane Doubts.
15. Right of Private Judgment.
16. The Oxford Tractarian Schools.
17. Recent Developments of Tractarianism.
18. Reason and Faith.
19. Revolution and Reform.
20. Treatment of Criminals.
21. Prevention of Crime.

muel Rogers's Recollections of Personal and Conversational Intercourse with
CHARLES JAMES FOX,
EDMUND BURKE,
HENRY GRATTAN,
RICHARD PORSON,
JOHN HORNE TOOKE,
PRINCE TALLEYRAND,
LORD ERSKINE,
SIR WALTER SCOTT,
LORD GRENVILLE, and
DUKE OF WELLINGTON.
Second Edition. Fcp. 8vo. 5s.

. Roget's Thesaurus of English Words and Phrases classified and arranged so as to facilitate the Expression of Ideas and assist in Literary Composition. Eighth Edition, revised and improved. Crown 8vo. 10s. 6d.

nalds's Fly-Fisher's Entomology: With coloured Representations of the Natural and Artificial Insect, and a few Observations and Instructions on Trout and Grayling Fishing. *Fifth Edition*, thoroughly revised by an Experienced Fly-Fisher; with 20 new coloured Plates. 8vo. 14s.

wton's Debater: A Series of complete Debates, Outlines of Debates, and Questions for Discussion; with ample References to the best Sources of Information. New Edition. Fcp. 8vo. 6s.

ssell (Dr.) — The Life of Cardinal Mezzofanti: With an Introductory Memoir of eminent Linguists, Ancient and Modern. By C. W. RUSSELL, D.D., President of St. Patrick's College, Maynooth. With Portrait and Facsimiles. 8vo. 12s.

herzer.—Travels in the Free States of Central America: Nicaragua, Honduras, and San Salvador. By Dr. CARL SCHERZER. With a coloured Map. 2 vols. post 8vo. 16s.

Mrs. SchimmelPenninck's Writings and Life, edited by her relation, CHRISTIANA C. HANKIN:—

Life of Mary Anne SchimmelPenninck. *Third* and cheaper *Edition*, with Corrections and Additions; complete in One Volume, with Portrait..................Post 8vo. 10s. 6d.

Select Memoirs of Port-Royal. To which are added Tour to Alet, Visit to Port-Royal, Gift of an Abbess, Biographical Notices, &c. from original Documents. *Fifth Edition*, revised..................3 vols. post 8vo. 21s.

The Principles of Beauty, as manifested in Nature, Art, and Human Character: with a Classification of Deformities; II. An Essay on the Temperaments (with Illustrations); III. Thoughts on Grecian and Gothic Architecture.......Post 8vo. 12s. 6d.

Dr. L. Schmitz's School History of Greece, from the Earliest Times to the Taking of Corinth by the Romans, B.C. 146, mainly based on Bishop Thirlwall's History of Greece. *Fifth Edition*, with Nine new Supplementary Chapters on the Civilisation, Religion, Literature, and Arts of the Ancient Greeks, contributed by CHRISTOPHER KNIGHT WATSON, M.A., Trin. Coll. Camb.; and illustrated with a Map of Athens and 137 Woodcuts, designed from the Antique by G. Scharf, jun., F.S.A. 12mo. 7s. 6d.

Scoffern (Dr.) — Projectile Weapons of War and Explosive Compounds. By J. SCOFFERN, M.B. Lond., late Professor of Chemistry in the Aldersgate College of Medicine. *Fourth Edition*, brought up to the present time in a *Supplement*. Post 8vo. with Woodcuts, 9s. 6d.

SUPPLEMENT, containing new resources of Warfare..2s.

Senior.—Journal kept in Turkey and Greece in the Autumn of 1857 and the beginning of 1858. By NASSAU W. SENIOR, Esq. With 2 Maps and 2 Views in chromolithography. Post 8vo. 12s.

Bowdler's Family Shakspeare: In which nothing is *added* to the Original Text; but those words and expressions are *omitted* which cannot with propriety be read aloud. Illustrated with Thirty-six Vignettes engraved on Wood from original Designs by

G. COOKE, R.A.
R. COOKE,
R. HOWARD, R.A.
H. SINGLETON,
R. SMIRKE, R.A.
T. STOTHARD, R.A.
H. THOMSON, R.A.
R. WESTALL, R.A.
R. WOODFORDE, R.A.

New Edition, printed in a more convenient form. 6 vols. fcp. 8vo. price 30s. cloth; separately, 5s. each.

⁎ The LIBRARY EDITION, with the same Illustrations, in One Volume, medium 8vo. price 21s. cloth.

Sewell (Miss).—New and cheaper Collected Edition of the Tales and Stories of the Author of *Amy Herbert*. Complete in 9 vols. crown 8vo. price £1. 10s. cloth; or each work, comprised in a single volume, may be had separately as follows :—

AMY HERBERT	2s. 6d.
GERTRUDE	2s. 6d.
The EARL'S DAUGHTER	2s. 6d.
The EXPERIENCE of LIFE......	2s. 6d.
CLEVE HALL	3s. 6d.
IVORS; or, the TWO COUSINS	3s. 6d.
KATHARINE ASHTON	3s. 6d.
MARGARET PERCIVAL	5s. 0d.
LANETON PARSONAGE	4s. 6d.

"TO the thoroughness and integrity, the absolute rectitude inculcated in thought, word, and deed, and to the tender charity extended to the erring and repentant, we are inclined to attribute the hold these works take on readers of all classes and all ages. The pure transparent sincerity tells even on those who are apt to find any work whose aim and object are religious, heavy and uninteresting. *The re-publication of these works in an easily accessible form is a benefit of which we cannot over-estimate the solid advantages.*" GLOBE.

Also by the Author of Amy Herbert,

Ursula: A Tale of English Country Life. 2 vols. fcp. 8vo. price 12s. cloth.

History of the Early Church, from the First Preaching of the Gospel to the Council of Nicea. 18mo. 4s. 6d.

Self-Examination before Confirmation: With Devotions and Directions for Confirmation-Day. 32mo. 1s. 6d.

Readings for a Month preparatory to Confirmation : Compiled from the Works of Writers of the Early and of the English Church. Fcp. 8vo. price 4s.

Readings for Every Day in Lent: Compiled from the Writings of BISHOP JEREMY TAYLOR. Fcp. 8vo. price 5s.

Sharp's New British Gazetteer, or Topo-graphical Dictionary of the British Islands and Narrow Seas : Comprising concise Descriptions of about Sixty Thousand Places, Seats, Natural Features, and Objects of Note, founded on the best authorities. 2 vols. 8vo. price £2. 16s.

Short Whist; its Rise, Progress, and Laws : With Observations to make any one a Whist-Player. Containing also the Laws of Piquet, Cassino, Ecarté, Cribbage, Backgammon. By Major A. New Edition ; to which are added, Precepts for Tyros, by Mrs. B. Fcp. 8vo. 3s.

Simpson.—Handbook of Dining; or, How to Dine, theoretically, philosophically, and historically considered : Based chiefly upon the *Physiologie du Goût* of Brillat-Savarin. By LEONARD FRANCIS SIMPSON, M.R.S.L. Fcp. 8vo. 5s.

Sinclair.—The Journey of Life. By CATHERINE SINCLAIR, Author of *The Business of Life*. New Edition. Fcp. 8vo. 5s.

Sir Roger De Coverley. From the Spectator. With Notes and Illustrations, by W. HENRY WILLS; and 12 Wood Engravings from Designs by F. TAYLER. Second and cheaper Edition. Crown 8vo. 10s. 6d. or 21s. in morocco by Hayday.—An Edition without Woodcuts, in 16mo. price 1s.

The Sketches: Three Tales. By the Authors of *Amy Herbert, The Old Man's Home*, and *Hawkstone*. Third Edition; with 6 Illustrations. Fcp. 8vo. price 4s. 6d.

Smee's Elements of Electro-Metallurgy. Third Edition, revised, corrected, and considerably enlarged; with Electrotypes and numerous Woodcuts. Post 8vo. 10s. 6d.

Smith (G.)—History of Wesleyan Methodism. By GEORGE SMITH, F.A.S. Member of the Royal Asiatic Society, &c. VOL. I. *Wesley and his Times;* and VOL. II. *The Middle Age of Methodism*, from the Death of Wesley in 1791 to the Conference of 1816. Crown 8vo. price 10s. 6d. each volume.

Smith (J.)—The Voyage and Shipwreck of St. Paul : With Dissertations on the Life and Writings of St. Luke, and the Ships and Navigation of the Ancients. By JAMES SMITH, of Jordanhill, Esq., F.R.S. Second Edition; with Charts, Views, and Woodcuts. Crown 8vo. 8s. 6d.

A Memoir of the Rev. Sydney Smith. By his Daughter, LADY HOLLAND. With a Selection from his Letters, edited by MRS. AUSTIN. *New Edition.* 2 vols. 8vo. 28s.

The Rev. Sydney Smith's Miscellaneous Works : Including his Contributions to The Edinburgh Review. Four Editions :—

1. A LIBRARY EDITION (the *Fourth*), in 3 vols. 8vo. with Portrait, 36s.
2. Complete in ONE VOLUME, with Portrait and Vignette. Square crown 8vo. price 21s. cloth ; or 30s. bound in calf.
3. Another NEW EDITION, in 3 vols. fcp. 8vo. price 21s.
4. The PEOPLE'S EDITION, in 2 vols. crown 8vo. price 8s. cloth.

The Rev. Sydney Smith's Elementary Sketches of Moral Philosophy, delivered at the Royal Institution in the Years 1804, 1805, and 1806. Third Edition. Fcp. 8vo. 7s.

Snow.—Two Years' Cruise off Tierra del Fuego, the Falkland Islands, Patagonia, and the River Plate: A Narrative of Life in the Southern Seas. By W. PARKER SNOW, late Commander of the Mission Yacht *Allen Gardiner*; Author of "Voyage of the *Prince Albert* in Search of Sir John Franklin." With 3 coloured Charts and 6 tinted Illustrations. 2 vols. post 8vo. 24s.

Robert Southey's Complete Poetical Works; containing all the Author's last Introductions and Notes. The *Library Edition*, complete in One Volume, with Portrait and Vignette. Medium 8vo. price 21s. cloth; 42s. bound in morocco.—Also, the *First collected Edition*, in 10 vols. fcp. 8vo. with Portrait and 19 Vignettes, price 35s.

Southey's Doctor, complete in One Volume. Edited by the Rev. J. W. WARTER, B.D. With Portrait, Vignette, Bust, and coloured Plate. Square crown 8vo. 21s.

Southey's Life of Wesley; and Rise and Progress of Methodism. Fourth and cheaper Edition, with Notes and Additions. Edited by the Author's Son, the Rev. C. C. SOUTHEY, M.A. 2 vols. crown 8vo. 12s.

Spencer.—Essays: Scientific, Political, and Speculative. By HERBERT SPENCER, Author of *Social Statics*. Reprinted chiefly from Quarterly Reviews. 8vo. price 12s. cloth.

Spencer.—The Principles of Psychology. By HERBERT SPENCER, Author of *Social Statics*. 8vo. price 16s. cloth.

Stephen.—Lectures on the History of France. By the Right Hon. SIR JAMES STEPHEN, K.C.B., LL.D., Professor of Modern History in the University of Cambridge. Third Edition. 2 vols. 8vo. price 24s.

Stephen.—Essays in Ecclesiastical Biography; from the Edinburgh Review. By the Right Hon. SIR JAMES STEPHEN, K.C.B., LL.D., Professor of Modern History in the University of Cambridge. Third Edition. 2 vols. 8vo. 24s.

CONTENTS.

Hildebrand.
Saint Francis of Assisi.
The Founders of Jesuitism.
Martin Luther.
The French Benedictines.
The Port Royalists.

7. Richard Baxter.
8. The Evangelical Succession.
9. William Wilberforce.
10. The Clapham Sect.
11. The Historian of Enthusiasm.
12. The Epilogue.

Stonehenge.—The Dog in Health and Disease: Comprising the Natural History, Zoological Classification, and Varieties of the Dog, as well as the various Modes of Breaking and Using him for Hunting, Coursing, Shooting, &c.; and including the Points or Characteristics of Toy Dogs. By STONEHENGE. With about 70 Illustrations engraved on Wood. Square crown 8vo. price 15s. half-bound.

Stonehenge's Work on the Greyhound: Being a Treatise on the Art of Breeding, Rearing, and Training Greyhounds for Public Running; their Diseases and Treatment: Containing also Rules for the Management of Coursing Meetings, and for the Decision of Courses. With Frontispiece and Woodcuts. Square crown 8vo. 21s.

Stow.—The Training System of Education; including Moral School Training for large Towns, and the Normal Seminary for Training Teachers to conduct the System. By DAVID STOW, Esq., Honorary Secretary to the Normal Seminary, Glasgow. Eleventh Edition, enlarged; with Plates and Woodcuts. Post 8vo. price 6s. 6d.

Strickland.—Lives of the Queens of England. By AGNES STRICKLAND. Dedicated, by express permission, to Her Majesty. Embellished with Portraits of every Queen, engraved from the most authentic sources. Complete in 8 vols. post 8vo. price 7s. 6d. each.—Any Volume may be had *separately* to complete Sets.

Memoirs of Rear-Admiral Sir William Symonds, Knt., C.B., F.R.S., Surveyor of the Navy, from 1832 to 1847: With Correspondence and other Papers relative to the Ships and Vessels constructed upon his Lines, as directed to be published under his Will. Edited by JAMES A. SHARP. With Sections and Woodcuts. 8vo. price 21s.

Taylor.—Loyola: and Jesuitism in its Rudiments. By ISAAC TAYLOR. Post 8vo. with Medallion, 10s. 6d.

Taylor.—Wesley and Methodism. By ISAAC TAYLOR. Post 8vo. Portrait, 10s. 6d.

Tennent.—Ceylon: an Account of the Island, Physical, Historical, and Topographical: with copious Notices of its Natural History, Antiquities, and Productions. Illustrated by 7 Maps, 17 Plans and Charts, and 101 Engravings on Wood. By Sir J. EMERSON TENNENT, K.C.S., LL.D., &c. 2 vols. 8vo.

COMPLETION
OF
THE TRAVELLER'S LIBRARY.

Summary of the Contents of the TRAVELLER'S LIBRARY, *complete in* 102 Parts, *price One Shilling each, or in* 50 Volumes, *price* 2s. 6d. *each in cloth.*— *To be had also, in* complete Sets only, *at Five Guineas per Set, bound in cloth, lettered, in* 25 Volumes, *classified as follows:*—

VOYAGES AND TRAVELS.

IN EUROPE.

A CONTINENTAL TOUR .... BY J. BARROW.
ARCTIC VOYAGES AND DISCOVERIES } ...... BY F. MAYNE.
BRITTANY AND THE BIBLE ...... BY I. HOPE.
BRITTANY AND THE CHASE ... BY I. HOPE.
CORSICA .... BY F. GREGOROVIUS.
GERMANY, ETC.: NOTES OF A TRAVELLER } .... BY S. LAING.
ICELAND .... BY P. MILES.
NORWAY, A RESIDENCE IN ..... BY S. LAING.
NORWAY, RAMBLES IN ...... BY T. FORESTER.
RUSSIA ...... BY THE MARQUIS DE CUSTINE.
RUSSIA AND TURKEY .. BY J. R. M'CULLOCH.
ST. PETERSBURG............ BY M. JERRMANN.
THE RUSSIANS OF THE SOUTH, BY S. BROOKS.
SWISS MEN AND SWISS MOUNTAINS } BY R. FERGUSON.
MONT BLANC, ASCENT OF ...... BY J. AULDJO.
SKETCHES OF NATURE IN THE ALPS } BY F. VON TSCHUDI.
VISIT TO THE VAUDOIS OF PIEDMONT } ...... BY E. BAINES.

IN ASIA.
CHINA AND THIBET........ BY THE ABBE' HUC.
SYRIA AND PALESTINE............ "EŌTHEN."
THE PHILIPPINE ISLANDS, BY P. GIRONIÈRE.

IN AFRICA.
AFRICAN WANDERINGS .... BY M. WERNE.
MOROCCO .... BY X. DURRIEU.
NIGER EXPLORATION .. BY T. J. HUTCHINSON.
THE ZULUS OF NATAL........ BY G. H. MASON.

IN AMERICA.
BRAZIL.................... BY E. WILBERFORCE.
CANADA................. BY A. M. JAMESON.
CUBA .... BY W. H. HURLBUT.
NORTH AMERICAN WILDS .... BY C. LANMAN.

IN AUSTRALIA.
AUSTRALIAN COLONIES ...... BY W. HUGHES.

ROUND THE WORLD.
A LADY'S VOYAGE .... BY IDA PFEIFFER.

HISTORY AND BIOGRAPHY.

MEMOIR OF THE DUKE OF WELLINGTON.
THE LIFE OF MARSHAL TURENNE............ } BY THE REV. T. O. COCKAYNE.
SCHAMYL .... BY BODENSTEDT AND WAGNER.
FERDINAND I. AND MAXIMILIAN II. } BY RANKE.
FRANCIS ARAGO'S AUTOBIOGRAPHY.
THOMAS HOLCROFT'S MEMOIRS.

CHESTERFIELD & SELWYN, BY A. HAYWARD.
SWIFT AND RICHARDSON, BY LORD JEFFREY.
DEFOE AND CHURCHILL .... BY J. FORSTER.
ANECDOTES OF DR. JOHNSON, BY MRS. PIOZZI.
TURKEY AND CHRISTENDOM.
LEIPSIC CAMPAIGN, BY THE REV. G. R. GLEIG.
AN ESSAY ON THE LIFE AND GENIUS OF THOMAS FULLER } BY HENRY ROGERS.

ESSAYS BY LORD MACAULAY.

WARREN HASTINGS.
LORD CLIVE.
WILLIAM PITT.
THE EARL OF CHATHAM.
RANKE'S HISTORY OF THE POPES.
GLADSTONE ON CHURCH AND STATE.
ADDISON'S LIFE AND WRITINGS.
HORACE WALPOLE.
LORD BACON.

LORD BYRON.
COMIC DRAMATISTS OF THE RESTORATION.
FREDERIC THE GREAT.
HALLAM'S CONSTITUTIONAL HISTORY.
CROKER'S EDITION OF BOSWELL'S LIFE OF JOHNSON.

LORD MACAULAY'S SPEECHES ON PARLIAMENTARY REFORM.

WORKS OF FICTION.

THE LOVE STORY, FROM SOUTHEY'S DOCTOR.
SIR ROGER DE COVERLEY.... } FROM THE SPECTATOR.
MEMOIRS OF A MAITRE-D'ARMES, BY DUMAS.
CONFESSIONS OF A WORKING MAN .. } ...... BY E. SOUVESTRE.

AN ATTIC PHILOSOPHER IN PARIS . } ...... BY E. SOUVESTRE.
SIR EDWARD SEAWARD'S NARRATIVE OF HIS SHIPWRECK.

NATURAL HISTORY, &c.

NATURAL HISTORY OF CREATION .... } BY DR. L. KEMP.
INDICATIONS OF INSTINCT. BY DR. L. KEMP.

ELECTRIC TELEGRAPH, &c. BY DR. G. WILSON.
OUR COAL-FIELDS AND OUR COAL-PITS.
CORNWALL, ITS MINES, MINERS, &c.

MISCELLANEOUS WORKS.

LECTURES AND ADDRESSES { BY THE EARL OF CARLISLE.
SELECTIONS FROM SYDNEY SMITH'S WRITINGS.
PRINTING .... BY A. STARK.

RAILWAY MORALS AND RAILWAY POLICY ...... } .. BY H. SPENCER.
MORMONISM .. BY THE REV. W. J. CONYBEARE.
LONDON .... BY J. R. M'CULLOCH.

Thirlwall.—The History of Greece. By the Right Rev. the LORD BISHOP of ST. DAVID'S (the Rev. Connop Thirlwall). 8 vols. 8vo. with Maps, £3. — An Edition in 8 vols. fcp. 8vo. with Vignette Titles, 28s.

Thomson's Seasons. Edited by Bolton CORNEY, Esq. Illustrated with 77 fine Wood Engravings from Designs by Members of the Etching Club. Square crown 8vo. 21s. cloth; or 36s. bound in morocco.

Thomson (the Rev. Dr.)—An Outline of the necessary Laws of Thought: A Treatise on Pure and Applied Logic. By WILLIAM THOMSON, D.D., Provost of Queen's College, Oxford. *4th Edition.* Fcp. 8vo. 7s. 6d.

Thomson's Tables of Interest, at Three, Four, Four-and-a-Half, and Five per Cent., from One Pound to Ten Thousand, and from 1 to 365 Days, in a regular progression of single Days; with Interest at all the above Rates, from One to Twelve Months, and from One to Ten Years. Also, numerous other Tables of Exchanges, Time, and Discounts. New Edition. 12mo. price 8s.

The Thumb Bible; or, Verbum Sempiternum. By J. TAYLOR. Being an Epitome of the Old and New Testaments in English Verse. Reprinted from the Edition of 1693; bound and clasped. 64mo. 1s. 6d.

Todd (Dr.)—The Cyclopædia of Anatomy and Physiology. Edited by ROBERT B. TODD, M.D., F.R.S., &c., Physician to King's College Hospital; late Professor of General and Morbid Anatomy in King's College, London. Assisted in the various departments by nearly all the most eminent cultivators of physiological science of the present age. Now complete in 5 vols. 8vo. pp. 5,350, illustrated with 2,853 Woodcuts, price £6. 6s. cloth.

Tooke.—History of Prices, and of the State of the Circulation, during the Nine Years from 1848 to 1856 inclusive. Forming VOLS. V. and VI. of Tooke's *History of Prices from 1792 to the Present Time*; and comprising a copious Index to the whole of the Six Volumes. By THOMAS TOOKE, F.R.S. and WILLIAM NEWMARCH. 2 vols. 8vo. price 52s. 6d.

Trevelyan (Sir C.) — Original Papers illustrating the History of the Application of the Roman Alphabet to the Languages of India. Edited by MONIER WILLIAMS, M.A., late Professor of Sanskrit in the East-India College, Haileybury. 8vo. with Map, 12s.

Trollope.—The Warden: a Novel. By ANTHONY TROLLOPE. New and cheaper Edition. Crown 8vo. price 3s. 6d. cloth.

Trollope's Barchester Towers, a Sequel to the *Warden.* New and cheaper Edition, complete in One Volume. Crown 8vo. 5s.

Sharon Turner's History of the Anglo- Saxons, from the Earliest Period to the Norman Conquest. Seventh Edition, revised by the Rev. S. TURNER. 3 vols. 8vo. 36s.

Dr. Turton's Manual of the Land and Fresh-Water Shells of Great Britain: With Figures of each of the kinds. New Edition, with Additions, by Dr. J. E. GRAY, F.R.S. &c., Keeper of the Zoological Collection in the British Museum. Crown 8vo. with 12 coloured Plates, price 15s. cloth.

Dr. Ure's Dictionary of Arts, Manufac- tures, and Mines: Containing a clear Exposition of their Principles and Practice. Fourth Edition, much enlarged; most of the Articles being entirely re-written, and many new Articles added. With nearly 1,600 Woodcuts. 2 vols. 8vo. price 60s.

Uwins.—Memoir and Correspondence of Thomas Uwins, R.A., late Keeper of the Royal Galleries and of the National Gallery, &c. Edited by Mrs. UWINS. 2 vols. post 8vo. 18s.

Van Der Hoeven's Handbook of Zoology. Translated by the Rev. WILLIAM CLARK, M.D., F.R.S., &c. Professor of Anatomy in the University of Cambridge. 2 vols. 8vo. with 24 Plates of Figures, price 60s. cloth; or separately, VOL. I. *Invertebrata*, 30s., and VOL. II. *Vertebrata*, 30s.

Vehse.—Memoirs of the Court, Aristo- cracy, and Diplomacy of Austria. By Dr. E. VEHSE. Translated from the German by FRANZ DEMMLER. 2 vols. post 8vo. 21s.

Von Tempsky. — Mitla; or, Incidents and Personal Adventures on a Journey in Mexico, Guatemala, and Salvador, in the Years 1853 to 1855. By G. F. VON TEMPSKY. With Map, Illustrations in colours, and Woodcuts. 8vo. 18s.

Wade. — England's Greatness: Its Rise and Progress in Government, Laws, Religion, and Social Life; Agriculture, Commerce, and Manufactures; Science, Literature, and the Arts, from the Earliest Period to the Peace of Paris. By JOHN WADE, Author of the *Cabinet Lawyer*, &c. Post 8vo. 10s. 6d.

Wanderings in the Land of Ham. By a DAUGHTER of JAPHET. Post 8vo. 8s. 6d.

Waterton.—Essays on Natural History, chiefly Ornithology. By C. WATERTON, Esq. With the Autobiography of the Author. 2 vols. fcp. 8vo. 10s.

Waterton's Essays on Natural History. Third Series; with a Continuation of the Autobiography, and a Portrait of the Author. *Second Edition*, Fcp. 8vo. price 6s.

Watson's Cybele Britannica; or, British Plants and their Geographical Relations. By HEWETT COTTRELL WATSON. 4 vols. 8vo. price 42s. cloth; or each vol. separately, price 10s. 6d. The fourth volume is devoted to general views and tabular summaries, showing the phyto-geography of Britain under various aspects.

Webb. — Celestial Objects for Common Telescopes. By the Rev. T. W. WEBB, M.A., F.R.A.S., Incumbent of Hardwick, Herefordshire. With Woodcuts, and a Map of the Moon 12 inches in diameter engraved on Steel. 16mo. 7s.

Webster and Parkes's Encyclopædia of Domestic Economy; comprising such subjects as are most immediately connected with Housekeeping: As, The Construction of Domestic Edifices, with the Modes of Warming, Ventilating, and Lighting them—A description of the various articles of Furniture, with the nature of their Materials—Duties of Servants—&c. New Edition; with nearly 1,000 Woodcuts. 8vo. price 50s.

Weld. — The Pyrenees, West and East, a Summer Holiday in 1858. By CHARLES RICHARD WELD, Barrister-at-Law. With 8 Illustrations in Chromo-xylography from Drawings by the Author. Post 8vo. 12s. 6d.

Weld's Vacation Tour in the United States and Canada. Post 8vo. with Map, 10s. 6d.

Weld's Vacations in Ireland. Post 8vo. with View. 10s. 6d.

Willich's Popular Tables for ascertain- ing the Value of Lifehold, Leasehold, and Church Property, Renewal Fines, &c.; the Public Funds; Annual Average Price and Interest on Consols from 1731 to 1858; Chemical, Geographical, Astronomical, Trigonometrical Tables; Common and Hyperbolic Logarithms; Constants, Squares, Cubes, Roots, Reciprocals; Diameter, Circumference, and Area of Circles; Length of Chords and Circular Arcs; Area and Diagonal of Squares; Diameter, Solidity, and Superficies of Spheres; Bank Discounts; Bullion and Notes, 1844 to 1859. *Fourth Edition*, enlarged. Post 8vo. price 10s.

Wilmot's Abridgment of Blackstone's Commentaries on the Laws of England, intended for the use of Young Persons, and comprised in a series of Letters from a Father to his Daughter. 12mo. price 6s. 6d.

Wilson's Bryologia Britannica: Con taining the Mosses of Great Britain and Ireland systematically arranged and described according to the Method of *Bruch* and *Schimper*; with 61 illustrative Plates. Being a New Edition, enlarged and altered, of the *Muscologia Britannica* of Messrs. Hooker and Taylor. 8vo. 42s.; or, with the Plates coloured, price £4. 4s. cloth.

Yonge.—A New English-Greek Lexicon Containing all the Greek Words used by Writers of good authority. By C. D YONGE, B.A. *Second Edition*, revised and corrected. Post 4to. price 21s.

Yonge's New Latin Gradus: Containing Every Word used by the Poets of good authority. For the use of Eton, Westminster, Winchester, Harrow, Charterhouse and Rugby Schools; King's College, London; and Marlborough College. *Sixth Edition*. Post 8vo. price 9s.; or with APPENDIX of *Epithets* classified, 12s.

Youatt's Work on the Horse, comprising also a Treatise on Draught. With numerous Woodcut Illustrations, chiefly from Designs by W. Harvey. New Edition, revised and enlarged by E. N. GABRIEL, M.R.C.S., C.V.S., Secretary to the Royal College of Veterinary Surgeons. In One Volume, 8vo. price 10s. 6d. cloth.

Youatt. — The Dog. By William Youatt. A New Edition; with numerous Engravings from Designs by W. Harvey. 8vo. 6s.

Young. — The Christ of History: An Argument grounded in the Facts of His Life on Earth. By JOHN YOUNG, LL.D. Second Edition. Post 8vo. 7s. 6d.

Young.—The Mystery; or, Evil and God. By JOHN YOUNG, LL.D. Post 8vo. 7s. 6d.

Zumpt's Grammar of the Latin Lan- guage. Translated and adapted for the use of English Students by DR. L. SCHMITZ, F.R.S.E.; With numerous Additions and Corrections by the Author and Translator. 4th Edition, thoroughly revised. 8vo. 14s.

[*September* 1859.

www.ingramcontent.com/pod-product-compliance
Lightning Source LLC
Chambersburg PA
CBHW032147010526
44111CB00035B/1232